We Need to Talk About Kevin Keegan

We Need to Talk About Kevin Keegan

A Bumper Book of Football Writing

GILES SMITH

PENGUIN BOOKS

PENGUIN BOOKS

Published by the Penguin Group
Penguin Books Ltd, 80 Strand, London WC2R ORL, England
Penguin Group (USA) Inc., 375 Hudson Street, New York, New York 10014, USA
Penguin Group (Canada), 90 Eglinton Avenue East, Suite 700, Toronto, Ontario, Canada M4P 2Y3
(a division of Pearson Penguin Canada Inc.)
Penguin Ireland, 25 St Stephen's Green, Dublin 2, Ireland
(a division of Penguin Books Ltd)
Penguin Group (Australia), 250 Camberwell Road, Camberwell, Victoria 3124, Australia
(a division of Pearson Australia Group Pty Ltd)
Penguin Books India Pvt Ltd, 11 Community Centre, Panchsheel Park, New Delhi – 110 017, India
Penguin Group (NZ), 67 Apollo Drive, Rosedale, North Shore 0632, New Zealand
(a division of Pearson New Zealand Ltd)
Penguin Books (South Africa) (Pty) Ltd, 24 Sturdee Avenue,
Rosebank, Johannesburg 2196, South Africa

Penguin Books Ltd, Registered Offices: 80 Strand, London WC2R ORL, England

www.penguin.com

Published in 2008
I

The articles in this book first appeared in the *Sunday Times*

The moral right of the author has been asserted

Set in 11/13 pt Monotype Bembo
Typeset by Rowland Phototypesetting Ltd, Bury St Edmunds, Suffolk
Printed in England by Clays Ltd, St Ives plc

978-0-141-03779-0

www.greenpenguin.co.uk

Penguin Books is committed to a sustainable future
for our business, our readers and our planet.
The book in your hands is made from paper
certified by the Forest Stewardship Council.

This book is dedicated to Sabine, Mabel and my matchday companions, Barney and Joe.

Contents

Contents

Introduction

E-mail to Tony Lacey at Penguin Books
From: Giles Smith
Re: *We Need to Talk About Kevin Keegan*

Tony,

Sorry to be quite so late with the text for the football writing collection. The photocopying involved has turned out to be a bit more time-consuming than I anticipated, not to mention the process of putting back the swearwords taken out by *The Times* sports desk (family paper, and all that). It's coming along pretty well, though, and I should be able to get something over to you by Thursday. Failing that, by the end of Friday. Monday/Tuesday at the very latest. Wednesday, first thing, tops.

In the meantime, it occurs to me that we had better start turning our minds to the important matter of whom we're going to get to write the book's introduction. Obviously, this is going to be a critical decision in terms of communicating the book's significance and status. At the same time, I don't want to overplay it or seem to be building the collection up into something that it isn't. It's a compilation of thoughts and reactions written over the course of three turbulent years in the game's history, pure and simple. Which is why I suggest we don't aim too high – just go for someone respected, with a modest public profile, who understands where I'm coming from, and whose endorsement would carry weight with people who know about football and perhaps just a little bit beyond.

I don't know what you think, but the name I keep coming back to is Nelson Mandela. Do you have any ins? It wouldn't need to be long. A couple of paragraphs in enthusiastic support of the project would do, and we could fill the page with a headshot and a big signature. And he could say something about football being the force that unites the world if he wanted to, though it's not my opinion. What do you reckon?

Tony,

Fair comment. And, no, I suppose I can't be confident that Mandela *is* a regular reader of my stuff, though, if you don't mind me saying, I think it's slightly hurtful of you to put it so bluntly. And, as a matter of fact, my instinct, contrary to yours, is that the former leader of South Africa *would* enjoy a 1,500-word joke about Steve Bruce, if he were in the mood for one. But let's not waste time arguing about this. What if we simply got Mandela to put his name to a statement, along the lines of, 'If there's one sports columnist I hate to miss, it's Giles Smith in *The Times*.' I mean, in a sense, that wouldn't even be a lie.

Tony,

OK, if that's the way you feel, forget it. But can we at least try instead for John Terry? An introduction from the Chelsea and England captain would get across the message that these were the views of a columnist respected both outside and inside the game. I'm told Terry's a big *Times* reader, which is a start. Also, you mentioned beforehand your concern that there are occasional moments when the essential objective purity that otherwise defines my writing gets slightly skewed by the fact that I'm a season-ticket-holding Chelsea supporter. I'm not sure I agree, but this would be a neat way of at least acknowledging the possibility. I think I have a number for Terry's agent. I'll send it over.

Tony,

Really? Christ, that's a lot of money. Still, I suppose when you consider what the guy earns for just a couple of hours' training every morning . . .

What if we go back to him and make a slightly reduced offer – say, £35,000 – but add in the condition that he refers to me at some point in the introduction as 'Gilo', 'Gilesy' or 'the Smithster'? And, obviously, it's not my business to go ghost-writing the whole thing, but if he could be encouraged to use the sentence 'He rocks my world,' it might work well.

Tony,

No, I hadn't realized these costs were recoupable against royalties. Scrap that, then. Back to the drawing board.

Incidentally, I'm intrigued by your feeling that this is the kind of book 'people are going to want to dip into'. I have to say, that's not my perception of it at all. I can see how the typography and the layout might give readers the impression that they are holding an assembly of bits and pieces, loosely organized. But my sense is that this is a book that people should feel obliged to read through in sequence, from beginning to end, extremely carefully, taking notes as avidly as if there were going to be a test at the end. But hey – your ideal reader, my ideal reader . . . it all comes down to individual perspective in the end. And they're all readers, right?

Tony,
I agree that Nick Hornby would, in many ways, be perfect. The fact that he is a Penguin author and therefore technically 'in reception' is also tempting. Plus I guess you could argue his career does need a boost. The problem is that Nick is a friend of mine so, in all honesty, I'd feel a bit awkward about asking him. Actually, it goes a bit deeper than that. Nick and I quite often e-mail each other about football, and you know how it is: you can't have any kind of conversation with a newspaper columnist without expecting to see your thoughts boldly appropriated and published a couple of days later. In fact, some weeks, when I can't come up with anything, I just cut and paste Nick's e-mails. (This is between you and me, you appreciate.) All in all, I reckon he would probably feel he's written enough of this book already.

What about getting a woman? Because it's not just meant for men, this collection, you know. It only seems that way. Does Zadie Smith like football?

One possible problem with that immediately, of course: people might think she's a relation.

Tony,
I did as you suggested, and asked the sports editor at *The Times* if he felt able to come up with a few opening words of praise and explanation. He laughed, very loudly, for a very long time. Then he said, 'That's the only funny idea you've had this year.' Then he hung up.

I'm not hopeful.

Tony,
This girl Nadine certainly does sound interesting. And I suppose I can see the value of, as you put it, 'going down the WAG route'. Nevertheless, is this exactly the message we want to be sending out about the book? And just because she says she once went out with Joe Cole, do we automatically believe her?

Tony,
Did you get my e-mail about John Updike?

Tony,
Are you there?

Tony,
Get back to me, would you? At this rate, I'm going to end up having to write the introduction myself and then it's going to look like we couldn't find anyone else.

2005

In which an over-refreshed Delia Smith sings like a canary on the pitch at Carrow Road, Steven Gerrard house-hunts suspiciously far from home and everyone is distracted, very briefly, by cricket. And in which we evaluate the full, terrifying implications of the curse which is 'tapping up', join Sven-Goran Eriksson's England on a trip to the home of soccer, and consider whether Lee Sharpe truly has it in him to go all the way on Celebrity Love Island. *But first, a cruel lie is nailed about Paul 'Gazza' Gascoigne's ice-skating abilities.*

Seaman on Ice

The world of sport was airborne with jubilation as, amid genuinely incredible scenes, David Seaman defied the odds to snatch glory in a bitterly contested, down-to-the-wire finale on *Strictly Ice Dancing*. Victory for this modest son of Rotherham ended nearly two years of hurt for sport, whose representatives have routinely struggled in celebrity endurance shows since the false dawn which was Phil Tufnell's triumph in the May 2003 series of *I'm A Celebrity . . . Get Me Out Of Here!* The pain is over; the healing can begin – especially for Seaman whose ankles must be killing him.

And to think that, as little as three weeks ago, joining the likes of Carol Smillie and Marcus Patrick from *Hollyoaks* in a nationally broadcast, pro-celebrity ice dance challenge would have been the last thing on the former England goalkeeper's mind. It should have been Paul Gascoigne on the night – and, inevitably, even in the overwhelming emotion of Seaman's big moment, the thoughts of a nation went out to the fabled Geordie, sidelined after picking up a niggle in training. Or, more specifically, after picking up Jimmy 'Fivebellies' Gardner in training and falling over, damaging his own neck.

That was the story, anyway, although there was precious little evidence of such an incident in the BBC's documentary footage last night, which seemed to imply that Gascoigne injured himself without help from anybody else. It couldn't be, could it, that one of the greatest sports news stories ever was a saucy hoax?

Whatever, Gascoigne was present to witness his understudy scoop gold after just eight days of preparation. As Seaman bowed to receive his medal from Bruce Forsyth, Gascoigne was visibly choked. Quite rightly. This one was for him – and also, of course, for the millions watching at home and the hundreds who had eagerly gathered rinkside for just a sample of Seaman on ice. (There's a schoolboy joke hovering somewhere in the vicinity of that sentence but you underestimate me if you think I'm going to go anywhere near it.)

Let nobody downplay the nature of Seaman's achievement here. Eight days is no time at all in which to put together a properly competitive ice dance routine – not when the competition includes Jessica Taylor from Liberty X and Scarlett Johnson from *EastEnders*. And not when everyone else has been at it for four weeks.

At least Seaman was drawn to dance last, which must have worked in his favour, nerves-wise. It also meant he knew exactly what he had to beat. By then, Smillie's challenge had gone south following some disappointingly 'square and blocky' arm-work and Marcus from *Hollyoaks* had been left to chew on a total mark of merely 12 out of 40 after a routine so wooden it could have formed the material for a church pew.

By contrast, confidence in Seaman grew during the on-ice introductions, when, in full flow up the back straight, he pulled off a thumbs-up to the watching Gascoigne. The laws of slapstick dictate that, if it was going to go pear-shaped for the retired keeper, this was the moment he would have flipped over and exited the arena on his Lycra-encased backside.

But no. He remained vertical. And so, accordingly, did the bright pink tie which Seaman had chosen to offset his black, sequin-spangled, diaphanous shirt – cleverly picking up the pink theme in the strips of dyed spaghetti that his professional partner, Zoia, was pretending constituted a dress. They danced to Tom Jones's version of 'Kiss', in a tight, fast routine which said to the judges, in so many words, 'Pick the sequins out of that, suckers.'

And the judges were impressed. 'You're the first one that's gone out there and really attacked it,' one said. There was one quibble: 'Your arabesque lines need a major look at.' Which sounded harsh, but the judge in question was really only expressing something the whole nation had said after that Ronaldinho goal in the 2002 World Cup.

But cometh the hour, cometh an unflappable Seaman. 'I just went out there and gave it a blast,' he said. Doors open for him. Who knows? He could kick on from here and step up to *I'm A Celebrity*. Meanwhile, an open-top bus tour must surely follow. The feelgood factor is self-evidently there. The question is, how to harness this victory to the London 2012 Olympic Bid and to the benefit of sport in the nation generally? We've seen that the country can stage major events at which sport is the winner. It's up to the administrators now.

Refereeing – Why a Little Technical Assistance Wouldn't Hurt

(*At Old Trafford on 4 January 2005, late in a match between Manchester United and Tottenham, Roy Carroll, the United goalkeeper, accidentally dropped a hoofed shot at least two feet behind his goal-line. The referee and his assistant, being some way up the pitch at the time, and otherwise preoccupied, failed to notice this indiscretion, and the score was allowed to stand at 0–0. The ensuing debates could so easily have centred on the failings of the modern goalkeeper, but, fortunately for Carroll, they centred on the failings of referees instead.*)

The argument is surely a simple one. If the technology exists, and if it is practical to apply it, there is no reason why football should hold back. And if it can be achieved without disrupting the all-important integrity of the game, then we say, by all means, let's see referees equipped with artificial brains.

In the past, when artificial intelligence was in its blueprint stages, it did not appear to lend itself straightforwardly to a refereeing application. Early human brain substitutes were unreliable and cumbersome, to the point where they would need to be carted about in a supermarket trolley – not a particularly viable notion given the famously hectic pace of the English game.

Our own times, however, have seen amazing advances in microchip technology and parallel developments in laser and keyhole surgery, such that intelligence for referees is no longer merely the dream of science fiction. Today's plastic brain is an insertion no bigger than a cereal packet and can be powered by a simple DC battery-pack, discreetly attached to a belt or 'bum bag'.

These ultra-refined units can spot arms raised in the penalty area, players going down too easily, balls crossing the goal-line by a yard and myriad other infringements which today's unassisted official inevitably has problems with. So sophisticated is this new generation of artificial brain, it can even detect and respond to a trip on a visiting attacker in the penalty area at Old Trafford, a feat of cognition which has defeated naturally endowed referees for years.

Scientists confidently predict that, in due time, they will have the means to create an entirely remote-controlled intelligence system, allowing officials to be propelled from the stands, or from a blimp – the so-called 'brain-box in the sky' option. It will mean the referee can be steered by someone who actually knows what they are doing, such as a fan, the referee's former woodwork teacher or Mark Lawrenson.

But that's for the future. In the meantime, the only barrier preventing football from sorting out the referees' brain problem is expense. What does it cost to replace a referee's brain?

Factoring in the materials and the surgeon's time, it's got to be at least 300 quid a pop, batteries not included. And when you multiply that by the number of officials required to work up and down the country, you're looking at an overall spend which could prove prohibitive, certainly for the lower leagues.

It may be, then, that we need to make the conversion in stages, first creating an elite, salaried corps of brained-up refs who are appointed to officiate at the big games. The braining programme could then be rolled out in increments. And as with DVD players that can record, so, presumably, with plastic brains; there is bound to be a 'price breakthrough' eventually, putting the technology within reach even of the Championship.

So much for referees' brains. As for the kind of external technical assistance that everyone has been hysterically screaming for following this week's oversight at Old Trafford, our advice would be for football to steer well clear. It's one thing to bring the referees up to speed, but quite another to burden the game and erode its crucial humanity with video replays and off-the-pitch deferrals.

The innovation with the most wind behind it seems to be a ball which reports on its own whereabouts via a cunningly inserted microchip. It will get no backing here. Such a ball would be disconcertingly open to tampering by agents – either Russian or sports. Also, how would you safeguard the system against interference from other electronic signals, such as mobile phone networks? The notion that one day, while innocently texting a friend on the other side of the ground, I might accidentally score for Tottenham is too awful to contemplate.

Why go to the trouble anyway? It's not even as if over-the-line debates happen all that often. The best efforts of the archivists this week yielded a maximum of five memorable incidents in forty years around the entire world. It's hardly a storm of controversy. It isn't even a subtle trend.

But if we must be panicked into incorporating a new coping device, let it at least be one which compensates for the loss of valuable amusement which is guaranteed to spectators by entrusting these matters to a fallible ref. Our suggestion in this area is for the replacement of the goal net by a Spiderman-style web, exactly a ball's width behind the line. You would know when the ball had crossed the line because it would stick. Goal! Boy, that one *really* rippled the old web! True, the disadvantage is that players, too, might get caught up in the stickiness. But it would serve them right for defending so deep.

Let's face it: most of the time, football is no fun at all. Most of the time, for multiple reasons, football is agony. It starts to be fun, however, when Roy Carroll drops the ball a mile over his line and neither the ref nor his assistant sees it. Moreover, if you decline all extraneous assistance, you leave alive the possibility that at some point in the future it will be a Manchester United player whose potentially match-winning shot is fumbled over the line in the ninetieth minute without the referee noticing. At Arsenal, say. At the climax of the season. And then Sir Alex Ferguson will have to give a post-match interview on the topic. You don't want to see that? You're not interested in football.

How to Guarantee Romance in the FA Cup

Jose Mourinho – not routinely an advocate of knockabout, Benny Hill-style comedy – suggested this week that Premiership sides should play their FA Cup ties away from home, irrespective of the draw order. It's an idea with a lot going for it, although, on the down side, it would deprive non-league players of the chance, just once in a while, to get changed in a dressing room with a radiator and some lavatory paper.

But why bother with a draw at all? Why not just fix it? If the point of the FA Cup is to be, first and foremost, a life-affirming romantic narrative, and only secondly a club football tournament, then why not get it arranged by the kind of people who understand that business? The draw should be assembled by a panel, consisting of television scriptwriters, playwrights, perhaps a prize-winning novelist. (Not the Booker, though. You want someone who understands storylines.) Input from Hollywood? Why not, if someone is willing to get involved and can demonstrate an appropriate depth of feeling for the task?

They'd find the Premiership club whose big-money striker was facing a court appearance; and they'd find the non-league club whose captain was a policeman. And, bingo: there's your Cup pairing. They'd find the struggling lower division side whose balls and cones had just been lifted by bailiffs and they'd hand them the lifeline of a money-earning tie at Anfield.

They'd find the brother of a Premier League star grimly plying his trade in the Conference and they'd match him up with his famous sibling, creating a massively moving head-to-head with family tensions to the fore, in which the neglected son made one last desperate, ninetieth-minute attempt to earn the love of his scornful father. And finally we'd have the FA Cup that people seem to crave – one with romance guaranteed.

Fortress KitKat: Why the Name of Your Stadium Matters Less than Your Choice of Half-time Snack

A powerful mixture of dismay and consternation greeted the grave announcement from York City FC. When a club changes something as central to its identity as the name of its ground, people are likely to feel the matter keenly. And when, as in this case, the change is from Bootham Crescent to KitKat Crescent, the debate is bound to grow unusually lively.

It was no surprise, then, to hear supporters of York denounce this naked confectionery-toting, declaring it to be further grim evidence of the relentless march of commercialism across the national game. 'Whither tradition?' was the helpless cry. Bootham Crescent, it was argued, is historically and geographically resonant, a name thickened with seventy-three years of association and buffed to a high lustre by its use across the generations, whereas KitKat Crescent is just a plug for a chocolate bar.

It's hard not to sympathize. I can barely begin to imagine

how I would feel if the club I supported suddenly announced that, following the securing of a new sponsorship package, it would from here on in be playing at the Malteserdome.

At the same time, let's not overlook the claim of Britain's best-selling chocolate bar to be honoured in this way. As York City have defensively pointed out, KitKat is a local product, and one of which the region is right to be fiercely proud. Perhaps one might further appease the disappointed historians by mentioning that the legendary Reg Baines, a veritable goal-machine for York in the 1930s, was a foreman in the chocolate factory. So in some ways, far from being a soul-less sell-out, this new KitKat association is a return to the club's roots.

Moreover, like York City, the KitKat turns out in red and white. And although the team don't yet share the KitKat's habit of wearing a layer of foil underneath, it could be an idea on the colder days. And, of course, if we were in search of cheap laughs here, we would point out that a KitKat can be very easily taken apart.

Much more than this, however, we should acknowledge the central position which KitKat already occupies within the game. For the football-supporting nation, it's without question the half-time chocolate bar of choice. Its carefully compounded layers of wafer-thin biscuit have long since made it the first-option comestible for fans seeking to take on board vital sugar during the interval. Divisible four ways, in most cases, it's a highly sociable snack, too, and thus more than commonly amenable to crowd-based consumption. Accordingly, more than any other, it's the chocolate at the heart of the football-going experience.

My loyalty to KitKat in a half-time setting is unwavering. OK, I'll admit that there was a brief period in the early 1990s when, on some ill-conceived glory-hunt, I switched my allegiance to Boost. But I was young and irresponsible and – as I realize, looking back – I didn't know myself very well. With age, and something like wisdom, I came back to KitKat. I think we all do in the end.

Don't get me wrong: I'm not running the Mars bar down.

I have been a user of Mars in the past, at half-time when there weren't any KitKats, and at other moments, and have found it to be of valuable assistance in no fewer than three key lifestyle areas: working, resting and playing. It's just that there's a kind of chewy, drawn-out self-indulgence going on there which is not entirely conducive to the half-time context, where a more focused, more brittle snack tends to be called for. Though not as brittle as a Crunchie, obviously. That would just be crazy.

To all those who would hold up the Snickers as a chocolate bar to be reckoned with in this area, I hear what you're saying. It's a busy and enduring snack with a vital peanut component. But, for me, it's asking for a Snickers which is the problem. It's just one of those words, like 'moist', 'wipes' and 'Van Nistel-rooy', which I have trouble bringing myself to say in public. Also, as with the Mars, the unshareability factor has to count against it in the long run. Ever tried halving a Snickers in a full house? You end up extracting a four-foot string of caramel from the hair of the bloke in front of you.

All in all, I can't see where the plausible challenge to KitKat's half-time supremacy is coming from among today's rival confections. Yorkie, though it has its feisty virtues, remains firmly a lorry driver's chocolate: it's likely to be confiscated at the turn-stiles as an offensive weapon and it doesn't answer to the way that football-going has opened up to women in the last decade or so. Lion bar? Too chewy and the bits get in your programme. Flake? Too flaky. Double Decker? Too horrible. Toblerone? Be serious.

As for the objection traditionally raised against the KitKat – that it 'isn't quite enough' – well, anyone clinging to that old canard clearly hasn't investigated the new 'Chunky' and 'King Size' variants. Granted, these products don't suit the original, finger-favouring purists, but they are still unarguably a KitKat at heart and a commendable addition to the KitKat family. (We'll draw a veil over KitKat Kubes. What's *that* about?)

So, KitKat Crescent: why not? I can, in fact, think of only one serious disadvantage. Assuming York City ever put together a commanding run of home form, it's going to be difficult for the commentators to refer, with the appropriate degree of seriousness, to 'Fortress KitKat'.

But think how much worse it could be. The makers of KitKat also make Dairy Crunch and Strawberry Nesquick. 'See you at the KitKat' at least has a swing to it, and an impeccable set of footballing credentials behind it.

Vinnie Jones: a Life in Pictures

To what was already one of Britain's most enviable CVs in light-entertainment television, Vinnie Jones this weekend added an appearance on *The Keith Barret Show*, the BBC's cod chat show on the theme of love and relationships. He wore a quality suit and was darkly charming in the face of many layers of irony, and it underscored yet again the point that, by dwelling on the former Welsh international's movie appearances, we risk undervaluing his talents as a small-screen player.

Don't get me wrong: Vinnie was good alongside Nicolas Cage in *Gone In 60 Seconds*. But he was even better, I thought, alongside Ainsley Harriott in *Ready Steady Cook*. More recently, Jones brought his undeniable leadership qualities to the repair of a Hertfordshire football club's changing facilities in ITV's *With A Little Help From My Friends*. Again, he showed himself to be a galvanizing small-screen presence while valuably indicating that menace has its place even in the operation of charity.

Then there was Vinnie's dedicated fly-on-the-wall documentary series, *Vinnie*, which was like *The Osbournes*, only without the Osbournes. The series certainly had things going for it, though. I'll for ever remember Vinnie's dexterity at letting himself into a locked house (his own, as it happened) with a credit card. But one thing the series didn't have was brevity. Did that programme really run every week for six months, or did it only appear to?

Yet, despite these unlikely achievements, attention tends to fall on the fact that Vinnie is the only former Wimbledon player ever to have forged a career in Hollywood. And with the club now transposed to Milton Keynes and struggling to fashion an identity for itself, it's a record that is not going to be broken for some time.

Yet, as he more than intimated on Friday night, he would rather we didn't harp on about his past. The phrase 'footballer turned actor' which inevitably crops up in articles about Jones, and which just cropped up in this one, grates on him wearyingly, he said. He seemed to be implying that it would be nice if people moved on and allowed him to be the person he has become.

Fair enough. At the same time, how could we possibly forget? Vinnie's career in football is the kind of thing a properly humane society wants to mark, and in a ritualized manner if necessary, if only to guard against the possibility of it ever happening again.

'Can I call you "Vin"?' Barret asked. 'No,' said Vinnie. But, with Tanya, his wife, alongside him on the sofa, he was warm enough to share intimate tales from the earliest days of their courtship. Apparently their eyes first met across a crowded cricket club bar, which the thirteen-year-old Vinnie had just forcibly entered. There was blood on his arm, Tanya recalled. 'It was the landlord's,' said Vinnie.

Their friendship suffered a setback, however, when some of Tanya's friends ran off with Vinnie's motorbike and Vinnie had to hit one of them with a crash helmet. But before long the couple were reunited and curling up in front of the cable television pictures that Vinnie had pirated by running in his own wire from a neighbouring junction box. Just a typical tale of young love in Watford, then – though, personally, I never tire of hearing the old romantic clichés.

Near the end, the couple were relaxed enough to play Barret's version of the old *Mr & Mrs* guessing game. And here one realized how the essence of Vinnie as a television performer is his flexibility within the limits he himself sets. He'll happily agree to sit on a television set in a blindfold and a pair of headphones whose earpieces have been made to look like house bricks, in honour of his past as a hod-carrier; and yet you still wouldn't want to cross him. Long may he continue to find work.*

House-hunting with Steven Gerrard

When reports suggested that Steven Gerrard of Liverpool had been seen hunting for property in Surrey, people were very quick to put two and two together and make a £1.75 million six-bedroom family house abutting a golf course. They were also quick to point out that, although there are no Premiership teams with a ground in Surrey, there is one with a training facility there, namely Chelsea.

Speculation hardly abated when Gerrard made some televised remarks to Gary Lineker in which, far from passionately committing himself in the long term to his present club – nor, indeed, to his present house which, perhaps tellingly, he didn't mention at all – the midfielder carefully made it clear that he would think about his future when he 'sat down' over the summer.

Footballers are always keen to do this kind of thing sitting down. 'Are you leaving?' you'll ask. 'I'll sit down over the summer,' they'll say. The inference is that they never get any other time to sit down. Certainly, there is no footballer in the world who will ever claim to have made an important career

---

* Later this same year, when Robbie Earle clinched victory in the BBC's *Strictly African Dancing* contest, the fabled Wimbledon 'Crazy Gang' had yielded a Hollywood film star (Jones), a British television ever-present (John Fashanu) and a televised dance champion (Earle), not to mention Dennis Wise. What an incredible breeding ground for British theatrical talent Plough Lane was. We won't arrive at a proper view of Wimbledon's place in history until we stop judging the club's achievements relative to the likes of Manchester United and Liverpool and start formally comparing its output, year-on-year, with that of the Sylvia Young Academy.

decision while standing up during the winter. That would be plain foolhardy.

Still, what with the equivocation and the house-hunt rumours, Liverpool fans have had ample reason to worry that their sturdy linchpin and adored homeboy has decided, 'Stuff this for a game of soldiers' and is off to London. But need they think so? There are, surely, plenty of perfectly innocent explanations why a recent afternoon might or might not have found Gerrard and his girlfriend outside a premium-priced des res somewhere near Godalming, testing the gravel on the drive for crunchiness.

Firstly, he might be planning to commute. True, Esher to Liverpool is not your ideal regular early-morning/early-evening drive. And when people speak of Surrey as 'classic commuter-belt territory', it's probably London that the belt is meant to be holding up, rather than Liverpool. Then again, if the M25 is working, and with a good run on the M6, I reckon Gerrard ought to be able to accomplish the journey inside four hours, door-to-door. Four and a half hours, tops. And I'm factoring in a stop at Banbury services for diesel and wine gums.

Alternatively, he could take the A322 out of Woking, hook up with the A4074 and join the M40 at Oxford, leaving out the M25 altogether. It's an idea, and doubtless Gerrard will have plenty of his own.

I can see, however, that just because the move makes sense from a practical point of view, it doesn't necessarily explain it to aggrieved Liverpudlians, who might be slightly hurt to see Gerrard so energetically distancing himself from the local community. If the manicured lawns of resplendent Southport, just north of Liverpool along the coast, were good enough for the likes of Tommy Smith and Alan Hansen, why should Gerrard need to seek his golf and his electronic gates in the snooty south?

It could be an emotional thing. Everyone who has ever house-hunted has been told by friends or estate agents, 'You'll know as soon as you walk through the door.' And it's just possible that

Gerrard and his girlfriend have walked through a lot of doors without getting that feeling. Maybe they started out looking in Skelmersdale and saw a lot of nice properties, but without ever thinking, 'This is the one.' And thus they have worked their way further and further down the country – through Newcastle-under-Lyme, down to Royal Leamington Spa and on to Bicester – until now, when they find themselves in and around Sunningdale.

Too picky? Possibly. But it's an important decision in the life of any young couple. You want to get it right. And it might not even stop there. They may yet push fruitlessly through Hampshire and end up on the Isle of Wight, from where the commute to Liverpool can be even trickier, what with the car ferry.

Or maybe it's got nothing to do with that. Maybe the proposed move is, straightforwardly, an act of homage to the heroes of light entertainment, many of whom, like Gerrard, set out from humble beginnings and clawed their way up until they were in a position to afford a home on a secure housing compound backing on to Wentworth. That was certainly the way Bruce Forsyth, for example, went about it, and you can see how a young man like Gerrard, with the fire in his belly, might want some of that action.

Or what about the theory that it's a retirement home – a remote place to which Gerrard can withdraw in satisfaction after many further years of glory at Liverpool? To which the obvious objection would be, why buy now? Well, maybe he's just taking a particularly cautious view on the stagnation of the property market and assuming that, if he gets things moving now, it might just about be possible to exchange and complete in forty years' time.

Unlikely? No more so, surely, than the thought that a footballer would house-hunt 270 miles away from home mid-season and risk sending out some pretty strong signals about his future intentions. And if you believe that, you'll probably also believe that the high-profile manager and managing director of a leading Premiership club would be daft enough to tap up a rival club's prize defender in a London hotel, rather than in the middle of a field in Wales where nobody would see them. As if.*

Tapping up — Your Questions Answered

Is tapping up one of the most terrifying evils confronting society today?
It is a canker which is eating into the heart of our civilization, even as it threatens the moral health of our children and promises to destroy every value that we hold dear and have fought so hard to defend. Or so you would think since the allegations surfaced about Chelsea having a word with Arsenal's Ashley Cole on the hush.

If these grave allegations are upheld by the Premier League's investigation, could any punishment be sufficiently steep for these vile miscreants who have had the wicked temerity to talk to each other about the possibility of a job-change?
Almost certainly not, although the leading suggestions are: that Chelsea should be docked as many points as might make the title race exciting again; that Cole should be fined to within an inch of his life for his disloyalty and flagrant opportunism; and that Peter Kenyon, Chelsea's chief executive, should be stripped naked and forced to ride a brindled mare up Fulham Broadway in public acknowledgement of his shame.

Does nobody have a good word to say for tapping up?
Only Sven-Goran Eriksson, who mentioned that it might not be altogether bad if, contrary to the current, peculiarly Victorian regulations, footballers were allowed to listen to job offers that

---

* Twice Gerrard teased Chelsea, and his own medal cabinet at home, with the prospect of a transfer. And twice his love for Liverpool, not to mention the less than delighted reaction of the local populace, caused him to change his mind. Never let it be said that the soul has gone out of the game. Although see p. 150 for some later confusion on Gerrard's part about the power of money.

intrigued them, without first requiring the permission of their employer. But for some reason, rather than being considered as a reasonable contribution to the debate, Sven's words were mainly dismissed as a gaffe.

At the very least, they were consistent with his personal philosophy. Sven politely listened to, and politely rejected, at least two job offers during his time as England manager – and was roundly abused for it by the kind of people who believe that managing the England national side is a manifest destiny rather than a job among many other jobs. These are the same people who would probably make the position hereditary if they could.

But Sven's point, in word and deed, is merely that footballers are being held to standards which would be unacceptable in any other form of employment. Excepting journalism, of course. Be assured that all the sports writers who have fulminated about the moral dimensions of the Cole case have never received a call from the editor of a rival publication, sounding them out about a better-paid job, and would hang up immediately if such a call ever came through.

Why would a football manager with a famous face and a footballer with an even more famous face conduct a supposedly secret meeting during daylight hours in the conference room of a busy London hotel rather than at a rural bus stop, or even, more simply, in somebody's kitchen?

One can only assume that the most obvious explanation – that Kenyon must be a very, very stupid man indeed – is a non-starter, even though it has its adherents. Better, surely, to believe that Chelsea's actions were so brazen, and so likely to be exposed, that they must have been deliberate and were done in order to get this issue out into the open, thus flying the flag for employees' rights everywhere – a bit like going to the European Court of Human Rights, if you like, except taking the long way round, via the *News of the World*.

What are the ethical implications of Chelsea allegedly offering to start Cole's salary as soon as he agrees to join, even though he won't be able to play for them until August at the earliest?

Think of it as a golden hello. Or perhaps a golden intake of breath prior to saying hello. Or maybe a golden nudge accompanied by a golden wink. It would also be a priceless instance of Chelsea loaning out a player before they had bought him, as opposed to loaning him out immediately after buying him (Alexei Smertin), or after buying him and finding out that he was about as much use in the Premiership as a penguin (Juan Sebastian Veron, Hernan Crespo).

If Ashley is smart, having agreed to accept a place to study under Mourinho at Chelsea in 2005–06, he will then request a deferral, or 'gap year', in the style beloved by students. Then he can go InterRailing — except that, where his fellow travellers will be eating bread and cheese and sleeping on station platforms, he will be on £85,000 a week and staying at the Four Seasons.

How will I know if I am being tapped up?

If it's Chelsea, they will have booked the Hammersmith Odeon and sold tickets. In most other cases, however, you will have to look out for a chief executive arching his eyebrows in a suggestive manner across a crowded wine bar. One benefit of making the formerly illegal approach legal is that it would straightaway eliminate this charade, with all its possibilities of misinterpretation. Also the economic benefit to the flowers, cards and trinkets industries will be immeasurable. It'll be Valentine's Day, every day.

I've been reading about this business for years and, in all that time, I haven't been tapped up by a Premiership club once. Am I doing something wrong?

Don't worry. Some people are tapped up by a Premiership club every day; other people go as much as a week, or even a fortnight, without being tapped up. Put it down to the little differences between us that make us human. Mind you, if you haven't had a call from Peter Kenyon by the end of next week, you should definitely have a word with your agent.

Delia Smith's Recipe for Premiership Survival

I suppose the key thing to say about the introduction of Delia Smith on to the pitch at Carrow Road during the televised match on Monday night is that it didn't work. But that's not to say it wasn't worth a try.

The Norwich City major shareholder and culinary legend had just witnessed a first half in which her points-hungry side had taken a two-goal lead over Manchester City, only to surrender it meekly and go in level at the break. For teams in the relegation zone, such slides tend to have a grim inevitability about them. You didn't need to be an astrologer or a student of ancient narrative forms to sense where the next goal was likely to come from – and it wasn't going to be from Norwich.

True, there was a glimmer of hope in the fact that Manchester City were managed by Kevin Keegan. And, as everybody knows, sides managed by Keegan tend to resemble a Rolodex in a strong wind; there's a lot of flapping and you're never exactly sure what's going to turn up. But even allowing for Keegan, it felt bleak for Norwich at half-time on Monday.

Now, confronted by such a situation, many of today's prissy, oil-drizzling TV chefs might well have been content to sit tight in the stands and let destiny run its course. But not Delia, who is from the old school where you roll your sleeves up, take the lard out of the fridge and get on with it. And so it was that the author of *Delia's Christmas* and countless other seminal works of the kitchen shelf, left her seat and walked out on to the playing surface with a microphone in her hand to make what is, these days, a rare television appearance.

An insensitive newspaper maintained that Delia seemed 'a little unsteady on her feet', but we are content to put that down to the condition of a tacky surface on a damp February night. It was clearly a pitch that would take a stud, but Delia was asking it to take a kitten heel, which is a different proposition altogether, from a balance point of view.

We are also sure that the odd, rasping drawl which Delia adopted – fully two octaves beneath the gentle soprano she always used while coaxing us to get the best out of our carrots – was a tactical decision, the better to underscore the urgency of her message to the people. After all, there's potatoes dauphinoise and there's relegation, and clearly each of them is going to call for its own, wildly different rhetorical approach.

Delia's sermon was addressed, necessarily, to the crowd, but one likes to think that its flavour and import were relayed to the players in the dressing room. That said, it didn't get off to the best of starts.

'A message for the best football supporters in the land,' Delia growled.

I don't think she necessarily meant to be ironic. The problem was, irony crept up on her somewhere, and she sounded as though she did. Irony can be cruel like that.

'We need a twelfth man here,' Delia continued. 'Where are you? *Where* are you? Let's be 'avin' you. Come on.'

Say what you like about the delivery, the dropping of important consonants in the word 'having' demonstrated her continuing mastery of the popular touch.*

Back in the Sky Sports studio, Dion Dublin was asked for an opinion but was unable to offer one because he was laughing too much. This was a shame because, in a long playing career, Dublin has worked under many managers, including Graham Taylor, and so might reasonably be thought to have insight to offer on the decoding of unusual or obscure half-time talks. But that's pundits. They always let you down.

Other observers have since chided Delia for her failure to be Martin Luther King. But Delia's approach has always been about simple ingredients, simply blended – to the point where some

---

* See also Tony Blair. And for a less successful demonstration, David Mellor.

critics have derided her for a patronizingly downbeat assessment of her audience's knowledge and understanding. Well, let them eat complicated cake. All I can say is that Delia's recipe for boiled egg is a firm family favourite round my way, and looks set to remain so.

Manchester City, of course, came back out and got their inevitable third goal, despite everything. The moral of this episode? You cannot stand in the way of destiny, any more than you can cook a decent steak with insufficient heat beneath the pan. But Delia's efforts were inspiring, in their own way. They showed what you can throw together even when there doesn't seem to be much in the cupboard. And let's face it, when did you last see Nigella Lawson get under the floodlights on a cold Monday night and urge the home crowd to do its business? I'll tell you when: never.

Remembering Eric

(Was it really ten years since Manchester United's gifted French legend went completely bongos at Selhurst Park and flung himself feet first into a Crystal Palace supporter's chest? Yes, it was.)

I must confess, until the business blew up about the masks, 'Cantona Day' had rather slipped my diary. Now the question of how best to mark the occasion – whether in public, with due ceremony, or quietly at home with friends – has become an issue for active debate, not just for me, but across the nation.

It's ten years since Manchester United's mercurial Frenchman broke a number of rules, both written and unwritten, regarding the practice of martial arts upon season-ticket-holding football supporters and, as a consequence, earned himself a nine-month ban from football and a two-week jail term, commutable to 120 hours of community service.

Now, no football supporters have a more finely tuned radar for an anniversary than Manchester United's. Remember the high moral dismay when Malcolm Glazer announced a bid for Manchester United within three days of the forty-seventh anniversary of the Munich disaster? Accordingly, United supporters had planned to turn this afternoon's revisit to Selhurst Park, the scene of the crime, into a kind of 'lest we forget'-style state occasion, with pomp and circumstance in the form of commemorative T-shirts and strap-on masks in the approximate shape of Cantona's rather magnificent head.

However, the management at Selhurst Park has warned United fans that anyone attempting to enter the stadium disguised as Cantona will be turned away. Furthermore, anyone who passes through the turnstiles as themselves and changes into a Cantona outfit once inside the ground, will be subject to immediate ejection 'on safety grounds'.

How these rules apply if the person entering the stadium looking like Cantona actually is Cantona is as yet unclear. But that detail probably needn't trouble us unduly. Cantona these days leads a largely blameless life as a French film actor, has shown scant inclination to mark 'Cantona Day' in the past and seems unlikely to behave any differently this year, just because it's the decade.

In the matter of the Cantona masks, one trusts the authorities to have made an informed calculation of the occasion's risks and to be acting according to that, rather than out of a desire to poop a party. That said, the more straightforwardly inflammatory act, surely, would be the wearing of masks depicting the face of Matthew Simmons. It was Simmons's abuse, after all, allegedly focusing on the Manchester United player's Frenchness, that brought out Cantona's inner Bruce Lee. So, in the absence of any clear steerage on this from the authorities, one assumes that Simmons masks are banned, too.

But does it then follow that 'Cantona Day' is completely ill-conceived as a festival, and that nothing should be done to commemorate that remarkable and in many ways era-defining moment of ten years ago? I don't think so, but I do think we need to be clear exactly what we are marking, if we choose to

mark it. I don't doubt that some knuckleheads continue to enjoy
the idea that, by battering one of the opposition's supporters,
Cantona was merely opening another front in their own ongoing
war. But we don't need to let the meaning of this episode get
co-opted and distorted by thugs.

On the contrary, Cantona's strike was, first and foremost, a
blow against racism – in particular, the idle, easy racism that
football grounds breed and tolerate. True, it's probably not the
route Mahatma Gandhi would have gone, faced by lippy dissent,
but there's no arguing that it made an impression, and not just
locally on Simmons.

More broadly, the idea that you might actually be answerable
to the abuse you dished out in a football ground was a new one
on supporters at Selhurst Park and beyond. Hitherto it had
seemed clear that a football stadium was a virtual world in this
regard. One didn't expect one's words and actions there to have
real consequences, any more than one expected the put-upon
villain in an Xbox gaming drama to crash out through the screen
and extract payback.

With one slightly inexpert piece of Kung Fu, Cantona, if not
dismantled, then at least queried this cherished illusion. And in
doing so, he opened up the chastening prospect that, if you
failed to adjust the scope of your shouting at a football match to
within the acceptable bounds of human interaction elsewhere,
you might well end up eating a footballer's boot.

This was no mean lesson, yet clearly it didn't get learned. At
the 2004–05 Carling Cup final, Jose Mourinho listened to eighty
minutes of potty-mouthed whining from the Liverpool fans
clustered around his dugout in the Millennium Stadium, before
politely advising them, with the gentle, finger-to-lips gesture
favoured by nursery school teachers everywhere, that a period
of silence on their part would now be appreciated.

In almost any other culture, he would have been instantly
awarded a civic prize for the upholding of civilized values in
barbaric circumstances. Instead, he is hustled down the tunnel
by the fourth official, Liverpool supporters leap about, honking

that they have been 'antagonized' (d'oh!), and most of the country's press expresses lofty surprise when the FA, in a rare moment of enlightenment, choose not to fine him to within an inch of destitution.

We appear to have learned very little. There is no glass screen between the stands and the pitch, but people continue to behave as if there is and what might have been the most lasting of Cantona's several legacies is left to dangle in the breeze. Maybe 'Cantona Day' is not a time for T-shirts and masks. But it could usefully be a time to remember and reflect.

Sam Allardyce at the Watershed

With Wayne Rooney scheduled to appear in a live teatime fixture, it will have been another twitchy Saturday for parents, teachers and other anxious guardians of the 9.00 p.m. watershed. As it happened, Rooney had one of his almost blameless, even decorous, days, at no point tossing from his pram the adult-oriented toys that could yet land live football a time-slot somewhere between *Porn: A Family Business* and *The Sky At Night*.

However, let rejoicing be severely limited, because, by then, an act of violence against the nation's moral fibre had already been committed – this time during the lunchtime fixture, and not by a player but by the manager of Bolton Wanderers.

The incident came in the seventy-first minute, when Sam Allardyce, with his side trailing by a goal and down to ten men, perceived that Arsenal's Antonio Reyes had, to use the popular phrase, gone down a little too easily. Arsenal got a free kick, and the producer cut to Allardyce, roaring off the bench at a speed later estimated to have been in the vicinity of 134 mph and with a face like a broken bottle.

Now, I'll admit in the spirit of openness that I have no official qualifications as a lip-reader. But I have watched a lot of football on television, so I have, at the very least, wide and concentrated experience in the field of lip-reading. And it's my perception

that the phrase used by Allardyce to convey, in the direction of
the pitch, his dismay at that moment is unprintable, beyond
mentioning that there were two words, both beginning with 'c'
and one of which was 'cheating'.

And all this at lunchtime, in the *Watch With Mother* zone. If
Captain Snort from Pippin Fort were alive today, he'd be spinning
in his grave.

Those of us watching in the company of children under eight
needed a firm hand on the tiller at this disturbing time, and
we got one, remarkably enough, from Jonathan Pearce, the
commentator. I don't think I am on controversial ground when
I suggest that Pearce is not famous for the canny deployment of
dry understatement. Indeed, he tends in the main to commentate
as if he is being vigorously boiled in a bag. So all credit to the
BBC's man for the quiet subtitle he added to these pictures by
merely remarking that Allardyce looked 'aggrieved'.

What are we to do about these almost daily offences against
propriety and their threat to the character of our offspring?
Well, FIFA has stepped in to pump up the punishment for abus-
ing the referee, which is something. It has also been suggested
that footballers and managers might consider toning down the
language altogether, but that's like asking for the game to be
played in wellingtons. Swearing is football's medium and always
has been.

Of course, the reason nobody much complained about it in
the past is that there were fewer extreme close-ups. Television
didn't use to have the cameras to dedicate to the drama of the
touchlines, nor did it have the zoom lenses to go in close when it
kicked off verbally on the pitch. So one option would be for television to get out of football's face and let the innocent remain so.

But that's not going to happen. So therefore, we've said it
before but we'll say it again: the simplest solution here is pixi-
lation. It's clean, it's safe and it's what television does with
exposed genitalia and celebrity number plates. So why not with
Sam Allardyce's head?

Recalling Chelsea with Claudia Schiffer

(Was it really 100 years since Chelsea were founded? Yes, it was. Any old supermodel could have told you that.)

It saddens me to relate that my invitation to this week's celebrity-studded party, marking the centenary of the founding of Chelsea Football Club, got lost in the post and still hasn't shown up. Weirdly, the same thing happened with my invitation to the christening of Romeo Beckham. A man could lose faith in the postal service.

Fortunately, however, some of the invitations to Chelsea's birthday bash did get through, and so the event was able to go ahead without me at the Butcher's Hook in the Fulham Road, which was the scene, on 14 March 1905, of the club's inaugural board meeting, back in the days when Peter Osgood hadn't yet invented himself and when Ken Bates was still just a surprisingly belligerent twinkle in his father's eye.

Had the late Gus Mears, who was in the chair on that seminal occasion, only known that the organism he was tenderly bringing into the world would one day grow and expand to the point where it would end up signing Vinnie Jones . . . well, he probably would have called the meeting to an end more quickly than he did and organized a game of darts instead. But many thousands of us over the intervening years have been grateful to him for sticking to the agenda.

And what a swell party Monday night's was, according to reports – one for the historians, indeed, as leading and legendary figures from Chelsea's present and past mingled animatedly. It's a rare night when Roy Bentley, the captain of the 1955 championship-winning side, gets to rub shoulders in the pub with Claudia Schiffer, the actress and lingerie model.

Roman Abramovich and Jose Mourinho were there, of course, and Ruud Gullit and Terry Venables, whose places in the Chelsea story are secure. And also present were Gordon

Ramsay, the television chef, who probably doesn't get to as many away games these days as he would like to, and Bernie Ecclestone, the Formula One supremo. I'm not sure whether or not Bernie supports Chelsea, but he definitely supports money, so it was entirely fitting that he should be there or thereabouts on the night.

It was an achingly stellar line-up, all in all, but the person with whom I most regret not getting to have a chinwag, fan to fan, is Claudia. I would have liked to ask her, over the sparkling white wine and caviar, whether she had a good day out at the Carling Cup final, what time she made it back to London and how many people she had in her minibus – just the ordinary kind of harmless but life-affirming chit-chat that football people exchange when they get together.

Claudia's old enough to remember when the West Stand was a carbuncle, accessible across a slagheap by a death trap of temporary stairways. She would be in a position to appreciate as well as anyone the full measure of how far the club has come. It would have been great to get her take on the club's history, particularly the Mears years. But who am I kidding? I'd probably never have been able to prise her away from her conversations with Bobby Campbell and Ian Porterfield.

Whatever, I'm left to wonder what Claudia is making of the Anders Frisk affair. This, after all, was the week in which Mourinho was declared 'the enemy of football' for his part in the resignation of the referee, who claims to have received death threats from Chelsea supporters since Mourinho was critical of his performance in Barcelona.

It's my conjecture that in this matter Claudia would be urging people to exercise greater discrimination in the separation of cause and effect. I don't know, because I wasn't able to ask her. But I imagine Claudia's opinion is that, if a manager thinks he sees the opposition's coach going into the referee's changing room at half-time, he'd have to be a saint not to want at least to mention it. It's not then that manager's fault if some knuckle-dragger with a misguided notion about his own part in the argument decides to go to war with the ref in question over the internet.

In any case, as Claudia would be the first to point out, the source of Chelsea supporters' irritation with Frisk had little to do with the half-time conspiracy theory, which has seemed muddy and incomprehensible to the layman from the start. It was the fact that Frisk sent off Didier Drogba for innocently contesting a 50–50 ball, a topic for debate on which Mourinho has been almost Gandhi-like in his restraint.

Now, I'm sure Claudia would come right out and say that no one should be hounded from their position in alleged fear for the safety of their family. But, at the same time, I reckon it would be very like her to add that, while we solemnly canonize Frisk as the first martyr of the UEFA elite officials' list, we ought not to overlook the fact that he was also a flouncing peacock, an incorrigible luvvie and a trouble-magnet – not 'an enemy of football', of course, because that would be a ridiculous thing to say, but definitely a distraction from it.

The Frisk affair, and its elaboration in the press and at UEFA, for all that it appears to be a debate about rectitude and the upholding of core moral values, has the unmistakable shape of a jealous swipe in the direction of Mourinho. It suggests that people, in the traditional English style, are growing impatient with his success. There will have been plenty of sympathy for him in the Butcher's Hook on Monday night, and beyond. Chelsea supporters are rapidly learning in this centenary year what it feels like to be successful and despised. Still, Claudia and I can remember times when the club was despised and useless. On the whole, this is better.

Vote, Vote, Vote for Sir Alex Ferguson

(*Tony Blair was about to go head-to-head with Michael Howard for the right to continue managing Britain at national and international level, and the country could hardly be expected to go to the polls without informed guidance from the Premiership's leading club manager.*)

Of all the political manifestos, none will have been more eagerly received and pored over than that of Sir Alex Ferguson, whose 'Why It Must Be Labour' – printed in full in the *Daily Mirror* – takes the form of a spirited and typically unequivocal, 600-word plea from the Manchester United manager for five more years of Tony Blair.

Of course, by speaking so openly (and optimistically, some might say) of Labour as 'the party of the working people', Ferguson does risk alienating the supporters who are the very core of Manchester United's fan base – the middle-class, home-owning, Volvo-driving people in the traditional Tory strongholds of the south. But that's the beauty, as well as the bravery, of Ferguson's endorsement, and one can see how delighted the Blair operation must be to have so potentially effective an agitator operating, as it were, behind enemy lines.

Anyway, I don't doubt that United fans of every stripe will be having a good look at themselves and their voting intentions following Ferguson's rallying cry. 'The health service is better,' writes Ferguson, without going into details. 'So are our schools. Kids are no longer thrown on the scrapheap,' he adds, before holding up the glimmering prospect of a society without prejudice, a land which rewards the humble and protects the weak, a country where all are equal before the law such that if, say, a manager of a leading Premiership club (let's call them Manchester United, and let's call him Sir Alex Ferguson) gets caught driving illegally up the hard shoulder of the M42 to avoid a traffic jam, he can claim a digestive problem and get acquitted by a court.

However, as well as being both visionary and polemical, Ferguson's essay is also a piece of moral instruction, a cautionary tale on the importance of persistence, as embodied in United's European Cup victory of 1999. 'Just think how you would feel if you don't vote and watch Michael Howard walking into Downing Street the next day,' Ferguson warns. 'You'd feel like I would have done if Bayern Munich had held on and the Champions League went to Germany not Manchester.'

Of course, even had Bayern held on, the Champions League trophy would not have gone, strictly speaking, to Germany; it would have gone to Munich, which, though indubitably a part of Germany, as Manchester is indubitably a part of England, is not quite the same thing. Note the subtlety of Ferguson's rhetoric here, and the appeal to deep-seated national prejudice in the insinuation that a victory for Howard is that most unacceptable thing – a victory for the Germans.

Clever old Fergie, then. Yet the analogy has its limits, and any United fan in a Tory marginal, inspired by the manager's words to have a change of political heart and, more than that, to deliver their Labour vote on 5 May right at the death, in the form of a Solskjaer-style, last-gasp, killer blow, should note that there is no time-added-on at polling stations. Miss the 10.00 p.m. deadline, and that's it, I'm afraid; the doors will be shut and the people manning the station will be inside, putting away the pencils. In this light, it might have been responsible of Ferguson to point out that voting, unlike winning the European Cup, is something which needs to be achieved within the regulation period.

However, it's only when Ferguson addresses the question of loyalty that his argument runs into major difficulties. 'As for Michael Howard,' he writes, 'there's only one thing you need to know about him. He supports Liverpool . . . and Swansea . . . and Folkestone . . . and Hythe Town . . . and Llanelli . . . He'll support anyone, say anything, to get your vote.'

Now, the politician who leans on football as a vote-clinching normalizer is a stock figure. Certainly anyone who sets out to become prime minister is, by definition, less interested in football than the job might eventually oblige him to claim to be. Life is about choices, after all, and if you are prepared to put yourself in a position where G8 summits, state visits, meetings of the war cabinet and so forth are likely to restrict your attendance at home games, then football is self-evidently not among the personal interests that you are carefully ring-fencing.

However within those strictures, it's not hard to see who has the best record of the major party leaders in this particular area. Howard's interest in Liverpool is longstanding and seemingly sincere enough; it certainly extends to watching them sometimes. And I'm not sure I see in what sense supporting Liverpool precludes a person from wishing well the non-league teams of Folkestone and Hythe, particularly if the Liverpool supporter in question happens to be the MP for their constituency. Similarly, there is no scandalous conflict of interest involved in supporting Liverpool while retaining a soft spot for Swansea City from League Two or Llanelli from the Welsh Premier League, clubs connected with Howard's past. Does Ferguson not look out for the results of Aberdeen?

Contrast Blair, who, famously, has his detailed and intimate recollections of supporting Newcastle United as a child. But equally famously, they turn out to have been impossible because the ground wasn't built or he wasn't alive, or because some other factual shortfall unnoticed by his press office obtains.

As for Charles Kennedy, never mind what he stands for; for whom does he stand up? Nobody really knows. Which means it's probably Queens Park Rangers. If, as Ferguson suggests, this really is 'the only thing you need to know', and if a politician's electability is to be judged by the depth and duration of his allegiance to his team, then I'm afraid there is no getting round this: Ferguson ought to have come out for Howard.

Of course, for many voters, other factors may well come into play, such as policies on immigration, taxation and hospitals. And for this reason our inkling is that Howard – despite the solid argument Ferguson inadvertently makes on behalf of his candidacy – may still be stuffed come the first Thursday in May.*

How I Learned to Love Chelsea and Stop Worrying about the Bomb

(*A draw at home to Arsenal put Chelsea within five points of their first league title for fifty years, with five games of the season remaining. But, for some of us, it was no time for complacency.*)

'*Chelsea will be champions unless someone puts a bomb here*' (*Arsene Wenger at Stamford Bridge*).

Until Wenger raised the bomb scenario, it hadn't really occurred to me. Which is surprising, given how carefully I have gone over in my mind the various combinations of events which could lead to Chelsea not ending up as champions this season. Call me paranoid, call me pessimistic or call me a Chelsea season-ticket holder: it amounts to the same thing. The point is we're not there yet, and until you're there a lot can go wrong.

The bomb, though: I hadn't thought of that. And it is a real worry. A slip-up against Fulham this afternoon; a victory for Arsenal at home to Tottenham on Monday night; a terrorist atrocity on Wednesday morning . . . how easily it could all unravel.

I know, I know: five points from five games. For the team that has lost just once in the league all season, this should not be, as they say, a big ask.

At the same time – five points from five games! That's a point per game for heaven's sake. Those players aren't machines, you know.

* I was absolutely right about this. Blair did win the 2005 election. You know, taking a hunch into print is always risky, especially on the really hard to call issues. But sometimes you've just got to bite the bullet and do it. The rewards, when you get it right, make all the anxiety in the meantime worthwhile.

If you care about this outcome, you are exiled for ever from the casual confidence of the neutral observer. I saw it written that, had they beaten Chelsea on Wednesday, Arsenal would merely have been 'postponing the inevitable'. The inevitable! If only. A fortnight ago, when Chelsea could only draw at home to Birmingham and their lead dipped from a potentially useful, if not remotely comfortable, thirteen points to a positively panic-inducing eleven points, it seemed to me that the title race had been blown wide open.

'I'm worried that Chelsea aren't going to win the title,' I told a friend. And he laughed more loudly than I have ever heard him laugh at anything. Which I suppose I might have found reassuring, if I hadn't found it so insensitive.

And that was before Wednesday, when the result did, I concede, bring the title within touching distance, but when Wenger had to go and mention the bomb – like I didn't have enough to worry about. For instance . . .

Scenario one: Chelsea lose all their remaining games, while Arsenal win all theirs. Arsenal thereby become champions instead of Chelsea. (This is in many respects the most simple of the scenarios. But that doesn't make it any less haunting at certain restless hours of the night.)

Scenario two: on the afternoon of Friday 13 May, with Chelsea taking a seemingly insuperable eleven-point lead into the final weekend of the season, the Premier League finds heavily against the club in the Ashley Cole tap-up case and imposes a fifteen-point deduction, making winning the title a mathematical impossibility.

Scenario three: Peter Kenyon does something so colossally stupid that the club automatically has its licence to operate rescinded. (Chelsea supporters of a nervous disposition inevitably spend a lot of time worrying about the next colossally stupid thing Kenyon may or may not do.)

Scenario four: at the general election on 5 May, with the league programme still dangerously incomplete, the country controversially elects a Taliban government, whose first move is to ban, on pain of death, kite-flying, professional football and all items of silverware. (In the event of this happening, the knowledge that I was likely to be put up against a wall and beaten about the knees for owning a CD-player would be little consolation.)

Scenario five: on 7 May, following a title-clinching home victory over Charlton Athletic, John Terry reaches for the trophy – only for a swarm of highly trained killer-bees to swoop into the stadium and sting it from his grasp. The bees then carry the trophy out over the rooftops and into hiding, and the season is declared void, pending a full investigation by journalists from *National Geographic* magazine.

Still, it's nice to realize it matters. One hears people saying that Chelsea's first championship victory for fifty years (assuming it happens) will mean little to its supporters, or possibly even deflate them, because the club has 'bought the title'. This would be in contrast, presumably, to the organic or 'naturally occurring' titles won by Manchester United and Arsenal over the last decade. It might be as well for all these late-onset friends of the earth to admit that, until such time as managers can wander dreamily into the sunshine and pluck a football team from the wild, we're probably stuck with a world in which people end up paying for them.

And that's not as easy as it sounds. You still have to be clever enough to pay for the right players, preferably having appointed the right manager to blend them together. Talk to Sir Alex Ferguson about it.

Meanwhile an article on the op-ed pages of the *Guardian* this week was claiming that Chelsea supporters would not sleep easily over their success, knowing that it was paid for with money gained by the privatization of formerly nationalized Russian service industries. Hold that champagne cork! While accepting that life presents many opportunities indeed to feel guilty by association, there surely comes a point for everyone where you have to stop whipping yourself in the interests of having some flesh left.

True, if I was a Russian peasant, I might retain a mild grudge or two about the flogging of my heating supply to a man who now lives in Sussex and has his own helicopter. But in the main, I'd be looking at what the likes of Arjen Robben, Petr Cech and Claude Makelele have brought to the Premiership this season and feeling that my gas bill had been pretty well spent. And when you think about the range of things that Roman Abramovich could be spending his money on (backing a South American military junta, for instance, or supporting the *Daily Mail*), then even the purchase of Hernan Crespo begins to look like an utterly innocent and life-affirming diversion. We say, long and happily may he spend.

We also say, may the Premiership be put beyond doubt as soon as possible. At the final whistle on Wednesday night, parts of Stamford Bridge joined in singing the great, traditional, end-of-campaign battle hymn. But not me. 'Oh, now you've got to believe us . . .' Not until we've won it, I haven't.

Did I get around to mentioning Scenario six? I don't believe I did.

Scenario six: locusts.*

The Golden Age of Fan Abuse

(*A Manchester United defender didn't like what he was hearing from an Everton fan and kicked a ball at him. Neither the referee nor the defender's manager was particularly impressed.*)

On the topic of Gary Neville and his sending off, Sir Alex Ferguson was crisp and to the point: 'You can't kick a ball at a spectator – not nowadays.' His words couldn't help but set one thinking fondly of those days when kicking a ball at a spectator was perfectly acceptable – that golden age when the game was

* Chelsea did win the 2004–05 Premiership title. There was no bomb. There were no locusts. The highly trained killer-bees, however, had to be intercepted by special forces at Heathrow.

played and run by real men, and you could give some lippy Evertonian a taste of the leather whenever you felt like it.

But that's all gone now. Take out a fan with a half-volley or simple drop-kick and the referee is immediately involved, not to mention the television cameras, stewards and police, and possibly even the social services by the end of it. The new lighter balls don't help, either. We're with Sir Alex, here. It's a different game these days, and not necessarily the better for it.

Manchester United in the Twilight Zone

The Football Association wants Sir Alex Ferguson to explain his claim that there may be something 'sinister' behind the lack of penalties awarded to Manchester United this season. Whether the United manager hands over the full weight of his research into this unsettling matter, or whether he confines himself to an outline of the salient points, his response is bound to make for fascinating reading when it plops through the FA's letterbox.

Of course, that response may be too big for the letterbox and, consequently, too big to plop. We don't yet know how far Ferguson's investigations have taken him, or how much inform-ation he has assembled. Clearly, however, Ferguson is not the sort of man who enters into anything lightly. It's perfectly poss-ible that we'll see piles of documents and computer printouts, possibly even boxes of forensically sealed evidence, and perhaps even one or two items carefully stored in polythene Ziploc bags, being carried over the next few days into the FA's offices in Soho Square.

Either way, let's hope the FA commits itself to full disclosure of the materials in its possession, rather than, as on so many similar occasions in the past, trying to hush the matter up and secure Ferguson's silence with a fine and a threat of further action if he ever says anything so silly again.

Because if there really are 'sinister' forces at work within the Premiership – and, let's be clear, we're talking about something which potentially goes way higher than Paul Dickov here – and if a senior leading figure within the game claims to have evidence that such forces are operating, then there can be no doubt that the paying public, upon whose support the game depends, deserves to know.

So far, Ferguson has only hinted at the shape of his findings, but the facts are indisputable: Manchester United haven't had a penalty since October last year – and that's despite trying as hard as everyone does these days to get one, and perhaps even harder than some, especially since Ruud Van Nistelrooy returned from injury.

'It is getting ridiculous now,' Ferguson told MUTV, after Alan Smith had a claim turned down in last Sunday's match against Newcastle United. 'I am not sure if they [referees] are instructed, but it is looking sinister to me. Since that penalty kick against Arsenal, it seems we are not going to get another one.'

However, our own research has indicated that the problem is broader than even Ferguson acknowledges. Chelsea have been awarded only four penalties in the Premiership this season, and not one of them has come at a particularly critical or match-turning moment. Indeed, one of the pens was in the ninetieth minute at home to Newcastle, when Chelsea were already leading 3–0, and so little did it matter that they let Mateja Kezman take it.

Eerie, no? But there's more. Arsenal, too, have been awarded merely four Premiership penalties (converting just three of them) in 2004–05 – and only one of those was this year. That's one more than Manchester United in 2005, true, but you'd expect a team with Robert Pires in it to be in double figures by this point in the season. There's only one possible explanation: that someone, or something, is working directly through the appointed officials to choke the penalty supply to the big clubs.

So who are they? What do they want? Who is implicated in the cover-up? And what is really going on when push comes to shove in the penalty area – or as Ferguson might care to think of it, 'the grassy knoll'?

These are the kind of questions which, with any luck, the manager's thorough explanation to the FA will address. But in the absence of that report, here's what I think might be happening – and it's the point that I suspect Ferguson has reached on this issue, too.

As David Icke, the celebrated author and cultural commentator, has already pointed out (and Ferguson, I'm sure, will be amply familiar with the theory), our world is governed by a master race of shape-shifting giant lizards, for whom the overt sources of power – the government, the royal family – are merely a front. (Readers new to this theory may care to visit Icke's website and go, in particular, to the section entitled 'The Reptilian Connection'.)

That much, I assume, we can all agree on. But if it's safe to say that shape-shifting giant lizards run the world, then it's no big leap of the imagination to suggest that those lizards might, at some point, want to extend their influence to the professional referees on the 'Select Group' list.

Hence the situation we're now in: the lizards are interfering with the referees' minds. In order to do this, they have created a new kind of highly intelligent weevil, which enters the referee's brain via the ear canal. The lizards might introduce the weevils at night, when the referee is asleep, or when he is out jogging. Either way, the referee feels and remembers nothing.

The weevil, however, goes to work to block vital neural pathways in the referee's brain, rendering him virtually immune to a tumble in the box if the player doing the tumbling belongs to one of the top three clubs, and especially immune to it if the footballer happens to play for Manchester United.

Why would the lizards be interested in doing this? Because they are part of the global conspiracy to bring down United? Perhaps. But, far more importantly, consider the implications of being able to render a human being grossly insubordinate, and completely oblivious to matters of size, history and standing within the community. And then consider what would happen if, having established the effectiveness of the weevils in this

controlled experiment with referees, the lizards were then to
unleash the weevils throughout society, introducing them into
the ears of the entire population.

The result would very quickly be anarchy and complete social
breakdown, creating a 'window of chaos' through which the
giant lizards could finally throw aside their disguise and assert
their dominion over, not just the United Kingdom, but the
entire earth. And Leicester.

One sees, with a shudder, how far this goes. It's why I am
urging the FA to hold a frank and open enquiry into Ferguson's
claims – and why I am urging Ferguson not to take the usual
£5,000 fine and a slapped wrist for an answer. After all, what's
important here: PR or the truth?*

Why 'Virtual Replay' is Spoiling it for Everyone

*(A Champions League semi-final between Liverpool and Chelsea. Luis
Garcia pokes the ball towards Chelsea's goal and controversy ensues.
But not for long.)*

Science moved quickly to adjudicate on the Luis Garcia 'goal'
for Liverpool in the European Cup semi-final, running the
forensic evidence through the computer and proving that the
ball came no closer to entering Chelsea's goal than the assistant
referee did. Always good to have the facts to hand, I guess, but
it must have spoiled the fun for those who were getting ready
to warm their hands round a Geoff Hurst-style debate – the kind
of football talking point which, with careful tending, might have
continued to give off a gently sustaining heat for a quarter of a
century or more.

Fat chance of that now. Was it a goal? No.

Still, some intriguing questions remain for our leisurely con-

* The contents of Sir Alex's dossier were never disclosed. Indeed, he went
very quiet on the whole issue. You go ahead and suspect a cover-up, if you
like. I'm saying nothing.

sideration. For instance, if the Virtual Replay system is so sophisticated, why, under the minutely accurate conditions of its reconstructions, do the players end up looking like characters from
children's television? The computer-generated animations from
Tuesday night conclusively demonstrate a number of things –
but nothing quite so memorably as the fact that Mr Ben couldn't
have been better placed to cover for the goalkeeper and that
Bob the Builder was fractionally offside during the approach
play.

Also, we are told that Virtual Replay is used on missiles by
the Israeli military, which sounds like a fairly awesome guarantee
of its efficiency. But, at the same time, it inevitably leads the
doubtful layman to wonder when, exactly, the Israeli military
needs to look at a replay of a missile, and to wonder what
controversies can possibly come up, in the missile-firing arena,
that Virtual Replay could usefully solve?

Missiles, after all, tend to be very much their own proof, in
this context, and questions of whether a missile crossed the line,
took a deflection, was offside at the point of launch, etc. look
fairly academic in the aftermath of its landing.

Still, the military parallel inspires one to suggest a potential
footballing development that would eliminate frustrating and
costly controversies such as Tuesday night's once and for all: a
ball that explodes on impact with the goal. I'm no expert on the
ins and outs of chemical reactivity, but it would surely be possible
in this day and age to fill the goal with a highly flammable gas,
such that, when the totality of the ball's specially designed coating reacted with it – ka-boom! Goodbye to not-fully-over-the-
line misery, and possibly to one or two other things as well.

Say what you like, it would take the pressure off the officials.
Surely even Roman Slysko, the assistant referee from Slovakia
who gave the Garcia goal at Anfield, wouldn't fail to notice the
fact that a bomb hadn't gone off.

Even without the intervention of Virtual Replay, though,
one senses that Tuesday's 'case of the goal that wasn't' might
not, with the best will in the world, have enjoyed a particularly

long and emotional public trial. It was noticeable that Chelsea's
players barely protested about the decision at the time. Partly
that must have been a response to the realization that losing a
goal was preferable to the other potential outcome that hovered
around the incident: losing a goalkeeper. (Petr Cech may have
been sent off for the contact he made with Milan Baros just
before Garcia scored – or rather, just before Garcia had his shot
cleared off the line.)

But partly, also, the Chelsea players must have understood
that a single Liverpool goal did nothing to change their mission
on the night, which was simply to score themselves at some
point. (A 1–1 draw would have taken Chelsea through on the
away goals rule.) It's why nobody connected with Chelsea is
talking right now about 'robbery' or seething with righteous
resentment. The fact that Liverpool were credited with a non-
existent goal is a small, fly-like irritation, almost an extraneous
detail, beside Chelsea's greater disappointment with themselves
for not scoring – the harsh and bitterly learned truth being, of
course, that if you can't score against Liverpool in 180 minutes,
then you don't deserve to win the Champions League.

Spare a thought for Garcia, though. History suggests that some
handsome-looking commercial opportunities were opening up
for him after Tuesday, until Virtual Replay crisply slammed the
door on them. At least Hurst had a good thirty-five years of
after-dinner speaking before the Israeli military got to him.
Garcia had less than twenty-four hours to work his story up into
something cute and anecdotal – not even time enough to get
himself booked on to a solitary cruise ship.

Accordingly, the legend of Tuesday night will remain un-
grown. What we're unlikely to see now, for instance, is any
development of Milan Baros into the Roger Hunt role. Hurst
always used to say that the reaction of Hunt in 1966 (who,
instead of hastening in to bury the rebound, turned to appeal
for the goal) confirmed him in the opinion that his shot landed
behind the line – an argument setting hearteningly great store
by Hunt's eyesight and instinctive integrity.

'What clinched it for me,' Garcia might have said in the talks he never got to give, 'was the way that Baros didn't bother to follow up. He knew, you see, that it was going in.' Alas, science has nixed that one.

Still, in the event that he meets with quibblers down the line, Garcia can take a leaf from Hurst's book. When people put it to the England striker that his second goal was an optical illusion suffered by a Russian linesman, Hurst would deal them the ultimate argument-settler: 'It was a goal on the day.'

It wasn't, of course.

Sven Does Dallas

Attention: All Players
From: The Football Association
Re: Summer Tour of the US

On behalf of Sven and everyone connected with Team England – welcome aboard! Firstly may we thank you for agreeing to come with us on this summer's upcoming national team tour of America, many of you at very short notice, at the end of what has been a long and demanding season, even in the lower leagues.

No doubt a few of you will have read some of the negative remarks in the press regarding the tour – how it's come at exactly the wrong time, how it's taking place in a country which is almost completely indifferent to football, and how, all in all, it's a complete waste of money and effort.

On the contrary, the tour will be a vital bonding exercise and a thrilling opportunity to grow the Three Lions brand in the biggest and most exciting sports market in the world.

You may also have heard it said that, what with the number of key players who have dropped out, variously claiming injury, exhaustion and fear of their club's manager, the tour is of limited, or even no, tactical use.

That assessment couldn't be further from the truth.

These days together give Sven what could be a critically important chance to examine his options in the event that, say, a nuclear incident at Sellafield devastes the north-west of the country on the eve of a major tournament and on a weekend that Chelsea and Arsenal happen to be in the region. And you know what they say: fail to prepare, prepare to fail.

A brief word on local custom. Americans refer to football exclusively as 'soccer' and mean, by 'football', an entirely different sport altogether. Indeed, if, at any point on the tour, someone invites you to 'come play some real football and see what you're made of,' we strongly advise you against doing so. You won't enjoy it.

So, again, thanks – and congratulations, too, especially to those who will soon be pulling on an England shirt for the first time, and, quite likely the last, as well. But, whether new to the set-up or old, please take a moment to familiarize yourself with the following itinerary, which has been broadly revised and replaces all previously issued itineraries.

Monday, 09.30. Arrival, Orlando. International press conference and photoshoot with David Beckham and members of the global broadcasting media, plus live internet feed.

Please note: this item is cancelled owing to enforced late arrival of David Beckham.

In its place: web-chat with Gareth Southgate. Followed by radio phone interview with Richie Hopeful at KSMOOTH, broadcasting easy-listening classics to the Orlando area.

10.00. Hotel meet'n'greet with representatives of our official tour sponsors – A1 Plaster Coving of Tampa ('the one-stop shop for all your plaster coving needs'); A Place For Pancakes, 2014 Main St, Delaware ('2-for-1 blueberry hour, 6.00–7.00 nightly'); and Big Dave's Furter Inc., 'America's premier offal and loose-meat processing concern'. Ceremonial exchange of goodie bags.

18.30. Tampa Bay Gator Dome. Match: 25-minute five-a-side, England v. George Duke III High School. As prelude to Roller Hockey Puckslam 2005, Philadelphia Moosejaws v. Cincinnati Burst.

(Please note: changing for this one will be on the coach. Also, the arena must be vacated immediately upon the referee's final whistle to allow the stage to be readied for Dwight Yoakam. Despite the strict time constraints, however, Sven is confident that all squad members will get a game. And don't underestimate George Duke III, by the way, They may 'only' be a high school side, but they were interstate champions in both 2003 and 2004. Not bad for girls!)

Wednesday: day off.

Thursday, 06.15. Internal flight to Dallas. Shuttle bus to hotel.

10.30. Training: a welcome chance to run up and down between some cones with Tord Grip.

11.30. Cross-promotional photo-opportunity: Dick Chad, chief strategy director of corporate affairs at Sugar-Me Donuts, and Wayne Rooney.

Please note, this item is cancelled, owing to lack of Wayne Rooney.

In its place: picture of Peter Crouch with a basketball player? (To be confirmed.)

14.00. Factory visit: Big Dave's Furter Inc. Courtesy of our sponsor, a rare opportunity to get a close-up look at life in one of America's premier offal and loose-meat processing plants. Find out exactly what goes into making the hot dogs and pies we take for granted. And find out exactly what doesn't go into them!

NB: this visit is compulsory, as is the wearing of hairnets at all times within the flaying and threshing halls. Representatives of the factory will be on hand throughout the tour to offer guidance on all sanitation issues – and, indeed, to answer any other questions you may have – but, if in doubt, cover up.

19.15. RomCom Stadium. Match: England v. Saratoga Vipers. As pre-match entertainment ahead of the 2005 Mega-Wired Monster Truck Fireball Derby. Forty minutes only. Rush goalies.

(The Vipers are, in fact, a Frisbee team, but we are assured that they regularly use soccer as part of their training workouts and so will be bound to give us a useful run-out. Again, we cannot stress too keenly the importance of vacating the pitch as quickly as possible before the arrival of the first mega-wired monster truck. If caught short, or otherwise in difficulty, stand still with your hand raised until a steward arrives.)

Friday: day off.

Saturday: another day off.

Sunday, 07.00. Internal flight to Detroit.

11.00. Pick-up basketball game.
   Shirts: Players registered with Premier League clubs.
   Skins: Players from Coca Cola Championship clubs or lower.

14.45. KY Arena. Match: England v. Bogota. Ten minutes each way. Barefoot, on sand. In run-up to Thunderslap Inter-zonal Tag-Wrestle Fest.

19.30. Flight to Heathrow. Please note that your personal baggage limit is 25kg, and that items containing loose meat and offal may not be imported into Britain without a full declaration to Customs.

Interlude: When Reality Hit Lee Sharpe

(*Or rather, when Lee Sharpe hit reality. One Fijian paradise, twelve castaway celebrities. But would the nearly man of football find love at the end of the day?*)

Even as Alan Hansen was vigorously engaging in a BBC 1 documentary with the question of how footballers cope with life beyond football, a thrillingly contemporary solution to the problem was proposing itself on ITV. Switch between the two channels and it was obvious that, if you're a player confronted with the inevitable waning of your physical powers, you can, essentially, go down one of two paths.

You can, like Dave Whelan, whose career was cruelly thwarted by injury, get yourself a market stall selling toiletries in Wigan and then, through sheer graft and application, diversify and grow the business, until eventually you sit at the head of a nation-girdling sports goods retail empire worth millions. Or you can take the Lee Sharpe route, and go on *Celebrity Love Island*.

Sharpe's is, of course, the more high-risk post-playing career strategy in the short term, and he must know that, however well it goes for him over the next fortnight on the show's sun-drenched Fijian set, he is unlikely to end up, like Whelan, owning and chairing a Premiership football club. He may, however, end up happily married to the girl of his dreams – or, more specifically, to one of the girls of the programme's producers' dreams. (As the old saying has it, you can't choose your relatives, but you can choose your friends. On reality television, though, you can't even choose your friends.)

And whatever happens, he'll have a tan. Still, to all footballers asking themselves the question, 'Am I a Dave or a Lee?' and answering, 'On reflection, I'm a Lee' – a note of warning. Not just anybody can walk on to a reality television show, even in the twenty-first century. For one thing, a cabal of repeat-performers largely sews up the available work. Among the homogenous

young love-seekers on *Celebrity Love Island* are Rebecca Loos
(ex *The Farm*, ex *Extreme Celebrity DeTox*) and Fran Cosgrave
(ex *I'm A Celebrity . . . Get Me Out Of Here!*). It's worse than
the civil service and, if this isn't already a crisis, it soon will be.
Hansen didn't get on to the subject for some reason, but it may
be necessary to bring in a kind of quota system limiting the
number of reality shows a celebrity can appear on in any season.
Otherwise, the opportunities simply aren't going to be there for
the youngsters.

Sharpe himself, of course, comes into this new show off the
back of the doomed *Celebrity Wrestling*. But – and, wannabe
Lees, again take note – *Celebrity Love Island* is a tougher ask
altogether for the former Manchester United star, calling, as it
does, for a completely different set of physical and mental skills.
Let's face it, it's one thing to try to push over John Fashanu with
a giant plastic bap, but it's quite another to share beach-based,
dorm-style living quarters with Abi Titmuss.

Yet the early signs are that Sharpe is bedding in well, if that's
a permissible expression in this context. One is aware, of course,
that *Celebrity Love Island* is a world where the transfer window
is always open. But, thus far, to the extent that Sharpe has signed
on with any of his fellow castaways, it has been with Jayne
Middlemiss from Channel 4's *The Games*. Sharpe was very soon
telling her about his house, a seven-bedroom Victorian semi
with, as Sharpe straight away mentioned, 'a cellar'.

This detail of the cellar, like anything said by anyone on
Celebrity Love Island, drew some smug hilarity from Patrick
Kielty, the show's presenter, but it's my feeling that Sharpe, far
from being gauche, was actually being tactically astute. If you've
got a cellar, you're best off being open about it as quickly as
possible. The longer you have a cellar that you don't confess to,
the more that cellar becomes a secret cellar. And a secret cellar
is not automatically a trump card in the dating game. It can put
people off.

Thus far, Sharpe's only stumble was in Tuesday's spelling
contest. (People wring their hands about falling standards and

the decline of human interaction on these kinds of shows, but frankly, most of the time, it's like watching life in a Victorian parlour.) Sharpe was knocked out early and, sadly, we didn't hear the word that felled him. But that might be just as well, for the producers were clearly in a cheeky mood and it was hard to decide what was more wickedly satirical on their part: getting Titmuss to spell 'inconsequential', or leaving Healy struggling to piece together the word 'celebrities'.

On that topic, one has seen bitterly conceived articles in newspapers this week referring to the cast of *Celebrity Love Island* as 'so-called celebrities'. Can we not rise above this now? To fall into that rhetorical trap is to ignore the massive linguistic shift undergone by the term 'celebrity' in our time – and thanks in no small measure to reality television. Now faintly pejorative, the word 'celebrity' is widely understood to mean something completely distinct from 'famous'. The idea of 'so-called' is, accordingly, implied within the term 'celebrity', and is therefore redundant, along with all those other tiresome qualifications such as 'D-list', 'Z-list' and so on.

Therefore, let's accept it: Sharpe is a celebrity – end of story. Or maybe beginning of story. We'll see.

It was Lee Sharpe's birthday the other day, and the occasion was marked in fittingly high style on *Celebrity Love Island*, with balloons, costumes and karaoke. Astonishing scenes. If you had told Sharpe, when he was a hungry teenager, setting out on a career in professional football with Manchester United, that he would celebrate his thirty-fourth year in a televised Fijian love nest, in school uniform, with Abi Titmuss – well, he would have laughed in your face. But such are the crazy twists of the sporting life, and who would argue that we aren't all richer for them?

The very next morning, though, a badly hung-over Sharpe was promptly dispatched to 'the Make or Break Boat' with Jayne Middlemiss, having been chosen by the viewers as the couple whose relationship would most benefit from three days of iso-lated counselling and therapy. For the record, Middlemiss's handmade card for Sharpe read, 'Happy birthday, knobhead.' 'I don't think it's anything major,' Sharpe explained. 'Just a little indifference, that's all.' But this is romance, where a little indifference goes a long way.

People have been saying that the contestants on *Celebrity Love Island* aren't necessarily the sharpest pencils in the box. And I suppose there is no point disputing the fact that Calum Best (the son of George) wouldn't automatically be first pick for the pub quiz team, even in a very small village. It's true also that the rear wall of 'the Beach Hut', the booth in which the celebrities confide their innermost thoughts to the camera, is a tropical fish tank, and that some harmless diversionary amusement can be derived from thinking of the slow, gliding motions of the fish in the background as a pictorial representation of the synaptic activity going on inside the brain of the celebrity who happens to be talking at the time.

Certainly, when Fran Cosgrave is in the Beach Hut, trying to find words for the myriad thoughts that have occurred to him during a long, hard day of sunbathing, and some weird bloater-derivative appears behind him, nuzzling a frond – well, at the very least, it's magical television.

But that's not to say that minds aren't being stretched here at all. The other night, for example, in order to win a snorkelling trip, the celebrities had to guess whether certain objects, tossed into the swimming pool, would sink or float. It's going to take a far more accomplished expert in the realm of sexual politics than me to unpack the full implications of Rebecca Loos's prediction that a melon wouldn't float because it wasn't hairy. Let's simply say that, when Germaine Greer, out of academic curiosity, signed up to do *Celebrity Big Brother*, she picked the wrong show.

Nevertheless, Loos and the rest of the girls did correctly surmise, after much conferring, that a mobile phone, if dropped into water, would go under – although the in many ways more urgent question of whether it would still be possible to play Beach Rally 2 on it afterwards sadly went unasked.

Sharpe, alas, was not on hand to bring his authority to bear on this game, which was a shame, because down the years he must have thought as hard as anyone on Love Island about the difference between sinking and swimming. But by this time, he was half an hour away by dinghy, having his palm read by a Fijian 'Love Doctor' called William. Not even England under Glenn Hoddle would have brought a footballer to this pass. 'You two are perfectly matched,' said the Love Doctor. 'But you both have to get rid of negative thoughts.' Sharpe was having none of it. 'It was all a bit random and a bit vague,' he said afterwards.

Those naughty producers deliberately disguised the temporary removal of Sharpe and Middlemiss as a permanent eviction, only breaking it to Sharpe later that he would not, in fact, be going home but would, instead, be spending three days alone with Middlemiss. Laugh? He nearly choked on his snorkel. 'So we've not been voted off?' Sharpe eventually said, and the sound was heard as of a penny, dropping. And sinking, as pennies do. Even the hairless ones.

Back on the island, where perspective is permanently off snorkelling somewhere, the apparent termination of Sharpe and Middlemiss gave rise to the kind of involved rituals of mourning which used to accompany the passing of ancient kings. Paul Danan, in particular, was taking the loss hard and appointed himself to the role of chief wailer. 'There was something really special about Lee,' he said, as his voice thickened to a paste with emotion. 'He loved wearing his hat.'

It will touch Sharpe, surely, to learn that this was how he was remembered by his peers on Love Island: as a man who wore a hat. But little do those celebrities know: the obituaries are premature, rumours of Sharpe's eviction are exaggerated, and he lives to sunbathe another day. He will rise and return to write another chapter in his *Celebrity Love Island* legacy, at the same time underpinning that great broadcasting truth: it isn't over until the viewers turn off in droves.

*

A major downturn of fortunes for Lee Sharpe on *Celebrity Love Island*: in a cruel twist, the public voted to pack him off for forty-eight hours to a five-star, fully catered Fijian beach-side apartment, complete with Jacuzzi, private pool and en suite bathroom with sea views, and in the exclusive company of a 33-year-old *Playboy* model called, almost inevitably, Nikki. Sharpe's reaction? 'It's killing me. It's boring the arse off me, to be fair. This has been garbage.'

So, as George Best was legendarily asked, in not entirely dissimilar circumstances: where did it all go wrong? There isn't a subscriber to *Playboy* who wouldn't have given his right hand to change places with Sharpe when the result of the voting was announced. And yet the former Manchester United star wanted out immediately and found himself, in his own words, 'shocked and stunned and a little bit gutted'.

Just to recap: this is a footballer being sent to hotel accommodation with a blonde model and describing the assignation as an onerous burden on his time and a general sap to his spirits. You can imagine Best shaking his bruised head in wonderment. Truly, it's a different game these days. The players throw their hands up at even the merest hint of physical contact.

Sharpe, I suppose, would argue that he simply got the wrong blonde model. Nikki is recently arrived from Los Angeles, whence she has been imported by the producers to bring a fresh pair of eyes to the situation on the island, and at the same time to raise the IQ level, which, in fairness, didn't start out all that high but has recently shown signs of sinking to dangerously low readings under the combined effect of more than three weeks of fruit-based cocktails.

Now, there's no arguing that Nikki, even on minimal acquaintance, seems to be a nice woman and, as *Playboy* models go, a very natural person – albeit, when someone from the home of 'Nip/Tuck' announces, 'I've got my mommy's lips,' there is always room to worry that she might be speaking literally.

The problem is that, even in advance of Nikki's arrival, Sharpe had grown eagerly attached to the idea of landing in the Love

Shack with Abi Titmuss, the calendar salesperson. And Titmuss has made no secret of her desire to shack up with the man whom regular viewers of ITV's celebrity romance-athon are allowed to refer to as 'the Sharpester'.

Thus when the public vote twinned Sharpe with Nikki, it seemed like nothing less than a perverting of love's true course. And Titmuss was in no doubt that it was the public who were, as it were, the perverts. 'They hate me,' she said. 'If they liked me, they wouldn't do that, would they?'

I don't know. But I was touched by her faith that this result was an expression of the popular will – or, indeed, of the popular anything. Patrick Kielty, the presenter, said there were 'tons and tons of votes', but how many, exactly, is tons and tons? And how did the voting divide? Also, where are the votes counted and who is the returning officer? It's clear that even now, in 2005, reality television falls some way short of offering transparent democracy. I'm not saying the producers make it all up on a whim. I'm simply pointing out that, in the absence of a full and frank demonstration of the political machinery, conspiracy theories are free to flourish.

On their first evening together, Nikki talked about her puppy and Sharpe mournfully cradled a glass of red wine and dreamed of Titmuss. 'It's as if I gave birth to it,' Nikki said. 'Oh, Monkey, I miss you.' Sharpe then gave a fathom-deep grunt, and Nikki went to bed.

You could gauge the full degree of Sharpe's indifference from the fact that he had a T-shirt on. Within the terms of the animal courting rituals on Love Island, that's the equivalent of a peacock deliberately stuffing its tail feathers into a wood chipper. It's why the show will stand if nothing else as a resounding tribute to the art of exhibitionism and by extension to the art of the tattoo.

Sharpe, for instance, from certain angles, looks like a page from a catalogue of reproduction Victorian railings. Best has the word 'Best' engraved across his lower back, which could be handy if he ever forgets or, like Paddington Bear, gets lost in a busy railway terminus. And Fran Cosgrave appears to have a month's-worth of back issues of *The Beano* laser-printed on his shoulders. People would be borrowing him to read, if people on *Celebrity Love Island* were interested in reading.

On the subject of which – ratio of bikinis to books packed for this five-week beach holiday: approximately 74:3. Ratio of swimming trunks to books packed by the men: 35:0. But I guess they must have known in advance that they would be busy, what with all the oiling each other.

A tropical storm lashed Love Island last weekend, causing awnings to billow, sun loungers to scatter and some of the celebrity competitors to move for the first time in several days. So severe was the meteorological uproar that, at its peak, Calum Best seemed to notice it. Were the gods angry or just, like the rest of us, slightly bored? We may never know.

It's not the first time, of course, that an ill wind has blown through the headquarters of ITV's celebrity snog-athon. Only a week ago, in a stand-out moment, relatively speaking, Rebecca Loos, the former PA to David Beckham, allowed her digestive system to get the better of her at the dinner table. Well, anything to move the conversation along, you might say. But it was an indiscretion which thoroughly alienated Best, who had been happily romancing Loos to that point, but who declared himself disgusted and cooled down their relationship forthwith. It appeared to be Best's opinion that a woman shouldn't do that sort of thing, or certainly not at the table, and definitely not at the table while on national television. He could have a point, at least about the television aspect.

However not even Loos at her most gaseous managed to cut off the island. Friday's lightning and thunder, on the other hand, meant that, for a short but alarming period, the celebrities were truly, rather than technically and career-wise, marooned. With only a week to go until the series ends, the grim possibility lingered that every one of the islanders would be sunk without trace and never heard of again, in which case the awesome power of mother nature would have brought forward the inevitable by at least a fortnight.

Amid chaos and inevitable anxiety, Friday night's eviction had to be cancelled because Patrick Kielty and Kelly Brook, the presenters, couldn't get across the water to perform the necessary ceremonies. Getting a boat ashore was out of the question, and, in the circumstances, they would have been struggling to land a chopper – though that, in many ways, is the story of *Celebrity Love Island*.

Still, it's exactly at such times of crisis that one looks for leadership, and it's a pleasure to report that one found it, on this occasion, in the form of Lee Sharpe. A stout refusal to panic has characterized the former Manchester United player's time on the island. When a Fijian Love Doctor was predicting a long-term future for Sharpe with Jayne Middlemiss, Sharpe kept his head down and continued to play his own game. And even when forced to enter solitary confinement with Nikki from *Playboy*, the man they call 'the Sharpester' manfully swallowed his disappointment, fixed his eyes on the far horizon, and saw the experience through.

It was no surprise, then, to find Sharpe co-coordinating the response to the storm, gathering everyone under a duvet in the porch area, and voicing appropriate concern when Nikki risked both electrocution and a home-run for satire by venturing out to the pool to retrieve her lip gloss.

Sharpe's public-spiritedness has been in stark contrast to the behaviour of Paul Danan, the former soap actor. If one has mild reservations about Danan, it's only because one has seen in the past how frequently the cheeky chappy persona can belie a 24/7 narcissist and borderline psychopath whose pint one would not wish to spill for fear of the consequences.

Nikki, though, clearly enjoys his company. Indeed, the pair have been intimate in the men's lavatory, the shower room and, controversially, the dormitory, which led their fellow celebrities to express horror that anyone could demean themselves so publicly. From the kitchen at this point could be heard the noise of

the pot and the kettle getting into a furious debate about colour.
Paul, however, is adamant that his feelings for Nikki are substan-
tial. 'I could imagine sharing a bit of a life with her,' he said.
But which bit? And whose life?

Against this garish backdrop, the burgeoning affection between Sharpe and Titmuss has come to look like something out
of Jane Austen, albeit in much smaller swimwear. Like the gallant
actors of old, who kept one foot on the floor during bed scenes,
Sharpe has worn a novelty sunhat for almost the duration of
their romance. Indeed, he stands revealed as a subscriber to all
sorts of supposedly outmoded gentlemanly codes and rules, such
as the one about not having sex with a woman on your first
reality television show. And while it is true that the pair have
been seen kissing and massaging each other from scalp to sole in
costly after-sun lotions, in the context of the shameless Danan/
Nikki alliance, it is as if Sharpe has merely sought Titmuss's
dance card and asked permission to mark it.

For this reason we urge the viewers still tuning in to *Celebrity
Love Island*, who could be at least 230 strong by now, to throw
the full weight of their phone-voting behind a Sharpe victory,
ensuring that he comes home with something more than sun-
burn and a vague sense of regret at the end of the five weeks.
Sport demands it, it goes without saying, but so does decorum,
and possibly the future of civilized romance.

AFTERWORD: *Incredibly, the viewing public did not heed this
call. The couple left standing at the end of the series were Fran Cosgrave
and Jayne Middlemiss – who weren't, in the romantic sense, a couple
at all. A weakness there, you could say, in the programme's format –
and one which, in tandem with unhelpful levels of viewer indifference,
could well have contributed to* Celebrity Love Island's *termination
one series later. The Sharpester? He went out at the semi-final stage.
From the nearly man of football to the nearly man of celebrity television.
But he's still out there, and the shows keep coming. It could still come
good for him.*

How to Qualify for Europe the Easy Way

(*An extraordinary second-half comeback from 3–0 down against AC Milan in Istanbul enabled Liverpool to land the European Cup on penalties. But would that earn them another go on the ride for free?*)

Win the Eurovision Song Contest, and you get to host the competition the following year. Win the Champions League, and you aren't even guaranteed a dressing room next time. It's one of the vital distinctions between these two great institutions of European life – institutions which, down the years, have grown to resemble one another in so many respects, not least their unreliability as cultural barometers. Or, to put it another way, if 'My Number One' by Helena Paparizou really is the greatest song we'll hear anywhere on the continent in 2005, it's possible that Liverpool really are the best team in Europe right now.

The question of whether UEFA should lower the hurdle to gymkhana level and admit Liverpool to next season's Champions League, has hovered for several weeks now, but, since Wednesday, obviously, it's been packed with added sentiment. David Moores, the Liverpool chairman, was biblical on the theme: 'It would be absolutely diabolical if we weren't allowed to defend it,' he said.

Meanwhile, Richard Caborn, the sports minister, was offering the opinion that it would be 'a travesty' if Liverpool were left out. And David Davies, the FA's executive director, asserted that Liverpool should be given a place 'for the wider interests of European football', which is certainly an interesting way to talk about Jerzy Dudek. 'The whole world will want us to play now,' Rick Parry, Liverpool's chief executive said on Thursday – conveniently ignoring that part of the whole world which supports Everton, and a number of other parts of the world, too, where the Champions League and its ideals and traditions are highly respected.

Somewhat more sinisterly, there are reports of the sponsors

being egged on to carry the fight to UEFA on Liverpool's behalf
– a chilly thought. Even Liverpool's own supporters, surely –
always keen to emphasize the club's legendary soulfulness –
would be uncomfortable to think that Liverpool were back in
Europe simply because PlayStation had got heavy on their behalf.

But, either way, here's the situation: not content with seizing
the biggest prize in club football, in an outcome that nobody in
their right mind would have predicted at any point in the season
– and certainly not at half-time on Wednesday night – Liverpool
now appear to want another prize for winning it. To be still
more specific about this – so we can accurately gauge the scale
of the presumption involved – they want another prize for
winning it *on penalties*. Talk about pushing your luck.

Of course, given the overwhelming sentimental pressure, it's
tempting to throw up one's hands and say, 'Why not?' The
competition is already so diluted – to the point where sides
finishing fourth in their league, and thirty points adrift of their
national champions, have been known to get in – they might as
well let Liverpool play. Hell, let them all in: Liverpool, Shakhtar
Donetsk, Herenveen, Didcot Town, the FA Vase winners –
even Middlesbrough, if necessary.

At the same time, some dim but still flickering notion of what
the Champions League is intended to be and to stand for inclines
one to think that there might be a principle worth battling for
here. There are, after all, two good reasons why places in the
Champions League are offered as rewards for league form and
nothing else: firstly, because league form is the only reliable
measure of a side's worth; and secondly, because if league form
is the only criterion for entry, participating clubs cannot afford
to concentrate on the Champions League to the neglect of their
domestic leagues.

For better or worse, UEFA is determined to market the
Champions League as the footballing equivalent of a plate of
smoked salmon; and, unfortunately, by the only standard that
UEFA applies (domestic league form), the current Liverpool
side is tuna and cucumber. They finished fifth. They weren't

just off the pace last season; they were thirty-seven points off the pace. They lost to Crystal Palace. They're not quite as good as Everton, who aren't that good, either.

What would UEFA in effect be saying by granting Liverpool a free ride? That this Liverpool side so bestrides the modern game that the rules must bend before them? That's a lot to conclude from a 3–3 draw with AC Milan – not to take anything away from that glorious comeback, on that amazing night: who could have thought a streak of luck could hold so long and so true?

That said, wouldn't any neutral, once in a while, like to see a Premier League side in Europe profit by cutting a swathe through the opposition, rather than grimly clinging on to snatch it at the last? It didn't happen with Manchester United in 1999 and it certainly didn't happen with Liverpool on Wednesday. It's the story of English football, I guess: never the irresistible force, always the immovable object.

Small wonder that the leading anthems of English football include 'We shall not be moved' and the theme from *The Great Escape*. What English clubs have a tradition of specializing in are lung-busting acts of tunnelling, frequently by people who have gone to elaborate lengths to bury themselves in the first place. (Rafael Benitez's heat-stroked decision to start with Harry Kewell on Wednesday night and leave out Dietmar Hamann showed that he, too, can be pretty handy in a hole with a spade when he needs to be.)

Now, one can be as much a sucker for those stories of narrow and implausible escape – those *Boy's Own* tales of chancing it – as the next person, without necessarily wanting to see them enshrined within the articles of the Champions League. The Champions League, after all, is not intended to be the Carling Cup with Air Miles; it's intended to be the rarefied stage on which the best performing clubs in Europe peel off their evening gloves to go *mano a mano*. And if UEFA has a genuine will to keep the riff-raff at bay, then it probably ought to use Wednesday night's slightly embarrassing outcome as an excuse to diminish the number of places available to each nation, rather than increase them.

That, one concedes, may be beyond UEFA's remit. But if the Champions League is to continue to mean anything – indeed, if the big sides are to continue to think of it as a club that they wish to belong to – then the law needs to be upheld, Liverpool need to be excluded, and the point needs to be firmly made that no one can seriously expect to blag a place in the Champions League merely by winning it. It's going to involve a lot more work than that.*

In the Groove with Jerzy Dudek

It was good to read this week about the Dudek taking off in Italy. You've never done the Dudek? It's the dance modelled on the distracting penalty shoot-out motions with which Jerzy Dudek, the Liverpool goalkeeper, brought a rare streak of Polish slapstick to the defining moment in the 2005 final of Europe's premier club football competition. Mostly it's about spreading your arms wide and wobbling from side to side, though there is also some more complicated torso-bending and palm-twisting to get involved with, for advanced Dudekkers.

Anyway, the Italian magazine *Gente* is tipping the Dudek to be driving them wild in the discos and beach bars of Italy this season and the television presenter Adriana Volpe has used her state-sponsored morning show to tutor the nation in the requisite moves, while at the same time pointing out the aerobic and muscular benefits which can arise from using the Dudek as part of your regular fitness routine. (It encourages, apparently, waist-narrowing, shoulder-broadening and buttock-tightening, though you probably have to get to an awful lot of European cup finals before the effects are noticeable.)

---

* A weedy compromise was arrived at whereby Liverpool were readmitted via the qualifying rounds. Some say the competition has never properly recovered.

Dudek, of course, is not the first Premiership goalkeeper to initiate a dance craze. 'Let's all do the Seaman' was a popular cry through the 1990s. That said, the Seaman (an exaggerated flapping motion with the arms above the head, paying tribute to the former Arsenal and England goalkeeper's touching vulnerability to shots from distance) was almost entirely confined to the stands at matches, and never ultimately made the all-important breakout into the dancehall arena.

No such problems, clearly, for the Dudek, which is already threatening to go continental in the manner of the shag, the twist and the watusi. But that doesn't automatically mean it's going to have everything its own way this summer, when the competition among dance crazes is stiffer than it has been for many years.

For instance, observers of the club scene are predicting some significant dancefloor uptake in the holiday season of 2005 for the Peter Kenyon. The object is to tour the floor, getting the phone numbers of as many other people's partners as you can – but doing it really clumsily, so that everyone notices. Rest assured – they'll be doing the Kenyon like nobody's business in the bars and Italian restaurants of Kensington and Knightsbridge this summer. Then again, it's probably not one for the popular resorts, and there's not much aerobic burn here for the health freaks. Also, although making an utter berk of yourself is part of the fun of any summer dance craze, there are limits.

More energetic and therefore, perhaps, more likely to score big numbers, dancefloor-wise, is the Lee Bowyer. Grab your partner by the hair, punch him in the face as if you just don't care! This traditional pas de deux, blending aspects of the mosh and the pogo, and modelled on the on-pitch set-to between Bowyer and Keiron Dyer, his team mate, towards the back end of the 2004–05 season, is destined to be huge in the Spanish resorts and on some of the larger Greek islands this summer – in fact, anywhere that Brits gather to holiday in numbers. Be warned, though: this one carries the risk of an automatic ejection from the club, and even of police intervention, if done properly.

Far more passive – yet undeniably aggressive in its own way – is the Michael Glazer. As you take to the floor, you hitch your trousers as high in the direction of your armpits as they will go. Then you buy the nightclub. Shortly afterwards, you announce that you are putting up admission prices, abandoning Ladies Night and reducing Happy Hour to ten minutes, suspended. Hey presto: you're doing the Glazer. It's not thought to be all that funny in the clubs of hard-to-impress Manchester, but it's considered pretty amusing elsewhere and is certainly a craze to watch as the holiday months unfold.

Meanwhile, what price an impressive showing this summer for the Harry Kewell? Also known as 'the Whingeing Aussie', this one's broadly inclusive simplicity – you merely have to limp around looking, in every sense, hurt – makes it a natural hit for the resorts and holiday camps. And the hairband is optional, which is a plus. No one is suggesting it has the potential pan-European pulling-power of the Dudek. But I think we can expect the Kewell to be a fairly dependable floor-filler come August. You dancing?

Team UK? Bring It On

Now that the 2012 Games are confirmed for London, the idea that there could be no hosting interest in the Olympic football competition is, surely, unthinkable. It's the national game after all – not to mention the curtain-raising event on the proposed timetable for 2012. Therefore the onus is on the relevant football associations to resolve their differences and agree to send out a representative Great Britain side for the occasion, pooling the available talent from the four home nations into a UK superteam.

It is a mouth-watering prospect. And there is fun to be had in the meantime by imagining that the event were happening tomorrow, and picking a side from the best that English, Scottish, Welsh and Northern Irish football can offer, to form your own fantasy Great Britain XI.

Here's mine. In goal: James (England). Across the back: Bridge (England), Terry (England), Ferdinand (England) and Ashley Cole (England). In midfield: Beckham (England), Lampard (England), Gerrard (England) and Joe Cole (England). And up front: Rooney (England) and Owen (England). Beat that!

Alan Smith: Voice of Reason

(Or why automatically saying yes when your country calls you isn't always the right thing to do.)

It is, inevitably, with large amounts of circumspection and an almost dizzying quantity of self-amazement that one finds oneself taking the side in an argument of Alan Smith, the famously unlovely Manchester United striker. But sometimes one sees a person so maligned that justice itself cries out in protest. And at such times, the usual obvious aesthetic considerations have to be laid aside and one must simply clip the clothes peg to the nose and wade on in.

Smith has seen what remains of his reputation kicked high in the air this week. His offence: declining the last-minute offer of a place on Sven's Magical Funbus to Denmark on the grounds that, if Smith travelled with England, he would miss an appearance for Manchester United Reserves *v.* Bolton Wanderers Reserves at Leyland.

That's not the United first team, note; that's 'the stiffs', as footballers like to refer to reserve sides. Stiffs before country, then. For many staggered observers, this was clearly a snub to rank right up there with, 'I'd love to, but I'm washing my hair.'

It was observed that Smith's invitation had only come belatedly, when Andrew Johnson of Crystal Palace ruled himself out with a hamstring injury. Accordingly, it was inferred that a petulant Smith was now relishing the chance to raise a middle finger in the direction of the entire Three Lions project. Parallels were drawn with the time that Chris Sutton turned up his nose

at a place in the England B team (stiffs, but at international level)
and was never asked back.

Eventually, the matter came to occupy Brian Barwick, the
chief executive of the Football Association, whose ability to rule
at the FA and yet remain blessedly free of controversy lasted,
one ruefully notes, only until he gave his first official newspaper
interview. Barwick described Smith's decision as 'not the clever-
est thing he has done', darkly implying that there would be
consequences for Smith's chances of getting picked for England
again. 'He was given the opportunity to play for England and
he has chosen to play elsewhere,' Barwick coldly said. The chief
executive underscored the profundity of his disappointment by
adding, mournfully, 'I never got the opportunity to play for
England.'

These remarks promised unhelpfully to destabilize relations
between the FA and Manchester United in a World Cup season,
and to call down the smoking wrath of Sir Alex Ferguson, which
is never pretty. Accordingly, the next day Eriksson felt obliged
to come out and meekly take the blame for everything, while
insisting that of course Smith remained (as the phrase has it) 'in
his thoughts'.

To understand Smith's motives, however, we need to consider why any player would resist Eriksson's silvery whisper and
say no to an England trip. True, in Smith's case this time, it
might not have looked all that enticing on the recruitment
posters: 'Now that our sixth choice striker has picked up a
niggle, your country needs you.' But even here, there could
have been plenty in the invitation to appeal to him.

An England trip routinely offers five-star accommodation in
a vibrant European destination, all expenses paid. Players enjoy
unparalleled access to cones put out by Tord Grip. (Few men
lay down a cone as well as the Gripster.) Otherwise, they have
little else to do but kick back and play a round or two of Beggar
My Neighbour with Jermain Defoe. In Smith's case, he would
have got a few days off training with Ferguson, which must
come as a fantastic relief to anyone who cherishes their nerve

ends. And, short of joining Manchester City, it's the only opportunity a player will ever get to flick David James on the ear on
the plane home. And all this for somewhere between twenty
and sixty minutes of utterly consequence-free football in an
international shirt (yours to keep or swap).

It's clear, then, that on at least one level Smith's refusal to join
the rest of the lads in Copenhagen this week was an act of
almost heroic self-denial. Offered the corporate jolly to end all
corporate jollics, and the dossiest doss known to man, he stayed
at home to work in the deeply unglamorous but necessary
circumstances of reserve football. And, doing so, he showed a
professionalism and an ability to make a sober assessment of the
circumstances that history has not necessarily taught us to expect
from him.

How unjust, then, that his actions should have been inter-
preted as an arrogant insult. Surely what he was saying, in fact,
was, 'Thank you, Sven and the FA, but right now, I don't think
I'm up to it. A midweek mini-break in Denmark with Jamie
Carragher inevitably has its charms, but on my present form, I
would be doing my nation a disservice by agreeing to come. Far
better that I stay behind and get some properly competitive
football under my belt, in the hope of becoming a better player
who may one day be of valuable service to his country, should
you ever again choose to look favourably upon his claims.'

And perhaps he was also saying, 'Have you seen Bolton's
second-string defence recently? Wet paper bag, or what? Even
I might nick one.'

And he did. Smith opened the scoring for United's reserves
in a confidence-boosting 3–0 rout. He will have looked no
further than that for vindication. However, one can hardly not
point out how subsequent events conspired to make Smith's
decision appear to be, as well as everything else, a tactical masterstroke. England's pathetic capitulation to Denmark on Wednesday left Smith looking like a man who had a ticket for the
Titanic, but chose to go on a bike ride instead, and was safely
home in time for tea. Professionalism, self-knowledge and

foresight then – all in the same package. Now tell me: who were the real stiffs?

A Permanent End to the No-score Draw

Congratulations to the organizers of this week's draw for the Champions League group stage, which touched nearly all the important bases. It featured a top-class array of Perspex tubs and vases, many of them new to the European scene; it was unstinting in its provision of brightly coloured plastic balls – piles of the things; it introduced into a superficially straightforward procedure at least three levels of strictly unnecessary obfuscation; and, lasting more than an hour in total, it was approximately fifty-eight and a half minutes longer than it needed to be. It was, then, the very model of a football draw ceremony in the twenty-first century.

Of course, one can quibble with some of the details. I was disappointed, for instance, to notice the lack of a dance number or musical interlude of any kind. Recent Olympic history teaches us that no publicly conducted administrative occasion is complete until Heather Small gets up to ask us what we've done today to make us feel proud. For all that it sounded a correctly impressive and inspiring note in its own way, Thursday's draw would have benefited enormously from the inclusion of an international singing artist of the calibre of, say, Sting, performing a specially commissioned, aspirational anthem – 'When My Ball Drops, I'll Be Dreaming', or similar.

Nit-picking aside, though, Thursday's draw, to my mind, amply delivered, and I'll have none of the carping from certain quarters that the show in Monaco was nothing more than a mark of pomposity, consistent with the Champions League's allegedly inflated sense of its own worth.

These will be people who can remember when the draw for a football tournament was performed unseen, by persons you had never heard of, with a velvet sack and some marbles. And I

suppose there's no getting round the fact that Thursday afternoon's exhaustive and exhausting business could easily have
been conducted by a solitary UEFA underling in a cupboard in
Switzerland, using a single sheet of A4, a pair of scissors and a
biscuit tin. But the problem with these backward-looking arguments is that they ignore what the Champions League has become,
and its status within the global sporting culture. This is, after all,
the greatest club football competition in the world, featuring the
domestic champions of Europe and also some teams that aren't
champions. You can't expect a contest so significant merely to
post its group stage draw on the net. There'd be uproar.

Indeed, the real question is how the draw ceremony can push
on from here and keep pace with the competition's ambitions
for itself in the future. I've heard it proposed since Thursday
that, what with all the holding up of cards with letters on them,
the draw already resembles an underdressed episode of *Sesame
Street*; and that, therefore, it wouldn't hurt to go that little bit
further and get Big Bird on board.

It's worth considering. I could see the reasoning behind inviting Paolo Maldini along to remove the balls with the team
names in them. The great AC Milan defender has a history
in this competition as storied as anyone's and deserved the
opportunity to write himself another chapter by giving the balls
the best of all possible stirs in Monaco.

At the same time, is Maldini pressing the right pan-European
buttons, demographics-wise? And he brought almost nothing to
the table in terms of movement and wisecracks. A big, colourful
Muppet would have sent a louder message. And Bear, from
The Bear In The Big Blue House, would have had still more
family-oriented cuteness and more presence.

Other aspects of the ceremony, too, are in danger of seeming
tired and stale. I'm sure I'm not alone in feeling that the plastic
fortune cookie device – the unscrewable ball which yields the
piece of paper bearing the team name or group letter – has run
its course. It was a delight when it first appeared, replacing
the outmoded, bingo-style numbered ball, and, what with the

additional hand-business involved in separating the ball's halves and unfolding the enclosed paper, it automatically expanded the time required to perform even the simplest draw by a factor in the region of 27. Result!

But familiarity has caught up with the device, breeding contempt. The time may have come to think more broadly about what can be done with the balls – perhaps even to wonder about the introduction of those glass chambers, used by pilots and astronauts to test lung capacity, wherein the challenge is to blow into a tube and see how long you can keep a ping-pong ball aloft.

Executives representing the poorer clubs could be brought on to the stage and required to blow into tubes in order to discover the identity of their seeded opponent, with the first person to run out of puff going into Real Madrid's group, and so on, all the way down to Liverpool. It would introduce the competitive element which the occasion so sorely lacks (it's a sports draw, after all), and in an extremely televisual manner – even more so if the chamber could be rigged up so that the dropping of the air pressure contrived to unhinge a bucket of gunk above the unfortunate chief executive.

Boom! Paired with Juventus and covered in orange goo. That's family viewing, right there. On the topic of which, would it hurt to get Noel Edmonds to have a look at the problem? Here's someone with a proven track record in family television. Don't forget that the format for *Noel's House Party* was sold right across the continent and, in the years of its pomp, pretty much defined what we think of as common ground in Europe.

You can see how such an idea would chime with UEFA, who must already be looking beyond the ratings dead-spot of a Thursday afternoon and thinking in terms of the far greater exposure and advertising revenues available in a Saturday-night slot. Don't get me wrong: this week, UEFA did the business. But they can go further. And they almost certainly will.*

---

* As it happened, Noel Edmonds was too busy devising *Deal Or No Deal* to get involved at this stage. It's football's loss.

Who's That with the Pope?

Amazement has greeted the story that the Pope failed to recognize Pele recently. His Holiness – no close follower of the beautiful game, it would appear – was allegedly spared an embarrassing 'And what do you do?' moment by the timely intervention of an aide. (And the moment could well have grown in embarrassment if Pele had chosen to explain that, right now, he is busy campaigning to expand awareness about erectile dysfunction.)

Then again, it's too easy to crow. Think about the number of people the Pope is obliged to meet in the course of his work. Small wonder if occasionally he can't put a name to a face.

Entire Country Gripped by Ashes Fever

(*In the summer of 2005, the England cricket team were advancing to victory over Australia in the Ashes Test series and few were the people who weren't enthralled – even those who were supposed to be preparing England for an international against Northern Ireland.*)

From the diary of Sven-Goran Eriksson, England manager

Tuesday
Sorted! Tord Grip and I get two together for Friday in the ECB enclosure, including complimentary finger buffet luncheon, courtesy seat cushion and a programme. Barmy Army! Of course, Tord immediately starts grumbling, going on about how he's never happy sitting with 'the corporates' and how he was really holding out for something in the Vauxhall stand, for the atmosphere. Plus he's worried that, if he goes in the posh seats, they won't let him wear his England baseball cap with the tinny-holster and novelty drinking straw.

I remind him, as politely as I can, that we both spent two and

a half hours this morning pounding the mobiles when we should
have been concentrating on the training, and that there was
absolutely nothing out there for less than silly prices. I also draw
his attention to the fact that it was me who eventually called up
the ECB because he was 'too scared' – and that, as a result, it
was me who went through the humiliating experience of having
to explain who I was. Not to mention taking the call an hour
later to the effect that Paul Daniels's people had been on to say
he couldn't attend, so they could probably squeeze me in with
a plus one.

As for the cap, I tell him there won't be a problem because
John Major wears one all the time. I'm making that up, though.
At least, I think I am.

'In the ground, Tord. For the Ashes, mate. That's what
counts, isn't it?'

Tord agrees and finally cheers up.

Wednesday
Instruct Ray Clemence to take training and spend the morning
in Tord's room, stencilling a hotel bedsheet with the flag of
St George and the slogan 'Freddie's Gonna Getcha'. (My idea.
Tord wanted 'Eat Ashes, Warne, You Lard-Arse', but I said I
thought that was a bit confrontational, especially for the ECB
enclosure.) The result looks pretty good, though there's an
awkward moment when a maid comes in, sees what we're doing
to one of her sheets and threatens to report us to housekeeping.
Tord has to slip her £20 to keep quiet.

When she's gone, Tord says, 'Blimey, twenty quid for a flag?
It's almost as bad as Cardiff.' We have a good old laugh about that.

Call Clemence at lunchtime to find out if there are any injury
problems and he breaks the news about Simon Jones. It's a blow,
obviously, but it need not be a terminal one, I think. We're still
hot to trot, in my opinion, and the Aussies are on the back foot.
Repeat after me: 'It's coming home, it's coming home, it's
coming – cricket's coming home.'

Use the afternoon to ring around a few pals, leaving messages on their machines, saying, 'I'm going to the Oval, I'm going to the Oval – you're not, you're not.' Well, you've got to, haven't you?

That evening we lose 1–0 to Northern Ireland, and inevitably there are intense discussions on the plane home. Steve McClaren thinks that the Jones business, coupled with the apparent return to fitness of Glenn McGrath, has frighteningly tipped the match in Australia's favour. But Clemence's view is that McGrath is now irrelevant, because it's Australia's confidence as a batting side that has collapsed and, accordingly, if Matthew Hoggard can get the ball to do a bit, the way he did at Trent Bridge, then there's no reason why it should go beyond day three.

'All I know,' I say – and then I leave a pause for dramatic effect, '. . . is that SOME OF US ARE GOING TO BE THERE!' And I stand up and make a giant 'four' signal to all corners of the plane – attracting the attention of the air hostess who points out that the seatbelt sign is switched on. Sit down like a good boy, before the situation escalates.

Thursday
Gutted. It's 9.30 when the woman from corporate entertaining rings and says there's a problem with the tickets.

'Don't tell me,' I say. 'Paul Daniels can make it after all.'

'Not to our knowledge,' she says. 'Security have been on to us, and they have some issues.'

I say, 'Look, if this is about Tord's beer cap, I can have a word.'

But she ploughs straight on. 'In the light of Wednesday night's result against Northern Ireland, our feeling is that we can no longer guarantee your safety and that we must therefore ask you to stay away from the Oval at this time.'

I say, 'Wednesday night? But the Ashes are on. Who even noticed?'

She says, 'We fear that your presence in the ground would, in the current climate, be an incitement to insurrection and that you would be a target for abuse and, possibly, beer cans.'

By this point, I'm in a panic and improvising wildly. 'I'll wear a helmet,' I say.

'I'm sorry,' she says, firmly. 'We have to consider the safety of our other guests.'

I shouldn't ask, but I can't help myself. 'Do you mind telling me,' I say, 'who's getting my pair?'

I hear her flipping through pages for quite a long time. Finally, she says, 'Keith Harris and Orville.'

Keith frigging Harris and Orville! What do they know about cricket? But, of course, they're all coming out of the woodwork now, aren't they? Where were the Keith Harrises and Orvilles of this world during the Atherton years, is what I want to know. The words 'sunshine' and 'trippers' come to mind.

I say, 'What if we reinforce the Volvo, black out the windows and go in the back way, like at Ulrika's house?'

She says, 'I'm sorry, Mr Svensson,' and hangs up.

I call Tord and I can tell that he's close to tears. 'Sixteen years of hurt, Sven,' he says. 'The Ashes up for grabs. How many times in our lifetime? How many times?'

'Don't worry,' I tell him. 'I'll sort it.'

Thursday afternoon

Tord comes over during the lunch interval and, with the telly on in the background, we set about cooking up a scheme that we can go back to the ECB with. My first thought is disguises. I'm going to need to look completely anonymous. Tord says, 'What about going as one of the early evictees off *Big Brother*? Nobody ever remembers them.'

But I don't fancy myself to pull it off, somehow, so Tord has a rethink, and his next idea is that I should dress up as John Major. 'If we get there early enough,' Tord says, 'you'll be ushered straight through.' Tord reckons I could do a very good Major. He thinks I'd have no difficulty passing for someone owlish, bewildered, promoted beyond his capacity to cope. Tord can be very cutting sometimes.

'But what happens when the real John Major arrives?' I say. 'It'll all kick off.'

'Fair point,' Tord says.

We both fall silent after that and watch the cricket. When Straussy reaches his 100, we're out of our chairs, obviously. But at the same time, the emotion of the moment seems to bring home to us what we're going to be missing. And, at this, Tord goes off on one, saying if I hadn't switched to 4–5–1, none of this would have happened. I say that's a bit bloody rich coming from him, given that 4–5–1 was his idea. Then he says, 'No, it wasn't,' and I say, 'Yes, it was,' and he says, 'No, it wasn't, it was yours,' and I say, 'Was it?' and he says, 'I think so.' And there's a pause and then both of us fall about laughing because we can't remember whose idea it was!

Soon after this, McGrath comes on and bowls Flintoff and we get miserable again. At stumps, Tord wheels his bike down the hall and doesn't even say goodbye.

Friday
Result! We're into the third over of the morning session and I'm doing the usual – telly for the pictures, *Test Match Special* for the commentary – when Tord rings sounding absolutely full of it, like yesterday never happened. He says, 'You aren't going to believe this, mate.'

It turns out that one of Tord's sisters works with a bloke whose cousin sometimes goes running with a woman whose aunt and uncle live in one of those flats with a balcony overlooking the Oval.

'I'm there already, Sven-boy,' Tord shouts. 'Get your backside over here. It's quality.'

I say, 'Do I need a disguise?'

'The owners are from Belfast,' Tord says. 'They love you like a brother.'

'Get the beers in, Tordy baby,' I say. 'I'm on my way.'

Come on, England!

Everyone with Prizes Shall Have Prizes

We were promised, by Denise van Outen, no less, 'an incredible night' and 'an incredible awards ceremony'. And, boy, did the inaugural FIFPro World XI Player Awards deliver on van Outen's plucky prophecy. Compacted into a two-hour special on Sky One, it produced scenes which stretched the bounds of the credible to a point where the elastic will be a long time recovering.

You would describe the event as surreal, except that, at the moment at which Wayne Rooney received a Young Player of the Year award from Jerry Hall, the Texan supermodel . . . well, Salvador Dali himself would have been getting his coat and asking the doorman to hail him a lobster. Rooney and Hall, Hall and Rooney – one had surely never imagined one would see these two, radically different cultural icons share face-time, outside of a bad acid trip. Yet there they were, and with neither of them quite seeming to know why.

Indeed, in an interview grabbed backstage, Hall reported the reaction of her children to the news that she was off to Wembley for the FIFPros: 'Mum, why are they having *you* there?'

'You?' 'There?' 'Why?' These were the questions that rang out through the night, and never more loudly than when Minnie Driver stepped up to read out the nominations for best midfielder. Or consider the following announcement, just ahead of the presentations to the prize-winning defenders: 'Ladies and gentlemen, please welcome Olympic gold medallist Darren Campbell and star of *Charlie and the Chocolate Factory*, Missi Pyle.'

Pyle, as I recall, played Mrs Beauregarde, the mother of a permanently gum-chewing, spoiled brat, but I'm sure no satire was intended. It wasn't that kind of occasion. Indeed, it provided a public stage on to which even Sven-Goran Eriksson could venture without hearing a murmur of dissent. There were video compilations, cut so fast that pretty much nothing identifiable as football was visible in them. There were musical interludes from Sean Paul and Zucchero (big in Italy). And, in one of those eerie coincidences that only televised awards ceremonies can yield, each of the five AC Milan players selected to sit in a satellite-linked room at the San Siro won an award – almost as if they knew, or something. Among them was Nelson Dida, who was voted best goalkeeper. At which point Katie Melua came on in a string vest and sang the Police classic, 'Dida doo doo, Dida da da'.

OK, I made up the stuff about Katie Melua. But this is true: Pele, winner of the night's obligatory legend award, could not be with us, but his message of acceptance was read aloud by Eamonn Holmes. Yes, at the FIFPro Awards, the part of the greatest footballer the world has ever seen was played by a former break-fast television couch potato. Maybe Willy Wonka was busy.

FIFPro: shame about the name. It sounds like a cat sneezing. But it stands for Fédération Internationale des Associations de Footballeurs Professionnels. And hence, the FIFPro World XI Player Awards – a dream team selection, assembled from the votes of 38,000 professional players in a project dreamed up by Gordon Taylor, the outgoing president of FIFPro and better known here as the chief executive of the Professional Footballers Association.

Taylor's vision of a kind of global works dinner is unobjectionable in itself. But the question one wants to ask is, why does Rachel Stevens have to be there? And why do television cameras have to be there? Let's overlook the misfortune of timing, whereby, even as pretty-boy might-have-beens such as Steve McManaman and Jamie Redknapp were larging it in their Versace lounge suits, directors of the Premier League were arranging crisis meetings to discuss overpricing, broadcast saturation and other matters possibly contributing to the present public perception that football is a gas-filled bore. That's not a perception I share, by the way. But you don't need to agree with it to feel that, while such a view is out there, it might be less than tactful of the sport to be seen raising a glass to itself in the company of Liberty X.

The point is, however you frame it, whomever you invite
and whenever you stage it, an awards ceremony for footballers
is wildly superfluous. Football is its own honours system. As
Minnie Driver will tell you, players are judged against each other
all the time in things called 'matches', which periodically lead
to the distribution of 'trophies' and 'medals'. Yet somehow the
notion persists that these mere footballing honours are not
enough and that there need to be bigger, overarching, showbiz-
style honours. Hence occasions like this week's, when people
get handed awards for having won awards. The technical term
for this is putting sugar on a sugared doughnut. It's an act of
over-provision which has already brought us the monumentally
emetic Laureus Sports Awards in (of course!) Monte Carlo. And
now this.

Satisfyingly, even as the FIFPros ran their jaw-dropping
course on Sky One, over on Sky Sports 1, on an occasion
notable for the complete absence of linen-swathed dining tables
and guest appearances by Kanye West, Grimsby were busy
stuffing Tottenham in the Carling Cup. Were you watching,
Jerry Hall? It simply doesn't get any more glittering than that,
so why pretend that it does?

TV Guide

Sir Alex Ferguson is refusing to cooperate with MUTV, Manchester United's in-house television channel, in the wake of a
perceived slight against the manager's tactics, so today's MUTV
schedule is revised as follows.

11.00. 'Our Leader Speaks'. Cancelled. Replaced by 'Our Leader
Is Good And Has Done Great Things' (rpt). Recap of the
1998–99 treble-winning season. 'These Whom Our Leader Has
Smiled Upon' (reserve match highlights) now moves forward
by thirty minutes to 12.30.

13.00. 'Thought For The Day, Featuring Our Leader'. Cancelled. Replaced by 'Behold The Fate Of Those Who Question Our Leader' (rpt). Another chance to see this 2001 documentary on the career of Jaap Stam.

19.00. 'Our Leader Bids Us Rest'. Cancelled. Replaced by 'A Book At Bedtime' with Carlos Queiroz.

In Passionate Defence of the Shush

By what dictatorial logic is 'shushing' a bookable offence? In the wake of his goal last weekend, Frank Lampard was shown a yellow card for putting a finger to his lips and recommending to Liverpool fans that a period of silence from them would now be most welcome. The words 'law' and 'ass' came to mind. Are Liverpool supporters so sensitive that they need to be spared the offence of this time-honoured gesture? It didn't sound like it the previous Wednesday, when they gave Lampard ninety minutes of lip on the subject of being fat. Can we not agree that, if it's a supporter's inalienable right to call a player fat, then it's a player's equally inalienable right to shush that supporter when he scores? Is that not called freedom of expression? And don't we value that above all in a democracy?

In the Name of That Bloke off London's Burning – Go!

In the end, you can only judge a manager on results and in this case the results speak clearly. Last year on *The Match*, the Celebrities lost to the Legends 2–1; this year the Celebrities lost 2–0. One cannot sidestep the obvious conclusion: celebrity football is going backwards under Graham Taylor.

Of course, one can quibble over team selection until the cows come home – or, as may be, until a podgy Ally McCoist rises at

the back stick in the seventy-first minute to nod home a second
goal and kill the game. But far more worrying are the signs that
Taylor has lost the dressing room. The manager had a week in
which to fashion this assortment of former soap actors and *Top
Of The Pops* dropouts into a workable football outfit, and in his
pre-match team talk Taylor presumably thought he was speaking
a language his players would readily understand when he said,
'This is your theatre. This is your stage. This is your audience.
All we want is a performance from you.'

But he seemed to be forgetting that a high percentage of his
squad hasn't worked for ages. That's why they're on *The Match*.
And what could talk of stages and performances possibly mean
to a winner of *Big Brother*? If Taylor had been looking to awaken
the giant in Anthony Hutton, he would have done better to
take him aside and offer him a personalized gee-up along the
lines of, 'This is your couch. This is your sitting room. Now go
out there and pick the hard skin off your feet.'

To be fair, Hutton needed no private rhetoric to inspire him.
He was stationed out wide on the left side of midfield but, as he
amply demonstrated during those long weeks of incarceration
in the Big Brother House this summer, he is someone who is
more than prepared to drop off, if the situation calls for it, while
also being supremely equipped to come inside and hang around
hopefully, waiting for something to happen.

Accordingly, Hutton walked away from the wreckage with
the consolation prize of a Man of the Match award – a prize
which he was, if anything, a little too consoled by, continuing
to beam and wave at his family in the stands during what was
obviously the regulation period of post-match head-hanging for
the rest of the team. But he is young: he will learn to fake that
'too gutted about the result to take any pleasure in my own
performance' stuff in due course.

The gravest disappointment, from the Celebrities' point of
view – and the detail that raises the biggest question mark over
Taylor's management – is that these Legends were clearly ripe
for the taking. Talk before the match suggested that this was a

leaner and meaner Legends side than the one which almost embarrassed itself last year. Meaner was right. Peter Reid expressed his admiration for the Celebrities by mentioning that he was 'hoping to get close enough to kick a couple of them' and his two-footer on Harvey, after just three minutes, was the hardest a member of So Solid Crew has ever been tackled by someone who wasn't a policeman.

Indeed, as temperatures boiled in the first half, it appeared the Celebrities had come through a week's training simply to earn a once-in-a-lifetime opportunity to get clattered by David Batty, and it was hard to remember that children's charities were benefiting from the money raised.

So, meaner, definitely. Leaner, though? In as much as many of the Legends appeared to have been preparing for anything, it was to audition for the part of the Fat Controller in a forth-coming *Thomas the Tank Engine* movie adaptation. Andy Gray, in the commentary box, kept talking up Neville Southall's brilliance as a goalkeeper, even now – and with reason. There was a reflex save from Hutton that would have flattered Gordon Banks in his prime. At the same time, Southall's size these days is such that, as soon as the ball enters the six-yard area, he can hardly help but get something to it.

John Barnes? Anonymous, even though he was, necessarily, given lots of space. Matt Le Tissier? Got a nosebleed when the ball hit him in the face and had to be substituted. Dean Saunders? Hamstrung. Peter Beardsley? Actually tripped over the ball at one point. As for Gary McAllister who, in the view of Harvey, speaking last Thursday, 'could pass the ball through the needle of an eye' . . . well, I thought that was a verbal slip when I first heard it, but, after McAllister's performance on Sunday, I realize it was a perfectly accurate scouting report.

Yet Taylor's Celebrities could not fashion a way through. Throwing on Andy Scott-Lee, the *Pop Idol* evictee, for Ralf Little from *The Royle Family* with fifteen minutes remaining merely smacked of desperation. And leaving Phil Tufnell on the bench throughout deprived us of the laughs which, after a week of these programmes, many of us felt we richly deserved.

Legends: N. Southall (Wales), V. Anderson (England), N. Winterburn (England), P. Reid (England), D. Walker (England), G. Pallister (England), M. Le Tissier (England), D. Batty (England), I. Rush (Wales), P. Beardsley (England), J. Barnes (England)

Subs: P. Shilton, P. Albert, G. McAllister, A. McCoist, D. Saunders, W. Barton, C. Woods

Celebrities: A. Lawler (*Dream Team*), N. Pickard (*Hollyoaks*), R. Little (*Royle Family*), B. Shephard (GMTV), D. Jones (Sky Sports News), T. Craig (*Coronation Street*), P. Olivier (*Brookside*), J. Wilkes (*Mother Goose*), D. Campbell (ex Olympics), A. Hutton (ex *Big Brother*), MC Harvey (So Solid Crew)

Subs: A. Scott-Lee, P. Tufnell, D. Young, W. Mellor, P. McGuiness, I. Thomas, J. Alexander.

Top Cops Await Their Chance

'British police officers, drawn from twenty-nine specialist football units, will travel to the World Cup next year to assist German police in coping with an expected influx of more than 100,000 English football supporters. Although no firm decision on numbers would be taken until December, a seventy-five-man squad was not out of the question' (news report).

So who, exactly, are the anti-hooliganism officers in the frame for Germany 2006? Here's your exclusive guide to the front-runners.

Deputy Chief Constable Roy Howard

It will take more than an 'easyJet bonanza' to unsettle this top-class football crime-stopper. Superb for many years in a holding role at Dover, Howard has also shown that he is easily capable of adapting seamlessly to the international game, which tends to involve more water cannons. He is also a mature reader of pressure situations and unflappable when push comes to shove, which it very often does at this level. No one has summed it up better than Joe Cole: 'Howard is quality plod.' A certainty for selection.

Detective Inspector Graham 'Nosher' Nugent

An indefatigable evidence-gatherer who is unafraid to put a foot in, 'Nosher of the Yard' will always be a legend in the game for the ninety-minute man-marking job he did on Leeds United's Dezzy Higgins during a fog-delayed Dover-to-Boulogne ferry crossing in 1999. Fitness has sometimes been an issue in the intervening years, though no one who saw Nugent at work during the 2004 European Championships in Portugal will doubt his ability to get up and down an airport departure lounge. A vital cog in the England machine in Germany, then, assuming he can avoid injury in the run-up period.

Chief Superintendent Barry Warburton

When people speak of this as the most promising generation of anti-hooliganism officers in living memory, they refer in particular to Warburton, who was nominated for European Bizzy of the Year in 2004 and was unlucky to lose out, on that occasion, to Dick Van der Pump of the Netherlands. What price, then, Warburton for World Bizzy of the Year 2006? It's not unthinkable. He commandingly led the line in Blackburn, Derby and Wolverhampton during the fabled 'dawn raids' of 2002, and is hugely effective at working the channels, English or otherwise. First class fuzz, bound to be there or thereabouts in Germany.

Community Beat Officer Darren Lapwood

Boy genius or petrol-soaked liability? Campaign-clinching hero or unwholesome reprobate, permanently on the edge of suspension? Lapwood's detractors point out that he totally lost the plot in Belfast last month when he went berserk and arrested himself. His seniors counter that he is still extremely young and that if you take that wilder element out of his game, you lose the

policeman. Either way, it's impossible to imagine England travelling to Germany without him.

Sergeant Bob Sanderson
Had an enormously disappointing European Championships in
Portugal, though he later claimed, with some justification, that
the continental-style plastic wrist ties had upset his natural
rhythm. Even then, Sanderson did little during the World Cup
qualifying period to mollify the doubters. But every side needs
a dog-handler, and, in the absence of any other obvious contenders, Sanderson simply *is* that dog-handler.

Police Constable Roger Ives
At almost any other period in history, the hapless Ives – inevitably dubbed 'Roger N'Out' by his team mates – would be in
nobody's mind for a prestigious World Cup spot, other than his
mother's. And even she might have her reservations. However,
at 6'8", this Cambridgeshire cop is fully ten inches over the
regulation height for entry into the force and could therefore
profit from the currently popular school of thought that someone
unusually tall inevitably 'offers something different'. As yet, there
is no clear indication of what that 'something' actually is, nor in
what sense it could be described as 'different'. And for as long
as that remains the case, fans will clearly continue to complain
bitterly that Ives is merely on board to wind them up by
obstructing their view. But if the selectors continue to set such
store by the presence of a token tall man, far from being 'Roger
N'Out', it could well be 'Roger N'In' for Ives – which would
be fantastic news for this modest, understated man, his lovely
Ukrainian wife, Ova, their children, Charlie and Tango, and
the family dog, Foxtrot.

Police Community Support Officer Colin Bayliss
It would be easy to overlook the claims of this young, emphati-
cally talented product of West Ham's legendary police academy.
Many questioned the wisdom of his move last summer across to

the Chelsea force, where stiff competition for places has led to him spending most of the current Premiership season outside the ground in a van. Bayliss, however, has persistently reiterated his desire to stay and 'fight for his place'. There is no denying that he has the game, and it could only take one outing – in a match against Tottenham, say, or perhaps in a Cup game against Leicester – to show what he can offer. An outside bet.

Telling the Players What They Need to Hear

We rise to salute John Enever and Andrew Peel, the Nottingham Forest supporters invited by Gary Megson to give the post-match team talk after Forest's miserably inept 3–0 defeat at Yeovil. 'The fans had paid an awful lot of money to travel and we produced a performance that was a disgrace,' the Forest manager explained. So he let the players hear it from the punters – having, apparently, issued those punters beforehand with the rather touchingly protective instruction not to make it 'personal'. And Enever and Peel, who seem like the kind of supporters any club would be glad to have, went along with it, delivering between them a five-minute address on 'basic application' to an apparently disoriented and entirely silent dressing room.

Talk about 'having your say'. But let's deal directly with the question that is bound to hover over this story, particularly in a period when Megson's managerial and tactical abilities are coming in for criticism: namely, did he pick the wrong fans? Many would maintain that, having decided to go down the supporter-in-the-dressing-room route, Megson would most efficiently have generated the kind of reaction he was looking for from his players by appointing thirty-five hard nuts to crowd in there and sing, 'You're so shit it's unbelievable.'

Our feeling, on the contrary, is that, by introducing Enever and Peel – by all accounts passionate and yet reasonable, coherent and eloquent – the manager brought off the greater shock. After all, how often in his career does the average footballer find himself listening to reason, least of all from a fan? And how often does he hear coherence and eloquence from anybody?

It's no exaggeration to say that this story has touched a nerve globally, as evidenced by a search on the internet. It's a rare news day when Forest make it into the *Sydney Morning Herald*, and an even rarer one when they appear on the sports pages of the *San Jose Mercury News* during a World Series. Fans, irrespective of their sport, are responding to the tale with a widening of the eyes and a shiver. We think we can manage. We manage from the stands all the time. But what if we were challenged to deliver? Would we cope, like Enever and Peel? Or would we go to pieces, like Barry Fry?

Barry Fry, or worse. I like to think that, invited into the dressing room in the right mood and at the right moment, I could slam a hand down on the treatment table, dismantle a few tea-cups against the ceiling tiles, wind up the hair-dryer to full blast, take out some overpaid, fancy Dan's eyebrow with a well-aimed boot. But would the full rhetorical impact of what I had to say be at all undermined if I then went round for autographs and, perhaps, a couple of mobile phone snaps to mark the occasion? For my children, you understand.

We can all dish it out in theory; but can we actually dish it out in practice, directly into the players' eyes, from less than ten feet away in a quiet dressing room, with the scent of Deep Heat in the air and a bath running in the background? In what we will come to regard as the innocent age, pre-Megson, this was never something we had to imagine – just as Matthew Simmons never imagined that the virtual conversation into which he entered with Eric Cantona at Selhurst Park in 1995 was a two-way exchange which would bring him into contact with the inescapable reality of the eccentric Frenchman's studs. Another cherished illusion down, then. But it does us no harm to reflect soberly on our behaviour in this area.

Coincidentally, as the empowerment of the humble punter soared to new levels in Yeovil, this was also the week in which Elfsborg, the Swedish First Division club, decided to issue refunds to every one of the 200 supporters who had travelled to Stockholm to see their team lose 8–1. An announcement on the club's website reads: 'This is our way of apologizing to all our supporters, members, sponsors and all the volunteers who work for our club. We are ashamed.'

Now, there's shame and there's shame. The defeat, we should notice, was to Djurgarden, who have just won the Swedish title for the third time in four years. (Elfsborg finished seventh.) But, in any circumstances, this would be a different way of going about things at the club/supporter interface and it sets a potentially awesome precedent. Eight goals against and your money back – that's football as a whole new commercial proposition. You didn't hear anything about reimbursement from Everton, when Arsenal stuffed them in the dying stages of last season. True, that was only 7–0, not 8–1, but I don't suppose it will be any consolation to Everton's travelling support to realize that they were, according to the Swedish way of looking at things, agonizingly just one goal short of a full refund.

Clearly we are entering an era of breakthroughs for fan power undreamt of in the days of David Mellor and his Football Task Force. How timid, how insipid, how utterly narrow the limits of that body's ambitions – to control the price of replica shirts, achieve a more affordable half-time pie, etc. – now appear. A place on the board for an independent supporters' representative? Pah! They should have been agitating for a place in the technical area and risk-free, performance-linked travel arrangements. That's the future.

The Vote of Confidence That Was Actually Confidence-boosting

'If Steve Bruce didn't win a match for the rest of the season, he would still be our manager' (David Gold, chairman of Birmingham City, 31 October 2005).

'*Do you really think that's wise, sir?*' (*Sgt Wilson*, Dad's Army, passim).

Herewith, exclusive extracts from David Gold's diary of the 2005–06 season.

Wednesday 2 November 2005
The papers have gone quite strong on my comments about Steve. Good. It gets the message out there. And if this really is, as one of the journos put it, 'the most remarkable vote of confidence ever given by the chairman of a football club to his manager' – then, good, too.

My point was a simple one: that Steve Bruce is the heart and soul of this club, its cornerstone both now and in the future, and nothing that happens on the field is going to change that. And if, by coming out and clarifying this point, I end up striking a small blow against the heartless, results-driven culture that has come to dominate the game, and the all-too-pervasive climate of fear under which football bosses labour, then so be it.

Most of all, though, my message was for Steve. I can't see how it won't be good for him. All those other terrified managers, scurrying about, unable to concentrate, wondering when the axe is going to fall – Steve doesn't have that distraction now. He's bullet-proof. He's Superman. Was Superman bullet-proof? I can't remember. But he could stop a speeding train with his bare hands, and that's how I want Steve to feel about himself. I've given him the platform. I'm confident he can build on it.

Saturday 5 November 2005
Went down 8–0 at Newcastle. Not pretty. Nevertheless, Steve – wearing an Hawaiian shirt, I noticed, which was unusual for him on a matchday – seemed to be making every effort to look on the positive side and was beaming all over his face when I questioned him in the dressing room on his decision to play Emile Heskey in goal. 'It was a bet, chairman,' he said. 'Hezzer's going to be cleaning my car from now until the end of the

season! Mug, or what?' Cue uproarious laughter from everyone
and much flicking of Hezzer's ears.

That's what I love about the man. There's no barriers between
Steve and the players. They respect him, and yet he's one of
them at the same time.

Monday 14 November 2005
Message from Steve to say not to worry if the training ground
seems quiet this week. He's decided to take the first-team squad
away for a bit of golf. It's a sensible notion and he has my
unconditional support. What the armchair fan tends not to
realize is that there's much more to management than simply
picking your best team every week. There's the psychological
side and the whole team spirit thing. And if that means a week
on expenses at Sea Island, Georgia, then great. They'll come
back the stronger for it, I know.

Saturday 19 November 2005
Lost 17–1 to Chelsea. Disappointing, obviously, but, on the plus
side, our 62nd minute consolation goal from Jermaine Pennant
was, as I put it to Steve afterwards, 'a real cracker'. 'Certainly
was, chairman,' Steve said. 'Only wish I'd seen it.'

Apparently, the bloke fitting Steve's new car stereo chose
exactly that moment to call him out to the car park to check a
couple of things about speaker positioning. But that's Steve
through and through: a complete perfectionist when it comes
to the details, whether it's his music or his football.

Monday 5 December 2005
Heard something interesting about a young Spanish player who
may become available to us during the January transfer window.
Rang down to Steve's office to get his thoughts.

A voice said, 'Sheldrake Ladders.'

I said, 'Steve?'

The voice said, 'No, it's Bob.'

I said, 'Who's Bob?'

The voice said, 'I'm Steve's brother-in-law. Who are you?'

It turns out that Steve is helping Bob out with an office and a photocopier during a 'transitional phase' for Bob's business.

Bob said, 'Do you need any ladders at all?'

'Not right now,' I said.

'Well, I'd better be getting on, then,' Bob said, and hung up.

I'm so impressed. Moved, in fact. There's a lot of lip service paid to 'football in the community', but how many other leading managers would actually put themselves out to stimulate the business life of the local area?

Saturday 24 December

Dropped round at Steve's place with a few seasonal offerings for the family, but there weren't many lights on. Eventually the housekeeper came to the door. 'They've gone to Jamaica for the new year,' she said.

Steve, of course, always was a forceful advocate of the winter break. And given the way the fixtures tend to pile up at this time of the year, I back him all the way in that.

Monday 2 January 2006

Steve's back, looking tanned and rested, but we've gone down 26–0 at Arsenal, the fans aren't too happy and the press are warming up for a field day. Even so, when I see Steve afterwards, he simply gives me a big, theatrical shrug, and with that lovely, wry smile of his says, 'Funny old game, Saint.' Fantastic. The man just never feels the pressure. It's what you need in a situation like ours.

Saturday 7 January 2006

Scramble a draw at home to Portsmouth with a last-minute equalizer from Walter Pandiani. Bump into Steve in the car park and he takes off his headphones and, despite a heavy carrier bag filled with magazines, manages to raise a cheerful thumb in my direction. 'That point could prove very valuable at the end of the season, chairman,' he says.

'Yes,' I say. 'Although, of course, it was the FA Cup third round.'

There's a kind of look that flickers in Steve's eyes sometimes, bless him (the dumb chairman, stating the blooming obvious!), and I catch that now, just before he says, 'Well, I know that . . .' But at this moment, his phone goes, so I never get to hear the point he was trying to make. Never mind. I'll ask him about it later. It's a permanent education, working with a top-class manager, because they are always thinking about the game in new ways.

Wednesday 8 February 2006
Reached Steve on his mobile.

'Man U this weekend, then, Steve,' I said. 'What are your feelings?'

He said, 'Is that this weekend?'

It was hard to hear him above the sound of rushing water.

I said, 'You in the shower, mate?'

He said, 'No. I'm marlin-fishing in Florida.'

Nice one!

Saturday 4 March 2006
Slightly surprised to see brother-in-law Bob from Sheldrake Ladders in Steve's seat in the dugout for this afternoon's six-pointer against Everton (lost 7–0). Took the opportunity to raise it with Bob when I bumped into him in the players' lounge afterwards. 'I couldn't get a ticket,' Bob explained. 'So Steve very generously said, "Use mine." You know what he's like.'

I asked, 'But where did Steve watch from?'

'Not sure,' said Bob, through a mouthful of peanuts. 'Though he did say something about needing a haircut.'

'Rubbish view from there, by the way,' Bob added. 'I should have brought one of my ladders.'

Saturday 11 March 2006
We're down, following a 9–0 savaging by Fulham in front of

the lowest attendance at St Andrews since the founding of the Premiership, so the mood is a fairly sombre one when Steve stops by at my office to open new contract negotiations. But I'm able to reassure Steve that loyalty is still the watchword at Birmingham City, and that however other clubs choose to behave in these situations is a matter for their own consciences. With that, the atmosphere lightens, and we're free to talk positively about the challenges that face us in the future.

'Any thoughts on purchases over the summer, Steve?' I ask.

Steve thinks about it for a while, and says, 'I might get a new telly.'*

Winston Bogarde: a Memoir

Like you, I'm sure, I will always remember exactly what I was doing when I heard that Winston Bogarde had retired. I was reading a newspaper. One knew, of course, that the legendary Dutch stopper couldn't go on earning for ever. But that knowledge in no way lessened the impact of the news when it broke.

A tug of sadness will have been felt throughout football, but especially keenly at Chelsea. True, Bogarde only made four first-team starts there, in the period of a four-year contract. And one of those was against Gillingham in the Worthington Cup, which is as close to a second-team start as a first-team start gets. Yet his salary of circa £40,000 per week ensured that the Rotterdam-born central defender was a towering presence on the club's wage bill, where he was an ever-present from the beginning of the 2000–01 season until the end of 2003–04. That makes him, by any standard, a Chelsea wage bill legend. Indeed, I would go so far as to say that no other player in Premiership history has put himself about on a club's wage bill the way that

* In the winter of 2007, amid uncertainties wrought by a potential takeover bid, Birmingham finally allowed Bruce to leave and become manager of Wigan Athletic. The terms of his new contract were undisclosed, but given that his deal at Birmingham was for ever, they must have been quite good,

Bogarde did. He was up and down that wage bill tirelessly for four seasons. I fully expect never to see his like on a wage bill again.

Certainly in terms of sheer tenacity, Bogarde was a one-off. There's an accusation you hear levelled at foreign imports all the time: sure, they're happy to pick up a pay packet while the sun is shining, but can they bank a salary on a wet Tuesday night in Bolton when they haven't been picked? And, if he did nothing else, Bogarde silenced football's cynical xenophobes with a resounding 'Yes, I can.' The hurly-burly of the Premier League wage bill suited his game.

He added to those four first-team starts with Chelsea a further eight appearances as substitute in the 2000–01 season, but for the next three years he made absolutely no appearances at all. Thus the suggestion of one news source this week that Bogarde was 'hanging up his boots' did inevitably beg some questions about the exact whereabouts of Bogarde's boots at this time. In his fourth and last season at Chelsea, he had no squad number and was training with the youth team. (He was also said to be commuting from Amsterdam, though Bogarde fiercely denied this.) Yet you could not budge him. In an age when footballers' contracts suddenly did not appear to be worth the paper they were written on, Bogarde took what will go down as the last great stand on behalf of the written deal. His word was his bond. He stuck by it until the end.

Assuming that Bogarde was on Chelsea's books for three years and ten months, he earned £8,240,000. If the story about commuting was true, then the club might at least have recouped some of its money in fines for lateness. As it is, Bogarde's average of £686,666 per appearance is positively Las Vegan.

But then, even the story of his signing is an example of the kind of fairy tales that only football provides. Merely four months before Bogarde arrived at Stamford Bridge, Chelsea had met Barcelona in a Champions League quarter-final. A plan was formulated, allegedly by Graham Rix, then Chelsea's assistant manager, to target the opposition's soft spot – namely, one

Winston Bogarde. Chelsea, with Tore Andre Flo on fire, bombed all over the floundering Dutchman and were 3–0 up by half-time. Alas, Barcelona's own formidable pressure was too much for Chelsea in the away leg and the Spanish side went through. Ripple dissolve to August, though, and there is Bogarde awakening to find the club that had identified him as the weakest link only a couple of months earlier is now beckoning him aboard on a Bosman with a big fat salary attached. It's *Boy's Own* stuff.

Needless to say, some critics have argued that circumstances at Chelsea were soon to leave Bogarde 'in the comfort zone'. But it takes a certain kind of character to earn £40,000 per week for three years for doing next to nothing. You must remember that this was in the pre–Sudoku era, when spare time was that much harder to manage. And as a footballer who never had to work weekends, Bogarde would have had some spare time to manage. I never saw his lawn, but I would wager it was a sight to behold. And he must have had the tidiest shed in Europe.

Now, though, Bogarde has obviously reached the stage where he wants to move on from football and seek new challenges. There has been a suggestion that he might run 'a music promotions company'. That would figure, although a more suitable proposal came up in discussion on the *Times* sports desk this week: farming. Under EU set-aside regulations, Bogarde could take a subsidy and get paid not to grow anything. Failing that, he would seem well placed to become a football agent.

If nothing else, his retirement will hasten me finally to get on and organize the plaque that I have been intending for ages to mount above my desk, as an inspiration and a comfort.

'I give my all every single day and I know that I cannot do any more than that' (Winston Bogarde, 2002).

Those words are drawn from the interview in which Bogarde famously described himself, with a refusal to self-dramatize that was typical of the man, as 'the biggest outcast in England'.

This was debatable. That he was the biggest-paid outcast in England was less so. But some traces of bitterness appear to remain. 'I won't miss football,' Bogarde claimed in his official announcement this week. 'The game has been good to me, with the exception of my period at Chelsea, but now I'm not interested any more.'

'With the exception of my period at Chelsea'? That hurts. I would like to think that the supporters made him comfortable, even if the club's £8,240,000 didn't. But while there is any doubt, the least the club can do is dispel any lingering resentment by offering Bogarde the traditional tribute for services loyally rendered – a testimonial. He never really got the chance to say goodbye to the fans. And, thinking about it, his hello wasn't all that clear cut, either. So let's see a Chelsea XI take on a Holland XI in the big man's honour. Of course, it would be just Bogarde's luck not to make the squad. But that needn't spoil the occasion. He could watch from the stands, or from home, and get the cheque sent on. And those of us in the crowd, though naturally sad not to see him, could at least console ourselves that it's what he would have wanted.

The New Wembley: Book Now to Meet Disappointment Head On

England's victory over Argentina last weekend apparently triggered a surge in ticket applications for the new, and as yet incomplete, Wembley National Stadium. On Monday, Wembley National Stadium Ltd reported taking £2 million in orders for the various packages reserving seats in the new stadium, from the Corinthian (£16,100 for a licence fee, plus £5,400 for a ten-year season ticket) down to the Club (£3,900 for a licence fee, £1,350 per year for a season ticket). 'This just shows how keen football fans are to see England play at Wembley,' Michael Cunnah, the chief executive of WNSL, remarked.

But worry not if your favoured package is now sold out. A

wide range of seating options in the new, £757 million stadium remains available, in styles to suit all tastes, and at prices to suit all pockets.

Five-Star Deluxe Utopian New Wembley Spa Pamper Package

Your day starts with a full-body aromatherapy massage in the Jamie Redknapp Healing Rooms. Then enjoy your choice of colonic irrigation, Hopi ear candling or a detoxifying body wrap in the company of Howard Wilkinson. After a light lunch, relax and watch the game from the vantage of your own salon-style treatment table while receiving an Indian head massage from Peter Shilton. Allow those stressful post-match crowds to clear by checking in for a reviving pedicure and body-brush, followed by a tour of the stadium with Nobby Stiles. What better way to enjoy the League Two play-off final, or any one of the eleven other big sporting occasions that form the Wembley season? Available as a ten-year debenture at only £4,273,301.35 per person, including VAT.

The John Terry's All Gold New Wembley Mascot Package

Your exclusive matchday laminate allows you to join the England squad on the morning of the game for a hotel breakfast, including Weetabix and a glass of freshly chilled Lucozade. Travel to Wembley on the team bus and accompany the players to the dressing room, where a replica England kit awaits you. (Please state sizes.) Then listen to Sven-Goran Eriksson's pre-match team talk and, indeed, find out whether he gives one. After that, it's down the tunnel and out on to the pitch, holding the hand of the player of your choice. Participate in the pre-match kickabout and then see the game from an exclusive seat in the home dugout. Unless you showed form in the kickabout, in which case replace Ledley King in the holding role. Price: £894,765, plus agents' fees. Caution: may involve rooming with Joe Cole.

The Platinum Sir Geoff Hurst Wembley Heritage Sensation
Fantastic *trompe l'oeil* tribute to England's 1966 World Cup hat-trick hero: three seats together which, on closer inspection and following careful scrutiny of the available film evidence, turn out to be just two seats. Who gets the non-existent seat? Loads of family fun, guaranteeing anything up to half a century of vigorous debate. Available on a match-by-match basis at £7,523. Price includes balloon, whistle and argument-settling half-time visit from Sir Geoff himself (subject to availability).

The David and Victoria New Wembley Golden Bridal Suite
The ideal England-watching opportunity for football-crazy newlyweds or for established couples looking to renew their vows ahead of, say, a friendly against Austria. Swathed in royal mauve, your tastefully appointed pitchside booth offers a queen-size bed, monogrammed towelling bathrobe, inflatable thunder sticks and a programme. Please ask at reception if you wish to purchase the bathrobe. Price: £47,598 per night, based on two persons, and no more than two persons, sharing.

Hercules Full-Trim Range-Topper Triple-A Prestige Silver-Lining Executive Corporate Package for Corporate Executives (originally offered as The Total Prawn Sandwich Stuffer)
Sold out.

The Below-Target Sales Rep in an Eight-Year-Old Vauxhall Vectra Ligging Opportunity
Slightly padded seat. Free cup of Kenco and a ginger nut. Price crash! £400 per year, ono. Sixteen thousand of these must go.

The Builder's Cleavage Early Riser Special
Join the on-site crew slinging up fibreboard as fast as is humanly possible. Get to watch the match from an upturned bucket over a strong brew in a chipped mug. Going rate of pay: £50 per day (unskilled). Note: the high possibility of cement dust means this

package is not suitable for allergy sufferers. Access to cranes is strictly by application to the foreman.

The 'It Were Different in My Day' Vintage Bronze Wembley Experience

An opportunity for the nostalgic, or the simply curious, to relive the golden age of football-going at Wembley, before the fall of the Twin Towers. Your highly collectible matchday ticket, complete with reproduction tout's thumbprints, offers an obstructed view, several miles from a toilet or acceptable catering facility, behind chicken mesh, in one of the old stadium's legendary and lovingly restored backless seats. Upgrade to the premium package to be located on crumbly terracing. Upgrade to premium plus to watch from the back of a white horse. (Horse not supplied.) Round your day off by getting chased up Wembley Way by a skinhead carrying a set of darts. Price, including Bovril and Wagon Wheel, £4,678 per match, plus tip for the skinhead, at your discretion.

Season Ticket in the IKEA Stand

In association with the new Wembley's distinguished business partners on the north circular, a sports-watching opportunity to suit the most demanding fan of DIY. On arrival at the ground, simply assemble and install your seat from the contents of the flat-pack provided. Slot tab B into groove A while simultaneously gumming joint D to recess E, allow concrete to set, and hey presto: your very own place in the venue of legends. Price: £12.99 for a set of six. Availability: considerable in the event of the building work overrunning, as widely predicted.

The Peter Crouch Gantry Pass

Great view from up here, albeit mostly of the surrounding countryside. For safety reasons, admission will be from 75 minutes into the match only, unless in exceptional circumstances. This is a standing-only zone, with limited wheelchair access. First come, first served.

A Few Words in Support of the Booing of
National Anthems

What's to be done about the booing of national anthems? The practice is so widespread now that it can be confidently numbered among the standard preliminaries of international football, certainly in Europe. The teams come on and stand in a line, and then the supporters compete to see who can more effectively drown the opposing side's national song beneath a barrage of whistling, jeering and, if necessary, aerosol horns. And then (to adapt Gary Lineker), the English win, the position of England in relation to anthem-booing being much like that of Brazil with regard to football: we may not have invented it, but we sure as hell beat the world at it now.

That said, it behoves no one to rest on their laurels in this department. Supposedly neutral Swiss supporters gave the Turkish national anthem a comprehensive caning ahead of a World Cup play-off in Berne the other week, and Turkish fans replied in kind before the second leg. With the Swiss coming through, you wouldn't bet against a dark horse causing an upset or two, booing-wise, in Germany next year.

Observers and commentators have long found anthem-booing a source of bitter disappointment, embarrassment and dismay – though, we should quickly point out, this is not everybody's position. Some people remain sanguine about anthem abuse, regarding it, not as culturally boorish and roundly undiplomatic, but as one of the few remaining strands linking international football to the golden days of music hall and pantomime. According to this theory, the crowd member who boos, for instance, the national song of Ukraine may not, in fact, be intending to pour inflammatory scorn on the entire history of that country and its struggles, but may merely be taking advantage of the opportunity to satisfy a widespread human 'boo-hiss' craving stretching all the way back to the theatre of ancient Greece and catered for in more modern circumstances by the entrance, stage right, of the Ugly Sisters.

The more vocal body of opinion, though, insists that the booing brings shame upon us all and that we would be happier in a world in which the national anthems at matches were 'impeccably observed', like a two-minute silence. Include among their number Sepp Blatter. The president of FIFA indicated this week that it might be best to stop playing national songs before football matches altogether. 'I consider the booing extremely disrespectful and, of course, disparaging to national pride,' Blatter said. 'I'm wondering whether it makes sense to play the national anthems. We should at least consider not playing them.'

This, obviously, is the zero-tolerance option: deny the booers the oxygen of an anthem. Yet the first thing to note about Blatter's thinking in this area is how contrary it runs to the general way of things in football, where the trend is overwhelmingly for adding anthems, rather than subtracting them. The Champions League has its own anthem (one to which, incidentally, none of the players appears to know the words and which nobody shows any inclination whatsoever to sing along with – a position that UEFA should urgently address). And a year ago, following suit, the Premier League introduced a specially commissioned, synthesized fanfare which no one has ever booed – strangely, really, given the incentives.

This proliferation of anthems has opened up whole new areas for diplomatic incident. At Chelsea last season, following a mix-up in the PA booth, the Premier League anthem was played before a Champions League match and a major international crisis was averted only, one felt, by the fact that not many people noticed, and that the ones who did notice didn't really care.

Blatter's willingness to contemplate abandoning anthems on the international stage must indicate his belief that everything else has been tried. And, indeed, our times have seen exhortations via the stadium's video screens, increasingly desperate PA announcements and special messages in the programme from David Beckham. At Wembley, during the 1990s, one recalls hearing a specially recorded announcement from Kevin Keegan, then the manager of England, urging 'respect'. The booing, when it came, was, if anything, more intense.

Yet one would be reluctant, surely, to see the anthems go – especially these days, when television's microphones get in close enough to pick up the sound of players singing along. And is it necessarily true that all the other options have been exhausted? To my knowledge, there has never been, for instance, an initiative in which fans were encouraged, not simply to listen in silence to the opposing side's anthem, but to join in with it and sing along, karaoke-style, with the lyrics unfolding on the big screen, accompanied by a helpful bouncing ball. It would offer a chance for fans from nations with deeply boring national anthems (the English, the German) to experience what it feels like to get behind a real belter (the French, the Italian) and for everyone to rank their own performance when given some of the tougher nuts to crack (the Danish, the Russian). Comic counterpointing with hooters, in the manner of the Last Night of the Proms, would be perfectly permissible and, indeed, encouraged.

Another untried option is to play both teams' anthems at the same time, creating a kind of all-in sing-off, in which supporters would be too busy coping with the demands of their own anthem to lay into anybody else's. The problem here, of course, would lie in creating a level playing field, given that national anthems can vary wildly in length. The Brazilian anthem, for instance, lasts the best part of a quarter of an hour. Overrun by the Brazilians – it wouldn't be for the first time.

Of course, any campaign against disrespectful booing could hardly end at national anthems. Blatter has not announced his position on booing the reading out of the opposition's team sheet, but, again, if he felt strongly enough about it, banning the public announcement of the teams would cut off this kind of booing at source. Similarly with the tradition of booing the opposition's appearance on the field for the warm-up: ensure that the warm-up takes place under cover and you remove the possibility of such booing.

One would be keen to know, however, whether the president has any ideas for coping with the ritual, blanket, all-weather booing of players such as Craig Bellamy and Alan Smith, an opportunity which a broad majority of customers quite reasonably considers to be included in the price of the ticket. Perhaps Blatter would support a regulation banning players likely to incite booing. But the problem with combating booing by removing the opportunities for booing, is that, in the football context, there may not be very much left by the time you have finished. And what would we all boo then?

Thierry Henry: the Perfect Example

Youngsters wanting to learn how it's done would do well to get hold of the video from Saturday of Arsenal's Thierry Henry. Look at the positions he takes up, the space he finds. Look at the concentration from start to finish. Note, above all, the patience. As a lesson in how to do an appearance on *Parkinson*, it was straight out of the coaching manuals.

Let's begin with the basics: his kit. It might be fusty to mention it these days, but a true professional takes pride in his appearance. Henry was immaculately turned out: a superb black suit, a white shirt open to reveal a plain black T-shirt. Then there was his achingly assured wave at the top of the stairs, followed by his consummate management of those stairs, incorporating traditional nonchalance about the in-house orchestra – again, textbook stuff. Then see how, once seated, Henry quickly adopted the perfect body shape, the torso purposefully forward, the left hand grasping the lower part of the chair's metal arm for balance, the head tilted in thought.

He was fluid, both tracking back to defend (the French underclass and its discontents) and going forward to attack (the racism of Luis Aragones, the Spain coach). Of the man who called him 'a black shit', Henry coolly shrugged and said, 'Maybe he doesn't have a lot of vocabulary.' This point was the greater for coming from a man who was speaking at the time in his second language. Indeed, Henry's idiomatic English very rarely betrayed him, except, touchingly, at the moment when, reflecting on the hardship of his upbringing, he said, 'I had the chance to have good parents.' If you have the chance to have good parents, seize it, seemed to be the message. Take good parents over bad parents every time.

But – take note, kids – it's as much about what you do when the ball isn't at your feet. Not even the greatest goalscorer in Arsenal's history gets an entire *Parkinson* to himself, and for much of the middle portion of the show, Henry was forced to concede possession to Sarah Lancashire from *Coronation Street*. It happens. The important thing is to be able to hold steady when it does, and soak it up without losing focus or going to sleep.

Even late on in the Matthew Kelly interview, the Arsenal man was still alert and looking for opportunities in the final third. Bear in mind that this was also a show in which Parkinson crossed the stage to risk a chat with Stevie Wonder, who rarely begins a sentence on a Saturday without the intention of concluding it the following Tuesday afternoon, at the earliest. Almost inevitably, a well-thumbed Wonder anecdote about jumping off roofs in his childhood took the show well into extra time. But Henry was still there at the end, demonstrating that all the silky skills in the world are nothing unless you can twin them with that old-fashioned, unglamorous chat show virtue: stamina.

They moan about him at Arsenal, of course – the over-elaboration, his apparent aversion to scoring goals that don't seem to demand instant commemoration on top ten video compilations or even by a special issue of limited edition china figurines. He has broken the club's scoring record and he is most likely the greatest Arsenal player any of them will ever see on *Parkinson*, but it's the paying fan's God-given right to grumble, so every now and again they grumble.

But then, they probably moan about Parkinson, too. The

received opinion is that his landmark show is now a soft launch pad for upcoming television programmes. And given that Henry's fame beyond football arises from his advertisements for Renault, it could be said that he, too, qualified for an invitation by virtue of having a series on ITV. But it's not Parkinson's fault that Bob Hope is dead. And as for 'soft', in an age in which interviewers set out to nail, ridicule and trivialize, isn't it worth having someone who understands the meaning of the word 'guest' and behaves accordingly?

'I'm not going to ask you whether you're leaving Arsenal,' Parkinson said to Henry. This may have frustrated Arsenal supporters who seek urgent reassurance on this matter. But what would be the point of asking that question? How self-deluded would Parkinson have to be about his influence? As if Henry is going to say, 'You know, funny you should mention that, Mike, but, between you and me, when the January window opens, I'm off to Liverpool in a surprise swap for Peter Crouch and a Nissan Almera.' At no point in the modern era has a footballer chosen to announce a major transfer deal through the medium of a Saturday-night chat show. Not even David Beckham.

Instead, Parkinson asked a question worth asking and got an answer worth hearing. Would Henry ever consider refusing to play in a country where football and racism were still locked in an ugly embrace? And Henry pointed out that racism had not stopped him moving to Juventus. Which means one cannot rule out Spain as a possible destination for Henry.* A sad thought. It will be harder for him to reach *Parkinson* from there. But we'll have the memories, if he goes, and the video.

* Indeed, Henry moved to Barcelona and was barely ever heard of again.

The Boy's Own *Story to End All* Boy's Own *Stories*

(*An in-house magazine for top-flight footballers? Edited by Jamie Redknapp? This we had to see. Except we couldn't, because it was only sent to footballers. Ah, well. It was probably mostly adverts, anyway.*)

STRICTLY CONFIDENTIAL

The following represent the minutes of an editorial strategy and early-stage planning meeting for ICON magazine, the publishing venture organized by Jamie Redknapp, the former England international, and his wife, Louise, with a view to developing a high-end, glossy periodical aimed exclusively at professional footballers.

Venue: the private dining room of the Lucky Boy Thai Restaurant, Bournemouth.
Present: Jamie and Louise Redknapp, Sol Campbell, Graeme Le Saux, Anton Ferdinand, Iain Dowie.
Apologies for absence: Michael Owen (hamstring), Rio Ferdinand (shopping).

The meeting was brought to order by Jamie Redknapp, who thanked everyone for finding time in their busy schedules to attend what he said was very much an informal think-tank. As he hoped everyone was well aware by now, the vision was to create a magazine that spoke directly to professional footballers about their lives and interests. In order to do so, he said, it was vital to hear from voices within the game, whose input would vitally shape the project and ensure that it ended up hitting the target rather than flying wide. He said he was grateful, then, for this opportunity to have an open-ended brain-crunching session with people whose opinions he valued as professionals and friends.

Iain Dowie asked if it would be possible to order soon because he was starving.

Food was ordered.

Jamie Redknapp invited everyone to open the file in front of them and consider the sheet detailing the results of some specially commissioned research into footballers' reading habits. Of 100 Premiership footballers polled, he explained, 39 per cent said they read *Nuts*, 48 per cent said they read *Shoot!* and 1 per cent said they read the *New York Times Review of Books* (but may have been kidding). Redknapp pointed out that there was clearly a gap for a publication that embraced a footballer's interests and that wasn't *Shoot!* or *Nuts*. He then invited Louise to bring the meeting up to speed with developments on the commercial side.

Louise Redknapp reported that advertisers had responded with enormous enthusiasm to the ICON project, particularly in the luxury retailing and fashion sectors. Prada, Philippe Patek watches, Louis Vuitton and Bentley were definitely on board and Sikorsky were keen to set up a promotional spot the ball competition in which the first prize was a helicopter.

Jamie Redknapp welcomed these indications of the project's strength and viability, but pointed out that the editorial challenge remained. Accordingly he said he would now like to throw the meeting open to the floor. Off the top of their heads, he wondered, could anyone think of any topics that today's footballer would instantly recognize as being of special or even unique interest to him?

Sol Campbell suggested blisters.

Jamie Redknapp said he wasn't sure that this kind of topic was strictly within ICON's remit.

Sol Campbell said that footballers get them all the time.

Jamie Redknapp said he didn't think that blisters would sit comfortably alongside adverts for Bentley and the Mandarin Hotel chain.

Sol Campbell said that didn't mean that footballers didn't get them.

Louise Redknapp suggested that maybe the way forward was

to take the subject of foot care and broaden it to take in moisturizing in general, in which case she thought she might be able to get Clarins interested in an advertorial.

Jamie Redknapp made a note to examine blisters.

Graeme Le Saux said he'd like to read an article on the 4–3–3 formation, or maybe a series of articles on formations in general – putting them in context, going back to their historical roots, explaining their advantages and disadvantages.

Jamie Redknapp said he could see where Le Saux was coming from with this idea, but not many players really understood that kind of stuff and he didn't want to risk intimidating the readership or turning them off prematurely.

Iain Dowie asked who was having the beef strips in ginger.

Anton Ferdinand said that one of the big issues facing young players coming into the game these days was what to do when you locked your car keys inside your car. Only the other day, he said, he had shut the key fob inside his self-locking Lincoln Navigator. And in fact, most mornings the car park at West Ham's training ground was absolutely thronging with players who had locked themselves out of their cars. Ferdinand said he would be keen to read an article which got to the bottom of this phenomenon, perhaps with the AA's phone number at the end.

Jamie Redknapp said he would think about getting a writer on to it.

Sol Campbell said that, on a related topic, he would love to see something in the magazine about the cars that referees drive. Most referees' cars, he said, were absolutely minging.

Graeme Le Saux pointed out that Graham Poll drives a Vauxhall Vectra. There was a five-minute adjournment for laughter.

Louise Redknapp suggested doing referees' cars as a makeover item – getting hold of a referee's car, perhaps without his knowledge, and completely restyling it, inside and out. She suggested calling the feature 'Pimp My Ref's Ride'.

Jamie Redknapp made a note to ring Len Randall at the Referees' Association to explore the idea.

Iain Dowie asked if anyone else had tried the chicken satay. He expressed the opinion that it was magic.

Graeme Le Saux wondered if there was any mileage in having a books page on which players were invited to review their own, ghosted autobiographies. It would be interesting to know, he said, if any of them recognized the life they were reading about. There was general agreement that this was a nice idea, but doubts were also voiced about whether players could ever be persuaded to read their autobiographies.

Anton Ferdinand asked if there were any plans to include a fixture list.

Jamie Redknapp said that they had considered doing so, but had decided it looked a bit boring. He pledged to have another look at the issue of fixture lists, though, if he felt the pressure was there from readers.

Iain Dowie asked if it would be possible to order some more prawn crackers.

Jamie Redknapp pointed out that the choice of a cover star for the magazine's launch issue would be critical in terms of establishing the magazine's tone and identity. Fortunately, he said, he had been able to call in a favour from a relative, gaining exclusive access to someone high profile and popular whose image on the cover would strike exactly the aspirational note the magazine was looking for. At the same time, Redknapp said, he didn't want to open himself up to the accusation of nepotism and he was keen to know what the meeting thought on this.

Graeme Le Saux said he didn't think Redknapp should worry at all. Frank Lampard was a model professional, in the form of his life, who was extremely well respected within the game and would be the perfect cover material for the magazine, irrespective of whether or not he was Jamie Redknapp's cousin.

Jamie Redknapp said he hadn't meant Lampard – he had meant his father, Harry. But now that Le Saux had mentioned it, maybe Lampard would look a bit better in the close-ups. Certainly he would look better wearing the Versace male thong. Redknapp resolved to have another think.

Louise Redknapp mentioned that debate was still ongoing about the possibility of a cover-mounted gift for the launch issue. Perfume, a DVD, a Hermes scarf or a set of leather-clad scatter cushions were all ideas under consideration. But she admitted that footballers already had a lot of perfume, DVDs and scarves and she wondered if anyone round the table could think of anything with a slightly greater 'wow' factor.

Sol Campbell suggested a jet ski. There was general agreement that a jet ski would be cool.

Jamie Redknapp said he thought there might be some practical issues relating to attaching a jet ski to the front of a magazine, but he said he would talk it over with distribution.

Louise Redknapp raised the question of the magazine's fashion coverage and expressed her hope that they would be able to find something fresher than the 'Jose Mourinho's coat' angle, which she felt had been done to death elsewhere.

Sol Campbell suggested doing Arsene Wenger's coat.

Louise Redknapp said that would certainly be different.

Jamie Redknapp said he would get someone to have a look at it.

At this point, Anton Ferdinand abruptly stood up and began patting his pockets. 'Not again!' he said, and left the room in a hurry.

Iain Dowie said he could murder a coffee.

The meeting broke up shortly afterwards.*

---

* As 2007 ended, ICON filed losses of £85,000 (or about a week's wages, in football terms) and arranged a debenture agreement with National Westminster bank to take care of its mounting debts. The general feeling was that, in a highly competitive marketplace, and despite having some cracking pictures of Frank Lampard in an evening suit, ICON couldn't finally loosen the grip on footballers' reading habits of other, established high-net-worth-lifestyle titles such as *Nuts*, *FHM* and *Stuff*.

Dressing up for Christmas

Photographs of Blackburn's Robbie Savage entering a nightclub in a Scooby Doo outfit stunned football this week. Across the country, professional players were emitting involuntary gasps, clapping their hands to their foreheads and crying, 'Why didn't I think of that?'

At Christmas party time, like at no other time in the season, the pressure is on footballers to come up with something novel. Hats off, then (or rather, dog-shaped hoods off), to Savage for this week's performance. I have searched my *Rothman's Football Yearbook* and I can find no record of any player in the modern era attending a football club's official Christmas bash dressed as the dumb, but lovable canine crime-stopper. Batman, yes; some kind of generic pirate, every year. But Scooby Doo, no.

The nigglesome midfielder scores extra points for pairing the outfit with some stylish, pricey-looking brown loafers, rather than the spongy, paw-shaped slippers which one assumes were supplied. I'm sure I won't be the first to point out that Savage hasn't always needed the help of a hired costume to resemble a cartoon animal. But that shouldn't detract from the carefully researched magnificence of his effort, best judged in the context of his team mate Paul Dickov's painfully thin Yoda from *Star Wars* disguise.

Christmas, as Sir Alex Ferguson might say: bloody hell. Perry Como was telling only half the story when he described it as 'the most wonderful time of the year'. The legendary American crooner hadn't seen Dominic Matteo dressed as Andy Pandy or Brett Emerton as an Indian chief, let alone Brad Friedel in an antique Burberry golfing outfit, looking like some kind of chav-tastic Payne Stewart. What a swell party Blackburn's must have been, and an unignorable testament to the fun-loving, all-smiling, emphasis-on-comedy, no-nasty-pieces-of-work-here attitude that Mark Hughes has bred at Ewood Park over the last year.

You can tell a lot about a club by its Christmas party: its morale, its attitude, its position in the league. For instance, not so much embracing the obvious stereotype as jumping enthusiastically into its arms, Chelsea celebrated Christmas this week at the Café Royal in London. There wasn't a Scooby Doo outfit to be seen. Instead, the word is, the players had prepared meticulously for the night, studying DVDs, specially compiled by Jose Mourinho and his staff, of previous Christmas parties in the same location, in order to be completely confident of the whereabouts of the bar, cloakroom, lavatories, etc.

Result: a hugely successful, if slightly unexciting evening. And another clean sheet. One newspaper reported that Eidur Gudjohnsen looked 'unsteady on his feet', but anyone who has been watching Chelsea this season will know that this needn't necessarily have been down to drink. Indeed, with competition for places as stiff as it was, Gudjohnsen can consider himself fortunate to have been picked for the Christmas party at all.

Far more noteworthy was how much energy all of the players, including Gudjohnsen, seemed to have in the party's second half. I don't suppose many other clubs will even come close to matching those fitness levels this Christmas season. What's more, sparing anyone the potential indignity of being discovered face down in Leicester Square by a street cleaner, a fleet of hired cars was on hand at the end to spirit the players safely to their homes. Carling don't do footballers' Christmas parties. But if they did, they would probably be like Chelsea's.

Word has it that Wigan's Christmas bash started surprisingly well, exceeding absolutely everyone's expectations, given the budget, but faded badly when the pop and Pringles ran out a third of the way through. Over at Manchester United, meanwhile, disappointment followed Ferguson's decision to hold this year's party at the centre of a set of covered wagons, circled so tightly that not even the players could get in. Staff allegedly spent about twenty minutes dispiritedly attempting to find an entrance, while from within came the muffled sound of Ferguson shouting Christmas carols. But eventually everyone gave up and drifted away. Sources close to the club described this development as 'worrying'.

Naturally, though, at this time of the year, even in the midst of revelry, one's thoughts turn to those less fortunate – namely, the players of Newcastle United. Last year, Graeme Souness got wind of the players' well-advanced plans to stage a Christmas bash in Edinburgh and, before you could say 'Grinch', the manager had cancelled it. ('Why Edinburgh?' you may wonder. But this slightly mystifying practice of staging club parties away from home appears to be widespread. Blackburn's fancy dress party this week took place in Manchester. Clearly, at some point in the planning stages, someone stands up and says, 'Let's go somewhere no one will recognize us.' D'oh!)

Now, it's true that, at the time of Souness's clampdown, the legendarily hard-partying Patrick Kluivert was still on Newcastle's books, meaning that there was every danger that the party soon would have moved on from Edinburgh and would most likely have ended, anything up to six days later, in a canal in Amsterdam. In this context, Souness's decision to declare a ban looks less like the act of an unrepentant Scrooge and more like a charitable gesture on behalf of already hard-pressed hospitals across Europe.

But even with Kluivert long gone, sources now indicate that Souness has again cancelled Christmas – or at any rate restricted it to a lunch at the training ground canteen, where the players can look forward to an individual serving of Turkey Twizzlers, followed by steamed pudding and Scott Parker's rendition of 'All I Want For Christmas Is Me Two Front Teeth'. Quite apart from the festive spirit, doesn't Souness recognize a team-building opportunity when he sees one? Consider the 24-carat boost to morale which would come from seeing Alan Shearer in a Tinky-Winky outfit. Let's face it, it comes but once a year. It only feels like it's more often.*

---

* Two years later, festive partying by Premiership footballers took a dark turn and Christmas had to be cancelled everywhere, indefinitely. See pp. 372–5.

Steve Bruce Gives Us a Wave

'It was an instinctive thing,' Steve Bruce explained, 'and as soon as I put my hand up I thought to myself, "I shouldn't really have done that." ' Well, perhaps not. But then again, maybe he should. It's a knotty one. Little can the Birmingham manager have imagined, when he waved to the Manchester United supporters during this week's Carling Cup tie, that he was opening up such a densely packed etiquette worm-can.

The problem is, we lack clear and definitive guidance in the matter of a football manager's public interaction with the opposing team's fans. In this delicate area, the book simply has not been written. It awaits its Lynne Truss. On the one hand, when something in the region of 3,000 people are singing your name in sentimental approbation, as the United fans were on Tuesday night (they think highly of Bruce, on account of his achievements at Old Trafford as a player), it would seem a little rude simply to ignore them. It would seem especially rude if you happen to be standing around not doing anything particularly important at the time, as managers tend to be during football matches. On the grounds of politeness alone, there is obviously some impetus to (in the accepted terminology) 'acknowledge the crowd'.

On the other hand, there's the reaction of your own crowd to think of. On Tuesday, Birmingham supporters responded to Bruce's wave with jeering and the affronted fury of someone catching their partner in the arms of an ex. The implication was that the manager was guilty of some kind of treachery, calling into question in the most fundamental way his dedication to Birmingham and perhaps, beyond that, his fitness to continue in the job. Accordingly, Bruce's carefully weighed post-match remarks on the episode contained righteous defiance and slightly anxious self-defence in equal measure. 'If our supporters were offended, then I apologize,' he said. 'If anyone doubts my commitment here, then they shouldn't . . . But if people want to hang me for this, that's up to them.'

I think we can agree that hanging would be going a bit far for an offence that, interestingly, isn't even a bookable one in the eyes of the Football Association. At any rate, the fourth official took no action against Bruce for waving to the wrong fans – though, of course, he may have been unsighted. (Without the benefit of video replays for these kinds of situations, we are destined to linger for ever in a limbo of judicial might-haves and maybes.)

Whichever way you look at this complex episode, the protocols for managerial behaviour, clearly, are non-existent. In those circumstances, I would argue, contrary to the disappointed Birmingham fans, that Bruce's instincts served him commendably well. His gesture was polite, brief and seemly. What's more, it was the right gesture. A simple raised arm towards another team's fans is always going to be preferable, in this context, to other, fuller responses, such as an extended bout of overhead clapping, the adoption of a Messianic pose with both arms outstretched and a tipped-up chin, or, perhaps worst of all, a stint of jocular 'I am not worthy' bowing. And, most importantly, it did not involve Bruce leaving the technical area – something that would have been necessitated by other, more vigorous responses, such as, say, a sprint along the touchline, rapidly collecting high-fives.

One applauds Bruce, too, for not attempting to take the furtive route with a quick, possibly backwards-directed, flick of the hand, in the hope that none of the Birmingham fans would notice. That kind of cowardly nonsense is all very well in La Liga, but we don't want it getting a toehold here, thank you very much.

Bruce's was, then, in many ways the model reaction – and in an area where a model was sorely needed. It could be usefully adopted as a blueprint by any other manager worried about being hymned by the other side's fans, and about how to respond in this awkward social situation. At the same time, managers ought to understand that not everything sung about them by other teams' supporters is an invitation to a two-way conversation. In the interests of clarity, then, it might be worth pointing out that chants it is perfectly acceptable to ignore, on the grounds that they are satirical or unflattering in intent, include: 'Wenger, Wenger [or similar], give us a wave,' 'Fergie, Fergie [or similar], what's the score?' and 'xxxx off, Souness [or similar].'

Meanwhile, the book is open on the first referee to 'acknowledge the crowd'. My money is on Graham Poll.*

The Goal Celebration: a New Breakthrough

A highly significant week for Nwankwo Kanu, who, after scoring for West Bromwich Albion against Tottenham on Wednesday night, became the first footballer in the televised era to involve a ball boy in a goal celebration. More than that, in the second half Kanu scored again, and by reprising the celebration at the other end of the pitch, promptly became either the second footballer in the televised era to involve a ball boy in a goal celebration, or the first player to do so twice, whichever way you want to think of it.

Let's make clear straight away that neither of the ball boys, plucked from their stations at the side of the goal and thrust into statistical history, objected. That said, the ball boy plucked in the first half (Kieran Day, aged twelve) possibly enjoyed it a bit more than the ball boy plucked in the second half (Mark Hingley, aged eleven). But then, Kanu wasn't to know that the second ball boy was a Tottenham fan.

Now, that would have to hurt, wouldn't it? Not only has your side just gone 2–0 down in the freezing cold, but you are in the arms of the goalscorer, with the onus on you to look jubilant about it in front of the cameras of *Match of the Day*. It is difficult to know how any of us would react in similar

---

* This was a cheap joke, and wildly wrong in any case. In a sense, Jeff Winter had already cracked this one out of the ballpark by kissing the medal he received for refereeing the 2004 FA Cup final. See pp. 121–4 for Winter's own account of this moment, and much more.

circumstances, but it is clear that not all of us could guarantee to show good grace under that kind of pressure, and Hingley can only be admired for displaying a poise and equanimity way beyond his years.

Day, too, came astonishingly good on the night. 'I got a couple of knocks on the head when they jumped on Kanu, but I didn't mind at all,' he reported. Again, someone with less composure and a less intuitive feel for the big occasion could have come horribly apart. Just the abruptness would do it. One moment you're minding your own business, standing about in your tracksuit, doing what ball boys do, which is almost nothing. (In the modern age of stadium construction, when stands tend to be built hard up against touchlines, the role of the ball boy is largely ornamental, much as it always has been in Subbuteo.) The next moment you are borne aloft in exultation by a Nigeria international, with the rest of the team fast approaching.

Being a football follower, and indeed a member of Albion's academy side, Day would have had some knowledge of the way that goal celebrations often pan out. Accordingly, it must have occurred to him, in that split-second after Kanu picked him up and turned with him in the direction of the pitch, that he could imminently find himself at the bottom of a pile containing most of the Albion first eleven. Worse, in a hellishly real version of a familiar performance-anxiety dream, Day could have discovered himself at the centre of some pre-planned dance routine, the product of hours of rehearsal on the training ground, and knowing none of the moves. Yet his face betrayed nothing of these anxieties, beyond a slight widening of the eyes. A pro.

And it's not as if Kanu's intentions were automatically obvious at the time. Watching on television, one's initial thought was that the striker was tactically deploying the ball boy as a human shield – realizing that, so long as he had an innocent child clasped to him, he was protected from the worst of the post-goal rough-housing that would otherwise come his way from his team mates. But Kanu later explained that his intention was to clarify to his watching wife that he was dedicating his goal to

Sean, their baby son. In the necessary absence of Sean himself, the striker had grabbed the nearest child to hand and was relying on his wife to make the imaginative leap from the specific child he was holding to their own. OK, so there may have been something less than watertight about the logic of the gesture. But you've got to credit Kanu at least with moving beyond the mimed baby-cradling by which other players now routinely celebrate goal-and-offspring coincidences.*

One could see Kanu's actions as an extension of a rich tradition of goal celebrations using things that happen to be lying around at the side of the pitch. Paul Gascoigne and Teddy Sheringham, playing for England during Euro 96, led the way in the adoption of extraneous water bottles. Lee Sharpe's use of the corner flag as a substitute microphone stand was, at least until *Celebrity Love Island*, pretty much the only detail anybody could remember with any confidence from Sharpe's professional career. And back in 1996, Robbie Fowler, then a Liverpool player, set a potentially disruptive precedent by picking up one of those tubular, sock-wrapped broadcast microphones, and waving it above his head – a rare example of sport interfering with television rather than television interfering with sport.

Post-Kanu, however, we probably have to accept that this is a seam which is now all but mined to exhaustion. True, as yet no one has commandeered a roving, touchline television camera and used it to film their own goal celebration in video-diary form – perhaps surprisingly, given how temptingly close those cameras get to the pitch, and given, also, the known fondness of some Premiership players (Keiron Dyer, for instance) for recording each other in action.

Otherwise, we await only the first goal celebration involving a fourth official. But that, presumably, will come in time. Let's face it, fourth officials are highly vulnerable in this regard, being easily accessed at the side of the pitch, like water bottles, and, if

---

* For an altogether more chillingly paranoid interpretation of this incident, see p. 238.

anything, even less busy than ball boys. All it would take is a
striker with enough energy to make a sprint for the half-way
line and enough political engagement to want to dedicate a goal
to the unemployed. With that, the history of the goal celebration
will be complete, and we can get back (none too soon, surely)
to a crisp handshake and a swift jog back to the centre circle,
the way these things used to be. Oh, please.*

* Two years later, Kanu was left for dust in this area by the dummy-sucking
Carlos Tevez of Manchester United.

2006

In which we investigate the full monetary cost of a lifetime spent following football – and discover that, comparatively speaking, it's actually quite cheap. And in which we join Sven-Goran Eriksson on his critical, potentially era-defining quest to choose the right hotel for England in Germany, see Graeme Le Saux grow closer than ever before to the Rwandan Mountain Gorilla and wonder whether it might be an idea if managers actually watched players play before deciding to sign them. But ahead of all that, a plea to Hernan Crespo to enjoy the Surrey nightlife while it's there to be enjoyed.

What's on in Cobham

We can all sympathize with a homesick footballer. Think what it must be like. You arrive at a Premiership club from Spain, say, or Italy, with nothing but your hand luggage, a basic grasp of the English language and a set of patiently instilled ideas about football and the best way to approach it. And you suddenly discover you are in a country where the game is played at an average speed of 954 miles per hour with a bizarre and maniacal intensity by people such as Paul Dickov. It is, truly, a different culture, and the fact that so many imported players stick it out and, indeed, go on to have long and illustrious careers here, is a testament to their genuinely humbling levels of flexibility, character and application.

This, though, has little to do with the particular brand of homesickness announced by Hernan Crespo, the top-class Argentina striker who plays, every now and then, for Chelsea. Crespo's pining to be elsewhere does not derive from matters on the pitch, where, he concedes, all is going swimmingly. 'We are thirteen points clear in the Premiership, we have the best manager in the world and Roman Abramovich worships me,' he said. However, he added, 'This life isn't all just about football and at the end of the year I want to return.'

Return, he means, to Italy. For Crespo, the question of what constitutes home is a slightly complicated one. He was born in Argentina but, for seven years before Chelsea signed him in 2003 and again last season when they loaned him to AC Milan, he worked in Italy and has clearly come to regard the country as his own.

Asked what he missed about Italy, Crespo replied, 'I miss everything, my friends, cinema, TV, theatre.' The absence of friends must indeed cause a pang – and if Crespo hasn't felt able to rely on Joe Cole to point him in the way of a good night out, ending shirtless and blackeyed in a minicab, then so be it.*

But at least he didn't mention the food, because then there really would be no arguing with him. As it is, the other things on Crespo's list give anyone who would like him to stay and be happy more than a chink of hope that he can be persuaded. There are, of course, plenty of things to miss about Italy for which Britain, particularly in the grip of a grim, low-skied January, can offer scant compensation. Had Crespo claimed to miss, for instance, Italian fashion and the sight of people carefully dressed in clothes that genuinely suit them, it would have ill behoved anyone British to quibble with him. And if he had said he missed Italian weather, one could only have nodded in frank and open understanding. But before Crespo, did anyone – even an actual Italian person – ever claim to miss Italian TV?

Eighty-five per cent of Italian nationals who emigrate cite as their main reason for leaving the country 'looking for something to watch'. OK, I made that up. But it sounds about right. Certainly the only thing anybody ever remembers about Italian TV is that nightly, close-down programme in which a housewife strips down to her underwear. All the rest is hysterical soap opera

* The Chelsea and England midfielder had recently arrived at a minicab office in the early hours of the morning, entirely bare-chested. Why? Because he needed a cab, of course. What a swell party that must have been, though.

and 1970s-era variety shows. Does Crespo really want that? And if he does, I'm sure that, these days, with the right satellite package, he could get it anyway.

As for Italian film, the Odeons of Milan, like the Odeons of London, are currently stuffed with *King Kong* and *Chronicles of Narnia* – except, in Milan's case, they are dubbed into Italian. Is this what Crespo, a Spanish speaker, is after – films dubbed into a language that is not his own? And if so, can that longing not be sated at home in England, with the miracle that is the multilingual DVD?

And with regard to the Italian theatre that Crespo claims to miss, it's not like he's been exiled to a cultural wilderness. The man is working in Cobham, for heaven's sake. There is a wide range of top-class theatrical experiences available to him in the Surrey area, if that's his bag. I'd be surprised if Jose Mourinho – usually so thorough in his approach to player-management – hasn't provided Crespo with his own, individually tailored dossier, entitled 'What's On in Esher and environs'. He would already know, in that case, that *Aladdin* is still running at the Victoria Theatre Woking, with Melinda Messenger and Bobby Davro.

And that's not all. *Saturday Night Fever* opens at the same venue soon and there's a one-off *Singalonga Joseph* coming up which the penalty-box predator would have to be physically unconscious, surely, not to enjoy. If, on the other hand, he fancied something a little more off-Broadway, what about Screaming Blue Murder comedy night at the Mitre, Hampton Court? Or there is always the Riverhouse Barn at Walton, which offers a variety of concerts, theatrical performances and crafts shows.

Crespo probably doesn't need me to point out, either, that Cobham is on the edge of one of the largest paintball parks in the UK, Campaign Paintball. The place is also very convenient for Chessington World of Adventures, where I can personally recommend the Vampire ride, though not necessarily on a full stomach. It's all about forgetting what you have left behind and immersing yourself in what you have come to. Which takes some effort, of course. But with the football going so well, it would be a shame if Crespo didn't at least try.*

The End of Punditry as We Know It

Some words of sympathy for Peter Schmeichel, removed from his post as a BBC football pundit for, allegedly, a persistent failure to come to the point. True, the former Manchester United goalkeeper will probably not go down in the records as one of British broadcasting's crisper orators, even allowing for the fact that his first language is Danish. Yet since when have such considerations been deemed critical in television football punditry? And what kind of anxiety must now be gripping the industry? If having a point and being able to arrive at it swiftly are suddenly the criteria, surely no one is safe.†

Transfers – Not Just for Christmas

By common consent, the debut for Celtic last weekend of Du Wei, a 23-year-old defender from China, was not glittering. After forty-five minutes of being barged about by Clyde players and looking about as miserable as a penguin on a sunbed, he was substituted. It would be unfair to suggest, as some of Du Wei's harsher critics did, that he appeared not to have played football before. But he did appear not to have played it for quite some time.

Impartial observers sat down to tuck into a full serving of scorn with the traditional side order of *schadenfreude*. How could a professional club like Celtic, with not inconsiderable resources,

---

* Journalism, sadly, doesn't always get results and Crespo returned to Italy and the comforts of his television set at the end of the 2005–06 season.
† It didn't get any easier for the Great Dane when he signed up for *Strictly Come Dancing*. See p. 231.

a full complement of back-room staff and an experienced manager in Gordon Strachan, get it so wildly wrong? There didn't
seem to have been a more cleanly drawn illustration of the great
transfer-market truth, 'nobody knows anything', since Graeme
Souness secured for Southampton the services of Ali Dia.

You may recall that Dia claimed to be a twenty-one-times
capped Senegal international and to come with a personal
recommendation from George Weah. You may also recall that
neither of these things (fairly straightforwardly checked, you
would have thought, but, hey, people are busy) was true. Souness
nevertheless waved Dia straight through to the Southampton
subs' bench for a match against Leeds, wherein, replacing an
injured Matthew Le Tissier after thirty-one minutes, the cour-
ageous impostor promptly began to make Du Wei look like
Franz Beckenbauer *circa* 1974, forcing a confused and almost
certainly quite cross Souness to sub the sub.

Astonishingly, nothing about this 24-carat cock-up prevented
Souness from continuing a highly paid career in top-flight English football management, where his unapologetic summary of
the Dia affair still ranks as one of the classic pieces of post-match
buck-passing: 'That's just the way the world is these days.'

Dia, though, was merely the subject of a hastily arranged (and
quickly cancelled) loan. Whereas, had there not been talk of
Celtic signing Du Wei for four years? Which potentially would
have multiplied the fun many times over. But no. The next
thing we heard, Celtic had smoothly rid themselves of their
Chinese acquisition, having exercised what was described in
some reports as a 'send-back option'. That forlorn half a match
is thus officially the extent of Du Wei's Celtic career, and by
Tuesday he was on a plane home to China. No second chance.
No talk of allowing him to 'acclimatize' to the hectic pace of
the Scottish game. He was off, leaving his Canada-based agent
to express the optimistic hope that this setback wouldn't prevent
Du Wei from acting as 'a trailblazer for Chinese players looking
to play in Scotland'.

A 'send-back option', though – this is a troubling development.

In an increasingly cautious global marketplace, we seem to be entering the age of the sale-or-return transfer. Ever more aware of their rights as consumers, and on ever tighter budgets, managers are beginning to demand satisfaction or their money back. The big stories of the January 2006 transfer window were either cagey loans (Wayne Bridge to Fulham) or deals involving a relatively modest down payment with further money predicated on future success (Theo Walcott to Arsenal), which is basically keeping the receipt by another means.

But whither then the vital comedy of a manager getting it hopelessly and expensively wrong in the transfer market – a comedy which has long been at the very heart of the game as we know it, and which yields one of the most important tools we have for objectively judging a manager on his performance? At a hastily convened fans' forum this week in London*, at which this matter was urgently debated, the disappointed and even angry consensus was that if Gordon Strachan signs an utterly duff player from China, it shouldn't be funny and embarrassing for forty-five minutes only; it should be funny and embarrassing for four years or the duration of the player's contract, whichever is the longer.

The risk-free transfer is a kill-joy arrangement, threatening to spoil things for the people without whom there would be no professional game – the fans. Supporters want to see managers back their judgement with hard cash and face the lasting consequences – not necessarily the managers of the clubs they support, but managers of other clubs certainly. One thinks glowingly back to terrible deals, such as the one in which Blackburn, under (that man again) Souness, spent £6.75 million on Corrado Grabi of Ternana, on the patently insufficient grounds that he had scored nineteen goals in Italy's Serie B. His subsequent Premiership strike rate: two goals in thirty appearances.

Or one fondly recalls the signing of Massimo Taibi by Manchester United for £4.5 million, and how that goalkeeper was

* Technically speaking, me and a friend in a pub in Camden Passage.

soon booking a place in the reserves by allowing Southampton to score three at Old Trafford. In both the aforementioned cases, think how the richness of the comedy would have been diminished had either Ferguson or Souness been able to exercise a 'send-back option' at the first unignorable sign that these baffling signings really weren't up to it. Or think how differently recent arguments about Ferguson's acumen would have panned out had he been freely able to take Kleberson, say, on a thirty-day trial before deciding that he didn't quite live up to the billing in the catalogue so he would return him in the packaging in which he had come, to obtain a full refund.

It is commitment, above all, that one longs to see in a transfer deal, and some kind of legislation which outlaws the feeble bet-hedging embodied by elaborate loan deals and so-called 'send-back options' could only be welcome. Our message to the authorities is clear, then: oblige managers to sign players like they mean it, or not at all.

Now is the Jeff Winter of Our Discontent in Hardback

The title of Jeff Winter's newly published autobiography, as printed on the jacket, is *Who's the B*****d in the Black?* A rare moment of enigmatic coyness, there, from the retired football official from Middlesbrough. Have you guessed what the obscured word is yet? Buzzard? Blizzard? Biscuit tin lid? Keep guessing.

The book had to be tenderly handled in discussions on *TalkSport* this week, where presenters felt compelled to refer to it as, 'Who's the [brief but pregnant moment of radio silence] in the Black?' Good to see a media outlet in this day and age taking people's sensitivities into account. At the same time, if you can't say 'bastard' when talking about Jeff Winter on *TalkSport*, where and when can you say it?

Interestingly, though, these days, the question 'Who's the bastard in the black?' is not much asked in football grounds –

not for reasons of nicety, but because when today's fans wish to berate a referee to the tune of 'Bread of Heaven', they tend to wonder, specifically, 'Who's the wanker in the black?' Perhaps Winter figured that, as a title for an autobiography, 'Who's the W★★★★r in the Black?' would have been an act of self-deprecation too far. Certainly it would have sent out an altogether different message. Still, there is no reason why terrace chants in this area shouldn't continue to present a rich seam for the titles of referees' books. At any rate, one eagerly awaits publication of 'The Referee's a W★★★★r: the Life and Times of Graham Poll'.*

We can't have too many books by refs, can we? Their struggles, their handball decisions, their games of Connect 4 with Paul Durkin during elite list training days at Staverton – these things are the very lifeblood of sporting literature and they come thrillingly alive in the 302 hardback-bound pages, plus index and plates, of Winter's life story. I say 'life story' because Winter's book ostensibly takes the form of an autobiography. Yet, as readers will rapidly discover, it's so much more than that. *Who's the B★★★★★d in the Black?* is, in its own way, a work of fantasy fit to rank alongside such classics of the genre as *The Hobbit* by J. R. R. Tolkien and Glenn Hoddle's *My 1998 World Cup Diary*.

Here, for instance, is Winter on his last game in charge at Anfield:

I had mixed feelings. On the one hand I wanted to finish the game a little early and get off the pitch before people saw big tough Jeff Winter in tears. Then again, I didn't want the game to end. Liverpool were 4–0 up, so it was in my hands. Nobody would care either way. In the end I played a little bit extra, waiting until play was at the Kop end, before sounding the final shrill blast – a bit like the Last Post. The fans behind the goal burst into spontaneous applause. It was longer and

* We didn't have to wait long. Poll published his autobiography in 2007, albeit under the altogether duller title *Seeing Red*. Find the book warmly welcomed into the canon of referee-related literature on p. 316.

louder than normal, even for a big home win. Did they know it was my final visit? Was the applause for me? They are such knowledgeable football people that it would not surprise me.

Note the referee's use of extra time as a dramatic device – not something you often see openly talked about. One had assumed, perhaps naively, that, when the fourth official held up the board on ninety minutes, the number on it represented a stipulated period to be added on, rather than a notional, ballpark figure for the referee to adapt according to his own emotions and his sense of the day's narrative arc. Does this seem shocking to you? Winter is clearly right that, with the score at 4–0, the material outcome of the match was unalterable at that point, beyond possibly trifling matters relating to goal difference. And even had a player, say, broken a leg in those added seconds while 'big tough Jeff Winter' waited for the ball to go up near the Kop, I'm sure they would have reasoned that it was all part of the emotion of the occasion.

It's an interesting question, though, that Winter asks about the fans. Do you suppose the appreciation heard at Anfield that day was for the club's players and staff following a 4–0 home victory during a down-to-the-wire race with Newcastle United for the final Champions League qualifying place (a piece of context strangely absent from Winter's tearful recollection)? Or was it the traditionally warm Merseyside send-off for a dearly cherished b*****d? Bear in mind that the final day of the season, the usual time for fond farewells of all kinds, was still a fortnight away, and that this was merely the Anfield leg of a schedule which Winter himself says 'sometimes felt like a farewell tour of the country'. My own hunch, for what it's worth, is that, what with all the other distractions, remembering to acknowledge Winter's curtain call would have taxed the concentration even of Liverpool's 'knowledgeable football people'.

Then again, maybe I haven't been watching closely enough. I go to quite a lot of football matches, and did so throughout Winter's professional career. Yet, to be perfectly honest, and

much as it may shame me to admit, I can't recall a single game
I have attended that Winter refereed. I mean, I know he was
out there on occasions and I was certainly vaguely aware of him
from time to time. But in terms of putting his face to specific
matches – nothing. It's clear to me too, now, that I must even
have caught him on his farewell tour and not realized. That is
a source of bitter regret to me, obviously, after reading the
autobiography. I would have held a lighter aloft – assuming it
was a night game.

Ah, well. I can use the book to fill in the gaps. It takes us all
the way from Winter's first appointment to run the line in the
Football League ('Congratulations, you bugger,' a friend tells
him, 'I knew you'd make it'), through to the climactic moment
where he kisses the medal presented to him as referee of the
2004 FA Cup final between Manchester United and Millwall
('I had lived the dream'). In between, we visit the City Ground,
Nottingham, for Winter's first Premiership match, where in the
foyer the pictures of Forest players with the European Cup seem
daunting to the rookie ref on the way in, but not on the way
out. 'I felt relaxed and confident,' he writes, 'and didn't even
glance up at the European Cup winners on the wall. I was in
the big league with them now and didn't need to feel inferior.'
And we join the official in his car when he takes the call
confirming his FA Cup final invitation. 'I felt an inner calm. I
felt exalted but in control. I sensed I was at the very pinnacle.'

And to think that Steve Bruce, the manager of Birmingham
City, called this man 'an absolute prat'. Sadly, of course, the
story is over. But the legend lives on, and in the interests of
tending its flame we now ask, did you see Winter on his farewell
tour? Were you there for Winter, one last time? At Fratton Park,
say? Or Portman Road? How was it for you? Emotional? Did
you keep the ticket stub or any other memento of the occasion?
Write in and tell us about it.

Football Phone-ins: the Way Forward

Tired of football phone-ins? Tired of people griping about their back four from a poorly connected mobile phone on the M62? Me too. But there is another way. When Brighton's Mark McCammon called BBC Southern Counties Radio to take issue with the panning he had been getting, he raised the possibility of a golden future for programming in this area in the form of a phone-in exclusively open to players. We want to hear from Rio Ferdinand on the A34 about the lacklustre displays by supporters at Old Trafford. We want to take a call from Noureddine Naybet on the M25 about the lack of ambition among fans at Tottenham. We want to bring in Nicky Butt on the B4176 approaching Telford and hear him say, 'Leave me alone, you sad swine.' The traffic has been one-way for too long. It's time the players had their say.

The Minnow: a Wildly Overrated Fish

'Divided loyalties for you, then,' a friend said, when Chelsea drew Colchester United in the FA Cup. He knew me to be a Chelsea supporter. He knew me also to have grown up in Colchester. He could imagine me gleefully watching Didier Drogba bear down on a panicked and badly misplaced Colchester defence, only for some long-dormant gene to awaken inside me, causing my sympathy to enlarge in an unexpected direction and leaving me willing the Drog to miss.

He was entirely wrong. I have visualized a full range of scenarios, in connection with my mental preparation for this first-in-a-lifetime experience of seeing these two teams on the same pitch, and the result is always the same. Not one part of me — not even the part of me that has paid for a ticket — is hoping to see a closely contested game of football. I have nothing but fondness for Colchester. Some of my best friends and all of my family are Colcestrian. One of my brothers is travelling 800 miles to see this game. But should Chelsea utterly wallop Colchester United, all the evidence is that it will rest perfectly easily on my conscience.

I admit that it hardly looks classy to say so. There is something about actively hoping to see Goliath shove David's sling where the sun don't shine which the human heart, in general, seems to react against, even leaving aside the question of whether that human heart went to school with David. We all know where we are meant to stand on the eve of this kind of FA Cup tie – behind the plucky bantamweight against the steak-fed heavy. Even the dedicated fans of the shark are meant to have some sneaky fellow-feeling for the minnow.

And, of course, one hears all the arguments – that the entire Colchester squad was assembled for less than Frank Lampard spends per annum getting his cars valeted; that Chelsea enjoy the comforts of a hand-crafted, leather-bound stadium, while Layer Road is a demolition order waiting to happen, and so on.

Yet how noble is it, in fact, to want to see greatness humbled and the successful humiliated? I think it was the contemporary philosopher Robbie Williams who pointed out that an American sees a rich man's house and says, 'I'm going to live in a house like that one day,' whereas a Briton sees a rich man's house and says, 'I'm going to get that bastard.' There could be no more perfect encapsulation of the spirit that infects the country in anticipation of a potential FA Cup giantkilling, and it is time that we rethought it, if only in the interest of the nation's sporting health and the continued pursuit of excellence.

To the objection that my roots should place me at the Colchester end, I would point out that football allegiance is often a matter of where your eyes fall first, and my eyes fell on Chelsea long before I was even properly aware that teams like Colchester United existed. This was in 1970, when Chelsea won the FA Cup, and you could call it a bang-to-rights case of the sunshine bringing out a very young tripper. At the same time, that was a pretty fine side – better than anything that followed it for at least a quarter of a century afterwards. And OK, so my hunch didn't work out too well in the medium term, but I still stand by the method behind it. The fact is, the decision about which football team to follow is far too important a matter to be decided by something as random and whimsical as the place you happen to have been born.

Still, I cannot deny that, for as long as it was impossible for me to get to Chelsea for important activities such as match-watching and autograph-collecting, Colchester served as a useful surrogate. Accordingly, I was the owner of a surprising number of signed pictures of Ray Harford and there was a period when Micky Cook's handwriting was as familiar to me as my own. I wasn't there on the defining afternoon when Colchester dumped Leeds – Jack Charlton, Billy Bremner and all – out of the FA Cup. But the photograph of a prone Ray Crawford, scissor-kicking the ball into the Leeds net, is as crisply imprinted in my mind as any other frozen sporting moment. And the tale – quite possibly apocryphal – of how Leeds fans cried in the streets of Colchester that day worked formatively on a young mind to create a vivid sense of how things might be, in the best of all possible worlds.

But that, alas, was a long time ago, and this, alas, is football. Get in there, Goliath.*

Wayne Signs On

Wayne Rooney stands on the threshold of a career as one of Britain's most prolific authors. The £5 million allegedly on the table from HarperCollins for the as yet unpublished Manchester United prodigy is believed to tie him to no fewer than five volumes of autobiography over the next twelve years – a lot of time at the laptop for someone with a parallel occupation in

---

* Final score: Goliath 3–David 1. Which, apart from David nicking one, was only right and proper in the end.

football, although having a day job as a postman famously didn't hinder the output of George Gissing, the Victorian novelist.

If it goes through, the five-book deal should put paid once and for all to the image of Rooney as monosyllabic, while at the same time spectacularly raising the bar for writing in this area. It puts the striker on track to pip fellow-author David Beckham, who may yet manage a fourth volume of autobiography – 'The Spanish Years' – to go with the three volumes already published, but who will surely struggle to add to that tally, without resorting to quiz books.

The Rooney book deal is also a wake-up call, not to mention a rap across the knuckles for the likes of Andrew Motion, who dusted Keats off in a measly single volume. What about going into a bit of detail next time, Motion?*

Wembley Stadium: What's a Short Delay Between Friends?

Our thoughts this week go out to Martin Tidd, the UK director of Multiplex, who announced as long ago as May 2005 that he would be watching this year's FA Cup final in the new Wembley Stadium. 'I can absolutely guarantee that the FA Cup will be held at Wembley,' Tidd said, 'and I can absolutely confirm that my seat is there and I'll be sat there.'

But that was before the FA anticipated, reasonably enough, that the cranes might get in the way and decided to stage the final in Cardiff. A quiet afternoon lies ahead for Tidd on 13 May 2006, then – apart from the noise of drilling and banging, of course. On the plus side, though, I'm sure some of the builders

---

* *Wayne Rooney: My Story So Far* came out in 2006. I bought my copy, eye-wateringly discounted from £17.99 to the intriguingly precise price of £9.97, in the Tesco superstore at Ryde, and tossed it into a trolley already containing yoghurt, bread, toilet rolls and washing-up liquid. People say online shopping has practically destroyed the traditional book-buying experience, but I'm not so sure.

will have the radio on, enabling him to keep up with the game. And parking should be a doddle.

In the months after Tidd made his bold declaration, optimism on the likelihood of a Wembley FA Cup final in 2006 quickly evaporated. By this week, it was the construction industry's worst kept secret. Paddy Power, the bookmaker, closed its book on the matter after only two days, having allegedly noticed (and this was surely the spot of the year) 'men in hard hats placing big bets in the Wembley area'. Superb stuff. The people Multiplex were backing to get the job done were, apparently, backing themselves not to. I'm looking forward to the episode of *Bob the Builder* in which Bob, Scoop and Dizzy pop into Ladbrokes to have a crafty fiver on themselves at 9–4 not to complete in time the underpass designed to spare the local hedgehog family. In the aim of disabusing our children, once and for all, about what the world of contract building is really like, this episode must surely come.

Even so, the FA's announcement prompted, in the papers, much tutting and derision and open accusations of bungling, most of it written by people whose experience of major construction projects is limited to putting up a shelf – or probably, to be more specific, to failing to get round to it. What is really surprising, surely, about the Wembley delays, is that anybody is surprised. As anyone who has ever extended their kitchen into their side return knows only too well, all builder's estimates are to an important extent an act of creative writing and each of them is to be taken with a pinch of salt – or, more specifically, with half a hundredweight of salt, due for delivery on Thursday, but delayed until Tuesday afternoon on account of a problem with the suppliers.

True, few of us see our kitchens, like Wembley, go over budget by more than £400 million, even if we end up choosing a more expensive tile than we had intended to and have to get someone back later to sort out the plumbing for the dishwasher. But it's just a question of proportion, and a builder's estimate doesn't suddenly start having a firm foundation in reality simply because he happens to be constructing a football ground. Where do you suppose the expression 'a ballpark figure' came from, if not from man's timeless experience of building sports stadiums?*

Accordingly, I don't go with the people beating up the FA for their part in 'the Wembley fiasco'. On the contrary, the FA seems to me to have played a fairly tidy game. The staggering £180 million lost by Multiplex on the Wembley project includes £14 million of penalties paid to the FA for delay. This was a fixed-price contract with all liability for lateness and overspend passed on directly to the contractor. Go out now and propose a similar arrangement to the builder working on your kitchen extension, and then stand back as the tea ejaculates, in a gale of derisive laughter, from his nose.

Also, as great planning disasters of our time go, the new Wembley barely measures on the meter. For truly award-winning budget-busting and for positively Olympic errors of time-management, you've got to hand it to the British Library – ten years late and costing £511 million, as opposed to the £32 million predicted. Alternatively, consider the Scottish Assembly building in Edinburgh which, when it finally opened, three years off schedule, had cost £431 million, a more than tenfold increase on the original budget. By these standards, the new Wembley is both cheap and on time.

In any case, I may not have been alone in finding the notion of 'rushing to complete' a 90,000-seat sports stadium a faintly worrying one. Call me overcautious, but if I am going to be joining that number of people in a newly built football ground, I would like to be able to reassure myself that a suitable period has passed for 'snagging'. I would prefer to think that the seats, staircases and toilet facilities, among other things, have been bolted on properly, rather than by some hyped-up screwdriver jockey who managed to get 9–1 with William Hill that he could finish the job by Wednesday.

Remember the Millennium Bridge in London? It swayed

* I'm not sure this is true, actually. But it sounds good.

because its designers had not adequately wondered about what would happen if people ever walked on it. Well, that's 'rushing to complete' in a nutshell. I want to be as confident as possible that the stand I'm sitting in isn't going to start bouncing in sympathy the first time more than fifty people jump up and down inside it in unison. And if that means a delayed opening, and a few more million down the pan for Multiplex, then I'm with the FA in saying, 'So be it.'

So it's going to be another five weeks or so late. So the FA Cup final can't be in London this year. So Jon Bon Jovi is going to have to wait a bit before he gets to say 'Hello, Wembley' in a pair of unfeasibly tight trousers. So what? The new national stadium will by all accounts be a thing of wonder, an arena to match any in the world and a sports and rock'n'roll mecca in which no unforeseen expense has been spared.

In the meantime, the Cup finalists and their followers must once again set up camp in the glorious Millennium Stadium, Cardiff, which can hardly be labelled a hardship. Incidentally, it is usually the Millennium Stadium that gets a mention, when noses are being thumbed in the direction of the new Wembley. But let's not forget that Laing, the contractor on the Millennium Stadium, lost £26 million on the project because of an over-spend. That's building, folks.*

Coming after Sven

'England's players are set to be given their say on who they think should take over from Sven-Goran Eriksson after the 2006 World Cup. The Football Association have revealed they are considering giving David Beckham and other senior members of the national team the chance to share their views as the search for a new manager steps up a gear' (news report).

---

* The new Wembley opened for the FA Cup final of 2007 and was very impressive. Bit sterile, maybe, but it didn't sway once.

Minutes of meeting held 11.00 a.m. on 2 March in the Michael
Aspel Conferencing Suite at the Crowne Plaza Hotel, Derby.

In the chair: Brian Barwick, FA chief executive
Present: David Davies (FA executive director), David Beckham
(Real Madrid), Rio Ferdinand (Manchester United), Joe Cole
(Chelsea), Paul Robinson (Tottenham Hotspur)
Apologies for absence: Frank Lampard (hamstring), Wayne Bridge
(ankle), Ledley King (broken satnav)

Brian Barwick opened by thanking everyone for their time and
readiness to convene at short notice. They would all be aware,
he said, that the time was fast approaching when the FA would
have to announce its choice of successor for Sven-Goran
Eriksson – a critical appointment for the future direction of the
national side. Recognizing the complexity of the task, Barwick
said, and wishing to arrive at the most informed decision possible, the FA was committed to taking soundings across football,
and in particular from the people best placed to provide valuable
input on this matter – England's players.

Rio Ferdinand asked if this was going to take long because
he had left his Lincoln Navigator in a disabled bay.

David Davies offered to go out and move it for him.

Rio Ferdinand threw the keys to David Davies.

Brian Barwick continued that the FA's own researches were
going well and that, as had been widely reported in the press,
there did indeed now exist a shortlist of six potential candidates
for the job, some of whom might even be prepared to accept it
at the right price. But as yet, Barwick said, nothing was set in
stone and blue-sky thinking was still welcome. He stressed,
however, that the purpose of the present meeting was not to
talk in terms of specific names so much as to create a broader
forum for discussion, enabling the FA to build a detailed picture
of what the players of 2006 expect and hope for from a national
coach, going forward.

Joe Cole said he thought it should be Martin O'Neill.

Brian Barwick said that obviously O'Neill was among the candidates whose suitability the FA was assessing, but he reiterated that he was not looking to name names at this juncture, but, rather, hoping to stimulate a general debate in a confidential but above all informal and relaxed setting.

David Davies came back in and said he couldn't get the doors to unlock.

Rio Ferdinand said he should try getting up really close and pressing the keypad twice.

David Davies went out again.

David Beckham raised the subject of cones. He said that all players recognized that putting out cones and getting everyone to run up and down in between them was a significant part of what England get-togethers were all about. Yet, in all his time within the England setup as captain and before that, there had never been a clear directive about whose responsibility it was to collect up the cones afterwards. This, Beckham said, had often led to ugly arguments between Tord Grip and Ray Clemence, and sometimes to Shaun Wright-Phillips being forced to do it because he was the littlest. He wondered if there could be some clarification of the whole area of cones and cone-collection under the new regime.

Brian Barwick said he felt sure he could guarantee this. Indeed, he couldn't see why it wouldn't be possible to find scope within any proposed coaching structure for a designated cones supremo, if the pressure from players was there.

Joe Cole said it sounded like a job for Stuart Pearce.

David Beckham said maybe Cole was right, but he wondered whether Pearce had enough experience to be trusted with the cones yet at international level, and maybe he needed a few more years with the cones at Manchester City first. Steve McClaren, on the other hand, had spent a lot of time with cones, Beckham said.

Brian Barwick said he would certainly keep those names in the frame and would try to take the temperature of the FA board on this, when appropriate.

David Davies came back in and said that he had managed to get into the car but that he couldn't start the engine.

Rio Ferdinand said that the engine was probably disabled and that he should get in, lock and unlock the doors using the keyfob and then depress the clutch before turning the key in the ignition.

Joe Cole wondered whether, given that the car's engine was disabled, it was now officially OK to leave it in the disabled bay.

Brian Barwick said he didn't think so.

David Davies left again.

Brian Barwick asked whether there were any strong feelings among the players about the future manager's nationality. Within the FA and some of its affiliated organizing bodies, he said, he had noticed a strong strand of feeling that the next coach of England should be English.

There was laughter. Rio Ferdinand asked Joe Cole to pass the biscuits.

Paul Robinson mentioned Sven-Goran Eriksson's extraordinary appetite for club football. Sven was always turning up, he said. Indeed, Robinson couldn't remember the last time he had played in a match that Sven had not attended. At first, he said, it had been quite flattering. But eventually it grew to be kind of spooky, knowing he was always there, watching. He said he appreciated that the bloke obviously had time on his hands, but, even so, would it be possible to have a word with any future incumbent?

Brian Barwick said he would note the objection of players to the England manager attending quite so many games.

David Beckham underlined the need for continuity. He said that under Sven the players had got used to working with a manager who said very little before a match, even less at half-time and absolutely nothing afterwards. If someone was going to come in at this point and start throwing his weight around and telling people what to do, it might not go over too well. The players, he said, got plenty of that at home with their clubs, and international duty would be bound to lose a lot of its appeal if it suddenly stopped being a chance to take a break, catch up with old friends and generally recharge the batteries.

Brian Barwick said he was duly noting the players' feelings in this area.

Joe Cole said he still thought it should be Martin O'Neill. Either him, he said, or the Dutch one.

David Davies came back in, holding a parking ticket.

Rio Ferdinand began pelting Davies with Custard Creams.

Joe Cole and David Beckham also threw biscuits.

As Brian Barwick moved to shield the paperwork on the table in front of him, Joe Cole accidentally caught him on the ear with an Abbey Crunch, requiring a plaster.

The meeting broke up shortly afterwards.*

When Refs See Double

What is the ideal number of referees for a football match? It would depend which referees you were talking about, I suppose. In some of the more award-winningly pernickety cases, one ref can feel like two or three too many, and I once saw a match at which there appeared to be five separate officials out there, individually piping themselves blue, although, on closer inspection of the programme, it turned out to be only Rob Styles.

'No refs at all' would have its advocates, but anyone tempted to join them should remember that football is still some way from being a self-policing sport. Give it another millennium or so, plus a couple of cold weekends in hell. In any case, you can't delete the ref without gutting the game of the vital narrative of blame that has brought so many fans so much pleasure down the years, and by which countless managers have held on to their jobs. In the unique architecture of football, the whipping

---

* After a botched attempt to snatch 'Big' Phil Scolari from Portugal, the FA eventually appointed Steve McClaren and the rest, as they say, is the end of history. So much for broad soundings.

post turns out to be holding up the entire building. Remove it at your peril.

How about two referees, though? According to Lars-Christer Olsson, the UEFA chief executive, UEFA will discuss over the summer the viability or otherwise of sending out a pair of referees per match, each charged with controlling their own half of the pitch. The theory is that doubling up and decreasing the officials' zone of responsibility in this way might place the referee closer to fast-evolving controversial situations.

I'm impressed by the potential of this idea, which is already standard practice in American football and ice hockey, and, of course, in cricket. Indeed, the only people I can imagine objecting to it strongly are referees themselves, who clearly enjoy being regarded as 'the man in the middle' and would be less keen to go under the slightly less zingy label 'one of two men, quite near the penalty area'. And then, obviously, the referee's match fee would have to be halved, from £320 to £160, to reflect the decreased workload, and the present generation of stand-alone refs would possibly take exception to that.

Nevertheless, the compensatory opportunity is clearly there for the more open-minded officials to rethink their role, forge new partnerships and maybe even become attention-grabbing double acts, winning a new place in the fans' hearts.

'Who is it today?'

'We've got Bennett and Dunn.'

'I like them. They're funny.'

Paired-up refs could develop their own interplay, maybe come up with some distinct hand signals, one to another, possibly even use some sign-off music at the end of the match, such as Morecambe and Wise's 'Bring Me Sunshine' – and with the famous silly dance, if necessary. It might defuse the tension which runs like steel wire through even the most innocuous of fixtures these days, and it would be better, surely, than the present solemn march-offs, amid boiling rancour, escorted by policemen and stewards.

There would be more to it than pure entertainment, as well.

Working as a pair, officials would have access to the 'good ref, bad ref' routine which has proved so reliable for extracting confessions from rock-hard crims in televised police work, and which could, by a process of confusion and dislocation, plausibly cause players such as Wayne Rooney to grow weary of getting in authority's face in such a tiresomely predictable manner.

Objectors will raise the obvious recruitment dilemma. If this idea goes through, football associations would be looking to double the number of referees at precisely the moment in history that no one in their right mind, anywhere in the world, wants to become one. Faced with a strikingly similar crisis, the teaching profession has gone heavily down the television advertising route, recently deploying a memorably compelling campaign emphasizing the enlivening effects of working around children. There is no reason why a similar approach might not work for refereeing – along the lines of 'Use your head: get to hang out with Peter Whittingham.'

But that might not be necessary because, under the new twin-ref regulations, the gates would suddenly open again for retired officials. Disappointment has already been voiced within the refereeing profession about the statutory retirement age, which is felt to be sidelining perfectly competent and highly experienced officials who, were it not for the regulations, might easily have had a couple more seasons in their legs. Inevitably it pained one to think that one had seen slightly less of David Elleray than one might have done, had the rules not been so inflexibly applied. A less physically demanding two-referee arrangement, though, would change the parameters on retirement entirely, potentially enabling the game to re-embrace the likes of Keith Burge of Tonypandy, or even Roger Kirkpatrick, who might not be able to get up and down a pitch the way they once did, but could possibly get up and down half a pitch.

Clearly, in terms of effective match-management, the twin-officials approach would be nowhere near as efficient as the so-called 'ref in the sky' option – whereby, while Keith Stroud and Norman Burtenshaw, say, ran their respective portions of the playing surface, and Mark Clattenburg covered the dugouts and technical area, you would have Graham Poll aloft in a chopper to pick up the bits and pieces and ruling on some of the narrower offside calls. It is important to the spirit and integrity of football, however, that any changes regarding the government of the professional game should be manageable at grass roots, too, and sadly, while it remains the case that only a limited number of Sunday League sides can afford to have the necessary helicopter on standby, this will have to remain an idea whose time has yet to come. Two refs, though? Easily done. And double the fun, surely.

A Hotel Fit for England and, Possibly, Peter Crouch

Sven-Goran Eriksson proudly showed members of the media around the England team's chosen headquarters for the 2006 World Cup – the five-star Buhlerhohe hotel, expensively aloft in the mountains above Baden-Baden, featuring top-ranking accommodation, a deluxe spa, state-of-the-art conferencing facilities, fine dining, a succulent wine list and all the things considered essential in preparing for a tricky group phase opener against Paraguay. According to Eriksson, twenty-five hotels were considered in all, and naturally in such a critical matter the Football Association's choice was made only after long deliberation and extensive research by the coach and Tord Grip, his right-hand man, leading to an in-depth scouting report, extracts from which are published for the first time below.

ATTENTION: FA executives only
From: S-G E
Re: Hotels, Germany 2006

. . . Moving on to the Grand Hotel Imperator at Muhldorf, single rooms were bright, simply but tastefully furnished, all of them ensuite and PlayStation-ready. Tord tested a range of beds on the third floor for bouncebackability and scored them an impressive seven. And the breakfast buffet was as good as any we experienced in Germany, offering both Cheerios *and* Honey Nut Loops.

Once again, though, we found ourselves coming up against the problem of bed length in relation to Peter Crouch. It has been a constant sticking point on our travels, I'm afraid. The management were prepared to go up to 6ft 5in with the mattress, but after that, as they rightly pointed out, the foot of the bed would be in the mini-bar. Only the Buhlerhohe (see sheet 17) is offering to go as high as 6ft 6¾ in, and even that is a quarter of an inch shy of Crouch's full length. It's the same old, frustrating story, then. True, Trixxi's Grosse Fun Keller in Hamburg was able to offer a seven-foot bed, but there were strange manacles attached to the wall and leather hoods all over the place and both Tord and myself found both the atmosphere and the conversation at breakfast a little oppressive.

I don't want to seem to be running away from the issue, but it occurs to me that we may be devoting too much time and energy to the question of Crouch's bed. He is, after all, just one player among many in the squad, and a player who, between you and me, is only likely to get on if things are truly desperate. As such, my notion is to have a word with Crouch about the possibility of his adopting the foetal position come June. I imagine he must feel like doing that a lot of the time, in any case.

. . . Otherwise, in the five-star sector, probably the closest rival we have seen for the Buhlerhohe was the Charlottenberg Schloss at Freising, which combines the grandeur and elegance befitting a party including the likes of Ledley King and Jamie Carragher with an imaginatively intimate approach to customer comfort. The provision of complimentary lederhosen, for instance, along with the more regular towelling bathrobe and slippers, was a nice touch, though Tord did later report some chafing. However, Tord felt able to score the Charlottenberg's king-size beds an acceptable six for bouncebackability, even though his testings were interrupted by a newlywed couple complaining from the floor below. For my own part, I would like to set on record that rarely in my career in football have I seen such a large wicker basket of free toiletries, and that Birgitte in the spa area gave me the best Indian head massage I have ever had. And wait until the players see the utterly fantastic, walk-in power-showers. Shaun Wright-Phillips is going to be blown away by the power-showers. Possibly literally. We should talk to the management about lowering the water pressure in his room.

However, Tord pointed out that Cartoon Network did not feature among the channels available on the in-room satellite service, which could be a problem among some of the younger players. And, if we're being honest about it, among some of the older ones, too.

An additional drawback was the surprisingly rudimentary conference room, where there were no PowerPoint facilities nor even a whiteboard, which, as I suggested to Tord, would seriously hamper me in getting the team together for impromptu talks on tactics. Tord replied that it would make a fat lot of difference, then. He added that the closest England had come to seeing a PowerPoint presentation during my period in charge was when Sammy Lee got up to have a little jab at the fourth official during the Argentina game . . .

. . . If we agree that privacy is a premium requirement for an organiz-ation as popular as ours, then we could do worse than cast an eye over the Kloster Brunnenkapell, a twelfth-century Cistercian monastery in the mountains above Traunstein. Days begin simply with prayers in the chapel at 4.30 a.m., followed by a breakfast of oats, followed by more prayers and then work in the gardens, before further prayers and lunch (bread). The afternoons are given over to meditation, and the evenings are dedi-cated to more prayer, before a glass of water and bed at 7.00 p.m. Mobile phones are completely forbidden and if a monk wishes to talk to his agent, he has to walk to the payphone, seventy-three kilometres away at Bernau. Clearly we are talking here about a regime which would be quite alien to our players, excepting, obviously, those who have worked under Sir Alex Ferguson. Nevertheless, on the plus side, the press won't come anywhere where there is no drink, and the phone ban promises to release the players from the distractions that have so badly hampered preparations in the past.

There are no on-site training facilities, as such, but the monks indicated that they would be more than ready to cordon off an area of the vegetable patch for our use. And Tord and I are both in a position to attest from our time in the Kloster that the order of silence during the hours of daylight grants an unrivalled opportunity for deep self-reflection in an atmosphere of worldly transcendence. David James, I know, would love it here. But I'm not sure Joe Cole would. Or anyone else, really. Also, the nearest road is a fourteen-kilometre hike by mule.

. . . I don't think we ought to waste too much time considering the Studentenhotel at Hersbruck, where neither Tord nor myself passed a pleasant night. It possibly didn't help that both of us were kept awake until the small hours by Danish backpackers singing Don McLean songs, but the complete absence of pillows had already spoiled our mood and the nadir was reached in the morning when a chemistry student from Lyons filched Tord's Head & Shoulders. Although the shared bathroom situation would be nothing that the players weren't already familiar with, I can't see those members of the FA executive who will be travelling with us responding warmly to having to keep a weather eye on their spongebags. Tord's bouncebackability rating: zero, although let the record show that, following what was in my opinion a highly contentious game of paper, rock, scissors, he was on the top bunk at the time.

. . . A warm Bavarian welcome is certainly guaranteed at Marta and Horst's Gasthaus, Holzkirchen. Tord and I had barely set our bags down in the hall before Horst was excitedly bringing out his home-cured sausage. Rooms were cosy and, downstairs in the lounge, the evening of traditional folk music and dance, hosted by Marta, was great fun, despite being compulsory. Marta also pours a generous schnapps, served with little squares of her own almond cake, described by Tord as 'ripper'. Worth bearing in mind, then, as a budget option. Not, I take it, that anyone is seriously thinking about the budget at this point.

A Short History of the Great Football War of 2005–10

(*As tensions rose between the G14 coalition of Europe's biggest football clubs and the game's official global governing body, and as squabbles grew over such divisive issues as money-sharing and the release of players for international duty, Sepp Blatter, the president of FIFA, darkly announced, 'If they want war, they will have it.' The rest was history.*)

Chapter 1. The Gathering Storm

Anxiety about the G14 coalition had been growing for some time. What did it want? What was it arming itself for? The fact that G14 turned out, on closer inspection, to represent not fourteen but eighteen clubs, only increased the sense that something underhand was going on. Also, if these were, according to G14's own website, 'eighteen of the most significant contributors to the success and quality of European club competitions', then, concerned citizens wondered, what were Bayer Leverkusen and Olympique Lyonnais doing in there? Frankly, what were Arsenal doing in there?

A dark rumour persisted that the G14 clubs were looking to seize control of the Champions League and bring about a world in which clubs were paid thousands of euros to release personnel for international service. Both these interests – and, indeed, the G14's very existence – set it on a collision course with UEFA, the governing body of European club football, and with FIFA, the international body.

Nevertheless, when David Dein, the vice chairman of Arsenal, returned from a summit in Milan waving a sheet of Marriott Hotel notepaper and proclaiming 'Peace in our time', many believed him. Two days later, however, the G14 clubs made their intentions clear by invading Poland. On the morning of 28 August 2005, Sepp Blatter interrupted radio broadcasts across Europe with the following announcement: 'I have to tell you that as of today we are at war with AC Milan and all those other jumped-up fuckers.'

Chapter 2. The World in Crisis

With surprise on their side, and the unreadiness of the opponent painfully apparent, the aggressors swept through western Europe. They were ambitious, disciplined and, above all, well fortified. Ajax sent its youth academy – some 400,000 men in total. G14 forces under the command of the president of PSV Eindhoven quickly annexed the Sudetenland. The swift capitulation of the entire French league was disappointing but not entirely unexpected. Many clubs suffered in the fighting, but FC Dynamo Dresden were particularly badly hit. In these early days of the conflict, panic among FIFA's allies was rife. Lennart Johansson, the president of UEFA, left Switzerland in a sealed train. Jose Mourinho departed from Chelsea in a sealed wicker kit basket. Shaun Wright-Phillips left Chelsea in a sealed trophy.

The future of the war clearly depended on which way Chelsea would fall. While the club was under the presidency of Ken Bates, G14 had excluded it for being too poor and too rude. Latterly, G14 had excluded it for being too rich and too rude. This would have made it a natural ally of FIFA – except that UEFA had not endeared itself to Chelsea by referring to it as 'the enemy of football'. At the same time, the club appeared to have global ambitions of its own. Peter Kenyon, Chelsea's chief executive, had unpleasantly spoken of 'turning the world blue', which sounded suspiciously like a suffocating manoeuvre, and it was widely believed that the club might seize this moment of upheaval to make its own move.

To Blatter's immense relief, however, after the hastily signed Cobham Agreement of 4 September, Roman Abramovich pledged himself to FIFA and immediately offered his submarine and naval fleet to the cause, along with a large number of polo ponies and some truly cracking helicopters.

Meanwhile, still under UEFA's struggling but valiant control, the Champions League raged on. On his way to commentate on a third-round qualifier between Levski Sofia and Artmedia Bratislava, ITV's Clive Tyldesley was assassinated with the poisoned tip of a hot dog, and Bulgaria was brought headlong into the conflict.

Chapter 3. Their Finest Hour

The G14 generals may have underestimated the will among the FIFA-led allies to prevent the Champions League from being taken. Resistance was formidable. Forces of the G14 sought to cut off the supply of vital equipment by closing roads along the

Czech and Hungarian borders – the so-called Umbro Line.
But the allies were undaunted. In Moscow, teams representing
CSKA and neutral FC Basle played a group phase match in kits
made out of newspapers and torn-up blankets. Before a group
B match between SC Heerenveen and Brondby, rebel forces
working in accordance with Operation Gatorade attacked the
lorry bringing electrolyte-replacing sports drinks into the stadium. However, after a sticky moment, the lorry got through
and the match went ahead.

Chapter 4. Victory in Europe
In what would prove to be a ruinous strategic blunder, with the
Champions League still not secured and their troops clearly
waning from the exhaustion of a long and physically demanding
campaign, G14 commanders recklessly opened up another front
and attempted a wholesale takeover of beach soccer on the
northerly coast of France. Thus overstretched, the G14 forces
were easily repulsed by British holidaymakers – as so many
people are. Routed, the G14 troops either dispersed or beat a
hasty retreat through the Alps, to huddle miserably in the Stadio
del Alpi and await arrest.

Blatter was driven up the Champs Elysées in an open-top bus,
accompanied by the managing director of McDonald's Europe,
the marketing manager of Amstel and leading representatives of
the Champions League's other top-line sponsorship partners.

Post-war reparations were punitive. Manchester United was
divided into four separate zones under Allied Control, to prevent
it ever again getting quite so far above itself. Barcelona was
required to spend ten years working solely as a feeder club for
FIFA-loyal Birmingham City. The Milan clubs were dissolved.
And following the notorious 'Poll Affair' and the subsequent
trial, Graham Poll, the FIFA official, was accused of having
collaborated with G14 forces and was suspended indefinitely.

A new age of hope and unprecedented opportunity dawned
across the democratic footballing world and Blatter was free to
pursue his vision of an internationally united professional game,

run benignly and without self-interest by central organizations, and preferably played by women in saucy strips.

(*Students wishing to research this period further may care to note that, upon entering the terms 'Blatter, G14' into the Google search engine, you will be asked 'Did you mean bladder?' Well, did you?*)

The Ball is Round – and Thermally Bonded Using a Patented Technique

The launch of 'the official ball of the 2006 World Cup final' means it can now straightforwardly be said that the tournament in Germany has inspired more balls than any World Cup in history – a truly unprecedented number of balls.

The latest, commemorative, gold-panelled issue of the Adidas Teamgeist ball joins the already announced black-panelled version, itself, you will remember, a 'breakthrough in ball technology', whose 'revolutionary new propeller panel shape' and 'patented thermal bonding technique' have been designed to 'minimize corners and create a more homogenous system in terms of performance and look' while allowing for 'a cleaner kicking area'.

'It only surprises me that nobody thought of it before,' said Franz Beckenbauer, referring to the little flash of marketing brilliance which sees the final get its own limited edition ball, marked with the date and kick-off time to avoid unnecessary confusion. But, of course, marketing being marketing, it won't stop there. So, bone up using our handy, at-a-glance 'Official Balls of the World Cup' guide.

The Official Ball of the 2006 World Cup Third Place Play-off
This specially commissioned, beige-trimmed edition of the Teamgeist ball, boasts a uniquely developed vario-valve, for that slightly deflated look. In addition, the incorporation into the ball's casing of a heat-sealed layer formed from recycled plimsolls

ensures that it is likely to absorb water at more than ten times the FIFA-approved standard, and, even dry, should provide no bounce whatsoever. Utterly lifeless all in all, then. What better way to mark the traditional consolation occasion for teams who, if they were being honest, would rather have gone home after the semi-finals?

The Official Group of Death Ball

Distinct from the Teamgeist in being made from vulcanized body parts and covered in hair and worms, the all-new Poltergeist is solely for use by teams in the group deemed by a hand-picked committee of television pundits to be the most deathly. The latest microchip technology enables the ball to be pro-grammed to emit a variety of blood-curdling screams and groans, while the deployment of a thin paste of radioactive materials in the coating makes the resulting sphere liable to move a bit in the air, and even more liable to burst into flames, laying waste to everything within a twenty-mile radius. Limited domestic take-up for the Poltergeist is expected post Germany, although Blackburn Rovers could possibly license it for use in the event that the club makes it into Europe for next season. Note: requires batteries and a concrete-lined carrier bag.

The Official Ball of the Almost Certainly Meaningless Group H Match Between Saudi Arabia and Tunisia

Exactly like the ball used in all the other Group H matches, and yet that little bit more meaningless, thanks to its construction from a carefully researched blend of surplus materials. Because of the ball's unique 'deadweight' structure, it can also double as an abdominal exerciser, or be hollowed out and used in the garden as a novelty planter.

The Official Light Training and Stretching Only Ball

The result of a long and detailed period of consultation with the England medical staff, this lightweight, sponge-style ball has been developed for use in the run-up to the tournament by players who have played in excess of eighty-five club games in the previous ten months and either wouldn't care if they never saw a football again or have broken something, or both. Fabricated from 100 per cent Metatarsalite, the Recupoball comes with a special Ralgex-based coating and features an inlaid Nurofen dispenser. This invaluable remedial tool has been scientifically demonstrated, with invaluable input at the R&D stage from Michael Owen, to lend itself ergonomically to light cones-work and mildly aerobic games of catch. Tinkly bell and string optional.

The Official Ball of the Opening Ceremony

Humungous tarpaulin sphere which automatically bursts open to disclose 1,400 local schoolchildren in national dress and a selection of drama students on stilts. A significant technological advance on the now legendary Guffball, first used at the start of France 98, the 2006 model offers superior roll, courtesy of an all-new, butter-based waxing treatment for the outer surface, and features a patented venting system which ensures a continued supply of oxygen to the schoolchildren in the event of any unforeseen delay or overrun in the scheduled show. Patently pointless and yet somehow essential. Warning: may also contain German light entertainers.

Management Gary Lineker's Granny's Way

(With Sven-Goran Eriksson and the Football Association having agreed to call it quits over the England job, debate was widespread about who should be England's next manager – and never more widespread than when the BBC's top sports presenter got involved.)

Gary Lineker certainly dropped a bombshell this week. The host of *Match of the Day* and well-known crisp advocate suddenly announced in a discussion about the credentials of 'Big' Phil Scolari and the advisability or otherwise of asking him to take on English football's top job, 'My *granny* could probably have managed Brazil to World Cup success.' However you frame it, that's a ringing endorsement for the coaching potential of an unsung senior citizen, and the more impressive for coming from a former player whose credentials as a judge of the international game are not in doubt.

Now, inevitably, the substance of Lineker's claim for his granny's managerial acumen will be subject, over the coming days, to far more technical scrutiny than we are qualified to perform here. But in the meantime, one is surely entitled to ask: Why are we only now hearing about Lineker's granny in relation to the England job?

How did it come to pass that a candidate apparently amply qualified to take a national team all the way in the game's biggest tournament failed to figure even briefly on the shortlists? And why did an FA delegation end up flying to Portugal in pursuit of the Brazilian Scolari if someone capable of organizing a World Cup victory was on the doorstep all along?

It's a bewildering oversight and one that can only bolster the current image of the FA as a sack full of thudding fools, blundering blindly from one disaster to the next. That certainly seems to be the opinion of Steve Bruce, the manager of Birmingham City, who accused the FA of 'making a nonsense of the whole thing' by again seeking a foreign coach for the national team, and asked, rhetorically, 'Would an English coach get the Brazil job?'

True, it's a mirthful prospect. And previously one might have been tempted to complete the simple logical circuit on Bruce's behalf, and point out that the reason this prospect is a joke is because English coaches aren't much cop and there is no one among the current batch who gives even a hint of being able to point a team in the direction of a world championship. Except now we know that's not true. There is Lineker's granny.

The question necessarily arises, though: did Bruce know about Lineker's gran? And if so, why didn't he say anything? Similarly, why did no one from the League Managers Association, whose chief executive, John Barnwell, is again left shaking his head sorrowfully, get behind Lineker's granny the way they rallied behind the candidacies of 'Big Sam' Allardyce, Stuart Pearce, Steve McClaren and Alan Curbishley? Why was no one keen to see Lineker's granny given a run?

One can hardly avoid lining up the usual suspects – prejudice against the elderly, knee-jerk age-ism, the routinely patronizing indifference to 'grey power' that, one is sad to say, increasingly typifies this nation's attitude to the old. Yet, now that Lineker has raised it, who in their right mind could not be drawn to the virtues of appointing as England coach someone who has, indeed, 'seen it all', even if they might have forgotten large bits of it, or be apt to repeat certain small bits of it over and over again?

We hear a lot about new brooms. Maybe what the job has been screaming for, all along, is an old broom – a broom from the days when they knew how to make brooms. It's not just one's eagerness to hear Peter Crouch greeted at Bisham Abbey with a wondering, 'Haven't you grown?' Nor is it necessarily one's interest in seeing the controversial, high-stakes gambling, which is said to be rife in the England squad, replaced by bingo and line-dancing. It's more what one knows about grannies – about their narrow-eyed mental strength, their focus, about the way they are no great respecters of reputation. Yes, they have their own way of doing things. But for today's increasingly flexible players, adapting to a routine of lunch at 11.45 a.m., followed by a sweet sherry and a handful of Matchmakers at 5.30 p.m., would be nothing.

Certainly one could feel confident that a granny would be more sure-footed in the England job than Sven-Goran Eriksson. There isn't a pensioner in the land who couldn't spot one of the *News of the World*'s fake sheikhs the minute he came up the garden path without the correct ID tag. As for coping with the pressure, why wouldn't a granny be as comfortable in an overheated dressing room as she is in an overheated sitting room?

And this is without factoring in the economic reasons, which are compelling. Scolari is said to be holding out for Eriksson's salary of £5 million per year. My hunch is that you could get a granny to do the job for as little as half as much as that, if a constant supply of Fruit Jellies and the occasional tin of Fox's Glacier Mints could be thrown in.

So, how might England have lined up under Lineker's granny? Probably in a solidly traditional 4–4–2, with a role somewhere for that nice David Dickinson from *Bargain Hunt*. Impossible to rule out a return for Lineker himself, too. Grannies love a grandson.

But it's all irrelevant now, of course. The FA, in its infinite wisdom, has again shown itself determined to favour proven experience over home-grown potential, with scant regard for the bigger social picture. Shame. Had Lineker's granny merely been interviewed, what an encouraging signal it would have sent out to a generation even now bracing itself for the axing of *Grandstand*, and facing up to the problem of finding something new to do with its Saturday afternoons. Memo to Gary: pipe up sooner next time.

Money in 'Can't Buy Everything' Shock

A staple objection to Chelsea's humungous wealth is that it enables the club to secure the services of any player it wishes. But, of course, a successfully completed transfer depends on other factors, including the player's willingness to move and the other club's willingness to sell him.

Nevertheless, this little nugget has become one of those 'things you have to say' when talking about Chelsea, so one probably ought not to have been too surprised to hear the notion expressed as fact the other day by Steven Gerrard of Liverpool. 'We know Chelsea can go out there and buy whoever they want,' the PFA Player of the Year said.

At the same time, without wishing to imply anything worrying about the capacity of Gerrard's memory, he does appear to be forgetting Chelsea's two unsuccessful attempts, in the summers of 2004 and 2005, to sign . . . er, Steven Gerrard. Or is he hinting that they should try again? Anyway, it's not true that Chelsea can have whoever they like. It only seems as though they can.

UEFA Pro Made Simple

The UEFA Pro Licence – it's the qualification you can't manage without. And that's official. The Premier League says so, and so does the League Managers Association. And, as a result, every week thousands of disappointed people like Glenn Roeder find themselves technically ineligible to manage a Premiership club in the long term because they lack the necessary piece of paper.

Are you a Glenn? Would you love to have the confidence and sense of achievement that comes from having a UEFA management certificate under your belt, but just haven't had the time recently because you have been too busy taking charge of Newcastle United on a temporary basis?

Well, you can change all that, thanks to TEACH YOUR-SELF UEFA PRO, our specially designed, easy-to-follow, eight-step programme, designed to take you all the way to a UEFA Pro Licence and the Newcastle job (subject to availability) in seven days, or your money back.

Why wait? Subscribe now to TEACH YOURSELF UEFA PRO and open up a whole new world of managerial opportunities at the highest level, joining the likes of such glittering UEFA Pro Licence holders as David O'Leary, Steve Bruce and Bryan Robson. This innovative, all gain/no pain self-tuition package is also available on cassette and CD, making it even simpler to study at a pace that you control, at the moments that suit you – while driving in to training, for instance, or on the coach going to an away game.

Lesson 1: Cones

The cone is, quite simply, the single most vital piece of equipment in a football manager's life. Not without reason is it often said: befriend the cone and you befriend the game. There are two main types of cone: the circular, quite flat ones, suitable for running between, and the altogether taller and more conical ones, suitable for dribbling around.

Coursework: Go into your garden with a number of cones. Arrange the cones in shapes of your own choosing on the grass. Notice how the space defined by the cones can be made to expand and shrink by moving the cones. Collect up the cones and go indoors again.

Lesson 2: Bibs

Second only to the cone in their indispensable nature, bibs generally come in high-visibility orange or yellow, but bibs in other colours are not unheard of. Some are easier to put on than others, but all have their place on the training ground.

Coursework: Using your imagination, devise three games involving a football likely to keep twenty-five young men in bibs amused for anything up to twenty minutes without any of them getting injured, and therefore not including British Bulldog.

Time left over? Drop a pile of bibs on to the ground. Estimate the number of individual bibs in the pile. Now count the bibs. Were you right? Try again with a different number of bibs.

Lesson 3: The technical area

Now that you have mastered training sessions, it is time to move pitch-side. Think of the technical area, even more than the dugout, as the headquarters of your managerial operation. For it is from here that you will do most of your shouting and pointing (see lesson 4).

Coursework: Watch a televised football match, paying particular attention to how often the managers step outside the technical area and by how much. Is Stuart Pearce ever actually in the technical area at any point? Notice the complete incapacity of the fourth official to do anything about this.

Lesson 4: Shouting and pointing

How important to top-level management is shouting and pointing? Put it this way: there has never been a top-level manager who did not shout and point, apart from Sven-Goran Eriksson. And look what happened to him.

Coursework: Standing in front of a mirror for reference, start pointing, left hand then right hand, building up the urgency gradually. Then move on to some of the more complex, hand-over-hand, tic tac-style arm motions. Don't worry about what they mean at this stage. Nor later, really. When you are happy with your pointing, do some shouting — of names, mostly. Alternate between two minutes of your best shouting and two minutes of your best pointing, until you are confident enough to try shouting and pointing at the same time.

Lesson 5: Man management

The chief function of a successful professional manager is to instil a winning mentality. He does this by working with his players' confidence. The trick is to know when to build a player's confidence and when to undermine it in a fundamental and lasting way, with criticism, ridicule and belittlement, in order to 'get a reaction'. That's a skill that can reliably come only with time and experience. In the meantime, a useful question to ask yourself is, 'How much bigger than me, physically, is this player?'

Coursework: Practise telling every player in your imaginary first team squad that they are the best in the world in their position. Where your squad contains two players in the same position, try to tell them this privately and instruct them not to talk to anyone else about this conversation.

Lesson 6: Diet and fitness

Contrary to what was thought in the 1970s, diet and fitness turn out to be intimately related. The modern manager must, accordingly, attain and pass on a workable grasp of nutritional basics. Numerous are the managers who have turned a new club around by putting a stop to a 'bacon sandwich culture'.

Coursework: Read through the following list of common food-stuffs. Then, using a pen or pencil, ring the item on the list which has, in your opinion, the least value as a natural perform-ance-enhancer. Pasta, chicken, steak, lettuce, fresh fruit salad, strawberry Chewits.

Lesson 7: Mind games

Every professional manager is, by default, a student of psy-chology – only with more money, obviously, and a nicer house. Use your understanding of this field to ensure that the match starts well before the referee's whistle.

Coursework: 'Obviously it is an important match for us. But the pressure is far worse for them because if they lose, I think their season is over, without a doubt. I think so, yes.' Analyse this traditional eve-of-big-match announcement from Jose Mour-inho, paying particular attention to its devastatingly wicked psychological brilliance.

Lesson 8: Understanding 'active' and 'passive' in everyday offside situations

Don't bother. Nobody does. They all make it up as they go along. So should you.

Now go back over everything you have learned. Lessons in place? Great! You're ready to manage Newcastle. Especially if you have already been doing so.*

---

* Official qualifications, or more precisely the lack of them, were the focus of attention again in 2007 when Avram Grant became the manager of Chelsea. See p. 333.

England Bonding Sessions: Fun for All the Family

'Stewart Downing, 21, single, the quiet man of the squad, likes to concentrate on his football and fitness' (newspaper feature on the wives, partners and children of the England squad who flew out with the players to Portugal this week for a pre-World Cup retreat).

Stewart Downing's Vale de Lobo diary

Monday
Nightmare flight. Babies crying, kids shouting, running up and down the aisle, playing with the seat-recliners, you name it. Had brought along Bryan Robson's autobiography to read, but no chance. Coach transfer no better. Worse, in fact. When got off, was lightly coated in crushed Pringles and had three Ribena stains.

Resort uplifting, though. Facilities look very promising. Good spread of pitches, including all-weather. Top-quality gym with decent range of static lifting machines. Big complimentary basket of fruit in the room, too, which was nice. Also a selection of organic facial treatments in a presentation slip-case and a giant teddy bear.

Apparently 'Vale de Lobo' is Portuguese for 'valley of the wolf'. No pets allowed, though, I notice. Ironic.

Tuesday
Kept awake most of last night by the wolf. The sound of the howling was astonishing – not something you could just turn over and ignore. Eventually, at about 2.30 a.m., phoned down to reception and asked, 'Can you do anything about that wolf?' Some confusion at first, but eventually they worked out it was Paul Robinson's newborn in the room next door, throwing a major all-night wobbler, so I just had to lump it.

At breakfast, sat with Becks and his family. Was glad of the chance to ask him about life at Real Madrid, particularly in relation to fitness regimes. I wondered whether they spent much time there on the purely aerobic side of things, or whether it was all working with the ball. Also, I've got this theory that the pace of the game in Spain is much faster than it is generally given credit for here, and I was naturally keen to get Becks's take on that. But what with him getting up all the time to stop his kids running up and down the buffet table, and what with Romeo dumping a bowl of Coco Pops in my Shredded Wheat, the conversation never really got going.

Good turnout of English tourists for the morning training session, which was nice to see. The boss took me aside and said, 'It's open to the media so try and look . . . you know . . . good.' Felt encouraged by that. Any sign that you are in the boss's thoughts at this stage has got to be positive. Training a touch disappointing, though. A bit of running, a bit of six-a-side, a few stretches, but not the thorough workout I'd been looking for.

Afternoon off. Resort seems to have everything. Rang John Terry to see if he wanted to try out the quad-biking. But he said that he and Toni, along with Rio Ferdinand and Rebecca, had got their names down for a mums-and-dads-to-be yoga session in the spa area. Took Bryan Robson's autobiography down to the pool, but there was too much shrieking and splashing, so went back to the room and played Beach Rally II on my mobile until supper.

Quiet evening. No one about. Considered asking Theo Walcott if he fancied a drink, but then remembered he wasn't old enough and went back to my room instead. Ate the roasted cashew nuts from my minibar. Quite good.

Wednesday
Another light training session – too light, really. I'd like to be pushing myself more. I had a word with Sammy Lee about it. I said, 'I didn't come all this way just to sit on an exercise bike in a pair of flip-flops.' 'Don't be daffy,' he said. 'That's exactly why you came all this way.'

It doesn't help that there's one or two injuries building up in the squad. Joe Cole got a toe caught in his partner's ankle bracelet overnight and could be out for a couple of days. And Frankie Lampard has trodden on a pull-along caterpillar, so he's going to be taking it easy for a while, too, until the swelling goes down and they can have a proper look at it.

Wandered around the resort a bit in the afternoon. It was pretty deserted, but eventually found a couple of David James's kids, playing with a ball out in the garden, and had a game of three-and-in. Did OK.

In the evening, the Champions League final was on. Buzzed Michael Owen to see if he fancied coming to watch it in my room and maybe get a pizza sent up. He said he might if he could get the kids settled. Watched on my own until the seventieth minute when suddenly the electricity went off. Louise Bonsall had plugged a bottle-warmer into their room's shaving socket and taken the power down across a quarter of the resort. It was an hour before the lights came back on.

In the bathroom, put the complimentary satsuma and tea tree oil mud mask on my face, just for a laugh. Looked quite like that one of the Incredible Four who stops a lorry with his fist. Washed it off again, though, because it started to itch.

Opened Bryan Robson's autobiography in bed, but fell asleep almost straight away.

Thursday

More injuries. Michael Carrick was hit by a chicken nugget at lunch yesterday and his eye is still quite puffy this morning. And Owen Hargreaves picked up a niggle on the way down to breakfast when he tried to step over a double buggy in the lift and it snapped shut on his leg. He looked in a bad way, but the medical staff say he should be up and running by the weekend, so long as nothing shows up on the scan.

Training negligible. Got told off for going in too hard on Theo Walcott. Think it was mostly frustration on my part. Plus the ball was there to be won. Drifted back up after lunch. Still feeling under-exercised, so decided to see how many laps of my

room I could do with the giant teddy bear on my back. Got up
to 704 before Elen, Frank Lampard's partner, came up and asked
me to give it a rest because she was trying to get her little one
off. Seven hundred and four, though: that's not bad, and I
reckon I still had enough in me to go all the way to 1,000.

In the evening, Jamie Carragher called up. He and Nicola
were thinking of having a quiet meal in the restaurant downstairs, maybe a drink afterwards. I said that was a brilliant idea
and I wasn't busy. Jamie said he didn't think I would be, and,
in that case, would I mind babysitting for their two, James and
Mia?

Couldn't really get out of it after that, but at least I drove him
up to £8.50 an hour. Spent the evening in Jamie's room watching *Thomas the Tank Engine's Peep Peep Party* and reading *The
Tiger Who Came To Tea*. Not bad, actually. Better than Bryan
Robson's autobiography, anyway.

Friday
Injuries: John Terry (carpet burns), Michael Owen (turned ankle
over on Brio train set), Peter Crouch (unfortunate bed-bouncing
incident).

Training, half-hearted. Lunch, chaotic. Hotel swimming
pool, a scene from hell. Will be glad when retreat is over and
can get a bit of peace.*

If the Salary Cap Fits . . .

The notion of a salary cap for footballers has been raised again.
It would, of course, be a heart-sinkingly retrograde step, forcing
football back towards the dark ages of the maximum wage,

* The quiet man of the squad he may have been, but aren't they always the
ones you have to watch? That certainly seemed to be the case when a reality
show called *WAGS Boutique* opened on ITV and Downing's girlfriend, the
superbly named Michaela Henderson-Thynne, suddenly found out that . . .
but don't read about it here, read about it on p. 248.

pre-Jimmy Hill. However, if by 'salary cap' was meant precisely that – a cap with a player's salary on it – then one could possibly warm to the idea.

Under this kind of salary cap legislation, players would be obliged to wear salary-revealing headgear at all times on the field of play. Presumably LED technology is sophisticated enough now that the display on the cap could be updated in real time, allowing it to incorporate performance-related bonuses, and thus providing an exact readout on the player's earning capacity at any point. Now that's what you call putting a price on someone's head. It would be a major step towards transparency in the game, and a formidably useful tool for performance evaluation.

Interlude – the 2006 World Cup, as Seen on Telly*

Controversy from the off, then, with the BBC electing to show only what Gary Lineker risibly described as 'a flavour of the proceedings' from the opening ceremony, rather than the total and unexpurgated coverage of this essential occasion for which many of us had been waiting anxiously for four years.

You're not going to tell me that the preamble in Munich didn't feature at least half an hour of bottomlessly puzzling pageantry involving drama students dressed as insects, not to mention a series of increasingly complex happenings necessitating schoolchildren and balloons. It's a contractual obligation in this day and age. But what did we get from the BBC? Six minutes at most of carefully selected highlights, parts of which were almost sensible.

On the other hand, the bell-ringers will live long in the memory – and the more so, possibly, for not being crowded out by other equally sensational images. They came after the Bavarian shoc-pattcrs and thigh-slappers, of whom an edited glimpse may actually, now one comes to think of it, have been

* It was cheaper than going.

enough. My feeling about lederhosen has always been that they must be more fun to wear than to see worn.

The bell-ringers, though – now, here was some collectable action. We were talking cowbells, but massive and golden and weighing, according to the BBC's Jonathan Pearce, whom one is inclined to trust on these matters, anything up to five stone a time. Which is an awful lot of cowbell for one person to be carrying on a football pitch before a major international, particularly if the bell happens to be attached to a leather belt and hanging, sporran-like, from the region of the ringer's groin.

In this apparently time-honoured German musical ritual, a sound is achieved by crouching slightly, gripping the bell firmly with both hands and making a thrusting motion with the hips. When a lot of people stand in a line and do this . . . well, it's quite a sight, especially when the music gathers to a fast-thrusting climax and especially when you remember that this was all going on well ahead of the traditional 9.00 p.m. watershed for scenes of an adult nature. As the FIFA slogan puts it, this World Cup is 'a time to make friends'. With a bell, if nothing else.

Follow that, indeed, because, frankly, when you've seen a line of traditionally costumed German gentlemen enthusiastically humping five-stone cowbells like tomorrow depended on it, there is little that a punditry panel featuring Alan Shearer can startle you with.

There are few greater tests of a commentator's steel than an early group-phase match involving Japan, so congratulations to Clive Tyldesley, who acquitted himself with style to spare, despite being handed a team sheet with the name Takashi Fukunishi on it. 'There is no other way of saying it,' the ITV commentator said apologetically, as offended viewers across the shires began their letters of complaint.

Even as Tyldesley spoke, Gareth Southgate, seated beside him in the commentary box, was demonstrating that there may, in fact, be as many as three or four different ways of saying Fukunishi to the country. Indeed, the new Middlesbrough boss showed that there are several semi-viable options for each of these Japanese players' names – and whichever one you choose, you may not entirely escape giving the impression that you are undergoing a ruinous attack of hay fever.

My feeling is that it might be wise to rest Southgate for a few days, or at least until his tongue returns to normal size. He's new to this co-commentary lark. You don't want to damage him by asking too much of him too soon.

At least he tried, though. For Mexico *v*. Iran, the BBC handed a World Cup 2006 studio debut to that renowned authority on football at the Iranian/Mexican interface, Lee Dixon. And the former Arsenal full back rose magnificently to the occasion by managing to get through the entire broadcast without noticeably mentioning a single player by name. Quality.

Yesterday Terry Venables didn't do much better with Australia, whose national team, remember, he once managed. Yet his pre-match remarks were limited to noting the presence in the side of 'the likes of Mark Viduka and Harry Kewell'. Come on, Tel. Most of us could have pulled those two out of the hat. It's a reasoned analysis of what Luke Wilkshire was intended to bring to the blend that we were all eager to hear.

Presumably there's some research involved in this television punditry lark – some videos of old games, a few chats with people in the know. At the very least, a quick flick through the Merlin sticker book. Or do they just pack a set of freshly laundered casual shirts and go out there and wing it? Perish the thought. That said, there remains the case of Ian Wright, who, given Holland *v*. Serbia and Montenegro to talk about, shruggingly concluded that he was only really interested in England.

Wright is officially wasted in Germany, and you can see the sadness of it in his eyes. He should be watching the World Cup on a giant screen in the centre of Kidderminster with a plastic Second World War helmet on his head and an inflatable thunder stick jocularly protruding from his trousers. But no. A World Cup comes round only every four years, and poor old Wrighty is cursed to spend it penned up on the telly.

Stay tuned, then, for news of our upcoming 'Fly Wrighty
Home' appeal, whereby, via a number of large-scale public
events across the country, we'll be looking to raise enough
money to get Wright airlifted from Gary Lineker-occupied
Berlin before the end of the group stage. And for one lucky
winner there will be the chance to fly the plane (air authorities
permitting – and you can't see them not).

Meanwhile, is it too early to be talking about advertising
fatigue? Ordinarily, I wouldn't expect to experience the symp-
toms of this until well into the second week, but here we are
on day five and there are already some ads on heavy rotation
whose chatty company I am beginning to tire of. In particular I
wish the makers of Pedigree Chum had chosen an occasion
other than the world's greatest sporting festival to ask us, 'What's
your dog's thing?' There's a World Cup on. The last thing any
of us need right now is to be distracted by the thought of our
dog's thing.

Ah, that old South Korean national anthem. So good, they
played it twice. Cue chaos among the ceremonial schoolchildren
accompanying the Togo players, some of whom took the com-
pletion of South Korea's big number for the second time as their
moment to leave the field, some of whom didn't and some of
whom got caught halfway. For a moment there, it looked like
an episode of *Tiswas*. Memo to mascots: it ain't over 'til the big
guy holding your hand sings.

We await the official observer's report, of course, but at
present no blame for this cock-up attaches to Graham Poll, the
sole English referee selected for Germany and the figurehead, or
snapped-off hood ornament, if you like, of Premiership offici-
ating, who was experiencing his long-awaited World Cup 2006
curtain-up.

Poll is often claimed – quite unfairly, surely – to have an ego
the size of Dortmund. Therefore it was widely held that it would
not chime well with his vision of his place in the scheme of
things if he drew one of the tournament's, shall we say, slighter

matches. I wouldn't say there was dancing on the streets of Tring when Poll was handed South Korea *v*. Togo. But there were one or two cheese and wine parties.

Poll, though, was heroically firm-jawed about this outcome, pointing out, on *Sky Sports News*, which faithfully filmed his departure from Heathrow, that it was an Asian team against an African team, meaning that he would know he was truly at a World Cup. He further emphasized the felicity by which the match was scheduled to take place on his wedding anniversary and underlined that there are no meaningless games at this level.

On which point I'm sure he is completely right. But let's just say for argument's sake that, by some freak of circumstance, it came about that there actually *was* such a thing as a meaningless game at this level. Wouldn't that game have to be South Korea *v*. Togo?

On reflection, though, if FIFA were going to give Poll any fixture at all, it was probably best that it was one featuring two countries unburdened by historical antipathy. Poll, his critics are apt to say, could start a civil war in a sock drawer. It's something in the way he smiles. Hands up if you were surprised when he was involved in only the second sending-off of the tournament.

Poll mildly fluffed the big moment, flashing first the red card and then the yellow. Was this a drop in his legendary intensity? In an interview early last season, our leading whistle-blower declared, with the self-effacement for which football fans know and love him, 'I prepare for every match the same way, be it a World Cup play-off or a domestic match. Form is not something you can turn on and off like a tap. As with players, if a referee drops his intensity by 5 per cent, it will show.'

Yet he also said, 'We work with a sports psychologist who tells us to treat every game as a rung on the ladder, and unless you are absolutely prepared you will never reach the top of the ladder. For me the 2005/06 season is like a long ladder through to the World Cup finals and the Carling Cup tie at Millwall represented my twenty-fourth rung on the ladder, with every rung as important as the others.'

Respect to the sports psychologist, of course, but wouldn't this ladder analogy only really work if Poll was envisaging himself reaching ever higher towards glory? Unless this particular ladder is lying flat on the ground. Or are some games more equal than others?

I don't know. Who among us is genuinely qualified to comprehend the mindset of the big-time referee? The important thing is, I reckon Poll did enough yesterday to warrant another major call-up. Is Angola *v.* Iran taken?

Have you noticed how difficult it is to get to see a doctor at this World Cup? It's worse than trying to arrange a home visit on the NHS. Players go down clutching their legs, shoulders, heads etc., in a manner that, in almost any domestic league in the developed world, would guarantee them the comfort of an emergency one-on-one with the family physio.

But then the referee steps in and tells the player to get up. If the player doesn't get up, the ref continues to tell him to do so for some time – in most cases until the player finally does get up, either out of embarrassment or boredom, or because by then his fracture has in fact healed. Thus, ironically, only the players with the sternest constitutions, the appetite for a fight and the guts to tough out a long-term stand-off with an A-list FIFA official get to have their knees sponged.

Clearly some sort of FIFA directive has gone out, instructing referees to allow medical staff immediate access to the pitch only in the event of actual, demonstrable limb loss. And even then it helps to have a note from your mum. Almost certainly this ordinance was set out a couple of clauses above the one entitled 'Restricting the delivery of water bottles during matches played in temperatures in excess of 34 degrees', itself a statutory part of the FIFA World Cup 2006 mission briefing, 'Giving these pampered ladyboys the sharp end'.

Even when the medics do get on, there is bad news for the watching millions: no automated stretcher-bearing devices. Since time immemorial (or, at any rate, since about 1990), a

World Cup injury has meant the emergence on the pitch of something that looks like a cross between a golf buggy and an ice cream van. The arrival of novelty vehicles was proven to have its own magically restorative powers, all but the truly leg-shattered footballer being resistant to the shame of leaving the pitch in a battery-operated bumper car.

Indeed, one wonders whether FIFA haven't missed a trick here. There is no one more vain about the kind of vehicle he is in than a footballer. By mechanically adapting a set of those coin-in-the-slot children's rides that one sees outside super-markets – a Budgie the Helicopter, say – and then licensing them for global use, FIFA could probably have reduced treatment stoppages across the international game by anything up to 90 per cent.

As it is, the medical SWAT teams in Germany are wielding merely the basic, hand-held plastic stretcher, a device which couldn't look more antique if it were horse-drawn. True, a satisfyingly tiresome health and safety initiative requires any player carried on this stretcher to be buckled up, twice, with the result that even players who aren't really injured at all appear to be leaving the field with two broken legs and a cracked rib. Yet there is no denying the overall loss to the drama the home viewer craves.

What chance of Mick McCarthy, one of the BBC's summarizers, needing some treatment before the tournament ends? Self-inflicted wounds would seem the most likely prognosis. McCarthy is a pint of umbrage in a mug. The mildly pedantic performance of a Russian referee the other day brought him to levels of dourness unheard of on television since Inspector Blake from *On the Buses* was in his pomp.

'Do you know what his job is?' McCarthy was asked. 'Traffic warden,' he grunted. (Schoolteacher, actually.) McCarthy wasn't finished. 'He's a wally in his part time. Mr Precious in his red shirt . . . I 'ate you, Butler.'

All right, I made up the bit about Butler. But if McCarthy doesn't run out at the finish of this World Cup with the Derek

Dougan Award for Analyst Most Like the Miserable Bloke
Behind You in the Pub, then the world will be upside down.

Rio Ferdinand said this week that it wouldn't matter to people
if England played badly in every game of this World Cup so
long as they won it. 'I'm the same, to be honest,' he said. Well,
Ferdinand knows his own mind, of course, but one wondered
about the accuracy of this reading of the national mood yesterday, when a grim and stodgy England left the pitch at half-time
against Trinidad and Tobago, with the score at 0–0, under a
blanket of catcalls and whistles.*

Maybe doing it with at least some degree of style does, after
all, matter to the gathered hordes of Kettering and Hatfield –
not to the degree that it matters to Portugal supporters, or South
Korea supporters, both of whom have been heard to heckle
their teams at this tournament for protecting a 1–0 lead, the
kind of luxury England fans can only dream of at present. But
maybe the style question counts to an important extent, hitherto
unconsidered by England's own players.

Well, one can hope. But it says everything you need to know
about yesterday's snoozefest that, before Steven Gerrard's goal,
its stand-out dramatic moment had featured Dwight Yorke, of
Trinidad and Tobago, who had to spend some time with his hand
deep in his shorts after an unfortunate ball-to-groin incident.

Clive Tyldesley, ITV's commentator, was sympathetic. 'I
don't know why we find it so funny,' he said. 'We've all been
there and it's agony.' Actually, speaking personally, I have to
confess that I have never been smacked in the privates by a
Gerrard volley during a World Cup group-phase match, but I'll
take Tyldesley's word for it. He is, after all, the Stuart Hall *de
nos jours* – albeit without the irony.

How badly did England let down ITV? The channel's cameras
had excitedly tracked the disembarkation of the team from the

* England went on to win 2–0 with a goal on eighty-three minutes and
another in injury time. By then they had already unimpressively defeated
Paraguay, 1–0, thanks to an own goal. It was all going swimmingly.

bus and released to an anxious nation the hugely reassuring sight of Wayne Rooney, wearing headphones the size of large squirrels. No one experiencing any kind of foot problem would risk putting on a pair of headphones that large – not because of the weight of wearing them so much as the risk of dropping them on the injured limb.

In the studio, Terry Venables wore a pink shirt, emphasizing his softer side. Stuart Pearce didn't. Sam Allardyce imaginatively said he was 'looking for Michael Owen to feed on the shoulder of Peter Crouch' – an interesting idea, but there's no meat on there, surely. A hungry striker would be better off feeding on the shoulder of a Rooney, surely, or even a John Terry.

The drafting of the eerily smiling Steve Rider into the ITV squad has certainly had a knock-on effect. He arrived in Germany late, citing a long-standing prior engagement at the Formula 1 British Grand Prix – surely no excuse that any football fan would understand – and presumably the idea was to settle the team down by bringing on board an older head. That's a reasonable enough approach, though, for my money, Rider lacks Gabby Logan's essential gravity and authority. Plus you know he would rather be watching golf.

Watching this strange power vacuum develop at the top for ITV, one can't help but wonder whether we might eventually see the promotion into more active service of Brad Lescarbo and Hal Butchgrass, the cod American hosts sponsored by Budweiser, who bracket the advertising breaks in little film clips – or, as we like to refer to them in the advertising game, 'bumpers'.

In all frankness, the comedy of Brad and Hal's combination of enthusiasm and ignorance is a bit hit and miss, but yesterday's effort was quite promising. Brad: 'And so the FIFA World Cup 2006 continues with England playing Trinidad *and* Tobago.' Hal: 'It doesn't seem fair, but OK!'

OK, indeed. And it didn't look fair, no. But that was England's fault – a style-free zone again.

*

So, that's the benchmark, then, right there: Argentina's second goal yesterday against Serbia and Montenegro. There have been goals scored in this World Cup from miles further out, involving shots of far greater power. But we have seen nothing to rival the sheer command and suavity of the twenty-four-pass move that led to Esteban Cambiasso scoring quite straightforwardly from twelve yards.

The opposition were completely carved apart. Indeed, if Serbia and Montenegro hadn't already decided to become independent states, that goal would surely have forced them to have a good, hard think about the idea.

The move had begun with the regaining of possession not far outside Argentina's own penalty area. Yet, of the twenty-four entirely unhindered passes that moved the ball patiently towards the penalty spot at the other end, and thence into the back of the net, not one travelled more than fifteen yards and in only one case was the ball required to leave the ground – a chip out to Sorin on the wing, who quickly chested it down on to the grass again.

One other thing: at no point in this move did any player perform a step-over. Can we finally be honest with one another about the value of the step-over? I know Ronaldinho does them. And Cristiano Ronaldo. But he's Ronaldinho. And he's Cristiano Ronaldo. In 95 per cent of other cases, the step-over is the showboating lightweight's way of saying, 'I haven't really got a clue what I'm going to do next, or where my nearest team mate is.' I don't know why FIFA has got such a bee in its bonnet about sliding tackles when yellow cards for step-overs are what the people genuinely want to see.

Did that Argentina move remind you of anyone? Not England, I'm assuming. Aerial photographs from the unmanned and mostly simulated mission against Trinidad and Tobago reveal a space roughly the area of Cornwall between the midfield and the attack, as five years under Sven-Goran Eriksson and three weeks of expensive fine-tuning in the Black Forest composted down into the solitary vision statement: 'Ping it up to Crouchy.'

Much was made on television at the time of how Trinidad and Tobago 'didn't seem overawed', but why would they have? In effect, they were up against MK Dons with a bigger hospitality budget.

Glimpses of Maradona in the crowd yesterday wearing a replica shirt and a patriotic rictus will have done nothing to stem the fast dissipating feeling that England in any way 'have what it takes' out there in Germany. The Argentina legend is one of those rare celebrities who has come, with the passing of the years, to appear more frightening than his *Spitting Image* puppet and accordingly, during his nation's anthem, he was, in all senses, animated.

'So passionate,' purred Jonathan Pearce. 'That's passion,' confirmed Ian Wright, the BBC's self-appointed passion correspondent, when the images were shown again in slow motion at half-time. You never see Sir Bobby Charlton threaten the integrity of his blood vessels in that way. Yet, when you come down to it, there is no reason why it shouldn't be a condition of his getting a free seat. But, sad to say, even England's legends appear to lack the wherewithal to turn it on when it comes to the big occasion.

The BBC has put up a sign by the message boards on its sports website requesting correspondents to tone it down a bit. Apparently, viewers, logging on to give Motty, Lawro and pals a piece of their e-mail, aren't holding back on what my mother calls 'choice language'.

You'll get none of that here, of course, where we take a far more tolerant and understanding line on commentators, pundits and their valuable work. We respect these people for the service they so selflessly offer at what must be a busy time of the year for them, what with there being a World Cup on and everything.

Indeed, we're not ashamed to say that we've got a lot of time for the carefully reasoned insights offered on the BBC by the likes of Martin O'Neill and, er, Martin O'Neill. And we very much enjoy it when Marcel Desailly enters the studio, with prodigious charisma intact, although we do wish Alan Hansen would stop licking him.

Altogether, in fact, we find that a beatific calm has settled upon us. Blissed out by all this gratifying football, we appear to have crossed over to a place where no analyst or commentator can touch us by means of inanity or hysteria alone, apart from, every now and again, ITV's Clive Tyldesley.

We observe, for instance, Lee Dixon mounting the argument, as he did this weekend, that England should make sure they win their group in order to avoid meeting Argentina until the final. And we note that he is completely wrong, because England and Argentina could meet as early as the quarter-finals. And we duly find ourselves obliged to conclude that whatever qualifications were necessary to become part of the BBC's punditry team in Germany, the ability to operate a World Cup wallchart was not necessarily one of them.

But do we therefore go directly to the BBC's website with our blood up and fire off a paragraph of crackling, semi-litigious opprobrium at the expense of Dixon and people close to him, in language to shame our mothers? No, we do not. We calmly split open another packet of chocolate and hazelnut Boasters (a prince among biscuits) and wait for the football to come back on.

For life is short, and World Cups are few – too few, surely, to be spoiled by the tiny slips of these peripheral figures. Not even Peter Drury screaming 'Equalizer!' when the score is 2–1.

That was during Italy *v.* United States. 'No Saturday-night feature,' Drury informed us, 'would ever match it' for its 'blood and thunder', its 'twists and turns' and, moreover, its 'everlastingly breathless plots and subplots'. Try running that one past Kasey Keller, the US goalkeeper.

'How would you describe today's encounter, Kasey?'

'The lads are everlastingly breathless in there, Peter.'

Alert, perhaps, to the rising levels of public disdain for the traditional pundit, in the staffing of Brazil *v.* Australia, ITV yesterday sent for Shane Warne, who, we understand, is an

Australian (wait for this) *cricketer*. Purists will complain, but if the job is essentially about being unable to understand a World Cup wallchart, then it might as well be a cricketer doing the misunderstanding as an ex-professional footballer.

Anyway, it was Warne's mission to be as Australian as he possibly could be, in the circumstances, and he fulfilled it admirably. Indeed, he couldn't have been more Australian had he attempted to keep his beer cool in the shadow created by Steve Rider.

Warne became the second high-profile cricketer to feature in the televising of this World Cup, following Andrew Flintoff's unsteady public embrace of Ray 'Shtubbsie' Stubbs on the first Saturday. Had the pie-eyed Flintoff been, say, a pie-eyed Robbie Fowler, the moral inquest would still be going on. But he's a cricketer, so it's fine. Cricketers can get away with anything. Unlike football pundits.

It's open season on John Motson at the moment. The BBC's Voice of Football is one of the few people in Germany who can genuinely consider himself to be having a rougher ride than Serbia and Montenegro. No sooner had a correspondent to the BBC website cruelly noted the similarity between Motty's trademark 'heh heh' chuckle and the sniggering noises made by the professionally juvenile cartoon characters Beavis and Butt-head, than stories began to appear, gleefully reporting that viewers 'in their thousands' have been giving Motson the digital elbow, using their red buttons to select the Radio 5 Live match soundtrack instead.

Can this be so? I don't really believe in the allure of this TV picture/radio sound phenomenon that people periodically evangelize about. I didn't really believe in it when you had to turn the sound down and stand the radio on top of the telly, and I don't really believe in it now that the digital revolution has put it at our fingertips.

For starters, this is Radio 5 Live we are talking about. (As of now, the option of teaming televised football with soft soul

classics on Heart FM remains but a digital dream.) And being
Radio 5 Live, the chances are that at some point you are going
to end up listening to Alan Green, the man who has done more
than any broadcaster on earth to narrow the gap between football
commentary and the sound of next door's car alarm. Give me
Motty every time, 'heh hehs' included.

Even during the blessedly Green-free experiment that I conducted yesterday – unfairly wiping out the undersung Guy
Mowbray midway through Togo *v.* Switzerland – the project
fell apart. You see – and I don't mean to get technical here – the
point of the radio commentary is to provide a suitable quantity
of information for people who haven't got any pictures. Thus
when you run a radio commentary next to some pictures, the
result is information overload.

It's like watching a film with subtitles, but when the film is
already in your own language anyway. I can see the appeal of
this setup for those who are not given to trusting the evidence
of their own eyes, such as, for instance, people in homes for the
bewildered. Otherwise I can only think it appeals to the kind of
viewer who likes to be able to say, 'Ooh, yes, look, he got that
right.' And these people think Motty is a nerd.

That said, yesterday I left on the radio feed after the match
had finished and was rewarded with the sound of an irate French
fan's voice emerging from the head of Ray Stubbs. 'Heh heh',
as Motty and/or Beavis and Butthead would say. Well, it passed
a couple of minutes innocently enough.

Would that the same could be said for the team in red yesterday. It is, I find, increasingly hard to feel neutral about Switzerland. The attritional play, the boggling lack of ambition, the
niggardly fouling in midfield, the aversion to flair or anything
that resembles it – these things force even the most equable
spectator off the fence eventually.

'They're not particularly attractive,' Paul Jewell said, 'but they
get the job done and you can't knock that.' I beg to differ. I
think we are perfectly at liberty to knock that from here to
Geneva and all the way back again, using big lumps of wood

torn out of our own garden fences if we so choose. This is, after all, a World Cup, licensing us to glorify the teams who turn it on, and pan the ones content to grind it out. I would probably have even stronger feelings about this if the team Switzerland most strongly reminded me of at this tournament wasn't England.

Of course, none of us will truly feel we've got England's draw with Sweden into even a semblance of perspective until we've checked the view of Ron Atkinson on the next of Big Ron's Big World Cup Podcasts. When not serving a penitential sentence as a World Cup pundit on the almost entirely unwatched UKTV, the disgraced analyst is currently offering the globe his suitably chastened thoughts via the SelfcastTV website, uploading his load, as it were, after each England game.*

Impressed? To adapt John Hodgman, the American humorist, not just anyone can broadcast on the internet. Odd, though, to find Big Ron of all people at the leading edge of twenty-first century infotainment. I have a hunch that, before this World Cup, you could have asked Big Ron to define podcasting and he would have guessed it was a town off the A619 near Staveley.

Now, though, with a whole new England saga to talk about, the only question is, where will Big Ron be this time? Thus far Big Ron has cast his pod from a variety of unexplained locations, including what appeared to be the bar and trophy room of his sumptuous home in the Birmingham suburbs, an abandoned cupboard, possibly in a media centre, and then, most excitingly, after England's game against Trinidad and Tobago, from a suite in a plush-looking hotel.

How plush? Well, beyond Big Ron's shoulder, no fewer than three pillows were clearly visible on either side of the king-size bed, making a feather-tastic total of six in all, so I think we can discount the possibility that it was a Travelodge.

Let me stress that at no point during this podcast did Big Ron

---

* Atkinson's media career was scuppered when an unexpectedly open microphone caught some of his, shall we say, antiquated views on Marcel Desailly's workrate. It's a long way back from there, even going via Sky One (see p. 203).

appear topless, which, sadly, tends all too often to be the way of things these days when celebrities turn up on webcams in bedrooms. On the contrary, Big Ron appeared to be dressed for a wedding, in a dark suit and silver tie. Which means that, although he didn't really say anything that wasn't said by a thousand other pundits in a thousand other media outlets ('the result was the important thing'), he looked a lot smarter when he said it. The man has standards, even now.

So bring him on. There is much to discuss – the Michael Owen injury, the Sweden penalty that wasn't, the Wayne Rooney/Peter Crouch partnership that also wasn't, the Rio Ferdinand injury, the Joe Cole goal, Steven Gerrard's second, the World Cup future of Theo Walcott, aged fourteen and three quarters, Roo's dugout punching and boot-tossing, and, above all, the question of whether, once again, the result (England 2 – Sweden 2, meaning both sides qualify for the knockout stage) was the important thing. All the indications are that Big Ron is going to be phoning down to reception for an even bigger pod.

Back in the world of real-time reaction, the ITV punditry panel crossed over from open-necked shirts into suits, to signal the gathering seriousness of the tournament. Thereafter, the kick-off almost had to be delayed to allow Terry Venables to come up with yet another way to pronounce 'Ibrahimovic', as in Zlatan, the injured Sweden striker. You say 'Ibrahimovic', Tel says, 'Ibrahemovic'. Tel also says 'Ibrahamovich'. Let's call the whole thing off.

Those Mexican fans: is it personal? Suspicion inevitably thickened yesterday when Clive Tyldesley became the third British broadcaster in Germany to complain on air about the disruption to his sleep caused by Mexico supporters staying in the same hotel. As someone who had apparently spent the previous night listening through the wall to hard-partying South Americans, a clearly bleary Tyldesley said that he could 'vouch for their [meaningful pause] . . . passion'.

The ITV commentator's lament comes only a week after

Jonathan Pearce, again while on air, mentioned having strong words in the middle of the night with a Mexican drummer in the hotel room next door to Pearce's in Munich. 'He [the drummer] now knows some choice phrases in Anglo-Saxon,' Pearce reported. Which may have seemed a little intemperate, even belligerent, of the BBC man and somewhat out of keeping with the spirit of what is, after all, intended to be an international festival of fun.

Remember, however, that a Pearce commentary will almost always involve him reading out whole pages of indigestible facts, relating to the exact age of the Spanish national anthem, perhaps, or the record as a penalty taker in international competition of Mabrouk Zayed of Saudi Arabia. Rest is, accordingly, as important to Pearce as it is to any other athlete at this World Cup and heaven forbid that he should have his performance impaired in any way by a freelance percussionist in a sombrero.

Since when Jim Beglin, too, has mentioned the sheer commitment to pleasure of the average Mexican fan, 'unless you happen to be in the hotel room next door' – this said in such a way as to imply that the ITV analyst was speaking from bitter first-hand experience.

Two such incidents would have been accounted a coincidence, but three begins to look sinisterly like some kind of vendetta and one wonders if the time hasn't come to bring in an external investigative authority. These connected events raise the worrying possibility of an organized team of vigilante Mexico fans, who are booking themselves into known media hotels specifically in order to keep awake high-profile British broadcasting talent, thereby critically undermining the coverage of the tournament in this country.

We don't know exactly who they are, we don't know exactly what they want. But we do know that their operation is alarmingly, chillingly indiscriminate. BBC or ITV, it's all the same to them.

It's the duty of all of us to be as vigilant as we can, but especially those currently travelling in Germany. Your information could be valuable. Keep an eye out for any Mexican with a drum insisting on occupying the suite underneath Peter Drury's. Be on your guard for mariachi bands creeping up behind Guy Mowbray. Contact ITV or the BBC and let them know what you have seen.

Also, think of ways in which you, personally, can make life easier for the media personnel who may be all around you. Offer them your seats in bars and cafés and on public transport, assuming they ever use it. When asked at reception whether you require a smoking or non-smoking room, simply request to be placed at least two floors away from any broadcasting talent, to create a zone of non-interference. If you must play wind instruments in your room, then endeavour to mute them with spare towels from your en suite bathroom. Before drumming, enter a wardrobe and close the door.

Above all, remember that not everyone at the World Cup has gone there to have a good time, and that, indeed, the person in the room next to you may be Mick McCarthy. Now, he *really* hasn't gone there to have a good time. 'Is that a badger hairstyle?' Pearce idly wondered the other day, referring to Danijel Ljuboja of Serbia and Montenegro. 'Skunk,' said McCarthy, with dark contempt. Maybe he's not getting enough sleep.

The World Cup on UKTV, the far-flung cable channel, looks quite like the World Cup on any other channel, I suppose, but less expensive. Unlike with certain other broadcasters we could mention, the budget has not run to a glass-backed, converted warehouse overlooking the Brandenburg Gate in Berlin. Instead it has run to a cloth-backed, unconverted warehouse in an undisclosed location, uncomfortably echoey and overlooking nothing at all, on account of the cloths.

Wind, or air-conditioning, ruffles the garish backdrop, light can be seen leaking beneath one of the drapes and a clock is occasionally heard chiming in the background. I quite like the clock. It's a comforting sign that time may not, after all, despite all other impressions, be standing still.

In this cheap and, if we're being honest, not all that cheerful

setting, Andy Goldstein, our host, and guests of the calibre of
Danny Murphy, the former England player, and Dave Gorman,
the comedian and author, do what they can to keep their spirits
up, and by extension ours. Meanwhile, one of the smallest
studio audiences you will ever see looks on glumly, giving every
appearance of having been marched in at gunpoint from a nearby
sandwich bar.

A sample of yesterday's conversation: Goldstein ribs Murphy
for not wearing socks. Murphy suggests that Goldstein's socks
probably have Mickey Mouse on them. Goldstein replies, 'I've
heard that Mickey Mouse has got a Danny Murphy watch.'
Ah, banter. By comparison, Lineker, Hansen and Shearer are
veritably the Marx Brothers of mirth and mischief.

Still, the point is that yesterday UKTV was the only place to
watch Ghana *v.* USA, live and unexpurgated. Thus, wobbly
scenery and bad jokes or not, the channel became a compulsory
stop for those of us who, over the last fortnight, have decided
that we rather like the cut of Ghana's jib.

And we were amply rewarded with victory and progress,
though not before a UKTV commentator had accused Ghana
of 'naïvety at this level'. Blimey, that took one back. In the
World Cups of yore, 'naïve' was routinely used by pundits in
the description of African nations and was, essentially, the default
synonym for 'black'. But as enlightenment slowly dawns, even
across the punditry business, 'naïve' has been seldom heard in
Germany. To the extent that the notion flickers on at all, it
seems to be in the shape of the slightly more politically acceptable
'gullibility', as in the following John Motsonism from earlier in
the tournament: 'I think there was a bit of Ghanaian gullibility
about that second goal, wasn't there?'

Of course, in terms of simple things like being able to pass
the ball, retain a formation or mark up at a set piece, whom, on
the evidence of Germany 2006, would you call the more naïve
– Ghana or England? Come to that, whom would you call
the more gullible? Anyway, Ghana march on, and thank you,
UKTV, for sharing it with us.

On a broader point of etiquette, one noted with some disquiet the failure of Rio Ferdinand to remove his iPod for an interview the other day. Now, one realizes that answering simple questions from the likes of Garth Crooks and Gabriel Clark is one of those low-watt activities that a person can perform perfectly well even while engaged in something else altogether more absorbing, such as watching a programme on television or doing the ironing.

Even so, it does seem a bit rude, not to say a touch discouraging, not to give Garth, Gabriel and co. at least the semblance of one's full attention when they take the trouble to come a-calling, so I think if Rio could try to remember from now on to get his plugs out, then we would probably all benefit in some small way and a standard of decorum would be maintained.

As they said on ITV at the start of this tournament, 'Let the memories begin.' And I, for one, will never forget what I was doing the night Graham Poll went into yellow card hyperdrive, booking Josip Simunic of Croatia so many times that the referee himself went dizzy and lost count.

And what I was doing, of course, as this momentous World Cup development and major human interest story unfolded, was watching Japan *v*. Brazil on another channel – a poor call, I now openly concede, and by some measure the worst decision I have taken since matches started overlapping, upping the pressure on the home viewer to a quite unacceptable degree.

I blame the BBC, though, for electing for some wild reason to hand the prime broadcasting slot to the Fancy Dan Brazilians, rather than encourage the nation to watch Australia-born Croatians and Croatia-born Australians kick lumps out of each other for a place in the second round.

And, like a sheep, I went along with it. For what? Yes, I got to witness the second coming of Ronaldo, and probably the hardest shot and best save of the tournament so far (Juninho and Yoshikatsu Kawaguchi, respectively). But what possible consolation is that when I could have been watching 'Polly' suffer the biggest loss of plot since that jumbo jet fell on *Emmerdale*?

People seemed aghast to see England's leading official attempt to pioneer his own, innovative 'three cards and you're out' legislation. But, in truth, the man from Tring seemed to be warming up for something special as early as his first game of the tournament, South Korea *v.* Togo, when he waved first the red card and then the yellow, thereby becoming the only official in this tournament so far to dismiss a player and then immediately book him. Talk about kicking a man when he's off.

Still, that hardly excuses the thinly concealed glee with which, we are ashamed to report, the nation's pundits greeted this second and more grievous mishap. On the BBC, Gavin Peacock was noting 'refereeing errors to the point I've never seen before' but sounding like someone who had just turned up £5,000 on a Lotto scratchcard. Over on ITV, Alan Curbishley had a brave stab at looking upset, but he's no actor. And was that just the hint of a smile on the lips of Jimmy Floyd Hasselbaink as he declared, with a shake of the head, 'If you are a World Cup referee, this is not allowed to happen'?

Whither this striking lack of sympathy for the man who has continually described himself as 'the Premier League's top ref'? It's the price you pay, possibly, for coming across like one of those disc jockeys who confuses playing records with making them and thereby presumes a prestige which doesn't quite tally with their fundamentally administrative position in the scheme of things. In this sense, the line of succession could be said to run from Dave Lee Travis, via 'Ooh' Gary Davies, to Jeff Winter and then on to Poll.

How much happier things seemed, all those days ago, when Sky Sports News tracked a Germany-bound Poll through Departures at Heathrow, for all the world as if he were Robbie Williams. Will the cameras be there when he returns? I don't know. But I fully intend to be – commitments permitting – and I think you should be, too, with all the flags and face paints you can muster.

Yes, he will most likely be returning in ignominy. No, he won't be going all the way to the final in Berlin. But he brought a lot of people a lot of pleasure along the way. Remember the turnout for the homecoming England rugby side after their 2003 World Cup triumph in Australia? Let's throng Tie Rack all over again – one more time for the Pollster.

As the national anthem played yesterday, ahead of England's 1–0 victory over Ecuador in the round of sixteen, the cameras cut to Posh Spice in the crowd. God bless you, ma'am. How proud we were, how proud. And yet Gary Lineker summed up the agonizingly contradictory relationship that the viewing nation has with these major England occasions. 'You look forward to them and then, when they're here, you dread them.' That was exactly right, I felt, except for the bit about looking forward to them.

Because, in all honesty, how many times can you watch England back-pedalling in bafflement and Paul Robinson doing his increasingly accurate impression of a peg-less tent before the prospect of seeing it again sheds the main part of its allure? 'It's England,' explained Lawrenson. 'It's called a roller-coaster.' Or a not very special team, depending how you look at it.

Doubtless it will prove fashionable to blame the coach for the grindingly unspectacular nature of England's progress. Yet let no one underestimate the efforts Sven-Goran Eriksson has latterly taken to reinvent himself in the public eye. Yesterday he was seen thumping the dugout in frustration – or, at any rate, lightly tapping it, as one might a Terry's chocolate orange. But it bodes well for the quarter-finals.

What's more, Eriksson's approach to line-ups has turned out to be surprisingly akin to the wags' approach to bikinis: he's packed a different one for every day. Which makes things more interesting. And would that the BBC showed anything like the same carefree willingness to experiment. They went into the knockout stages yesterday with, as usual, Alan Hansen in the holding role, Alan Shearer bedded down in a chair to stop any conversation developing in the final third, and Ian Wright out wide, though not as far out wide as many of us would like to see him.

I'm still waiting for Adrian Chiles to be given a proper run-out. He's shown on the highlights programmes that he is more than capable of mixing it up a bit, and moreover he is one of a very small number of broadcasters in Germany capable of talking about football in the way that people do who aren't on television.

Yet his sole contribution to yesterday's national festival was to helm the 'five silly things you didn't know about Ecuador' package. Chiles, surely, as much as any other presenter of his generation, is wasted telling us that Christina Aguilera's father is from Ecuador – a job which could easily have been left to Garth Crooks. I feel about Chiles the way some feel about Theo Walcott. What's the point of taking him if you don't intend to use him?

On a broader theme, I don't know what you think about the ceremonial exchange of balls that has taken place before every game of this World Cup. (Note: this particular ceremonial exchange of balls is entirely separate from the ceremonial exchange of balls taking place between pundits before, during and after the matches.) My own feeling, however, is that it has not been an unalloyed success.

The idea is that, directly after the toss, the opposing captains exchange, as well as the traditional pennants, the ball of friendship. Or is it the ball of fair play? It's the ball of something wholesome, anyway. The point is, the ceremony lacks a little in the dignity department – perhaps inevitably, given that it features a man trying to press a size five football on someone who is simultaneously trying to pass a size five football in the opposite direction. It looks like the kind of game you might play at a party to break the ice.

Also, it's kind of an obvious gift between players, isn't it? It prompts the image of a FIFA brain-crunching session ahead of the tournament at which someone suddenly jumped up and shouted, 'I know what they'd like – a football.' Maybe tokens next time?

*

Italy's shirts for this World Cup feature a design masterstroke: built-in sweat patches. For Germany, the *azzurri* are wearing blue smocks with an inset panel of darker blue under each armpit, for that very contemporary, failed-to-apply-the-Right-Guard look. Thus even players who have essentially coasted on their reputations for ninety minutes, then nicked it with a penalty in time added on, get to walk off looking drenched, as if they have been up and down the pitch all afternoon.

You have to ask, why didn't England think of that? Before ITV's coverage of Australia *v*. Italy yesterday, there was further analysis of the Ecuador snooze-athon, with salient replays, and it hadn't got any more exciting overnight. And this despite the fact that ITV had found a new close-up of David Beckham's now famous technicolour yawn – surely just a yawn of boredom which went wrong.*

Word that Beckham had kept his illness from the management did not go down well with the pundits. Sam Allardyce, in particular, thought that we had narrowly escaped a situation in which 'we'd all have been left with egg on our face'. *All* of us? That would have been some up-chuck. And was it egg, in any case? It looked more like Lucozade Sport to me. Still, I bow to Allardyce's greater experience in this area.

I have to say, though, I came quite close to joining Beckham in some loss of lunch yesterday when Steve McClaren proudly told ITV, 'We nullified Ecuador.' That would have been a depressing sentence no matter how it was said, but was the more so for coming with one of those Marmite-like coatings of self-satisfaction for which McClaren is famous. Apparently to ask for anything more from England than 'a result' at the moment is to reveal oneself to be a close relative of Fotherington-Thomas, the classic, mincing aesthete from the Molesworth books. 'Hello, clouds, hello, sky, hello, quick passing movements through midfield.'

---

* The England captain had used a quiet moment in the match to lose a small amount of internal excess baggage.

Then again, World Cups only come round every four years, so perhaps people are not being merely artsy-fartsy when they dare to hope for something more special from the occasion than nullification. That argument wouldn't get very far with Allardyce, though. Yesterday, the Bolton Wanderers manager picked a small fight with Andy Townsend for bravely insisting that England are, by some measure, the dullest team on show in Germany. 'I'm sorry,' Allardyce said, 'but entertainment has to go out of the window sometimes.'

Moments later, however, the conversation turned to fussy refereeing and the unhappy fact that you can get a yellow card in Germany for coughing without putting your hand over your mouth and a straight red for eating with your mouth open. And, in this matter, Allardyce conceded the strictness of the officials was 'spoiling the World Cup for me'.

So even for Allardyce, clearly, there is such a thing as a World Cup that can be spoiled. Can we, though, infer that he would accept it if the referees told him they were sorry but entertainment has to go out of the window sometimes?

So, the World Cup has a new all-time top goalscorer. Or, as Peter Drury on ITV put it: 'No one has gorged themselves more on the World Cup feast than Ronaldo.'* I wasn't too sure about the wisdom of going for a food analogy in the context of a player whose weight and general lack of condition were, only a week ago, inspiring viral internet jokes.

Sample: Ronaldo goes into Burger King and asks for two Whoppas. The assistant says, 'OK. You're not fat and you haven't lost it.'

The point about Drury, though, is that one is never entirely sure whether he is commentating on the football or writing a pastiche of Henry James. His problem, it strikes one as the tournament heads towards its business end, is ITV's in a nutshell:

---

* We mean the, by this point, somewhat lumpy, Brazilian Ronaldo, not the svelte, Manchester United showpony. So many Ronaldos, so little time.

over-excitement. The tempo of their coverage and the heat placed underneath it by commercial breaks require the channel to promise (in the words of the increasingly influential Brad Lescarbo from the Budweiser advertisements) 'mind-bending, pants-ripping, jaw-dropping soccer action' – and then to look a little hurt and confused if, as in the case of Argentina *v*. the Netherlands, it finishes flat and goalless.

Now, one despairs of the BBC, too, on occasions, such as the moment the other night when Leonardo used the words 'a Brazilian' in relation to a picture of some women in the crowd and drew a gust of sniggering and chortling from Gary Lineker and Mark Lawrenson, who are, I would tentatively suggest, old enough to know better. About forty years old enough, in fact.

Yet what the BBC seem to have eternally over ITV is the ability, not just to rise to the big occasions, but to cope with the bad matches when they come. Ukraine *v*. Switzerland, for instance – a match so endemically dull it contrived to yield the world's first unexciting penalty shoot-out, an outcome previously thought impossible.

Afterwards, Alan Shearer, on the BBC, simply said, 'Thank God for that, it's finished,' a sentence pretty much unimaginable on ITV, where there are high-end advertisers to placate and where some sort of red-faced apology would probably have been mustered.

In truth, the omens for ITV in Germany didn't look good from the moment they chose for their theme music a cloth-eared cover of David Bowie's 'Heroes' from which most of the chord changes had been patiently extracted. It seemed an implausible selection, even leaving aside the question of what Bowie's tale of being mashed out of his brain in Berlin on psychologically alienating chemical substances has got to do with the World Cup. Wake up, everyone: Maradona has *retired*.

Still ITV have had enough faith in this theme to make it available to viewers, which means that we, in turn, have had the rare pleasure of hearing the words 'digital download' on the lips of Steve Rider – as dislocating, in its own way, as seeing a shot of Sir Stanley Matthews wearing Nike.

There has been something wide of the mark, too, about ITV's World Cup competition, offering us the chance to 'live like footballers' via the prize of a weekend break in Cannes and a £28,000 car. But footballers don't really go to Cannes for the weekend, do they? And, as for spending just £28,000 on a car – well, £28,000 would barely keep today's Premier League stars in wing-mirrors. Indeed, in the modern football culture, the mother and father of all dressing-room ribbings awaits the player who spends as little as £28,000 on a pair of trousers, let alone on a car.

A tiny detail, perhaps. But these little misreadings of the tone do in the end add up to something, which is why ITV, in these later stages, appear to be merely making up the numbers while the BBC, despite the puns and the sniggering, charge on towards Berlin and glory.

Day off, rest day, interval – doesn't matter how you dress it up, the concept doesn't get any less ugly. After nineteen consecutive days of live football, this present interruption to the service is not just a body blow but also an insult to the stamina of the television viewing public, some of whom have been in training for this event for four years and don't take kindly to the sugges- tion that they can't hack it through to the end without a breather.

Mind you, on Tuesday night Ruud Gullit told *World Cuppa*, ITV's late-night review show, that he was looking forward to a break. This was doubly odd, given that Gullit has hardly appeared to be running himself ragged over the last fortnight – unless a gut can be bust by sitting comfortably in ITV's strangely luminous pitch-side booth and setting off on a series of mazy, gently loping sentences which sometimes (but by no means always) end in the discovery of a main verb.

I've kept away from *World Cuppa*, having found it, on my first visit at the start of the tournament, only marginally more amusing than an outbreak of mouth ulcers. But, perhaps subconsciously aware of the drought that lay ahead, I found myself back there after Spain *v*. France and was entranced to discover that Lee Trundle was a special guest.

Now, the list of subjects on which one wouldn't automatically seek the view of Swansea's knuckle-headed striker and all-purpose trouble magnet is long, but the World Cup would have to be quite near the top of it. That's *World Cuppa*, though. In previous years, a programme that tackled from behind like this might have gone unpunished. But the disciplinary regime has tightened. It's a straight red, I'm afraid.

Enough of that, though. If this dire FIFA-led hiatus has any positive effect, it will be in enforcing a temporary ceasefire in the bitter war that is currently being waged countrywide on all commentators and pundits. Of course, flinging flak in the direction of the TV chatmongers is a time-honoured World Cup staple — part of the fundamental panto of the occasion. This time, however, the amusement seems to have hardened into something altogether more caustic and vituperative. I merely refer you to the www.goalhanger.com website, where T-shirts inscribed 'Let's kick Tyldesley out of football' are currently available for purchase at £16.

Now, trust me, you'll find no such T-shirt worn here. Not until the price comes down a bit, anyway. We merely wonder what it is about ITV's chief commentator that might inspire a screen-printer to such devilish satire. Not the sanctimony or the funny gurgling noises at moments of excitement, surely.

One thing you could say about Tyldesley is that he is among our time's busier commentators, to the point where he appears to be jockeying unfashionably for a job on the radio, and when he comes out with a sentence such as 'Now he tries to slide it through to the full back,' he could be said to be providing illumination in a brightly lit room. I used to think this loquaciousness, which is somehow exclusive to ITV's commentators, had to do with the fact that they didn't get under the spotlight all that often, having only the Champions League games to work with, so they had to make the most of it when they did. But in the World Cup, these people are on pretty much every other night. They could afford to relax.

Actually, right now they've got no choice but to relax, and neither have we. Let's struggle through this dark time together, occupy ourselves as best we can, and hope to come out intact on the other side.

The break in the action from Germany was, of course, unacceptable and entirely avoidable, but there have been some positive outcomes. For instance, no one has been sent off for almost forty-eight hours now, which ought to bring the daily average down a bit. Also, there is every chance that, with the benefit of rest and recuperation, the feeling may have returned to Mick McCarthy's extremities.

You may remember that when we left the BBC's blunt-as-a-sausage match summarizer, Ukraine and Switzerland were between them contriving to produce the dullest game of the tournament after England *v.* Trinidad and Tobago, with potentially lethal consequences, inevitably, for those in the commentary box. And sure enough, after a long and worrying period of radio silence, McCarthy abruptly announced, 'R've gon nom', a phrase which, when later scrutinized by specially flown-in translators, was broadly accepted to mean, 'I've gone numb.'

A couple of days in a darkened hotel room, though, and McCarthy may even be getting a little tingle as the quarter-finals loom. Come to think of it, maybe all of us will benefit, energy-wise, from the break, which has allowed us among other things to go two whole days without hearing Steve Rider issue the dread words, 'Let's get the latest from the England camp.'

Ah, those reports from Baden-Baden. Cue Gabriel Clark standing shiftily in some trees with, off in the distance, a building which may or may not be England's hotel. And then cue a close-up of, say, Rio Ferdinand, propped up in front of an advertising hoarding and explaining to the world's press why playing badly is actually part of a cunning masterplan that will lead eventually to global domination.

Small wonder some conspiracy theorists believe these pictures aren't coming from Germany at all, but are entirely mocked up by the FA, under conditions of intense secrecy, in a studio in Southall, the evidence for this being the general air of unreality and the fact that Clark's lips don't seem to move when he's talking.

For me, though, such theories founder on the mighty figure of Garth Crooks, the BBC's official England-botherer, who, let's face it, could not be made up. For Germany 2006, Garth is experimenting with a whole new range of supplementary hand gestures, the like of which we have not seen from anybody on television before, with the result that this most extravagant of performers seems to be simultaneously signing his reports for the deaf, or, as may be, the gently snoozing.

Crooks ended an interview with Steve McClaren, Sven-Goran Eriksson's agreed successor, the other day by stating that he was looking forward to 'crossing swords' with the next England coach in the coming months, and it is, indeed, a joust to be relished – the self-styled D'Artagnan of the mixed zone versus the FA's very own ginger Zorro. Book now, folks.

One other small blessing from the tournament hiatus: Graham Poll didn't have to hurry home from Stansted yesterday to avoid missing the highlights. As predicted, FIFA told 'Britain's dopiest ref' (the *Sun*) to pack his whistle and scram and, according to news reports, poor Polly is now 'considering his future'.

Heaven forbid, though, that he should resign on the back of this solitary humiliation. On the contrary, if he acts media-smart, it could be the making of him. Think Hugh Grant after he was copped for kerb-crawling, or George Michael after that business in the gents. Poll should steel himself and do the chatshows – Richard and Judy, Des and Mel, Jonathan and Ross – taking care to laugh the incident off, fling up his hands and make copious play with the sentence 'What *was* I thinking of?' He should then, possibly, release a single – 'It Don't Mean A Thing If You Don't Come From Tring', maybe.

Graham: call me. I'm pretty sure I can see a way out of this.

*

There were some early candidates for yellow cards yesterday afternoon in Berlin, I felt – players whose offences would have commanded a routine caution under the new, tighter regulations we have been experiencing in Germany. On the Argentina side, for example, there was Juan Pablo Sorin (hair too long) and Hernan Crespo (shorts too high), while Germany had Bastian Schweinsteiger (silly name) and Jens Lehmann (nothing specific, but just generally rubbing people up the wrong way).

As it happened, though, the referee was amazingly relaxed, booking just one player in the whole of the first half. I don't know whether he could actually get ITV on that headset he was wearing, but this is exactly how David Pleat was telling him he should run things. 'He must referee it as sensibly as possible,' Pleat said – a blindingly brilliant recommendation, and a corrective for any referee thinking, 'I know: I'm going to go out there and officiate like a giddy goat on stimulants.'

The assumption throughout the coverage of this tournament has been that we will get a little anxious if we are obliged to go through more than an hour of World Cup television without getting a confirmatory report that the England hotel is still standing. Personally, I think we see enough of these players in the commercial breaks, what with Steven Gerrard kicking his Pringles about in a car park (not recommended, I would say, unless you like your crisps crunched up to look like something that's come out of the Hoover), and David Beckham carefully shaving his golden cheeks (not those ones), not to mention Owen Hargreaves looking mean, moody and magnificent on behalf of Calvin Klein underpants.

OK, I made that Hargreaves one up. Even so, I think it's fair to say that our incidental face-time with England personnel, even on days when England aren't playing, means we are not particularly at risk of forgetting them.

Still, ITV did at least widen the scope ahead of the quarter-final against Portugal by bringing on Ray Winstone, the film actor, who seems to have been appointed unofficial motivation expert to the national side, in these critical times. The post

wasn't advertised but there appears to be a feeling that, with
Sven in charge of England's morale, the players could use a
supplementary, freelance boost from a deeply menacing man
with a frightening haircut who can give it some cockney oik.

Asked how he would motivate a player like Wayne Rooney,
Winstone, who was clad in a replica England shirt, looked
directly into our living rooms for added effect and said, throatily,
'No one strikes the ball as cleanly as you – and Steven Gerrard
and Frank Lampard.' Hang on – that's two other people who
strike the ball as cleanly as Wayne. Over-complication in the
final third! You're losing him, Ray, you're losing him.*

In search of further succour, ITV visited Michael Owen at
home. The interview was shot in the now obligatory, impatient,
MTV style, with the camera closing in tight on Owen's teeth,
performing a rapid pan along his eyebrows, occasionally peering
into his ear canal. They'll be doing a nit-check next.

Nevertheless, it was good to see ITV exploring the channels,
as it were, because in other respects their coverage is staunchly
defensive. In Germany *v.* Argentina they had a clash of super-
powers to serve us. So whom did they pick to sit alongside the
eerily smiling Steve Rider and set the scene? Sam Allardyce,
Andy Townsend and Ally McCoist – an Englishman, an
Irishman and a Scotsman. It sounds like the beginning of a bad
joke, and I'm afraid it worked out a bit that way, too.

I have seen the incident replayed a thousand times and reproduced, over and over, in photographs. I have pored over the
evidence submitted by countless lip-readers, both amateur and
professional. And I have absorbed the competing and slightly
shifting public claims made since the event by its protagonists,

---

* Even with Winstone for inspiration, England couldn't beat Portugal. Wayne
Rooney ended up stamping on Ricardo Carvalho's genitals and the team lost
on penalties, thereafter flying home into a wide and lasting storm of scorn
from the nation which, among other things, ruined the commercial possibilities
for a large number of pre-written autobiographies.

not to mention the account rendered by the mother of one of the protagonists.

Yet, even after all that, I have read no more plausible or compelling a description of what was actually said by Marco Materazzi to Zinedine Zidane in the World Cup – just before the latter headbutted the former and was sent off in ignominy – than the one circulated widely by e-mail this week: 'There's a wasp on your head.'

Summarizing the shimmering opportunity a World Cup provides, shortly before Italy lifted the trophy Mick McCarthy had put it well. 'No better stage, mate.' True enough. Ask Zidane. But who, among the golden generation of broadcasters in Germany these last five weeks, truly found it within themselves to rise and grace that stage?

Not Ian Wright on the BBC, I would say, whose tribute to Sven-Goran Eriksson's substitution technique ('I'm just here crapping myself what he's going to do at half-time') was accounted a new low for publicly funded sports analysis.

Others tried harder – Peter Drury, for instance, who seems better placed than anyone alive to lead football commentary back to the formal eloquence that it last enjoyed during the Restoration. At one point, the ITV commentator dipped his quill and said, 'The defensive talisman of the Ivorian elephants is a little discomfited at the moment.' Ian Wright would have said, 'That Ivory Coast centre half is crapping himself.' You take your choice.

What is unarguably clear, post-Germany, is that we have reached the point where, in terms of simple wordage, television commentary can no longer be distinguished from radio commentary. This is now officially the age of the gabfest and Clive Tyldesley, in particular, seems to think a pregnant pause is an expectant cat.

In this competitively noisy context, the men who shone in Germany were not the big-time Charlies (the Tyldesleys, the John Motsons, the Jonathan Pearces) but the squad players – your Steve Wilsons, your Guy Mowbrays: modest illuminators, naturally disinclined to poach the occasion's glory with a status-enhancing punchline.

In the studios and pitch-side booths, it was in the main a miserable World Cup for the pundits. The historians of Germany 2006 will argue long and hard about which object at the tournament was less worth the effort of packing: Sven-Goran Eriksson's tactical whiteboard or Leonardo.* True, Alan Hansen worked diligently in the 'shaded areas' – a computer graphic used in the main to show large pieces of pitch with no England players in them. But that alone could not prevent the nation's traditional, mildly irked resistance to punditry boiling up into something much uglier and possibly permanent this time.

Accordingly, it may seem perverse right now to argue for *more* pundits. But bigger squads would, at the very least, have allowed for increased rotation and lessened the build-up of irritation in the sitting rooms.

As it was, both ITV and BBC had their set line-ups for the big occasions (the Hansen/Shearer/Wright formation, the Venables/McCoist/Townsend combo), with the result that a lot of pundits were taking their selection for granted and nobody seemed to be playing for their place. The heights of spread-legged complacency reached by Alan Shearer in particular, in his BBC chair, suggest that it will be some months before he manages to get up again, and presumably they will be putting the Geordie legend on a plane today with that chair still clamped to his thighs.†

On a sunnier note, the person most often seen in close-up was Franz Beckenbauer (24,312 shots), followed by Victoria Beckham (21,256 shots), with, in third place, the official Adidas World Cup 2006 ball (19,798 shots). I used to wonder about the purpose served by those full-screen ball shots, until my children began to pester me for the £15 replica version, at which point the scales fell from my eyes. No better stage, mate.

---

* Brazilian hunk, paid to sit still and smoulder, in the manner made famous in earlier tournaments by David 'Because I'm Worth It' Ginola.

† A year later, Shearer was forced to weigh the merits of media work against the merits of a proper job. Tough call. See p. 375.

Whatever anyone says about World Cups, humankind has yet to devise a more efficient way of making five weeks seem like forty-eight hours. Now what are we supposed to do? There's nothing left but to lie down in one of Hansen's shaded areas and dream of South Africa 2010, all the while mulling a trenchant prediction made by McCarthy: 'Four years from now, you'll see a World Cup with no physical contact at all.'

I'm not sure we will, actually. But bring it on, anyway. And, in the meantime, eh, Roberto – pass the Pringles.

Why Shouldn't England Fly EasyJet Like Everyone Else?

This week's reports that British Airways may no longer volunteer for the honour of carrying the mighty England football team and its equally mighty FA entourage were designed to paint a humiliating picture. Dumped on by Portugal and then snubbed by their own airline – could there be a more graphic measure of the dismal public and commercial standing of the Three Lions project since its low-watt showing in the World Cup?

Of course, it turns out that BA's arrangement with England is merely due to end in a couple of weeks, and, for all anyone knows, the company may once again at that point see the brand-enhancing value of offering Owen Hargreaves a business class seat and a complimentary copy of *Highlife* and renew. And even if they don't, BA is, allegedly, looking at ways to cut costs at the moment, so it will probably be about streamlining the business rather than about taking a dim view of Frank Lampard's recent inability to hit a German barn door.

Nevertheless, the fact that the BA deal is up for renewal inspires one to see an opportunity here, and a moment in time that Steve McClaren at the onset of his reign would do well to seize. For we can see nothing but benefit accruing to the national team if in future England routinely flew easyJet out of Stansted.

I know; it's not what they're used to. Indeed, by all accounts, no team at the 2006 World Cup lived as high on the hog as England did. While Argentina manfully billeted themselves in a glorified Travelodge on the edge of an industrial estate, England lorded it in the leafy remoteness of an astronomically pricey hotel and spa facility, with round-the-clock aqua therapy opportunities and hot-stone massages on demand.

The official thinking behind this extravagance appeared to be that multimillionaire Premiership footballers have their standards and that it would destroy the confidence of, for instance, Steven Gerrard, to spend so much as a month away from expensively marbled bathroom surfaces and a daily-replenished wicker basket of gratis skincare products, just because his country asked him to.

Unofficially, of course, one noted that the FA executives who plotted England's trip were destined to get their heads down in the same spot, and, as historians would attest, those people certainly know a jolly when they see one.

But either way, the result was embarrassment – five-star accommodation for a three-star team, run by a two-bit organization. And the problem was that, each time England failed to impress, they did so, unavoidably, against the background of this presidential cosseting. England revealed themselves against Ecuador to be no more competent than a mid-table League One side. Yet the supporter at home knew that, within a matter of hours, the players would be back inside their deluxe compound, living like Romans and padding about on the terrace in monogrammed towelling robes and sponsored flip-flops. Little wonder public feeling so rapidly hardened against them.

Would somewhere a touch less ostentatious have hurt? Somewhere with thinner towels and slightly substandard lavatory paper? It didn't seem to hurt Italy, or France, or Portugal or even Germany, all of whom went further in the competition than England while staying in worse hotels. Not that any of those teams stayed in bad hotels, exactly. But they did stay in the sort of hotels that touring football teams stay in when they aren't saddled with cosmic delusions about their status.

Still, a revolution in the way England conducts itself could start now, and it could start with the choice of airline. By the simple expedient of selecting easyJet, and perhaps agreeing to do his own bookings online, McClaren would, at a stroke, put the national team back in touch with its supporters – unavoidably so on the Stansted terminal transit, which can get pretty crowded at peak times.

True, there is no allocated seating on easyJet, which tends to make boarding a bit of a scrum. Yet even here there lies a bonus, because inadvertently the situation would yield, at last, a copper-bottomed reason for including in the national squad an utterly untested teenage striker. For even the budget airlines tend to offer a courtesy pre-boarding period 'for those travelling with small children', meaning that, with a Theo Walcott figure in the party, McClaren and the squad could be waved through early and have their choice of seating on a practically empty plane.

Having moved England on to a low-cost footing airline-wise, McClaren could then begin the process of downgrading hotel accommodation, before bringing about – by 2008, say, and the European Championships – the switching of the air-conditioned team bus for a couple of Transits. It could be the move for which he is remembered, forging a stronger connection between team and nation and, importantly, guaranteeing less derisive criticism when it all goes pear-shaped.

We stand, then, trembling on the brink of a new budget-class era for England – an era of hope, most certainly. And who could argue that McClaren – himself the beneficiary of a cost-cutting exercise to the extent that the FA clearly wouldn't have minded whom they got, as long as he was cheaper than Sven-Goran Eriksson – is not self-evidently the man to lead us there?

Ashley Cole and the Wild Mushroom Tartlet

Oh, to have been a scattered rose petal on the floor at the wedding of Ashley Cole, of Arsenal and England, to Cheryl Tweedy, of Newcastle and Girls Aloud. Oh, to have been a deluxe canapé on a waiter's silver salver at the stately home reception – a 'wild mushroom tartlet', maybe, or one of the 'Thai beef salads on a tempura coconut fritter'. The sights one would have seen, the things one would have heard, at what *OK!* magazine is calling 'the celebrity wedding of the year'.

As it is, those of us who were not among the chosen ones must merely press our grubby noses against *OK!*'s exclusive window pane and see the magic unfold across thirty-one pages of this week's issue, offering (count 'em) thirty-nine full-colour photos of the industrious left back on the day he plighted his fairy tale-tastic troth. Talk about covering the subject from every angle – although, as so often on these big magazine occasions, one doesn't feel one is thumbing through the wedding album so much as poring over the photographer's contact sheets from which the happy couple will later make a selection of the good ones.

All the details are here, though – the rings, the flowers, the colours of the ushers' waistcoats, the choice of processional music (Alicia Keyes), plus those all-important canapés in full. Well, almost in full. The 'salt and pepper squid' was, evidently, wrapped in 'Asian newspaper cones', but we are not told which particular Asian newspaper.

For Ashley, Roberto Cavalli, the designer, came up with a wedding ensemble so shiny you could shave in it – a 'beige, single-breasted tailcoat suit with cream silk lapels and a cream satin tuxedo strip on the trousers'. Seen full length and from the side, the defender looks endearingly like an unusually self-conscious roll of Bacofoil, at least in this respect confirming the wedding planner's touching impression of him as 'so down to earth'.

As for the guests – my dear, simply everyone was there

who wasn't on holiday. David and Victoria Beckham sent their apologies and the mother of one of them. Or, as *OK!* put it, using the correct Court and Social protocol, 'The Beckham family were represented by David's mother, Sandra.' Of the 'Boys of 06', meanwhile, only Sol Campbell appears to have been present, with Jermaine Pennant flying the flag for the lower orders.

How different the spread would have looked, though, if a few members of the England squad hadn't consulted their diaries and found that they were busy holidaying. Had these photographs thronged with World Cup underachievers, swathed in pricey clobber and grinning broadly, the spectacle would have seemed, like one of Ashley and Cheryl's lamb shashlik skewers marinated with Chinese honey, sesame and Szechwan peppercorns, a bit rich. This, after all, is the first time a member of this 'golden generation' of England footballers has been seen larging it in a celebrity slobber-mag since the various humiliations in Germany, and it would be hard not to notice the deflationary effect.

It happened too late for Cole, of course, whose wedding plans and supporting publicity deals were already in place, but one wonders whether one of the unlooked-for consequences of England's feeble, expectation-adjusting showing this summer might be to undermine, however temporarily, the plausibility of footballers as the subjects of thirty-one-page wedding exclusives. Had England won the World Cup, or even gone down in a blaze of glory, one might have read of the globe-conquering left back setting off in 'a Victorian-style ivory carriage upholstered in ivory leather and drawn by a pair of rare Glad Ruby white horses' and happily accepted that he was seizing his due as an eternal star in the sporting firmament. As it is, he simply looks a tit. Cruel game, football.*

* The course of true love never did run smooth, even with a liberal sprinkling of Szechwan peppercorns – and perhaps especially with one of those – and in January 2008 the Cole alliance was rocked by newspaper allegations of infidelity on the male side. Ashley Cole, a two-timer: who'd have thought?

Lean Times Ahead for Sacked Villa Boss

So, David O'Leary leaves Aston Villa 'by mutual consent'. He
has been in charge for three years, the last two of which have
seen the club in a slump that the manager has shown little sign
of being able to arrest. His achievements within the job have
included the mastery of the dismally self-exculpatory post-match
interview, and a number of other things we're sure, although
nothing else that springs immediately to mind.

He has certainly not won any trophies, although at the end
of his third year, he took substantial steps towards managing the
previously unthinkable feat of replacing the chairman as the
focus of the supporters' anger. So comically uncertain did his
position eventually become within the club's political hierarchy
that he was forced to deny the charge that he secretly encouraged
the players to slag off the chairman to a local newspaper journalist.

So what, then, would be the fitting end to this less than
dizzyingly brilliant reign? A light pelting with soft fruit by
season-ticket holders of particularly long standing? A period of
penitential community service in the Birmingham area? No. A
pay-off to the alleged value of £2 million. Which can be added
to the alleged pay-off of £3.8 million that O'Leary received
when it all went pear-shaped at Leeds United. Making a grand
total of £5.8 million for doing two separate football clubs the
favour of going away. We should all be football managers. We're
mad to be anything else.

England Fly Back through Time

It would be no exaggeration to say that recent events have
somewhat overtaken ITV's *Luton Airport*. Filmed at the start of
the summer, this gentle docusoap about daily life in and around
the check-in desks of a typical British air terminus now appears
to depict a golden era of travel in which passengers in manageable

numbers flow relatively smoothly towards on-schedule flights. No one is commanded to leave their copy of *The Da Vinci Code* in a specially provided dump-bin, nor consume their babies' carrot and turnip puree to prove that it won't blow up. It was a big moment in this week's episode when someone accidentally triggered a fire alarm. If only. Maybe the producers would consider preparing a DVD version of the series in sepia.

The waves of nostalgia started to come even more thickly when the programme showed the England football team passing through Luton on their way to Germany for the 2006 World Cup. Ah, the piercing memories, the aching innocence of those times. David Beckham leaned out of the pilot's window and waved the flag of St George above a sign reading 'Pride of the Nation' – an unthinkable liberty, given what we now know.

Also, this was back in the days when you could take Wayne Rooney on a British Airways Airbus A320 without having to place him in a clear plastic bag first. Days when inessential items of hand luggage, such as Theo Walcott, weren't automatically taken off you at the gate. Days when Sven-Goran Eriksson could turn up at the airport without guilt, even though his journey wasn't strictly necessary.

And then there were the onlookers, thronging the airport fence, their faces, fascinatingly from another era, shiny with anticipation and the thrill of it all. People whooped at the sight of the team bus, happy to catch even a glimpse of these outgoing heroes and to share with them this sense of being on the brink of greatness. It couldn't have looked more like archive footage if every bystander had been in a trilby and smoking.

I tried to explain to some nearby youngsters. 'You see, children, back then there was a real feeling in the land that this England side was capable of going all the way in the World Cup and bringing home the trophy for the first time in forty years.' But they weren't listening. They were too busy wondering why Rio Ferdinand hadn't been required to stow his iPod in the hold. In any case, bring home a big metal trophy on an aeroplane? As if.

ProZone – Your Questions Answered

Steve McClaren swears by it, Sir Clive Woodward reckoned it was indispensable and twelve out of twenty Premiership clubs have signed up for it in the 2006–07 season. We're talking about ProZone, the computerized data analysis system that's setting the football coaching world alight.

Want to know the exact total distance in kilometres run by Stewart Downing during England's friendly against Greece on Wednesday night? Want to see every movement made by Gary Neville reproduced in the form of a coloured arrow? Want to see Peter Crouch expressed as a graph? You'll be needing ProZone – or access to McClaren's briefcase where, every indication is, these critical statistics are now carefully filed.

Yet, even as its hold on the professional game tightens, and its disciples increase in number, mystery continues to shroud this leading-edge diagnostic tool – about how it works, about what it really tells us, and about exactly what the coaches do with all those hundreds of computer printouts when they have finished looking at them. Allow us, then, to settle your minds, dispel some of your anxieties and answer your most pressing questions to date about ProZone.

Do you need a prescription for ProZone, or can it be bought over the counter?
ProZone is freely available, in software and hardware form. McClaren first introduced the system during his time at Derby County and there is no evidence to suggest that he was under the doctor at the time.

How does ProZone function?
An elaborate system of cameras and sensors tracks the movements and actions of every player on the pitch, ultimately revealing the number and duration of their sprints, jogs and dribbles, the distance and destiny of their passes, and how much time they

spent getting in the face of the assistant referee. The information is then made available for analysis in highly confidential statistical printouts and in two-dimensional pictorial reconstructions, which tend to look to the untutored eye – and possibly even to the tutored one – like the onset of a particularly horrible migraine.

Can I get ProZone by pressing the red button on my remote?
Not yet. As of now, alternative red button services during foot-ball matches are mostly restricted to betting opportunities and fans shouting at each other in an unhelpful way. Occasionally, one of the more technically advanced television pundits will make an educational point using 'the electronic pen', which leaves a quivering white line, or 'snail-trail', across the screen. But these efforts stand in much the same relation to ProZone as cave paintings do to cinematography.

How much would it cost me to install my own ProZone system for 2006–07?
The best information is that £200,000 secures a full Premiership-style ProZone package for the coming campaign, though note that Carling Cup ties may not be included in the price. For some reason, people tend not to be particularly interested in analysing those.

Two hundred thousand pounds? Isn't this another example of the ordinary fan being priced out of the game?
Almost certainly. Eventually, of course, the technology will be broadly available, but in the meantime remember that, by using the more affordable DIY ProZone, it is perfectly possible to collect your own data for processing at a later stage.

Try, for instance, making a mark on a piece of paper every time your team scores and every time the other team does so. (You might want to divide the paper down the middle to make this easier.) Calculate and compare these totals at the end of the match. Use these figures to attain a readout on the efficiency and general standing of your team. Once the season has been running for a while, you may also wish to factor into your analysis your team's league position.

Eventually, supporters of a truly analytical bent who really want to get under the skin of the game may venture on to some of the more advanced forms of information-gathering. Does your central midfielder keep passing to someone in a different-coloured shirt? Does your expensively acquired winger seem more likely to pass to you, seated in the crowd, than to someone in a promising position in the penalty area? Are people around you shouting, 'For fuck's sake, get *back*, Drogba'? These are indications that the players in question may not be functioning to the optimum and you should log such details carefully in your personal files, prior to converting them into resentment.

How can I tell if my favourite player is on ProZone?
Many experts cite Rio Ferdinand as the classic example of a player who looks like he has been on ProZone for the best part of his career. We're not sure about that, but the tell-tale signs are a slight widening of the eyes and a hunted expression, consistent with understanding that every move you make is being monitored by cameras and sensors, and that deliberately getting muddy and making sure to breathe heavily at half-time no longer cut it as evidence of significant workrate at the highest levels of the game.

Does ProZone work for coaches, too?
Certainly – and the figures garnered from Steve McClaren's England debut at Old Trafford are already providing a fascinating insight into the ways of the new England coaching regime. When it came to shouting, for instance, McClaren made forty-six shouts, an impressive twenty-four of which were grammatic-ally complete sentences, eleven of which were inaudible and two of which were unprintable. The new coach also used his arms to make an undecipherable chopping-and-changing movement twenty-nine times and stood up and sat down fifty-one times.

All of these figures compare favourably with the statistics generated by Sven-Goran Eriksson's performance in the technical area in the last match of his reign, versus Portugal in the World Cup. (Shouts completed: 0. Undecipherable arm movements made: 0. Bench-rises attempted: 0.)

McClaren also registered a seventeen-fold increase over the previous incumbent in the use of facial muscles. These are widely thought to be encouraging signals, although remember that Kevin Keegan's ProZone numbers in this area were off the charts and everyone ended up thinking he was rubbish.

Why Does Everybody Keep Picking on Roo?

Sir Alex Ferguson certainly raises an interesting theory when he maintains that Wayne Rooney gets sent off, not for the acts of violence, but 'because of his name'. One has to wonder, though – is the name 'Wayne' that offensive these days? It's a perfectly acceptable name now, isn't it? OK, so perhaps among the more snobbish, unreconstructed referees, it might generate some kind of knee-jerk reaction and trigger jokes about car sun strips. But even then, in increasingly classless Britain, it would only be a yellow card, surely, and not a red.

Troubleshooting with Big Ron

A short while ago, the long and painful road to televisual forgiveness and a restored place in the nation's heart led Ron Atkinson to Provence, for the BBC's extraordinary celebrity language tuition show *Excuse My French*. It now brings the disgraced pundit to Peterborough for Sky One's equally bizarre and, in its own way, no less embarrassing *Big Ron Manager*. Surely even Big Ron must occasionally wonder, in his quieter moments, whether he wouldn't be better off staying at home in disgrace.

Within the bold remit of *Big Ron Manager*, Big Ron is the

sports world's Sir John Harvey-Jones. He is going to ease his Mercedes into the car park of a cash-strapped and malfunctioning lower league club, assess the damage from the Olympian heights afforded him by his experience in the game, effect a startling turnaround and leave with a wry smile and a shake of his lusciously tanned head.

Nice idea. In the event, though, Big Ron's very arrival precipitates all manner of chaos which could almost certainly have been avoided if he had driven his Mercedes straight past the gates. The programme's most hilarious caption labels Big Ron a 'Football Troubleshooter', which in this context is only accurate if we accept that a troubleshooter is someone who brings trouble with him and proceeds to shoot it all over the place.

In the now received style for reality makeover shows, the first episode of *Big Ron Manager* combined gritty fly-on-the-wall documentary observation with pieces of staged drama that would have looked implausibly camp even in the setting of a Spanish daytime soap. Witness the highly collectable scene wherein Big Ron got the alarm call from Barry Fry, the owner of Peterborough United, and promised to 'turn the car around' and get over there straight away.

Strangely unmentioned during this conversation, or at any other point, were the four weeks Big Ron and the cameras had already fruitlessly spent at Swindon Town before the manager, Iffy Onoura, saw exactly where all this was leading and respectfully asked them to leave and take their microphones and masking tape with them.

But that was then, obviously, and this was now. Fry greeted Big Ron like the old friend that he is, explaining that he had run out of money-making ideas. Not quite, he hadn't. Why, here was Big Ron and his cameras, presumably bringing along a handsome fee for their access.

Managing Peterborough at this point was Steve Bleasdale, a volatile Liverpudlian, promoted from coach after the departure of Mark Bright. One had seen, one had to admit, more firmly lashed cannons, and differences in style and approach from, say,

Arsene Wenger were quick to emerge. In rapid succession, during an away game at Notts County, we saw 'Bleo' offer to fight a lippy supporter and threaten to 'fookin' chin' the referee.

His pre-match talk in the dressing room was a homage to Alf Garnett, but also to Bob the Builder. 'Can you do it?' he bawled. 'Yes, you can.' Nevertheless, at the point at which Big Ron took Fry's call, Peterborough had won four of their last five matches and had entered the League Two play-off places, with thirteen games of the season remaining. Bleasdale seemed to be doing OK.

Enter Big Ron, though, and suddenly all sorts of insecurities and destabilizing uncertainties relating to authority arose. How could they not, with the chain of command now forced to accommodate a new link? Painfully, Bleasdale greeted Big Ron using the title 'gaffer'. 'No,' said Ron. 'I'm Ron. You're the boss, the boss of bosses.' This must have sounded encouraging to Bleasdale, but confusing at the same time. At any rate, there was room to wonder whether anyone who was genuinely 'the boss of bosses' would end up being asked to accept a made-for-television overseer, whose last managerial post ended seven years earlier, and who had spent much of the intervening period in the ITV commentary box, playing Eddie Large to Clive Tyldesley's Sid Little.

Sure enough, Bleasdale was soon feeling sorrowfully under mined, Big Ron was feeling spurned and valuable time and energy that might have been devoted to the team were going into distracting arguments about who was allowed in the dressing room and when. 'I'm not going to hang about corridors like a lollipop,' complained Big Ron, ruefully. One was witnessing, one realized, the first recorded attempt to steady a ship by blowing its bows off.

If you don't want to know the outcome, look away now. The outcome is a shipwreck. Observant viewers may already have noticed that Peterborough remain in League Two for 2006–07. Bleasdale walked out on the club in April, an hour before a match, declaring, 'I won't have four or five people picking the team.'

What madness all round. But its lesson may still be a pertinent one: money from television doesn't always help a club.

Scents and Sensibility

No surprise to find 'Intimately Beckham', the 'his and hers' perfume range launched by the Real Madrid midfielder and his wife, grabbing the scent-related headlines this season. 'Intimately Beckham For Her', we read in the press release, conveys 'the essence of the Victoria known only to the people closest to her', and 'opens with the pure fresh notes of bergamot and rose petals' before 'sensual orange blossom leads to a seductive base of voluptuous vanilla, rich sandalwood and an elegant layer of musk'.

By contrast, 'Intimately Beckham For Him', we learn, 'leads with the intense freshness and sparkle of bergamot, tangy grapefruit zest and zingy cardamom', and then gives way to 'a virile blend of nutmeg and star anise', before 'finishing down with warm sensual undertones of sandalwood, patchouli and amber'. All of which provides 'a heady mix of energy, vibrancy, comfort and warmth', projecting 'the edgy, sexy side of David'.

Sounds enticing. But what about some of the other fragrances that we're going to be wearing, in and around the stadiums, this year?

'Lava' by Roy Keane
Explosive debut scent, personally sourced by the incoming Sunderland manager, which boasts a wickedly dangerous head note of petrol and spent matches, middle tones of tangy grapefruit peel and prawn sandwich, finishing down with a base of wet Labrador. A real sock to the jaw, this abrasive confection actually foams on application. A special edition for sensitive skin, 'Lava for Muppets', comes online later in the year. In the meantime, nothing says 'take that, you cunt' quite so spectacularly as 'Lava', by Roy Keane. Refrigerate after opening.

'Possession' by Jose Mourinho

Painstakingly researched, ravishingly intimate and edgy but at the same time subtly guarded fragrance, going under the slogan 'Possession is nine tenths of the law', and designed to reflect not only the transition from defence to attack but, equally importantly, the transition from attack to defence. Suitable for a woman or a man. But they must have the attitude of champions. This is important. If they do not have the attitude of champions, they can sit in the reserves or go to Arsenal. Warning: repeated use may cause sudden and violent hair-shrinkage.

'Eau de Harry Redknapp'

Surprisingly durable, no-nonsense aftershave, blended from the produce of many countries, distilled on the south coast, and yet distinctively East End in aura. Available – bish bosh – from that bloke with a suitcase at Romford market. Or occasionally someone might come round the pub with some in a holdall. Tenner to you.

'Randy' by Martin O'Neill

All-new deodorant spray from the well-received 'Eau Neill' collection, launched when consumers finally ran out of patience with the 'House of Eau Leary'. A unique, 25-feet-tall pump-action dispenser releases across most of Birmingham an uplifting burst of lavender and wild rose, utterly intoxicating, embodying joy and relief, with – right at the very heart of the scent – the great smell of American money. Splash it all over.

'Clattered' by Craig Bellamy

Deeply energetic body spray, opening with a breathtaking salvo of diesel and Listerine, over a base of Cillit Bang kitchen cleanser intercut with used fire blanket, with just the slightest hint at the edges of lime Starburst. Some critics note a faintly unpleasant after-waft. Unusually thick, too, having, in fact, the consistency of fabric conditioner. But advocates insist this is a fragrance which never gives less than 100 per cent. Good, also, for shifting those difficult, burned-on stains. Comes in an innovative leg-tag container.

'Prone' by Michael Owen
Seemingly innocuous scent that, nevertheless, lays you out for a year. Also available, in packets of twelve, in steri-strip form and as a pre-fragranced support stocking.

'Forgotten' by Sven-Goran Eriksson
Handy Swedish odour-eater. Insert in your shoes and hey presto – nothing. Four and a half million pounds per year.

Dressing the Transfer Window

How was your transfer-window party? Did you throw your own, or go to someone else's? I'm assuming you did one thing or the other. The countdown to the shutting of the transfer window is, after all, the closest thing that football offers to sitting up on election night watching the results come in. 'Were you still up for Portillo?' people famously asked each other, after the Conservative-toppling election of 1997. Similarly, the question everybody was asking yesterday was, 'Were you still up for Ashley Cole?'*

Or maybe not. Somehow the closing of the transfer window doesn't grip us as it might. It's exciting, but one has the impression it ought to be more so. Take that Cole deal. I *wasn't* still up. I went to bed at midnight, when the transfer still hadn't been declared. Call me old-fashioned, but I assumed this meant it was now impossible. In the event, the 'official announcement' was not made until 1.25 a.m. Where's the fun in that? And what's the point of having a midnight deadline if people aren't actually running to beat it?

* The Arsenal left back completed a long-expected and rancour-inducing transfer to Chelsea, thus ending the intense personal agony of being on only about £50,000 a week.

The solution, it seems to me, is to create a far smaller window than the one currently on offer. Let's face it, on Thursday night, the excitement only really gathered in those last minutes, when the countdown clock thoughtfully organized by Sky Sports News was into double figures and a whole summer of transfer activity appeared to be boiling down to whether Chelsea and Arsenal had any ink in their photocopiers and whether Roy Keane would break the record for most players signed in the shortest space of time or explode first.

But imagine if those last minutes *were* the transfer window? At the moment, clubs get the whole summer, and another month in January. What if the window were twenty minutes annually? Think of the frantic action. Think of the panic and the highly televisual mayhem. Clubs would end up signing players by mistake – and then, when they realized, try to sell them on within the same window. And players, under the mistaken impression that they were signing for club A, would, in their confused haste, sign for club Y instead.

True, there wouldn't really be time, under this more stringent arrangement, for medicals. Good, though. That's another random element, right there. Has your club just spent £12.5 million on a player who is, technically speaking, missing a knee? Wait and see, folks. It's the thrill of the ride and the luck of the window, if the window were designed with drama in mind.*

---

* In a hectic trading period in the dying seconds of the January 2008 transfer window, Harry Redknapp, as manager of Portsmouth, bought Jermain Defoe from Tottenham with the money generated by the simultaneous sale of Benjani to Manchester City. Except the Benjani transfer wasn't completed in time, leaving Harry £8 million in the bunker. Now, that was the kind of drama we were looking for from a transfer window. Or it would have been if the Benjani transfer hadn't been completed a few days later, when the technicalities were ironed out. The transfer window may be less stiffly framed than any of us realize. In the end, if you are important enough, it may not really be a window at all – more an open-plan, flexible, walk-through area.

How to Get the Big-money Move You Always Wanted

Chelsea's extraordinary allegation that William Gallas was ready
to score an own goal if picked to play for the club, and therefore
needed to be bussed out to Arsenal at the earliest opportunity,
raises numerous urgent questions, not least among them, what
kind of own goal did Gallas have in mind? A scruffy and seemingly accidental deflection from a corner at some random
moment in the second half? Or a first-minute, forty-five-yard
solo run through a baffled defence, rounding the goalkeeper and
tucking the ball into the bottom corner, before wheeling away
in the direction of the Chelsea bench with his finger over his
lips? I'm thinking the latter. Gallas was, after all and by all
accounts, very keen to move.

Either way, this affair clearly has repercussions way beyond
the small cast of people involved. Straight away it casts into
suspicion, both in the future and retrospectively, all own goals.
Until this week, it was simple: an own goal was the occasion
among spectators for either unlimited hilarity or a particularly
excruciating form of despair, depending who scored it. We are
now obliged to judge whether that slightly overhit back pass
was a genuine misunderstanding or the frighteningly literal strike
action of a 'want-away' defender with the hump. The distinction
between basic incompetence and a desire for regular first team
football under Arsene Wenger is suddenly an extremely hard
one to draw.

Overall, the art of agitating for a move has bounded so far
ahead in this single incident that from now on, when the topic
of wanting away comes up, it will probably make sense to speak
of the eras pre- and post-Gallas. Clearly, in a world in which
players are opting out of pre-season tours and threatening large-
scale on-pitch sabotage, it is no longer enough merely to get
your agent to feed the press a few feebly destabilizing lines about
'interest' from Spain.

Nevertheless, the political wisdom of Chelsea's unprecedented retrospective disclosure in this matter has looked highly questionable this week. 'Why do they have to wash their dirty linen in public?' wondered Gordon Taylor, the chief executive of the Professional Footballers Association. To which Chelsea appear to be saying that they acted in self-defence. According to the club's statement on Gallas, 'Despite leaving, he continues to attack Jose Mourinho and this cannot be left unchallenged.' Yet I've looked around for a major, public, post-Chelsea, dirt-dishing Gallas interview – 'Jose Mourinho kept me in a basement and made me call him master,' or some such – but so far in vain. Maybe the attacks were more private than that, in which case perhaps they could have been defended more privately, too.

Nevertheless, openness also has its value, and if Chelsea had not gone public on Gallas, we would all be in a state of dangerous innocence, blithely unaware of the lengths to which today's players are allegedly prepared to go in order to wriggle out of their contracts. And if every club adopted Chelsea's policy, and issued official clarifying statements each time they sold someone, we might arrive at the truth behind many more recent big moves.

Craig Bellamy, Blackburn Rovers to Liverpool

'Blackburn Rovers feels that it owes it to the club's supporters to point out that the sale of Craig Bellamy followed the player's persistent and, in the club's view, deliberate invasion of the manager's personal space. Shortly after Liverpool's interest in Bellamy became known, the player began to make a point of standing extremely and unnecessarily close to Mark Hughes during training ground briefings, while waiting for the team bus and in many other day-to-day situations. Hughes repeatedly asked the player if he "wouldn't mind stepping back a bit", and although the player readily complied, it was noted that before very long he had sidled back to his original proximity. Hughes eventually deemed this situation not just uncomfortable but unworkable, and brought the matter to the attention of the board who agreed to release Bellamy to Liverpool for a fee in the region of £6 million.'

Damien Duff, Chelsea to Newcastle United
'Season-ticket holders should be aware that, ahead of the penulti-mate game of the 2005–06 season, during which the player had struggled to hold down a regular first-team place, Duff was found to be in possession of – in direct contravention of club rules – a whoopee cushion. He also had about his person at this time materials suitable for the manufacture and launching of paper pellets. In the club's opinion, it was the player's express intention to employ the said whoopee cushion and related materials for the purpose of undermining the manager's auth-ority. Inevitably, this was felt to be untenable, and talks opened immediately with prospective buyers.'

Jose Antonio Reyes, Arsenal to Real Madrid
'That Reyes wished for a prompt return to Spanish football is well documented. What supporters may not be aware of is the disappointing manner with which the player sought to force Arsenal's hand in this regard – namely, by repeating everything that Arsene Wenger said. "Don't copy me," Wenger would say. "Don't copy me," Reyes would reply. "I'm not going to tell you again," Wenger would say. "I'm not going to tell you again," Reyes would reply. Naturally, the coach grew extremely irritated with this situation and, following consultation with the board, it was decided that the club had no option but to release Reyes from the terms of his contract forthwith.'

Ruud van Nistelrooy, Manchester United to Real Madrid
'Manchester United would like it to be known, in the interests of full disclosure, that van Nistelrooy had a habit of hiding in the cupboard in the manager's office and then abruptly jumping out, causing the manager sometimes to cry out in shock. Van Nistelrooy also once concealed himself beneath a tartan blanket in the back of the manager's car, waited until the vehicle was

underway, with the manager at the wheel, and then leapt up, shouting "a-haargh!", causing the manager to brake violently and swerve, narrowly avoiding a collision with a bus shelter. Matters reached a head during the pre-season tour of South Africa when, as the manager lay in his hotel bed reading, van Nistelrooy burst from the wardrobe, swathed in a white sheet. Subsequent to this, Manchester United reluctantly took the decision to sell van Nistelrooy abroad.'

The Price We Pay for Football

According to someone with a calculator and a spare half hour at Virgin Money, the cost to the supporter of a lifetime of football-following is just short of £100,000. That's a ballpark figure, of course – or, as we should probably say these days, an out-of-town stadium figure. But, assuming an adult supporter's lifetime to be fifty-two years, and including tickets and travel, home and away, Virgin Money reckon the dedicated fan will almost break six figures investing in his or her habit.

I think what we're all meant to do at this point is honk '£100,000!', throw up our hands in despair, emit a high, keening wail on behalf of the so-called 'people's game' and wheel out our memories of a time when tuppence bought you a grandstand seat and a programme, and still left you enough over for fish and chips on the way home and the down payment on a Morris Cambridge.

Then again, when you think about it, £100,000 actually sounds quite reasonable. It's a lot of money, obviously – especially considered in a big lump like that. But you've got to factor in inflation. And you've also got to ask yourself, what does £100,000 buy you these days? For instance, it is now over-whelmingly clear that, at 2006 rates, £100,000 won't reliably secure two weeks' work from Ashley Cole. Indeed, if you even suggest the idea, he goes ballistic at the sheer effrontery of the notion and writes a book. Now, what looks more reasonable –

a fortnight's industry from the easily hurt left back or a lifetime of memories, some of them quite good?

Or consider it from a literary point of view. Plausible sources indicate that Wayne Rooney will receive £5 million for the five-volume masterwork he intends to complete over the course of his career. Volume one recently came in at 311 pages, including index. Assuming that his rate of production remains stable for the course of the contract, Wayne is on £3,215.43 per page. Is anyone going to tell me that fifty-two years of engagement with a football club, with all that it entails in the way of storylines and human drama, isn't worth a little over thirty-one pages of prose from Wayne?

Or let's put it in an even broader context. As a fraction of the UK defence budget for 2005–6 alone (£30,945 million according to 'UK Defence Statistics 2005'), £100,000 across a lifetime is clearly loose change – coins down the sofa. It would barely run to the exhaust pipe on a tank. Football supporting is also a politically neutral, pacifist activity. Well, in some cases.

What else could you spend £100,000 on in a lifetime? Ten extremely basic loft conversions? But think of the upheaval. One good thing about football: no dust. A hundred thousand pounds would also buy four top-spec Ford Mondeos. A lifetime of happy motoring, perhaps, but in a really boring car. Can anyone seriously suggest that a lifetime of football isn't worth that much? At least football is exciting *some* of the time.

How about essential foodstuffs? Even here the cost of football-supporting can look eagerly competitive. Assuming the price of a two-pint carton of semi-skimmed milk to be 64p (source: Sainsbury's), £100,000 would enable you to bring home 156,250 cartons of milk. But that's a heck of a lot of milk. You'd be bored with milk, in a way that you rarely are with football. And some of it would go off.

Here's the clincher, though. According to 'Family Spending 2005', a report by the Office of National Statistics, the average household spends £15 per week on insurance. That's £40,560 over a fifty-two-year period. In other words, the dedicated supporter spends only twice as much on football as everyone else gives away to insurance companies, only to discover, when their televisions get stolen, that there's a £250 excess that they didn't know about and that the effect of claiming will be to boost their premium at the next time of asking by a sum slightly larger than the amount claimed.

One sympathizes entirely with Malcolm Clarke, the chairman of the hugely valuable Football Supporters' Federation, who responded to the publication of Virgin Money's lifetime figure by saying, 'We need a new deal for the match-going supporter.' At the same time, in the context of insurance payments, one can't help but conclude that the dedicated football fan is getting a right old bargain.

My feeling, however, is that Virgin Money's £100,000 may be, if anything, a little on the shy side. The company says that its figure includes an allowance for club merchandise. I don't see how it can do – not given the vast and ingenious expansion that we have seen in that area over the last decade. There was famously a period when the Chelsea Megastore, for example, was offering a moped in club colours at £2,500. People are always on about the price of replica shirts, but wait until your kids start nagging you for replica vehicles.

Accordingly, my own calculations are based on a decent run in the Champions League and at least one visit to Cardiff (necessitating the inevitable purchase of pirated flags), followed by a pre-season tour of the Far East, where even a cup of tea can cost £26. My sum also allows for full accessorizing – including clothing, keyrings, mousemats and automobiles – along the way.

As a result of which, I arrive at something closer to £23,452 per annum, including half-time KitKats. That's £1,219,504 across the stipulated lifetime period. Steep? Possibly. But it still looks like pretty good value to me, relatively speaking. At any rate, it's a mere 390th of what it cost Arsenal to put up the Emirates Stadium. And you could always cut out the KitKats, maybe.

Of course, the report really worth conducting would be into

the cost to the lifetime supporter in emotional terms, rather than in purely material ones. But isn't that typical of the moneymen? Always thinking of the bottom line.

In Defence of the Penalty Shoot-out

Even as Sepp Blatter rounded on the penalty shoot-out this week, his words betrayed him. 'When it comes to the World Cup final, it is passion,' the president of FIFA, in one of his reliably amusing and now pretty much fortnightly sound-offs, explained. 'And when it goes to extra time, it is a drama. But when it comes to penalty kicks, it is a tragedy.'

A tragedy? Exactly. The highest form of theatre known to man. Long may the game give us penalty shoot-outs. Argument over.

Except that's not what he meant, of course. Blatter now belatedly joins those who believe the penalty shoot-out is 'no way to decide a football match', and certainly not a match as important as the World Cup final.

On the contrary, it is a brilliant way to decide a football match – any football match. At any rate, it is the best way that anyone has come up with to decide a football match that couldn't be settled by 120 minutes of football.

You only have to start considering the alternatives to realize exactly how brilliant the penalty shoot-out is. Coin tossing, as in days of yore? Too casual – almost dismissive. Awarding the match on the basis of corners won / shots taken / goals scored throughout the tournament? Depends how enthralling you find the thought of someone deciding a game with a calculator. Paper, scissors, stone? A bit complicated for some captains. A game of Kerplunk between the managers? As good an alternative as any.

Or given the FIFA president's publicly acknowledged predilection for body-hugging sportswear (you will remember his gallant assertion in 2005 that the women's game would gain immeasurably by the shrinking of a few kits here and there), perhaps the trophy could go to the team with the tightest shorts. (Result, if retrospectively applied to the 2006 World Cup final: a veritable romp home for the Italians. Why, if memory serves, the French barely turned up, in tight shorts terms.)

Blatter vaguely mentioned the hoary possibility of readopting the golden goal and systematically withdrawing players from the pitch to induce its arrival. But how would that work? The sight of ever fewer players chasing each other around an ever more open pitch would end up looking like something from *The Benny Hill Show*. We know Blatter doesn't want tragedy. Would he really prefer farce?

Better, surely, to stick with the high art and handsome ritual of the shoot-out. The prospect is many things – gruelling, harrowing, behind-the-sofa horrible – but it is never boring. The fact is that thirty-six years of history since it was invented can only produce one example of an unexciting penalty shoot-out – Ukraine versus Switzerland in the World Cup of 2006, when the Swiss confirmed their reputation for stultifying caution by showing themselves reluctant to put men in the box even for a penalty. (They missed three kicks in a row, while Ukraine were scoring all of theirs, diminishing the inherent drama somewhat.)

Yet, even accounting for that solitary blip, the shoot-out stands unchallenged as (and this, at least, you would think, would interest Blatter) an audience-winner. Even people who don't really click with football get the penalty shoot-out. Television-viewing figures routinely swell for shoot-outs, indicating that though people may dismiss them in the abstract, very few find them a turn-off in practice. And in all honesty, what else would fans of England have to talk about in their absence?

The consequences are, of course, grotesquely painful for the loser. But even there, the penalty shoot-out works its magic, granting the defeated team and its supporters a cushion of consolation ('well, it was a lottery, wasn't it?') of a plumpness that is quite simply unavailable to sufferers of the standard, open-play defeat.

And yet, amazingly, Blatter has indicated that an alternative arrangement could be in place as soon as the next World Cup, in South Africa in 2010. One weeps at the grim thought of the shoot-out's passing, even as one trembles to imagine what they might replace it with. Frankly, we won't feel even remotely consoled until we know that at least three of the following five potential solutions are jostling for serious consideration on the FIFA deadlock-releasing agenda.

1. Bumper cars: revival of the playground classic in which everyone has to fold their arms across their chests and then hop around, banging into each other. Fall over or leave the designated area (the centre circle would lend itself most obviously) and you're out. Last player standing clinches the World Cup on behalf of his grateful nation.

2. The Lotto Extra method: a big, ornate Perspex machine containing all sorts of not strictly necessary gubbins and given an antique and slightly alarming girl's name, is wheeled on to the pitch at the end of extra-time and randomly pumps out six numbered balls and one Thunderball. The team matching the most numbers with the squad numbers of the players left on the pitch at full time, triumphs. In the event of a tie, the World Cup simply rolls over to next time. Could feature Ian Wright in some capacity. Or Anthea Turner, if Wright is unavailable.

3. Phone vote: viewers call in and, at a cost of around 48 pence, say who they would like to win the World Cup. Has its drawbacks, not least with regard to democratic transparency, but is these days the method used to decide almost every other matter of significance to our lives, so why not?

4. Cock fight. Advantage: definitely no such thing as a draw here. Disadvantage: illegal.

5. Riot: fans of the opposing sides spill on to the pitch and fight it out. Highly popular as an unofficial game-settling device in

South America, and had its moments in English football during the 1970s and 80s, but is now rarely seen, except when Cardiff are involved. Spectacular television, though. And the pundits have a field day.

What Today's Busy Manager is Wearing

High praise, as ever, from the fashion world for Frank Rijkaard. For Chelsea, the Barcelona coach was wearing a black, waist-hugging, tailored suit jacket, emblazoned across the back in gold with the legend 'Sacoor – Prestige' – a reference to the company that supplies suits to the Barcelona football team.

This unconventional, boundary-pushing outfit was felt to fuse a fun and frothy splash of High Street bling with the earthy, workaday feel of a milkman's overall – the whole ensemble given a very twenty-first-century spin by those almost ruthlessly strong commercial overtones. Many commentators are still fanning themselves cool and hailing the world's first designer sandwich board.

Not everybody loved it, though. In a cruel blow for touchline menswear, and fashion-as-art in general, UEFA officials requested that Rijkaard remove this future-embracing garment at half-time. The Dutchman came out for the second half in a jacket that was entirely without gold lettering. Or any other kind of lettering. It was just (can you believe it?) a jacket.

UEFA's issue, as far as we have been able to establish, was not with gold logos on tailored jackets *per se* – although there are undeniably important arguments to be had in that area. An objection arose apparently because the logo in question did not belong to one of the Champions League's official 'sponsorship partners', who pay an awful lot of money for exclusive exposure on these occasions.

Had Rijkaard's jacket borne the logo of PlayStation 2, say, or Vodafone, he could almost certainly have worn it with impunity for the full ninety minutes, although it should be noted that, in the latter case, he would have been open to the risk of someone stopping him in the tunnel to ask about switching to the Anytime 350 package and to request a phone upgrade.

Even with Vodafone on his back, though, Rijkaard could still have found himself attracting concern from UEFA, who are contractually obliged to ensure equal exposure for all sponsors. To settle UEFA minds fully, what the Barcelona boss would have required in his jacket was a back panel capable of flipping between advertisements, across the full sponsorship range, in the manner of the electronic hoardings around the perimeter of the pitch.

Such a device would have been cumbersome, though, and likely to tug the collar down at the back, spoiling the jacket's line. And he would probably have kept tripping over the mains lead. It will be some time, I think, before we see managers fully 'switched on' in this sense.

Still, you can trust Rijkaard to be at the leading edge of managerial menswear. This is the guy, remember, who introduced the metallic-finish, mid-thigh rain mac into the world's dugouts, at a time when everyone else was going knee-length. And he single-handedly pioneered the use of wet-look hair gel in the technical area, now widely taken up across the European game. Even Sir Alex Ferguson's hair has a little shimmer about it these days. On a rainy night in an unprotected dugout, anyway.

All in all, the Rijkaard influence is right across this autumn's collections for managers, which demonstrate an enlivening move away from the Umbro car coat, and similar off-the-megastore-peg numbers, and towards suitage at the casual/formal interface. Jackets are loosely constructed. Dark greys are very now. Tie knots are fat. Shoes are polished.

True, the highly retro, badged blazer (UEFA can't touch you for it) in pastel shades lives on, courtesy of Arsene Wenger. But the wearing by managers of football kit – track suit pants tucked into sports socks and worn with football boots to give that once-popular 'I'll come out there and do it myself in a minute' impression – seems to have gone out of the game at the highest level with Alan Curbishley.*

These days, dressing in kit is *so* League One – a response, one assumes, to the realization that today's top managers (Jose Mourinho, Rafa Benitez, Wenger, Ferguson) weren't much cop as footballers originally, and see little value in pretending to be footballers now. Also, managers have finally wised up to the embarrassment of being seen to wear something you so obviously got for free. Everyone except Stuart Pearce, that is.

For autumn 2006, from Harry Redknapp at Portsmouth across to 'Big Sam' Allardyce, the look is very suited, very clean, very straight-up – one might even say, very post-bung allegation. Expect to see the closely fitted, nothing to hide / nowhere to hide it look gather some real steam across Christmas and on into the spring. Some observers are even saying the suspiciously padded coat that has traditionally found favour among coaches could be entirely extinct by the end of the season, or sooner if Lord Stephens's inquiry into unofficial payments really gets among the dirt.

Today's styles also happily adapt to changing physical conditions in the modern dugout, where increased comfort is the byword. Even allowing for the transformational, 'early-adopter' work done by Rijkaard and Jose Mourinho, the overhaul of the managerial look has, at its root, the demise of the wind-blasted concrete-box-plus-splintered-bench combo of yore.

The increasing prevalence at pitch-side of underfloor heating with Recaro seating in stitched leather, and the move towards all-weather carpeting in the technical areas, has had a massive effect on the coaching wardrobe, almost entirely ridding the professional game of sheepskin and of untreated animal hides in general.

Footwear is among the chief benefactors here. The modern dugout takes a polished brogue or suede ankle-height boot far

* Only to return, of course, in 2008 with Kevin Keegan. We really must talk about him at some point.

more readily than it takes a stud, and at this season's shows, much of the chatter has been about which manager will be the first to push the indoor-wear as outdoor-wear trend the whole way and wear carpet slippers. (The big money is on Neil Warnock.)

Are today's Premiership fashion-hounds ready to follow Rijkaard into gold logos? Maybe, give it a year or so. Meantime, Aidy Boothroyd is as good an emblem as any of where we all stand in 2006. Commonly in a dark suit and dark shirt, with a well-chosen tie and quiet accessorizing, in the form of belt and buckles, the Watford boss remains suave and in control, even if his team looks ragged as a roped-up sack worn over a bin liner. It's good to see.

The Dangerous Book for Footballers

By Conn and Hal Iggulden-Goal

(*Like* The Dangerous Book for Boys, *only healthier.*)

Introduction
In this world of computer games and mobile phones, footballers need a book about conkers, spy gadgets and stories of incredible courage. Only this week an investigation by Radio 5 Live revealed that players are shutting themselves away in hotel rooms, playing on-line poker, visiting porn sites and watching *Kiss My Whip in Sweden* (digital and satellite viewers only). It's time they could be using to make crystals, build a rabbit hutch or construct a swing from some rope and an old tyre.

Nowadays we protect our footballers as never before. If they are in their rooms watching *Kiss My Whip in Sweden*, we know where they are. And better that, we reason, than getting up to all sorts of dangerous mischief in the open. It's the health and safety mentality. And as a result, we are losing sight of what it means to be a young footballer – of the full and lasting richness of the footballer experience.

Because, even as we cosset him, we know deep down that what a footballer really wants to be is self-sufficient, capable of building a papier mâché mountain for a model railway or growing cress on blotting paper, and able to navigate his way by the stars.

This compendium arose from thinking back to the golden seasons of the authors' past – not so long ago, in fact. Those were the halcyon days when Rodney Marsh would spend his spare time happily making models of his racing pigeon from matchsticks. Days when Stan Bowles was content to occupy himself by honing a slick routine of dazzling coin tricks.

If we don't pass on these old skills, they die out. Our hope is that, many years from now, someone will dig this book out of the attic and give it to a footballer who is home from training on a wet Tuesday afternoon, whose laptop has frozen, and who is staring out of the window at the rain falling into his infinity swimming pool and wondering what to do.

How to build a treehouse

There is little to beat the thrill and adventure of creating a miniature home high above the world, amid the leaves. Use offcuts or pieces of discarded wood, such as the crate your Italian marble his'n'hers sink unit came in. Alternatively, have your personal shopper source some bits of 2x4 and a few sheets of hardboard.

Choose your tree carefully. Best of all, ask your agent to choose it, at the usual percentage. Short fruit trees are generally a bad idea. Ditto rosebushes. Older, thicker-limbed trees provide the more solid platforms. There may well be one at the bottom of your garden, assuming you didn't bulldozer it when you extended the snooker room. The gardener will know.

You will need to test your treehouse rigorously for stability. The best method is probably to send up Robbie Savage and get him to jump around for a while. House still intact? Hey presto – you're in business, and it's time to wire the place for sound and heating.

*

Knots

Every footballer should know a few knots, although in this age of Velcro fastenings and elasticated laces, good knotsmanship is a fast-vanishing art. This is a shame, because there is nothing more satisfying than being able to execute, for instance, a perfect Swedish Whip Knot. Fold the velvet cord in half. Loop through the shower rail and pass twice around the wardrobe doorknob before tying off on the Corby trouser press.

How to build a go-kart

The real and lasting satisfaction in building a go-kart lies in using salvaged materials – pram wheels, old wooden boxes, string, a few old nails – in order to make something virtually from nothing.

Then, for a truly bangin' ride, pimp your kart with the following wicked essentials: massive chrome rims, retro cream leather and a maxed-out sound system. Man, that go-kart is blessed with the mad flava! You're going to be real big out there!

Great Men of History, no. 14: Malcolm Allison

Long ago, before the invention of Jose Mourinho, there lived a football manager who took clothes very seriously. He was called Malcolm Allison, but Allison is a girl's name, so the world knew him as Big Mal. Big Mal enjoyed bespoke suits and well-shone shoes and was famous for wearing collars that would have broken the neck of a lesser man. Some of the hats Big Mal wore made such an impression that they ended up eclipsing anything else he achieved in the game. Even now people pass on the tale of Big Mal's fedora and ask aloud, 'How did he get away with it?' And people answer, equally aloud, 'We have no idea.'

The moral of this story is that being nicely turned out, with polished shoes, never hurt anybody.

Keeping a guinea pig

Available in an amazing variety of breeds and colours, guinea pigs make extremely pleasant pets and are relatively undemanding to keep – although note that most guinea pigs require cleaning out at least once a week. Get an apprentice to do it when he's finished cleaning your boots.

True, they may not be as impressive as dogs, but, well treated and properly fed (no steak), guinea pigs can be affectionate creatures and surprisingly intelligent. With the right training, who knows? One day your guinea pig may even lead your team out at Wembley. It would be a proud moment for you.

The stars

Major stars are Tom Cruise and Jennifer Aniston.

Minor stars are Jonathan Wilkes and Nikki from *Big Brother* 7.

Porn stars are Ben Dover and Annika, the Swedish Whip Girl.

How to make a tin whistle

You will need a thin, hollow metal pipe, around eight inches in length and one inch in diameter, such as might, for instance, form part of a hotel's central heating system, or be nailed into the bathroom wall as a towel-hanger. Detach and trim as necessary.

Make six, evenly spaced holes in the pipe using a drill, ideally, or the corkscrew from your minibar if no drill is available. Make sounds with your tin whistle by blowing gently into the pipe at one end and using your fingers to cover the holes in various patterns.

Tunes you can play on your tin whistle: 'Baa Baa Black Sheep'.

Tunes you can't play on your tin whistle: 'Freakum Dress' by Beyoncé; 'Grown Man Business' by Mos Def; anything by Ludacris.

Games for long journeys

Even the most gruelling coach trip (usually to Blackburn) can be made to fly by with a game of numberplate cricket. This game is probably best played away from the training ground car park, where a big total can be slow to accumulate (JT 1, AC 1, FL 1, etc.). Fortunately, as you will rapidly discover, not everybody on the road has personalized numberplates, so you'll soon be racking up quite an innings – until you are bowled middle stump, that is, by an overtaking green Austin Allegro!

Many of the classic Victorian party games adapt well to the travel situation. A moving coach certainly enlivens a game of Pin the Tail on the Donkey. Alternatively, try a round of Pin the Whip on the Swedish Nurse. Usually goes down well.

The Bouts We Want to See

(Passion boiled over in the technical area and two Premiership managers found themselves chest to chest. Unfortunately for fight fans, it was the wrong two managers.)

Hugely disappointing scenes at Upton Park. Clearly the public is as ready as it ever will be to embrace managerial fight action, but the promoters got it badly wrong on this occasion. The appetite was never going to be there for a bout between Alan Pardew and Arsene Wenger.

Who was responsible for this tepid match-up? If it was you, Frank Warren, then I hope you are hanging your head in shame. Right time, right place, wrong managers. Wenger may have shown the odd flash of something down the years but the grey-faced, whippet-thin, French intellectual has rarely persuaded anyone in the fight game that he was a major contender for serious belts.

As for Pardew, even Glenn 'Rocky' Roeder might have brought more to the table, attitude-wise, than the West Ham boss did on that fleeting occasion. It was like watching Colin 'Sweet C' Macmillan – a gifted, quick-footed fighter but one who always seemed to be struggling against the overwhelming niceness of his own nature. Little wonder Sunday's bout devolved into a tiresome stalemate, leaving the punters to drift off into the night wondering whether what they had seen even amounted to a fight.

The great fistic match-ups, the ones that pull in the paying customers in quantity and yield them legends to marvel over for years afterwards, require context – retribution, grudges nurtured through time, a story. A handful of archived xenophobic comments from Pardew about Arsenal's policy on English players clearly couldn't hope to cut the mustard in this respect. How would you even begin to bill a rematch? 'Pardew *v.* Wenger II: This time it's technical.'

Of course, for many analysts now sighing in resignation, the absence of spectacle was all too predictable. There is a robust and growing school of thought that believes the entire division is a busted flush – that the game is now littered with fancy continentals who spit out their gumshields at the first sniff of the cornerman's bucket, and that, for people who could really throw their weight around in the dugout, and who mattered to the world as fighters, you would have to go all the way back to the days of Don Revie.

How fantasy fight fans and the nostalgic in general ache to melt the barriers of time and bring back Revie, stripped and oiled as we best remember him in his prime, and ready to dish out the mother and father of all pastings to, for example, Watford's Aidy Boothroyd. We can but dream.

But perhaps this is not, in fact, the moment for unhelpful despair. The sport could be in better health than the critics allow and it would take only one promoter with flair and initiative to demonstrate as much. Certainly it is hard to imagine that a significant audience would not happily pay premium prices to be ringside for Sir Alex Ferguson *v.* Harry Redknapp.

It cannot be denied that Redknapp has fought lighter than he presently does. Some observers think the south coaster could possibly stand to lose a jowl or two to be at his optimum fighting weight. Against the veteran Scot, he would also be at a straight disadvantage in terms of both height and reach. Yet it cannot be denied, even by his most vocal detractors, that the Portsmouth man remains a master of the bob and weave and there is little in the game to match the mesmeric violence of his attacking flourishes when he is mad as hell.

Sir Alex, it is routinely said, possesses a glass jaw – particularly since he entered his sixties – and there are some who profess to be dismayed at the sight of this storied pugilist hauling himself into the ring for further damage at his advanced age, when there is so patently little left that he needs to prove beyond his own durability.

Yet the knight who, having found in the sport a legitimate means to channel his natural aggression, now fiercely protects his reputation as an unrelenting fighter with a simply gigantic upper cut and will, apparently, never be content merely to sit back on the ropes and hope to counter-punch his way to a payday. It's why Ferguson *v.* Redknapp represents such a lip-smacking prospect. It would be everything that Pardew *v.* Wenger so significantly was not.

Similarly, surely only rekindled enthusiasm and renewed faith await the spectator at a dust-up between 'Big Sam' Allardyce and Neil 'The Mouth' Warnock, could it only be arranged. Big Sam has always warmed to those almost monastic levels of self-denial that characterize long periods of the training fighter's life and as a result is widely agreed to possess one of the most vicious jabs the game has seen, as well as a tirelessly shrewd ability to put the combinations together.

As for Warnock, his repeated claims to be the real deal may just be a layer of rhetorical bluster designed to cloak the possibil-ity that he is merely a sparring partner who got lucky. Even so, it would be hard to imagine this fight not spectacularly going the distance, with the Mouth talking all the way through.

Even lower down the divisions, many observers grow increas-ingly excited at the prospect of a big-purse match-up between Roy Keane of Sunderland and Dennis 'Wisey' Wise of Leeds. We, however, elect not to add our voice to this clamour.

The fight game enjoys a sometimes too elastic relation with the codes of civilization. That is its nature. But wilfully pitch-ing the Manchester enforcer against the London fire-starter would seem like an outright invitation to lawlessness and open horror, at the end of which the gross mutilation of Evander

Holyfield by Mike Tyson would come to resemble but the lightest and most innocent of snacking opportunities. Even in 2006, surely, no television outlet would want to show such an R-rated encounter, except possibly the National Geographic channel or maybe ITV4. And who would volunteer to clean up afterwards?

The prospect, however, of Rafa Benitez, the wily Spaniard, slugging it out against a big-engined Stuart Pearce, with Steve 'Bring It' Coppell *v.* Iain 'Wowie' Dowie on the undercard – this we unconditionally rise to. The time is now. Let's get it on.

Chesterfield on a Budget

When Terry Brown, the chairman of West Ham, criticized his team after their embarrassing defeat by Chesterfield in the Carling Cup (a pub team could have done better, he is reported to have said), he allegedly framed his anger in the context of the £16,000 it cost West Ham for an overnight stay and coach travel on that trip.

What a waste, was the implication. Indeed. Assuming a party of forty travelled (sixteen players plus coaching staff and directors), West Ham would appear to have stayed in a £300 per night hotel and spent £4,000 on a coach. Four thousand pounds! You can *buy* a coach for not much more than that. At any rate, if you were travelling regularly (as West Ham presumably are), you would soon reach the point where owning a coach seemed like the sensible option.

Let's have a look at how much more cheaply the trip could have been done, shall we? My research indicates that the Legacy Hotel in Chesterfield is running a 'Money Saver' offer, cutting the price of a double room with 'television, telephone, hospitality tray and complimentary toiletries' to just £34.50 per night, midweek, based on two people sharing. Good central location, and use of a swimming pool, too.*

* Please call ahead. These rates may no longer apply.

Meanwhile, a call to Redwing Coach Hire yields a quote on a forty-nine-seater coach hire from east London to Chesterfield, returning the next day, at £945, plus driver's accommodation.*

Again assuming a party of forty, I reckon I could have brought the trip in at just £1,669.50, not including a supplement on the driver's unshared double room. It's about cutting your cloth, I guess. Certainly, set against that kind of spend, rather than £16,000, a defeat by Chesterfield might have been easier for the chairman to swallow.

Incidentally, before anyone gets any ideas, you are not allowed to field a pub team in the Carling Cup. Your reserves, yes. A pub team, no.

Are Refs 'Cheats' or Just 'Shite'?

James McFadden's defence against his sending-off for foul and abusive language appears to go as follows: Graham Poll, the referee, thought the Everton player called him a 'fucking cheat'. But McFadden maintains that what he said was, 'That's fucking shite, ref.' So therefore, according to McFadden, he shouldn't have gone.

Do you get it? The argument, as far as I understand it, seems to be that 'fucking cheat, ref' is properly foul and abusive, whereas 'that's fucking shite, ref' represents something closer to innocent literary criticism, and should go unpunished.

This is clearly barking. And yet referees buy it. For them, the unforgivable term of abuse is the c-word – 'cheat'. It is the c-word that seems uniquely to ignite a referee's anger – despite the fact that, when directed at a referee, it is meaningless.

Referees, after all, can be guilty of many things (blindness, smugness, you name it), but not, strictly speaking, cheating. What sneaky advantage does Poll gain by deciding that, for

---

* These rates may no longer apply, either. But I bet you can still do it for less than £16,000.

example, Andy Johnson has fallen over in the penalty area again? In what sense, in this situation, does Poll gain anything useful to himself by underhand means? He doesn't and, accordingly, 'cheat' is a completely lame insult to throw at him.

And yet, for some reason, 'cheat' is the worst thing you can call Poll – something that unmans him so fundamentally that he has no option but to reach for the red. But, in the name of reason and our common language, can we not agree that it is far worse for a referee to be called 'fucking shite' (which does make some sense) than to be called a 'fucking cheat', which doesn't make any sense at all?

Peter Schmeichel Gets Outfoxed by Emma Bunton

The elimination of Peter Schmeichel from *Strictly Come Dancing* was no less poignant for occurring on his birthday and all the more startling for happening after a foxtrot. Time and again in this competition, the former Manchester United goalkeeper has impressed in the traditional ballroom disciplines and struggled to impose himself in the more free-form, Latin-based dances.

It long ago reached the point at home where, as long as Schmeichel was formally attired, in white tie and tails, one felt one could relax. It was only when the Denmark international burst through the curtains in shiny bell-bottoms and a jewel-encrusted shirt that the danger signs, along with the shirt and trousers, flashed.

Also, if he was going to go, then surely it would have been after the samba round, when the judges' scores plunged him right down into what long-term observers of the pro-celebrity ballroom scene know as Quentin Wilson territory. (The television presenter is statistically the worst dancer in celebrity ballroom history, followed closely afterwards by Fiona Phillips of GMTV.)

'Heinous' was one of the verdicts on that samba of Schmeichel's. The sportsman said he didn't know what that meant. My dictionary has 'shockingly evil or wicked', which is possibly a bit strong for looking a touch clunky during some shoulder wriggles and failing to pull off a set of hip thrusts. But this is top-ranking light entertainment television. Temperatures run high.

Heinous or not, Schmeichel was spared by the public phone vote and anyone looking for a reaction from him this week will have been encouraged to see how good his foxtrot was looking in training. 'I love this dance,' Schmeichel admitted, with a carefree openness about his enthusiasm for ballroom that might have escaped him during his years in professional football.

He didn't let himself down in the performance, either. Perhaps he didn't quite boss the area as he used to in his Old Trafford pomp. But he stood up tall when he had to and made himself big, to the extent that Bruno Tonioli felt able to announce, 'The flying Dutchman is back.'

Wrong country, of course. One can only assume that, having long ago exhausted the 'Great Dane' pun, Tonioli felt he had no option but to move slightly south. It's all Europe, in any case. And as it happened, being mistaken for a Dutchman was the least of Schmeichel's problems on a night when Bruce Forsyth, apparently suffering a brief synaptic power cut, addressed him as 'Michael'. Still, no one said these shows were easy.

The point is, even after the judges' critique, Schmeichel looked well placed to survive and go forwards into the round of six. True, Arlene Phillips had accused him of having a 'cumbersome bodyline' and urged him to 'pull out right through the centre', which can be painful, especially for a retired sportsperson, and is tricky enough for anyone while wearing a cummerbund. Even so, it sounded like advice for the immediate future, rather than an end-of-term report.

But no. The lights went out over the seven couples until only two remained. Who ever thought Schmeichel would come off worse in a 50/50 challenge with Emma Bunton? But it happened.

Whither Michael, the flying Dutchman, now? Retired sportspeople notoriously have terrible problems adapting to life, post-celebrity challenge show. They miss the adrenaline, the training, the banter. It is, for many of them, the only real life they have known. It's a struggle for them to find something to occupy themselves, though a friend was quick to point out that Schmeichel has the ruddy complexion and stout thighs necessary for seasonal work as a department store Santa. It's a thought.

He needs to find something to engage him, or he'll end up as another pro-celebrity dancing victim, mournfully rueing what might have been. And how close he will feel he came. Yes, Mark Ramprakash has made himself hard to beat, but Matt Dawson and Carol Smillie have frequently looked vulnerable, and the path to *Strictly Come Dancing* glory must have seemed to open up enticingly for Schmeichel when Jimmy Tarbuck was forced to withdraw following a dizzy spell in training.

Clearly that was a major disappointment for the show, although you could argue, by way of consolation, that it was the first time in recent memory that the comedian had come over funny on television, so *Strictly Come Dancing* was privileged to capture it.

In the end, though, Schmeichel was fighting a battle he couldn't win against his own physique. Dance ruthlessly favours the more willowy figure and Schmeichel is, however tightly you dress him, a couple of oak trees straddling a warehouse.

We saw the same thing on ITV's *Dancing on Ice* with David Seaman who, no matter what steps the former Arsenal and England shot-stopper took to counter the gulf in size between himself and his partner, couldn't help looking like a passage from *Gulliver's Travels*. It may be that we have to accept, however reluctantly, that working expressively across the full range of the dancing disciplines is, in the end, not what goalkeepers were cut out to do.

Razor and the Troublemakers

On *Football Saved My Life*, a weekly series packing them in on Bravo, Neil 'Razor' Ruddock is attempting to transform the lives of fifteen troubled men through the power of football alone. Well, almost alone. The power of reality television is also involved, as is the power of calorie-controlled dieting, not to mention the power of a number of alternative therapies, just to make the show more interesting.

Patients must embrace a new work and fitness regime under Razor's grizzly tutelage, and the carrot at the end of the show's splintery stick is the chance to take on a team of ex-pros in a televised match. The road to personal redemption is a long and hard one, as ever, but in this case it goes via Neville Southall, which is nice.

The series is a bit like Sky One's *The Match*, with its climactic annual clash between Celebrities and Legends, except that the trainee footballers here need help, rather than exposure. The programme calls them 'fifteen of the laziest, greediest, binge-drinking louts in the business', which seems to sum it up fairly concisely, although don't let's forget the gambling.

Big drinkers from London, Razor's troublemakers are remarkable for their nicknames. These include Mad Dog, Arafat, Flatscreen and (my favourite, simply because of its utter implausibility as a name) Billy Joel. The programme's central pleasure lies in hearing Ruddock mulling over his options as a coach, and saying, perfectly casually, 'You look at Mo, Puke, Mingle, Landlord . . .'

One of Ruddock's managerial dilemmas is whether or not to play Puddles just behind Salad Bar in a diamond formation with Puke dropping off. Whoever the manager ends up picking, though, it's clearly going to be the best roll call television has heard since the Trumpton fire brigade last lined up – a flat back three (Pugh, Pugh, Barney McGrew) with a triangle across the middle (Cuthbert, Dibble, Grub).

Ability is mixed, except in swearing, where everyone seems to be capable of performing at Premiership level. Combing through the footage and calming it down with a bleeper must be providing work for an entire team of technical operatives working in shifts. I'm not sure why they bother, though, given that the show is going out on Bravo, whose channel slogan is 'Entertaining men since 1985' and where the chances of anyone watching who would be offended – indeed, of anyone watching at all – must be remote.

Still, it's something of a shock to hear the bleeper applied to Dr Adam Carey. The nutrition and fitness consultant looks like butter wouldn't melt when he's briefing the weight-watchers on ITV's *Celebrity Fit Club*, but it turns out he can send the air blue with the best of them when the need arises and when he's on Bravo with Ruddock.

Some would question Razor's credentials for this job. He never really cut it in football management, nor, as far as I am aware, in psychiatric counselling or any of the main branches of social work. His sessions with the squad have certainly been tenuous and chaotic up to now. But he is, without question, the hardest footballer who ever made the grade as *A Question of Sport* team captain, where he amply demonstrated that he would be exactly the sort of person you would want on your shoulder, in the event that it all kicked off on the Picture Board.

Plus he was in series three of *I'm A Celebrity . . . Get Me Out Of Here!* True, he didn't get very far. But he shared a damp clearing with Peter Andre, so respect is for ever due. What the former Liverpool enforcer has in spades is an appetite for being on television which jobs like these demand and which would thoroughly test the mettle of most of us.

In any case, rest assured that, come the day of the big match, viewers will be rooting for Flatscreen and Puddles to put one over on Matt Le Tissier, thus raising the flag for the semi-inebriated amateur. It's the British way. Contrast *Pros vs. Joes*, an American series, where 'ordinary' citizens take on retired sports professionals in various disciplines, and lose. Meanwhile the Pros snicker at the Joes for their presumption, hector them aggressively from the sidelines and generally make jocular hay with their names. (On the episode I saw, a man called Kevin Steinke, in particular, was having a hard time.)

The implication is that America has too much invested in the generic superiority of the sportsperson, even the retired one, for things to be otherwise. If any old Kareem or Charlie could rise off his sofa in Hackensack and outperform a professional, the world would be upside-down.

As a refreshing antidote to the culture of the underdog, *Pros vs. Joes* has everything going for it. Unfortunately, as a dramatic television programme it is hopeless. Steinke stunk at baseball. Who'd have thought? You'd say this much for *Football Saved My Life*: its outcome is uncertain. Go for it, Puke.

Throwing in the Towel, and Other Ball-boy Misdemeanours

It is not clear who emerged with greater dignity from the major towel controversy at Watford's ground this week, but for the moment I'm going with the towel. Noticing that the ball boys were drying the ball before returning it to home players, but were not extending this courtesy to the away side, Neil Warnock, the Sheffield United manager, grew exorbitantly aggrieved – something of a pastime for him, but still good value when it happens. 'A disgrace', Warnock called it, adding, 'You can't do things like that in the Premier League.'

At half-time, Warnock raised the matter with the fourth official. But whatever the fourth official is employed to do, apart from hold up the number board and act as a buffer between fighting coaching staff, he evidently has no brief to deal with matters of possible favouritism arising from ball-boy towel use. So nothing happened.

Still stewing, Warnock then dumped a towel of his own by the half-way line – more a gesture of protest, one felt, than a delivery to his players of much-needed emergency supplies. (The players, we should note, remained utterly unmoved by the towel war unfolding around them, and were possibly oblivious to it, what with having a game of football to play and everything.)

This in turn caused Adrian Boothroyd, the Watford manager, to wonder after the match whether Warnock needed that extra towel to dry 'the new perm he's got for the Premiership' – a completely unhelpful remark. You don't want to go towel-drying a perm. You'll ruin it.

And now only rancour and mystery remain. Were Watford guilty of manipulating the ball boys to hand their players an unfair, dry-ball advantage at throw-ins, reasoning that anything is useful which helps you to gain that extra 1 or 2 per cent? Or, in this case, that extra 0.00017 per cent. Or had Sheffield United neglected to request the full ball-boy moisture-removal service? Sometimes you need to ring down to reception in advance to secure an extra facility such as this, or even ask for it at the time of booking to avoid disappointment.

Either way, observers could hardly fail to notice evidence in this complex saga of football's increasing namby-pambyism. After gloves, roll-neck vests and Lycra leg warmers, it was only a matter of time before footballers started wanting to have the ball cleansed of residues before touching it. You never saw the likes of Ian Hutchinson getting his ball polished for him, and he could throw it over the stand on the other side.

In fairness, though, the modern player is working with different equipment. The sleeves of the old, durable cotton jerseys, if pulled down and anchored by the fingers in the palm of the hand, in the received style of ball-drying long-throw experts since time immemorial, were far more absorbent than today's synthetic fabrics, which are designed actively to repel surface moisture, making them all but hopeless in a liquid-removal situation.

Nevertheless, this week's incident has done nothing to dampen the anxieties of those who believe we are witnessing a worrying spread in the covert use of ball boys to influence matches at the very highest level. Though it is hard, at this stage, to get anybody, apart from Warnock, to go on the record about this, footballers are slowly coming forward to protest that they are subject to campaigns of intimidation by those seemingly innocent, and frequently extremely cold, small boys in tracksuits.

For instance, several Premier League players now talk privately of being on the receiving end of hard stares from ball boys at away grounds. 'There was this one at [name of leading English stadium withheld]. I could feel his eyes following me round the pitch,' a player recently recalled. 'It was really upsetting. And the worst thing about it was, there was no one I could tell.' The player was in no doubt that the ball boy had been 'put up to it' by the home team's coaching staff. 'This went all the way to the top, I'm sure of it,' the player said.

This solitary anecdote would seem insubstantial if it could not be coupled with disturbing reports of incidents of ball boys returning the ball with spin. 'I put my hands out to take the ball on the bounce,' a top-flight goalkeeper, who wished to remain anonymous, said. 'Of course, I wasn't expecting the spin, was I? It veered off to the left slightly and I took the full weight of it on the end of my ring finger. I wasn't myself after that for the rest of the game.'

Other players claim to have been adversely affected by ball boys rocking backwards and forwards on their plastic stools in 'a really irritating way'. And it is not only away sides that worry. Some players are now concerned that their own ball boys might have been 'got at' by the visiting side in the run-up to the match and offered incentives, including chewing gum and KitKat Chunkys, to work as 'double ball boys'.

It's a growing school of thought that when Kanu, then with West Bromwich Albion, clasped a ball boy to himself in the act of celebrating a goal last season, he was actually frisking him for concealed devices. Had he done it only once, no one would have suspected anything. It was the fact that he did the same thing again in the second half, to a different ball boy, that aroused people's fears that something systematic might be going on.

Now that Towelgate has blown the lid off underhand ball-boy

use, perhaps the Football Association, which has thus far, typically, turned a blind eye to this whole area, will finally feel obliged to investigate and act. If Warnock achieves nothing else in his career, at least he will be able to claim credit for that. Something needs to be done. Otherwise, how long will it be before the game is awash with a new breed of wildly emboldened ball boys, not afraid to go nuclear and deploy the ultimate psychological weapon in their armoury – not giving the ball back at all?

Vote, or the Gorilla Gets It

Can Graeme Le Saux save the Rwandan mountain gorilla? It's a big ask for the former Chelsea and England left-sider. It doesn't matter who you have faced in your career, those gorillas are always going to be unsettling in a one-on-one situation. They don't come much bigger or much harder, wildlife-wise. Nor more threatened, as it happens.

And then you look at the quality of the opposition. On *Extinct*, ITV's new pro-celebrity conservation smackdown, Le Saux is going up against Anneka Rice with the polar bear. We're talking a gigantic, bleached-white icon of the natural world with a huge sentimental pull when it comes to generating viewer response. And the polar bear has its fans, too.

Then there is David Suchet, representing the ever-popular giant panda. The big-eyed bamboo-chewer is bound to be somewhere in the reckoning when the phone votes are counted at the weekend and when Sir Trevor McDonald and Zoe Ball announce which endangered creature is going to be saved and which ones are going to the wall.

Actually, the winning animal gets half the prize money spent on it. The other half is divided between the losers. So, by choosing to vote for Graeme's gorilla you aren't automatically agreeing to wipe out, for instance, Sadie Frost's orangutan. Which is probably good, from a conscience point of view.

Le Saux is slated to make his pitch anon. On the launch show, there was a tantalizing glimpse of him giving it the full David Attenborough, whispering into the camera from a crouched position in some tall grass as, over his shoulder, several tonnes of male ape was debating with itself whether or not to eat him. Quality work from Le Saux, although, if we're being picky, Attenborough never looks quite so terrified.

At the risk of speaking prematurely, I think we can write off Michael Portillo and the macaw. No disrespect to the macaw, of course, but the decision to twin a retired politician with a soon-to-be-ex parrot can probably be dismissed as the exercise in easy satire on the producers' part that it almost certainly was.

Stiffer challenges for Le Saux are likely to come from Miranda Richardson, who is bound to get a big performance out of the Asian elephant, and Pauline Collins, who is championing the Bengal tiger – always there or thereabouts when the big extinction prizes are being handed out.

We're backing Le Saux and the gorillas, though, to pull off a surprise here. Rumours on the grapevine that the gorillas were hoping to get Sandi Toksvig are surely just so much jungle tittle-tattle. The personable and articulate full back has more than enough in his locker to get the nation behind the mountain gorilla. And behind is the best place to be, when those guys get going. You definitely don't want to be in front of them, anyway. Come on, then, Soxy. And come on, the gorilla.

Vote, or the Gorilla Gets It: Part 2

Congratulations to Graeme Le Saux who, by the time the viewer votes had been counted at the end of *Extinct*, ITV's endangered fauna phone-in, had hoisted the Rwandan mountain gorilla into the top three. Unlike the gorilla, Le Saux is only human, so he will almost certainly have been disappointed not to go the whole way to the top. But his opponents were David Suchet and Pauline Collins, who have years of pro-celebrity conservation work behind them, and anyone who is up against both the giant panda and the Bengal tiger in an extinction face-off is going to know he has been in a scrap.

As it happens, it's the tiger who will enjoy the lion's share of the raised funds, with the remainder being divvied up equally between the other contending animals. So everyone's a winner – even Michael Portillo's hyacinth macaw, which was very much the underdog here. In the circumstances, for Soxy to take the gorilla as far as he did on the resources that he had can be regarded as a small miracle of survival in itself. Plus a top-three finish presumably guarantees a place in Europe next season, and it's more years than we care to mention since the mountain gorilla had one of those.*

---

* Not content with using his public profile to make a difference in the life of the gorilla, Le Saux pushed on from here to reinvigorate a set of old gameshow formats. See p. 298.

2007

In which we hymn the forgotten heroes of '66, follow Rodney Marsh into a camera-infested jungle clearing and consider whether it is entirely smart of footballers to wax the hair from their legs when a game on a plastic pitch may be just around the corner. And in which we take a personal phone call from Liverpool's new American owner, receive a lesson from Craig Bellamy in how to hit someone with a golf club so that they stay hit, and discover Ken Bates advertising double-glazing. But, before any of that, a visit to the offices of LA Galaxy where anticipation is high in advance of the arrival of the world's first gazillion-dollar footballer.

David Beckham Goes West

From Peter Neumann, Head of Personnel and Rookie Integration, LA Galaxy

Dave!

On behalf of all of us here at the club, can I just take this formal opportunity to say, this is *so great*, dude. We know there were many prestigious places you could have gone at this pivotal moment in your career, including Sunderland, so the fact that you have accepted $250 million to join the party here at the Galaxy . . . well, it makes us humble, Dave, is what it does.

Humble and, of course, proud to have facilitated the record-breaking deal under the terms of which you now become the latest in a long and glittering line of British greats who have graced American soccer down the decades, such as Rodney Marsh and, more recently, Ricky Gervais.

You join the Galaxy at a hugely progressive time for us in general. The team has certainly come a long way under the gritty direction of coach Buzz Crumbleapple IV, and many of our outfield players now show almost no inclination to catch the ball whatsoever. Trading Buster Stinkenberger from Cincinnati Hooters last October sent a clear message to the world about the seriousness and depth of our intentions, which our unprecedented arrangement with you now further underscores. Come grow the brand!

By way of an induction process, we hope you will join us in July for our annual summer chilli cook-out over at Alexei Lalas's place. Let me tell you, the Lexmeister serves up the best buffalo wings this side of the Rockies, and a mean ol' dipping sauce, too. After last year's party, some of us were still tasting that sauce at Christmas! Anyway, this summer, in honor of our backers, Lex is planning to make it fancy dress on a *Chronicles of Narnia* theme. Should be a lot of fun. Bring the kids and your swim things.

It'll also be a nice chance for you to hook up in a relaxed setting with some of the other guys on the team. You will already know, I'm sure, Wexler Cornball, who rushed forty-seven yards in his first trimester and is currently 52 and 0 with the bases manned at the bottom of the ninth. Then there's Spud Berkeley, of course, who was Moosejaw High's MVP 417 times in the space of one extraordinary Spring Break back in 1997. I know Paddy O'Token is looking forward to saying hi. And so is our promising Hispanic teenage wide receiver, De'ath Drums-Fernando. They're good guys, Dave. Rowdy and a little unfocused, maybe. But good guys.

I'm pleased to confirm that your request for the heritage blouse number, 7, has been readily acceded to by our Squad Numeral Assignation Co-Ordination Unit. It did belong to our defensive line-backer Tad Crinklemeyer, but when he learned how much we were paying you, he was completely happy to give it up. However, have you completely abandoned the idea of retaining the number 23 that you wore with Madrid? I only ask because promotions point out that the Michael Jordan allusion would play extremely forcefully with our target demographic, neatly making a link in the public's imagination between yourself and someone they have heard of. Can I leave that thought with you?

Something else, Dave – do you have a game face? We've seen the Gillette campaign, obviously – and excellent work that was, too, by the way. But that would be a shaving face, right? Any chance you could work up something with a little more attitude between now and the end of the summer? People go a lot on that here.

Let me have promotions fax over some 10 x 8s of the present squad so you can see where we're coming from in this area. Check out the shot of Merckus de Johnelle, in particular. If he looks about ready to bust a squad car windshield with a hooker's purse, that's because he was! You'll enjoy working alongside Merckus, I think, just as soon as his parole comes up, which should be within a year or so now, our defense and litigation team informs me.

By the way, we've fully taken on board the concerns you had regarding press access to the locker room after games, and completely understand your sensitivities in this area.* At the same time, we don't want to risk potentially destabilizing relations with the press by denying them access which they expect. Therefore our intermediate solution is to have our Works department design and install an articulated frosted glass tube linking the shower area directly to your personal locker. Writers seeking post-match quotes can approach the tube and tap on the glass, and you can speak to them from there without undue loss of privacy. Trust me, it works. I've stood in the tube butt-naked myself, Dave, talking to my personal assistant, Shanice, and she was none the wiser.

Pre-season training starts July 17 – but, hey, see how you feel. You'll have places to go and people to see, I know. Even if you

---

* In America, it's perfectly conventional for the press to troop into the dressing rooms after games and push their recording gadgets under the noses of players who may at this point be wearing only towels or less. Now that's doing media access properly.

just came down a couple of times at the end of sessions to clap
the guys off, it would mean a lot to them.

   With regard to matchday kick-off times, when can you make
it? Afternoons suit you best, or mornings? Have a think about
that nearer the time and let us know. We can have a town car
sent over to your place, bring you down here twenty minutes
or so beforehand, giving you time to pad up, maybe sink a cold
one – however you want to play it is fine by us.

   Dave – again, a privilege. Let's go to work!

Pete

PS Would you, by any chance, happen to have a number for
Diego Forlan?

Gubba Gabba Hey!

Grandstand may be gone, but Tony Gubba marches on. The
legendary BBC football reporter and fabled Saturday-afternoon
'bits and pieces' man is seeing heavy frontline action as the voice
of *Dancing on Ice*, ITV's pro-celebrity skate-athon, cheeringly
underscoring the old adage that when one door slams, another
one opens, leading, if you're lucky, to an ice rink.

It's Gubba's star-spangled duty, at this massive event, to
review the celebrities' routines, pinpointing the salient moves
and features of interest – a job he rises to with the fluency and
authority that come only after years of dubbing commentary on
to random footage of goals from the Hawthorns for *Match of
the Day*.

'That's the back flip . . . then the helicopter spin . . . that's
the compulsory spiral . . .' Thus Gubba on Lee Sharpe's performance, one which saw him pass through to round three with
relative ease. The former Manchester United player has revealed
that he finds the preparation for ice dancing 'far harder than
football training', although the question of how hard exactly

Sharpe trained as a footballer was always an open one, especially with Sir Alex Ferguson.

The judges on *Dancing on Ice*, though, seem happy enough with his input thus far, not least Natalia Bestemyanova, the Russian Olympic champion, who said the Sharpester's bodyline was 'obsolottly porficked'. He'll be happy with that.

Gubba, though, had no time to sit back and reflect. 'The one-handed drape lift . . . good flow over the ice . . . the bridal lift to finish'. That was his handy breakdown of the routine offered by Kay Burley, the news presenter, who, following an unfortunate head to ice coincidence in training, danced with a black eye this week and looked a bit like Chris Eubank after Carl Thompson had finished with him.

But again Gubba steamed on, effortlessly familiar with the technical minutiae and inviting us to consider 'a pike-lay, over the knee' and, slightly less obscurely, 'that flying big one'. Moreover, unless my hearing misled me, he drew our attention in Lisa Scott-Lee's routine to 'a half-crucifix, a half-stag and an attitude leg'.

An attitude leg! It was round about this time that the famous move in which the male dancer grabs his female partner by the ankles and wheels her over the ice with her chin skimming the surface became, in Gubba's rendering, 'the handle-less Hoover'. At which point, a chilling thought occurred. You don't suppose he's making this all up as he goes along, do you?*

Anyway, no one could deny that Gubba has been wholly liberated as a wordsmith by this contest, and in particular by the costumes. Emily Symons from *Emmerdale* was all in orange for round two. 'She's like a succulent satsuma, waiting to be squeezed,' breathed Gubba, hotly. I stand to be corrected here, but I don't think he ever said that kind of thing down the line

---

* This suspicion didn't go away in series three of *Dancing on Ice*, which hit the screens in 2008. Herein, the newly crowned voice of celebrity ice dance claimed to spot 'a scoop lift', 'a threading-the-needle slide', 'a koala lift', 'a teapot, forwards then backwards, followed by a wooshka' and 'a big lighthouse sit-lift to finish'. The man was wasted on *Football Focus*.

from Turf Moor on a chilly January afternoon. And, if he had, the chances are that Frank Bough in the *Grandstand* studio would have cut him off without ceremony.

A succulent satsuma waiting to be squeezed? Note the alliteration. We're talking nothing short of improvised poetry here. That said, who squeezes a satsuma? Peel one, maybe, or break it into segments. But squeeze it? In my experience, that's courting disaster, fruit-wise.*

Gubba was even wilder about the dress chosen by Kristina Lenko, one of the professional partners. 'It's like an extra skin of gold leaf,' explained Gubba. 'When Kristina said she needed help getting into that costume,' he added, 'she started a stampede.' How the years fell away. There hasn't been a line like that on Saturday-night television since Bob Monkhouse was in his light entertainment heyday.

WAGS Open for Business

Where are we up to with the sex war? A man – and/or a woman – could get confused. On the one hand, evidence of important female freedoms, courageously won, is all around us. Take *WAGS Boutique*. Back in the unenlightened 1970s, it was always the footballer who opened the boutique. In ITV2's reality show, it's the footballers' partners who do so – two boutiques, in fact, which must battle for custom.

So that's another glass ceiling smashed through. On the other hand, what kind of free-living, self-determining, emancipated woman is happy to trade under – indeed, to embrace and wear as a large, diamanté-encrusted brooch of honour – the subordinate term 'wag'? Were the founding mothers of feminism content to be packaged as some bloke's wife or girlfriend? No, they were not. True, none of them ever went out with Marc Bircham

* For some further thoughts on fruit, but from Jose Mourinho this time, see p. 308.

of QPR. But even if they had, defining themselves exclusively in relation to him would almost certainly have been a political no-no.

Still, *WAGS Boutique* has found ten women ready to work the wag brand while the working is good, and to hell with the ideological battleground. However, viewers turning on in the hope of seeing wagging done well will quickly notice that disappointingly few members of this expensively outfitted crew have wagged at the highest level. Only Michaela Henderson-Thynne, the impressively double-barrelled girlfriend of Middlesbrough's Stewart Downing, has international experience in Baden-Baden (the definitive campaign medal in the wag trophy cabinet).

Otherwise we're talking largely unfamiliar Barclays Premiership wags and even a sprinkling of Coca-Cola Championship wags, plying their trade with partners from clubs such as Cardiff, Crystal Palace and West Bromwich Albion. 'You'll be down there soon,' Mrs Kevin Phillips told the girlfriend of Bobby Zamora of West Ham. They can be very cutting, those wags. Fair readers of football, though.

Traditionally, the reality challenge show format seeks an unlikely transformation, asking, for instance, whether a 69-year-old arable farmer from Pebmarsh can pass muster as a club DJ in Manchester. In this context, you've got to wonder whether handing wags the run of a boutique is necessarily taking them all that far out of their professional comfort zone.

Sure enough, the women didn't look particularly overtaxed by the contest's opening exchanges, which saw them divide into two teams of five and decide on names for their stores. This latter task involved getting together for what the show knowingly described as 'a brainstorm' – almost inevitably the kind of storm in which you could have got away without a mac.

The idea of calling one of the boutiques 'Silhouette' drew shouts of approval when mooted, but had to be shelved because no one could get past the third letter when spelling it. Subsequent enthusiasm among the women for the name 'Eleven'

was a runic mystery to Cassie Sumner, the sometime girlfriend
of Michael Essien of Chelsea, until it was explained to her that
there are eleven players in a football team. But give me one
good reason why she should know that. It's a squad game these
days, in any case.

Eventually, the women on one side of the divide settled for
'Better Half', while on the other – having dismissed the competing claims of 'Cinderella', 'Players Lounge' and 'Glad Wags' – the
contestants chose 'Bows'. Both stores then opened for business in
Marshall Street, London, where anyone who fancied popping
along and dropping £3,000 on a handbag (profits to charity)
could do so. As the show definitively put it, 'Cashmere jumpers
for goalposts.'

Incidentally, more than one competitor declared herself on a
mission to demonstrate that wags are 'not dense and stupid'.
Well, it's early days, of course. But there was plenty to support
that optimistic view in episode one, where Charlotte Mears,
who is the girlfriend of Jermain Defoe, claimed to have 'heard
of' Kent.

Reality has intruded on ITV's *WAGS Boutique*, to the inevitable
distress of everyone involved. After all, the last thing a reality
television show needs is for reality to come along and spoil
everything.

And if ever a programme seemed unlikely to be troubled by
the outside world, it was *WAGS Boutique*, a show combining
footballers' partners and the fashion retail business, and therefore
ostensibly as close to Disneyland as makes no difference. Alas,
midway through the series, with the rival boutiques open to
customers, Michaela Henderson-Thynne has separated from
Stewart Downing. Worse still, it has subsequently become apparent that the so-called quiet man of the England squad has a child
that Michaela was unaware of.

Until then, we had known about Michaela's personal background only as much as the show had told us – namely that
she sat with Victoria Beckham during the 2006 World Cup in

Germany and that her favourite crisps are cheese and onion. It thus changed the tone and footing of our relationship somewhat to find her sobbing into her mobile phone in the stockroom and saying, in effect, 'he might have told me', only using more swearwords than that.

Too much reality. Michaela was then required to explain herself to the show's cameras. 'Being with someone for four years, and him having a baby – it's a bit of a shock, really.' Indeed it is.

Here's a question, though: can one still be registered as a wag after one has separated from one's footballer? It may seem heartless to proceed directly from this human drama to plain administrative matters, but the inescapable fact is that Michaela's dilemma has left *WAGS Boutique* with a vexing problem regarding her continuing eligibility for selection.

It's a grey area, not to mention a potential legal minefield. Further blurring the boundaries, Danielle Lloyd, the controversy-mired beauty queen, who this week graced the show with an appearance as a guest shopper, was referred to by the voice-over as 'an on/off wag', a tactful-ish reference to the less than concrete status of her relationship with Teddy Sheringham. But in those moments when a woman is an off-wag, is she really, technically, a wag at all? Or is the rule once a wag, always a wag? It's a major headache for the administrators.

Incidentally, Lloyd, it emerges, was all set to join up with the *WAGS Boutique* squad, having passed the medical and agreed personal terms, when *Celebrity Big Brother* came calling and lured her away with the promise of first-team racism alongside Jade Goody. File under 'seemed like the right thing to do at the time'. It's sobering to reflect that, instead of playing her part in the ignition of a global row and effectively signing the death-warrant for her chances in daytime television, Lloyd could have been harmlessly selling designer T-shirts to bemused tourists with Michael Chopra's girlfriend in Marshall Street, London. Still, if you don't push yourself when the opportunity is there, what do you ever learn?

In other news from the series that nobody you meet is talking about: the Bows boutique are 2–1 up over Better Half, their rivals, in the weekly challenges; Mrs Kevin Phillips has attempted, with mixed results, to boost customer relations by serving in a nun's outfit; and Elle Isaac, the girlfriend of Paul Ifill of Crystal Palace, has filled a moment of downtime with some breakdancing, flat out on the shop floor, attracting excited interest from an unexplained and, mercifully, leashed bull mastiff who happened to be shopping in the store at the time. Amazing scenes, and almost certainly the first televised instance of the dog tailing the wag.

Meanwhile, charged with creating a theme for a fashion-shoot, Charlotte and Cassie have excelled themselves by coming up with the snappy line 'Never too busy to be gorgeous'. The trouble was, they forgot it almost immediately, and, despite much furious brain-racking, only ever partially recovered it. (Charlotte came closest with 'Not too busy to be beautiful', which was less snappy.) It's the age-old problem, of course: over-elaboration in the final third.*

Exciting Times Ahead for the Liverpool Reds

'Long-time favourites Dubai International Capital made a bitter exit from Liverpool this week to leave American entrepreneur George Gillett Jr on the brink of a £450 million takeover. The shock withdrawal came after the Liverpool board decided that they needed more time to look into the proposal from Gillett, sixty-eight, a former owner of the Harlem Globetrotters' (news report).

---

* Eventually we had a winner – Krystell Sidwell, the wife of Steve Sidwell, then with Reading but thereafter with Chelsea. Krystell's prize was a column in *Reveal* magazine, and all credit to her. They don't just give those away, you know.

From Peter Crouch's diary

17 February 2007
Meeting today at Anfield with the Americans. Me, Stevie
Gerrard and the gaffer. Quite surprised to be asked along, but
can't hurt to show your face. First impressions, very favourable.
Lots of stuff said about 'taking the franchise forward' and 'growing the brand on the Pacific rim'. Not really my area, to be
honest. But very friendly atmosphere. I even thought the main
man, Mr Gillett, took a bit of a shine to me. He was definitely
looking at me a lot, smiling and nodding encouragingly. It was
a bit hard to tell behind the glasses, but I think he even winked
a couple of times.

I was looking to Stevie for his reaction. I knew he had met
some of the Dubai boys when they were in the frame, and had
felt they understood the culture of the club. Plus they seemed
up for dropping a bundle on loads of new players and a stadium,
so he couldn't see a problem. Anyway, he seemed to like the
Americans, too. Handshakes and smiles all round.

Slightly strange thing at the end, though. As he was showing
us out, Mr Gillett grabbed my elbow and said, 'Can you bounce-
pass?' I must have looked confused. He said, 'I'll bet you got a
pretty cute bounce-pass, don't you?' I just smiled and nodded,
as you do, and he roared with laughter, clapped me on the
shoulder and shut the door.

24 February
Say what you like about the new regime, it's certainly freshened
up training. And it's great for me, personally, to find myself at
the centre of so much of it. The figure eight weave offence is
coming along well. So is the set-piece routine where Jermaine
Pennant runs to the back post with a step ladder, Dirk Kuyt
legs it up the ladder and knocks it down to Xabi Alonso, and I
turn a cartwheel and knock it in with the back of my head.
There was a bit of a setback when Dirk slipped on the second
rung and did his knee. But it's only his posterior cruciate

ligaments, fortunately, so he should be back before the end of the season.

27 February

Lost 9–0 at Wigan. Disappointing, but obviously some of the new ideas will need time to bed down. Midway through the first half, I've gone to the crowd with the bucket of water, except it's actually full of shredded paper – only I've got the wrong bucket, so I've ended up soaking this woman in row B, and she's now threatening to sue for distress, and also for ruining a family-size tub of popcorn. Avoidable, maybe. But, in my defence, it's a lot of buckets to have to think about. I'll get the hang of it eventually.

8 March

Got sent off in a 6–0 defeat at home to Manchester City. Jamie Carragher has fed me the ball and I've tucked it under my shirt and set off up the pitch, running with my knees up high and my hands in the small of my back. It's something we worked on all week in training, and the crowd absolutely lapped it up.

But not Graham Poll, of course. He's straight over to me with the cards out. Couldn't believe it when I saw it was red. I said, 'For Christ's sake, Polly. It's called entertainment, you ★★★★.' He just doesn't get it, though. Never has, and never will.

Incidentally, people say the soul went out of Anfield when the Americans bought in. I don't agree. When the whole of the Kop stands with scarves raised before kick-off and whistles 'Sweet Georgia Brown', I don't think there's anyone who wouldn't feel the hairs stand up.

12 March

I've got off with a token fine and a one-game suspension for the Man City business, but I reckon we're in for much worse after it kicked off big time in the 16–0 loss at Sheffield United tonight – mass riot in the technical area, both benches getting stuck in, Lucozade bottles flying everywhere, Neil Warnock heavily involved, it goes without saying. And all for what? Because Rafa Benitez came on the pitch on a bicycle and squirted party string over Phil Jagielka. You'd think some of these people had no sense of humour.

18 March

I was up before the FA today, charged with deliberately switching the official matchball for another ball, identical in outward appearance yet altered as to its physical properties, such that it would bounce in a random and unpredictable manner, causing unsuspecting players to swipe at the air, fall over on their faces, or otherwise look silly.

The club's lawyer argued that I was merely working in a hallowed comedic tradition which has brought pleasure to millions around the world and was once honoured with its own specially syndicated Hanna–Barbera cartoon series. Even so, the FA have thrown the book at me: five-match ban and a £300,000 fine. The gaffer's incensed. Reckons they're punishing me on account of my reputation. I think he's got a point.

14 April

Lost 32–0 at Blackburn and dropped into the relegation zone. Got summoned to see Mr Gillett. Found him looking tired and pale, staring mournfully at the framed pictures on his wall.

'Know who this guy is?' he asked me. I didn't. 'That's Fred "Curly" Neal,' Mr Gillett said. 'Best dribbler in the history of the Harlem Globetrotters. Know why they called him Curly?'

I took a stab. 'Because he's bald?'

'Correct!' At this point, Mr Gillett went into a long, helpless laughing jag, not fully recovering until he had taken out a handkerchief and blown his nose.

He then pointed to another of the pictures. 'That's Reece "Goose" Tatum. The Goose had a hook shot so good, they retired his goddamn shirt. And this one? Wilt Chamberlain. The legendary Wilt. These guys were *funny*! Show me our

Meadowlark Lemon, our Robert "Showboat" Hall. Where is our William "Pop" Gates, our Junius Kellogg?'

I said, 'Steve Finnan does a quite good impression of the ladies from *Little Britain.*'

Mr Gillett ignored me. 'You want to know about winning? One time, the Globetrotters had a 2,495-game winning streak. The night it ended, back in '71, against the New Jersey Reds – unforgettable. It was like laughter itself had stopped. You know which comedy great was made an honorary Globetrotter? I'll tell you who. Bob Hope!'

I said, 'We've got Jimmy Tarbuck, though.'

Mr Gillett looked at me coldly. Then his face kind of melted and tears came into his eyes and he let out the biggest sigh I've ever heard. 'I had such high hopes for you, Crouchy.'

Then he went and sat back at his desk with his head in his hands. 'Just go,' he said.

4 August

Optimistic about the new season. Yes, it's Championship football, but we've just got to get on with it and come back stronger. And with the new arena going up, this is an exciting time to be around Liverpool. Plus the owners have delivered on their promise to attract top talent to the club, using the summer window to bring in Michael 'Wild Thing' Wilson, who holds the record for a vertical slamdunk (twelve feet!). Obviously his arrival puts me under a bit of pressure, personally, but I have vowed to stay and fight for my place. You've got to, haven't you?

Exciting Times Ahead for the Liverpool Reds: Part 2

'*When I arrived in Liverpool, I picked up a paper and there were four or five letters to the editor about us from people who don't even know us. I've asked my people to get numbers for those fans, and I will ring them personally*' (George Gillett, at the announcement this week of the takeover of Liverpool FC by American businessmen).

Call No. 1

'Is this Distraught from Allerton?'

  'Come again?'

  'I have Mr Gillett for you.'

  'Who?'

  (Period of silence lasting fifteen seconds.)

  'Mr De Stroud, how are you today? George Gillett here – from the franchise? Just wanting to touch base with you about that letter, see if we can talk you out of setting fire to that programme collection of yours. Believe me, I understand that feelings are running a little high right now. It's always the way with new owners. My point is, though, I don't really see it as ownership, in this case. I see it more as custodianship of the legend.'

  'I don't want insurance. Is this about insurance?'

  'You see, if I was to put down a list of the top objectives that I have for the franchise, "money" would not be the first word on that list. Not at all. The word "winning" would be the first word. So would the word "tradition", and the word "legacy". That's three first words, I know. But it's a big list, on a big piece of paper. You with me?'

  'I'm trying to have my tea here.'

  'You know where you said you'll never walk alone? I'm impressed by that. You know why? Because I'll never walk alone, either. In fact, let me be absolutely clear about it: neither myself, nor any of the people in our organization, have any interest whatsoever in walking alone. Trust me, this is, from top to bottom, a non-solo walking operation. Am I setting your mind at ease?'

  'I'm not buying anything over the phone.'

  'A privilege to have shared this time with you.'

Call No. 2

'Can I speak with Tommy Smith?'

  'You're speaking to him.'

  'George Gillett calling. Saw the letter in the paper. Phewee!

Strong words you wrote there, Tom. The stuff about the polished jackboots of the infidel stamping the culture into powder? Very powerful. And I want to thank you for that, because passion is something we truly value here at the Liverpool Reds.'

(Strange low growling noise.)

'Something else we value? Actions. Actions over words, every time. Let me tell you something. We don't only talk the talk. We also walk the walk. So why don't you walk the walk with us, Tom? I can promise you: you'll never walk the walk alone.'

(More growling.)

'Stick around, won't you? We're going to have a lot of fun together. Say, Tom, do you ever get down to the stadium at all? We're going to be doing something over the next few home matches, a kind of goodwill thing – opening up the family enclosure to a few guests, giving a few people such as yourself a chance to visit with the franchise, see what you make of us. We'll have our promotions people rustle up a little take-home bag – a Reds pennant, maybe, and a bumper sticker, some balloons, nothing fancy, just a little token of our appreciation. Sound good to you? Just call up, tell them we spoke, and say you squared it with me. And come join us someday, at the field we call An. What do you say, Tom? Tom . . . ? Tom . . . ?'

Call No. 3

'Am I speaking to Deggsy?'

'Who's asking?'

'Deggsy, hi. This is George Gillett at the Liverpool Reds. Thank you for your graffiti. Such a vibrant colour and altogether a lot of energy there, although, incidentally, that's not how you spell "scumsuckers".'

'Fair point.'

'Listen, though: I understand the concern of fans such as yourself, who worry about this new regime coming in and changing the Liverpool way of doing things. But what if I tell you that, not only are we going to build you a spanking new, mega-capacity enormodome, we're also going to continue the Liverpool tradition of blowing millions on Spanish reinforcements in the summer transfer window?'

'Brilliant!'

'Anything else I can help you with today?'

'Gizza ticket for Barça.'

'Great talking with you, Deggsy.'

Call No. 4

'Is this Bezza?'

'Depends.'

'Hey, Bezza, this is George Gillett. I got your brick. Now listen to me, punk, and listen good. You try another stunt like that on my property and I'll have your puny little Limey ass in the slammer before you can say Roffa Benitez. Understood?'

Through a Glass Brightly with Chairman Ken

In a development which very few cultural analysts saw coming, Ken Bates is the new Ted Moult. Picking up, with typically brazen aplomb, the mantle of the deceased countryman who, back in the golden age of double-glazing adverts, famously urged the nation to 'Fit the best, fit Everest', the Leeds owner and perpetually bristling controversialist is the new face of Safestyle windows of Bradford.

The television advertisement arising from this spectacular alliance has yet to see heavy rotation in the primetime slots, although, to be fair, news of it got a decent showing on *The Glazine*, the weekly e-mail bulletin for the glass, glazing and fenestration industries. And if an underoccupied afternoon should happen to find you watching repeats of *Emmerdale* on ITV2, you, too, may be privileged to catch sight of a dashingly bearded gentleman with a twinkle in his eye and a window over his shoulder. (I mean behind him. We don't see Bates humping the things around. That wouldn't be dignified.)

The advertisement transports us to the balcony and sitting room of Bates's sun-dappled retreat in Monaco where, the implication is, a well-fitted window would certainly shut out the noise of the riff-raff and assorted Eurotrash, enabling our host to enjoy in peace the company of his clear-glass coffee table and rather firm-looking armchair.

If Safestyle really is the company Bates chose to fit the windows to his Monte Carlo apartment, it would be slightly surprising, the customer testimonials on the company's website tending to be from closer and more taxable locations, such as Doncaster and Gillingham. Even so, there can be no denying the lure, wherever you are, of Safestyle's 'buy the front, get the back free' offer, something which, if it could only be adapted for the football transfer market, could make life a lot less miserable for many of the lower league clubs.

It's a straightforward ad, but word is that the campaign is about to get more complicated and that, in the planned follow-up, Bates will be seen standing on one side of a Safestyle window and holding one of Dennis Wise's team sheets. Upon the hallowed instruction, 'Let her go, Fred,' a technician on the other side of the glass fires up a giant wind turbine. Bates then allows the team sheet to drop and, amazingly, thanks to the quality sealings tested and given an all-weather guarantee by this award-winning West Yorkshire company, it doesn't blow into the hands of a Crystal Palace player.*

As Half Man Half Biscuit wrote in the pop classic 'D'ye Ken Ted Moult?', 'Rain, shine or gale force nine / His frames remain intact.' What chance an update for 2007: 'D'ye Ken Ken Bates'? These twin champions of the replacement window have more in common than you might think. Moult, of course, was a Derbyshire farmer who turned panel game contestant. Bates, too, was a farmer, in Buckinghamshire, although, admittedly,

* In the early days of Dennis Wise's unlikely tenure as manager of Leeds, one of his own players was said to have passed the Leeds team sheet into enemy hands at Crystal Palace – a rare breach of confidentiality and not an altogether good signal about team spirit at the time.

one for whom *Ask Me Another* and the dictionary corner on *Countdown* somehow never came calling.

Another similarity: while Moult is widely credited with pioneering the concept of 'pick your own strawberries', Bates is widely credited with pioneering the concept of 'fry your own supporters on an electric fence'. It's the same, laterally thinking, go-ahead spirit.

We should have known something was up when a 'platinum sponsorship' deal made Safestyle the 'official home improvement partner' of Leeds United for the 2006–07 season. Safestyle have a tradition of commissioning celebrity-led television advertising campaigns, meaning that the former Chelsea chairman now takes his place in a starry cast list that includes Ken Morley, who plays Reg Holdsworth in *Coronation Street*, Cannon and Ball, the legendary TV funnymen, and Cheryl Baker from Bucks Fizz, not to mention Safestyle's own creation, the infamously loud 'Windowman'.

Inevitably, cynics will look at Bates's seemingly late-onset passion for the fenestration industry and accuse him of a marriage of convenience. People will easily imagine him taking an animated and sincere shine to the defenestration industry, but not to the fenestration industry. It may even be suggested that commercial breaks have seen nothing so haunting since Phil 'The Cat' Tufnell first signed off on the peerless misery of a loans company commercial with the catchphrase 'Happy days'.

In which case, now, perhaps, would be the moment to tell the story of the time when Bates dragged me into a public lavatory. The lavatory in question was in the West Stand at Stamford Bridge, which at the time had been recently completed under Bates's formidable aegis, and the then Chelsea chairman was leading a group of journalists on a tour of the new facilities. The particular and sustained fierceness of his pride in the quality of the porcelain fittings and the tiling is still a subject of wonderment among those of us who were fortunate enough to be there that day.

So, why not turn to the confrontational chairman and prime

driving force behind the brick compound which is Chelsea
Village for a steer on a decent window? Let's face it, he's built
more hotels than Ted Moult ever did.

A Round with Bellamy

(*During a Liverpool warm-weather training break in Portugal, the
reliably high-maintenance Craig Bellamy took exception to his team
mate John Arne Riise's refusal to join in on the karaoke and attacked
him with a putter. Later, though, the pair were to commemorate this
extraordinary low point in their friendship in an elaborate goal celebration
together. So that was all right, then. Anyway, here, in the first of an
occasional series of golfing tutorials, Craig Bellamy of Liverpool discusses
the vexed and critical matter of club selection and talks us through his bag.*)

It's no exaggeration to say that club selection is 80 per cent of
my game. On occasions, it might be as much as 90 per cent.
And there was one time, outside a nightclub in Prestwich, when
it arguably went all the way up to 115 per cent. That's how
important it is. The plain fact is, it doesn't matter how much
you've been working on your swing, your stance and all the rest
of it: at the end of the night, if you haven't got the right club in
your hand, you're not going to be getting the results you're
looking for.

For me, it's not all about ripping it and going for distance,
either. There's a culture of that in the game at the moment,
thanks to Tiger Woods mostly, and I'm not sure it's entirely
helpful. Sometimes you'll see a situation develop where it pays
to leave the big clubs in the bag and select a three iron, for the
greater control that it affords.

Say, for example, you've been out on the razz during a
training camp get-away in Portugal and some Norwegian
pooper in your crowd has spoiled the night by point-blank
refusing to get up on the karaoke. Now, in the inevitably ensuing
confrontation back in the hotel lobby, some players I know

would want to get out the driver straight away. For me, though, this kind of situation begs a long iron every time. What you sacrifice in terms of distance, you can more than make up for in accuracy.

That said, I'm not denying that there are times when you need to give a team mate a really big wallop and for those occasions I carry a square-faced Nike SasQuatch Sumo 2 and an r7 Superquad with a beautifully firm, yet subtly whippy shaft and an enormously forgiving sweet spot. All credit to the guys at Taylor Made for this lovely piece of engineering.

Time was when I would never go out without at least a couple of fairway woods, ready for those moments when you want to give someone a crack off a clean, central lie. But, again, I found the length of the shaft meant that I was quite often bringing hazards such as bystanders and parked cars into play. The younger, more impatient me would unhesitatingly go for the spectacular. But with experience, and as I've grown older and calmer, I've become more content to lay up, if necessary. In fact, I passed the fairway woods on to Robbie Fowler, who seems to have had a bit more joy with them.

Nowadays my favourite clubs would have to be the short irons. I'm never happier, really, than when I'm in the groove and working from a moderate stance with a seven or an eight iron. You can't overestimate the importance of being able to get up and down and, if anything, it was the long hours that I invested in my short game that eventually gave me the confidence to go up against Graeme Souness.

It's something a lot of people have trouble with, though. I had a letter recently from a guy – a perfectly respectable weekend club-goer. And he said, 'Craig, I'm in real difficulty here. I've gone out with some people from work, and this guy from personnel has refused to play me at darts, saying he didn't really feel like it. And I've swung at him with a lofted sand wedge, completely missing him, but now the police are involved and there's some danger I'm going to lose my job at the end of it all. What can I do?'

To which my reply was, 'Choke down a bit on the grip. With the lofted sand wedge in particular, it doesn't hurt to try and gain a bit more control with the hands.'

And then, of course, there's the putter – probably the most important club in the bag, being, as it is, the big finisher. My fastidiousness in this area has frequently paid off and long ago earned me the nickname 'the nutter with the putter'. You see a lot of the modern players working with the new broom-handle-type putters, which is fine, although to my mind if you're looking to cause that kind of light-smashing, aerial mayhem, you might as well use a pool cue. My preference is for the conventional, shorter-length shaft, nicely weighted, with a good, thick, mallet-type end to it. Cobra make some very handy ones.

In the end, though, the difference between success and failure with a golf club in your hand comes down to a blend of so many things. That's what makes this game the endlessly fascinating and at times downright frustrating business that it is. I suppose if I had to offer only one piece of advice to someone who was just starting out and feeling their way towards hitting someone with a golf club for the very first time, I would stress the importance of a pre-shot routine.

All of us, I know, experience at some point or other the temptation to rush a shot and get it completed before the police or the bouncers arrive or before the landlord can get round from the other side of the bar. In the long term, though, the best favour you can do yourself is to establish a pre-shot routine you feel comfortable with and then, most important of all, stick to it firmly, whatever the shot, whatever the situation.

Some of you may be familiar with the concept of the swing thought – a talismanic phrase or mantra to promote focus and to discipline the rhythm of your swing. It's an approach I thoroughly recommend. My swing thought for some years now has been 'Alan Shearer'. It was an idea that came to me while I was at Newcastle United, and I've found it invaluable since then in terms of putting myself in the right space mentally. It's 'Alan' on the backswing, and then 'Shearer' down to impact and all the way up to the top of the follow-through and the finish.

Try it for yourself. 'Alan . . . Shearer. Alan . . . Shearer.' It works for me. It could work for you, too. Happy clubbing.

Ray Stubbs Does Fame Academy

'Come up and see me,' Ray Stubbs urged us, 'make me smile. I'll do what you want,' he added, 'running wild.' Hands up if you found aspects of this proposal unlikely, particularly the last bit. All those years of fronting *Football Focus* and darts from the Lakeside have rarely allowed Stubbs to vent the side of himself that runs wild.

Never underestimate, however, the transformative power of celebrity-based challenge television – in this case *Comic Relief Does Fame Academy*, by enrolling for which the amiable BBC sports presenter has surely booked himself a place in history as the first former Tranmere Rovers player to go up against Tricia Penrose from *Heartbeat* in a nationally televised singing contest.

Stubbs, of course, has previous in the Comic Relief arena. Two years ago he volunteered to be mechanically carried aloft and plunged into a pile of cardboard boxes. The more money viewers pledged, the higher Stubbs was winched. Last year he was attached to a pole and pelted with hundreds of plastic balls. Mock if you will, but thus, in the twenty-first century, do people in remote and troubled areas of the world get fed and educated. Stubbs's willingness to suffer advanced bruising in tender areas in order to equip an African schoolroom was an example to us all.

But there is a world of difference between being tied to a stake in a hail of balls and taking on the likes of Tara Palmer-Tompkinson in a celebrity karaoke tournament – even if it seems to the casual viewer that there is no significant difference at all. And if Stubbs's rendition of 'Make Me Smile (Come Up And See Me)' was a touch on the stiff side, then we should all go easy, because there is no obvious way in which watching the late results come in with Gavin Peacock on *Final Score* represents adequate preparation for convincingly inhabiting a pop classic from the 1970s in front of a live studio audience.

Credit to Stubbs, then, for surviving the weekend's preliminary cull and going through to the competition proper, which begins tomorrow. He might even fancy his chances in a weak field. Certainly it was hard to hear Linda Robson of *Birds of a Feather* do 'I Will Survive' without thinking, 'You'll be on your own, then.'

Far worse, Rowland Rivron performed Dolly Parton's 'Stand By Your Man' in a pair of fake breasts. Some things aren't funny, even for charity, and how heartening it was that the watching nation decided that they didn't want to see this incorrigible chancer ever again and voted him off.

Stubbs might be quietly confident, in the circumstances. However tough it gets up there, it's got to be easier than a volley of plastic balls to the genitals, hasn't it?*

Sorting out the Peacemakers

Andy Gray was on to something. The Sky Sports football pundit pointed out that at least half the players involved in the mass punch-up at the end of the Champions League match between Valencia and Inter last Tuesday were trying to stop it.

It was the same story in the already legendary fight involving Arsenal and Chelsea players during injury-time at the Carling Cup final. By far the larger part of the starry cast performing in this wide-screen skirmish were players attempting to prevent those with a genuine interest in hitting each other from doing any such thing.

And it was the same scenario yet again when trouble broke

* Stubbs survived eight separate evictions before he met his end – and only then because he had picked up a nasty upper respiratory tract infection, which is one of the great perils of celebrity karaoke in the winter months. The eventual winner was Tara Palmer-Tompkinson, who was quality.

out between Arsenal's and Chelsea's reserve teams recently. In the ensuing, necessarily muddled crowd scene, those players bent on unbridled mayhem were but a small minority compared with those bent on bringing the violence to the swiftest possible end.

The message is obvious. It's time to clamp down on the peacemakers. Football will never adequately come to terms with the culture of violence at its heart unless it deals with the players who rush in to stop it. Look at the damage they do and the confusion they spread, separating players and restoring calm. At best the peacemakers cause the game a legal and administrative nightmare that can take whole weeks to unravel. At worst they ruin the amusement of the paying spectator who, frankly, after a 0–0 draw as punishingly drab as the one between Valencia and Inter, could legitimately feel that he was owed some entertainment.

The increasing proliferation and influence of non-combatants presents a problem as serious as any the game currently faces and threatens to make an ass of the law as it stands. Why did none of the officials see Emmanuel Eboue floor a suspiciously weak-kneed Wayne Bridge at the Millennium Stadium, requiring the FA to post-evaluate the offence later, using video evidence? Because, on the day, a crowd of self-appointed peacemakers was in the way, holding each other and jostling, as peacemakers will, and causing a massive and unhelpful obstruction, so that none of the officials saw the real business happen.

How much simpler it would be if peacemaking were itself a straight red card offence with an automatic three-match ban attached. Go in with your hands not raised, and you're off. Attempt to defuse the situation and suffer the stringent consequences. Get involved only if you want to get involved. Players would surely think twice then about casting themselves as mediators and wading in to restore sanity, and the subtly nuanced and perhaps finally irresolvable question of whether Emmanuel Adebayor was positively involved in the fighting or simply passionately interested in its abatement would become irrelevant.

Under new, easily imposed legislation, everyone who wanted

a fight could still have one — and suffer the penal consequences, of course. Everyone who didn't want a fight, however, would be required to sit down on the pitch with their legs crossed, firmly making their position as non-aggressors clear. And that includes all managerial and coaching staff in the technical area, who should also indicate their attitude by sliding off their seats and sitting on the ground, arthritis or other medical conditions permitting. Unless the managers want to storm on to the pitch, of course — which is fine, but they need to know that they will be judged accordingly.

This new zero-tolerance approach would make identification of the genuine perpetrators so simple that even a football referee should be able to manage it without recourse to television evidence and a panel of his seniors several days later. What's more, those of us in the stands or watching on the television would see a new kind of stripped-back scrapping in which everyone's intentions were clear. And that's got to be a boost.

Too often, as things stand, the action on the pitch is frustratingly incomplete. Consider, for instance, the germinal incident that prompted the Carling Cup final bundle. Exactly how angry was Kolo Toure with Jon Obi Mikel for pulling his shirt and thereby conceding a free kick in a dangerous area? How angry is it possible for a man to become in those not particularly provocative circumstances? We will never know the answer to this intriguing human question because all those other players intervened before Toure could finish expressing himself.

We have an opportunity here to weed out the game's most notorious peacemakers. Frank Lampard is one. He's always in there, causing peace. Lee Hendrie is another. Whenever it kicks off big time, you can bank on the Aston Villa midfielder to be right in the thick of it, attempting to bring about a peaceful resolution. Chris Powell of Charlton, too. In the event of any situation involving argy and its inevitable accompaniment, bargy, he'll be straight across to calm things down by encouraging people to talk the issues through. It's high time these people were stopped.

Eliminate them and you eliminate, too, their sinister repertoire of peacemaking moves – the sickening, police-approved, reverse arm-lock, the frustrating tug of the arm, the exasperating full frontal body hug, with accompanying backwards shove away from the mêlée towards the nearest touchline, the ceaseless instructions to 'just leave it'.

No one wants to see these kinds of things creeping into the game, least of all the children for whom these players are role models. Which is why we now say to the peacemakers, 'You've had your fun. Enough is enough.'

Americans Learning Fast

Note to George Gillett Jr and Tom Hicks, the new owners of Liverpool. I know how hard you guys have worked to get your heads around the concept – chiefly alien to the American sporting mind – of a draw. How unfair it was, then, that on your first visit to see the Liverpool Reds franchise in action – a 0–1, second leg, Champions League home defeat against Barcelona – you should have been obliged to chew on something even more elusively left-field and culturally baffling: the loss which, when you do the basic maths, adds up to a draw but, in fact, officially amounts to a victory.

It's all down to this thing called the aggregate score, and this other little thing called the away goals rule.* Let's not get bogged down too much in the technicalities here. The important point is, when you thread Wednesday night's defeat through these little loopholes, it explains something which must have mystified you greatly at the time – namely, why going down to Barcelona could be described on BBC news as 'an amazing night at Anfield'. It also explains why nobody laughed when Steven Gerrard said, straight after losing at home, 'We fear no one.'

* Having won 1–2 at the Nou Camp, a 0–1 home defeat was enough to send Liverpool through on away goals.

And why everyone was jumping around at the end despite not scoring and losing.

Crazy, no? But, hey – stick around. You could grow to love it. And just wait until you get to the whole 'extra-time and penalties' thing. That one will really drive you nuts.

The Abramovichs Separate: Who Gets the Tea Bar?

Analysts have been quick to describe it as 'the biggest divorce in history' – and it certainly seems to involve more and larger yachts than most divorces do. Six or seven additional houses and one or two further private aeroplanes as well, now you mention it. Yet, as Roman Abramovich, the billionaire Russian oligarch and owner of Chelsea Football Club, separates from his second wife, Irina, a former Aeroflot air hostess, mystery still shrouds the exact terms of the separation agreement that the couple drew up under protective legislation in Russia.

Who could fail to respect their fierce desire for privacy in this matter? The stripping apart of a couple's collective assets is always painful, even harrowing. During the course of a shared life, objects become invested with sentimental value way beyond their intrinsic worth. Take those four enormous yachts, for example. That might look like a cool £189 million of ocean-going hardware to you or me, but you can be sure that, to the Abramovichs, the boats are worth so much more than that. Logistically, the division of property raises its own tricky problems, too. What good is half a yacht to anybody?

It's nobody's business but the Abramovichs, of course, how they agree to divide their property. At the same time, when the owner of one of the country's biggest football clubs sits down with his soon-to-be-former wife to apportion their assets, the public may feel it has a right to know at least some of the arrangements. Hence our own painstaking enquiries behind the scenes, yielding the following account of the separation, which, though it may not be accurate in every detail, is probably as reliable as any other report on the divorce that you will read this week.

With regard to Stamford Bridge, then, our understanding is that Mrs Abramovich gets the East Stand and the South Stand (formerly the Shed End), while Mr Abramovich retains the West Stand and North Stand, also known as the Matthew Harding Stand. This is to include all relevant snack bars and their commercial pie-heaters. Mrs Abramovich also receives ninety corporate dining tables, each seating twelve, with an appropriate number of stackable chairs and forty-five yards in total of dismountable screening.

Allegedly, Mrs Abramovich has also been awarded one half of the bar known as 'Ossie's', located to the rear of the North Stand, including related taps, kegs and bottled mixers. It is not known whether this asset comes with any obligation to manage or staff the bar, which can get pretty hectic on match days.

From the dressing room area, meanwhile, Mrs Abramovich is understood to have had her lawyer's request for the home changing room's luxury floor-to-ceiling lockers in reproduction ash declined, but to have been given by way of consolation the shower attachments from the away changing room and, from the referee's room, all of the clothes pegs and the lock off the lavatory door.

Moving on to the Megastore: it is understood that Mrs Abramovich was extremely keen to keep the Chelsea curtains. Also the Chelsea duvet and pillowcase sets and matching lampshades. However, Mr Abramovich, who is also reportedly fond of those items (and understandably so, for they are quality), may not have made this easy for her. Accordingly, Mrs Abramovich may have settled instead for 450 Chelsea egg cups, a broad selection of silver-style keyrings and 60,000 unsold copies of *Totally Frank* by Frank Lampard, with the rights to republish or pulp as she sees fit.

From the club museum, Mrs Abramovich is understood to have been granted the following items:

• One pair of boots as worn by Ron 'Chopper' Harris during
the club's successful 1969–70 FA Cup campaign, slightly blood-
ied and bearing traces of gristle. Resale value via e-Bay: between
£50 and £150.

• One complicated electronic interactive entertainment device,
enabling Mrs Abramovich to take penalties against a grippingly
realistic computer simulation of Petr Cech, valued at £3,500,
including shock-proof rubber floor mat and easy-assembly,
screw-in wall mountings.

• A signed photograph of Micky Droy, slightly foxed, worth
£1.25.

It is believed, though, that Mrs Abramovich generously intends
to leave the above items *in situ* at the museum for the enjoyment
and enlightenment of future generations. She is, however, seeking to take item one, Chopper's boots, on loan periodically, in
order to be able to enjoy them, suitably cased, in the privacy of
her own home.

Turning now to Cobham, the site of the Chelsea training
complex: Mrs Abramovich is the recipient of four six-a-side
goals, with nets, and is believed to have secured all of the
orange cones. Mr Abramovich retains the yellow cones. Mrs
Abramovich receives the blue bibs and the white bibs. Mr
Abramovich keeps the yellow bibs and the green bibs.

In addition, under the heading 'Stamford Bridge sundries',
Mrs Abramovich seems to have received a lawnmower (petrol-
powered, sit-upon), a garden fork, several plastic crates suitable
for carrying Lucozade, and four bales of electric fencing, unused,
with plug, believed to be the property of the former owner of
the club, who may yet dispute this award.

Mrs Abramovich also gets Andrij Shevchenko. This item was
apparently uncontested by Mr Abramovich.

New Wembley Goal Threat

The gala opening of the new Wembley is, inevitably, an occasion for great and uncomplicated joy. Nevertheless, a worrying shadow hovers over the event. For the decision to lift the curtain on the ground with a match involving celebrities has raised the possibility that the first goal at the new national stadium could be scored by Chris Moyles. It's an outcome that would be likely to test the limits of any Radio One DJ's modesty, and would certainly tax Moyles's. We would, it is fairly safe to say, never hear the end of it.

It can still be prevented, though – and must be. Nothing less than the history of football in this country demands that some-body – a self-sacrificing hero – man-mark Moyles today until the critical moment has passed. Possibly three people. Sitting on him, if necessary. Even if, with Moyles pinned down on the edge of his own penalty area, the honour ends up going to Ben Fogle, the presenter of the BBC's Crufts coverage, or to one of the blokes from Westlife, it would, surely, be something the game could more easily live with when the record books come to be written.*

Beckham: Just One of Us, Only Richer and More Handsome

Members of England's 2006 World Cup squad were quick to refute the allegation made by Pini Zahavi, the influential Israeli football agent, that jealousy of David Beckham and his superstar status was behind the team's abject failure in Germany last year.

'Nothing could be further from the truth,' claimed Stewart Downing. 'Becks was the genuine, down-to-earth bloke that

---

* Worry over. Mark Bright, the Radio 5 Live pundit and former Crystal Palace striker, got it.

he's always been. For instance, sometimes he let us have a go in his helicopter. Not often, it's true. He made it pretty clear that the helicopter was for his own personal use, first and foremost. But there were a couple of times when he wasn't using it and he got one of his personal assistants to arrange for a few of us to have a little ride. We went up about forty feet and then down again. It was brilliant. I made sure I went to thank him afterwards. "It's not a problem at all, Neil," he said. "Now, back behind the velvet rope, please. You're in my light."'

'Jealous of Becks? Don't be daft,' said Peter Crouch. 'There's no ego with him. He's a squad man, through and through and it was the same in Germany as anywhere else. Take breakfast time, for instance. It was my job to test Becks's orange juice and make sure it was the right temperature and consistency, and then to pour his Cheerios. But I didn't have to do it on Wednesdays. He always gave me that day off and got someone else to do it. That's the Becks I'll remember from the World Cup: always thinking of others.'

'These stories are always going to come up,' said Gary Neville, 'and I'm sick of it, frankly. Just because a player's worked hard and got himself into a position where he has his own separate changing room, it doesn't mean he's responsible for wrecking the squad's morale by causing petty divisions. None of us resented the way things were. On the contrary, we all looked at it as an inspiration and a positive challenge to each of us. I think we all understood that if we worked as hard as Becks, especially in the shaving advertisements, we, too, would get to travel to games in a blacked-out town car rather than some dingy old bus.'

'It's such nonsense,' said Rio Ferdinand. 'Pini's my agent, but I think he's gone off on one here. Sven would never have let any one player get above himself and start dominating proceedings. I remember when we checked in at the hotel in Baden-Baden and it became apparent that we didn't have enough rooms for Theo Walcott. Sven went up to Becks's suite to have a word with him about it, and Becks, quick as you like, gave him a cushion off one of his sofas, almost without having to be asked.

And that meant that Theo got a good-ish night's kip in the corridor. And people are now talking about jealousy. Give it a rest.'

'Jealous of him?' said Joe Cole. 'I'll tell you what I was jealous of: I was jealous of the man's abilities as a leader. I was jealous of the effort he put in during training. I was jealous of his commitment to the cause and the charismatic way he united us behind him as Team England. That's what I was jealous of, and all the rest is cobblers. Although I did quite fancy his money. He had *loads* of the stuff. And my own chef, masseur and pedicurist – I wouldn't have minded that, either.'

'He brought us together, is the truth of the matter,' explained Paul Robinson. 'How many captains have I played under who have put Tom Cruise on speakerphone so we could all hear him talk? I'll tell you how many. One. There's only one Becks.'

'He was huge for me,' said Frank Lampard. 'I was working hard on my book during the tournament and it's invaluable for a first-time author to be able to speak to someone who's been published already and just get advice and encouragement. And I'll never forget the day I finally managed to get through to Becks on the phone in his room and told him about a couple of difficulties I was having, mostly with pacing. And I asked him what he would do. And he said, "Don't bother. No one's going to buy it anyway." Like with a lot of the best advice, I can remember feeling a little bit hurt by the bluntness of it at the time. On reflection, though, I now see that it was exactly what I needed to hear. That's the sort of captain he was.'

'Personally, I'll never forget the impact he had on me,' said Theo Walcott. 'It wasn't just the sofa cushion. It went much further than that. There was a night, early on in the tournament, when I couldn't sleep at all. You know, I was very young and a bit overawed by everything, and I needed someone to talk to who could calm me down a bit. So I went up in the lift to the floor where Becks's suite was. Unfortunately, security refused to buzz me in, but one of the bouncers there was extremely nice and loaned me a copy of *Stuff* magazine. So I had something to read when I went back to bed and it took my mind off things and I was soon asleep. It's acts of kindness like that that you remember, early in your career.'

'Did we lose in the World Cup because of divisions about David?' said Sven-Goran Eriksson. 'Incredible that anyone could think that. Clearly, we lost in the World Cup because I was manager.'

David James Lucks Out

Is David James, the Portsmouth goalkeeper, the unluckiest man in football? He has played for no fewer than fifteen different managers in his career so far, but only two of those managers have not been English. What a bummer. Talk about short straws. Merely the statistical odds on that outcome, in the modern, foreign-led era, must be highly improbable. And thus an intelligent player, who might have responded well to the civilizing influence of foreign coaching, has been bizarrely denied the opportunity to do so.

For the record, the non-English managers James has worked for are Graeme Souness and Gerard Houllier. The list of English managers, on the other hand, includes Graham Taylor, Dave Bassett, John Gregory, Alan Pardew, Kevin Keegan, Stuart Pearce . . . a veritable catalogue of the great tactical geniuses of our time. You can only feel sorry for the man. How different his career might have been.

England: a Rite of Passage

'I'm proud of the players. Quite a few of them grew up tonight' (Steve McClaren, speaking after England had beaten Andorra 3–0 away from home).

For Rio Ferdinand, the realization that something life-changing had happened was immediate. 'People talk about those pivotal moments in life – well, this was definitely one of those. You could see the difference in people's eyes as we left the pitch – calmer, wiser. We'd just seen off the team ranked No. 163 in the world, after a bit of a struggle, and that's always going to be a rite of passage in which you leave boyhood behind and emerge as an adult.

'What surprised me, I suppose, was how immediate the effect was. For instance, we usually play this game on the plane where we take it in turns to creep up behind Wazzer Rooney and flick him on the ears. Coming back after Andorra, it didn't even enter our heads. Everyone was too busy reading the *Economist*. Same in the baggage hall: not one of us tried to push Peter Crouch on to the luggage carousel and nobody attempted to tip Wazzer's trolley over. It was like a whole new age of maturity had dawned.

'The next morning, I took all my clothes to the charity shop and bought two pairs of relaxed-fit chinos and some polo shirts. Then I traded in my Lincoln Navigator for a five-seat Vauxhall Meriva. The seats fold down very easily to create a really useful load space, and I'm getting thirty-seven miles per gallon at the moment, which I'm very happy with.'

'It's hard to explain,' Steven Gerrard admitted, 'but when I put that second goal in, I just had this overwhelming feeling that I had finally come of age. It was as if an enormous weight had been lifted off me. All those years of desperate questing fell away and I felt settled, grounded, in a way that I never had before.

'Naturally, the first thing I wanted to do when I got back was sort out the garden. So I went up to Sainsbury's Homebase and bought a strimmer and a hose-tidy. It'll be nice to be able to sit out there, with the evenings getting longer.'

'I think I was a very anxious person before Andorra,' said Stewart Downing. 'I don't think I really knew myself, or what I wanted, at all. But after ninety minutes of pitiful scampering about against no-hoper opposition, everything suddenly fell into perspective. As a result, I'm a more sensible, more certain person, and have already begun to conceive of a future for myself beyond football, possibly in synthetic wall-claddings.'

'It all happens so suddenly,' Aaron Lennon pointed out. 'And aspects of it are a bit frightening, to be honest, or certainly confusing – the growth spurts and the hormonal changes, which no one really talks to you about. But the fact of the matter is, when I got back to the dressing room, my trouser legs were an inch and a half too short for me, my voice was an octave lower and I realized I needed to shave. Also, my Nintendo DS suddenly seemed really boring. There's no question for me – I walked into that stadium a boy, and, a 3–0 victory over part-time opposition later, I left it a man.'

'I definitely grew up against Andorra,' confirmed Micah Richards. 'My only anxiety is, did I grow up too fast? It's Estonia next. At this rate, I'll be an old man soon, muttering in an armchair.'

'None of us will ever forget that night in Barcelona,' avowed Ashley Cole. 'Some of those postmen can really play, you know. And I don't care what anyone says: when a team is getting six or seven insurance clerks behind the ball, they can be next to impossible to break down. We went to hell and back out there. But having been through it together is incredibly bonding. Whatever else happens to us now, we'll always have Andorra. Do you think there might be a book in it?'

'I got into a running battle with their centre back,' Wayne Rooney said, 'spent the night swearing at everyone, was lucky not to get red carded for stamping and had to be substituted after sixty-one minutes to prevent me from exploding. Grew up? That's fucking bollocks, that is. I went backwards, me.'

Criticism: There's a Time and a Place

John Terry was quick to condemn as unhelpful the booing that was flung at the national team by impatient fans during the match against Andorra this week. 'It would be better if they waited until after the game,' the England captain suggested.

It's not only booing, though. Cheering, or other outbursts

indicative of support, can sometimes seem a bit previous, too. Consider, for instance, a situation in which fans sing 'England's number one' at Paul Robinson, and then, an hour or so later, he fails to stop a Gary Neville back-pass in highly slapstick circumstances.

Or what about a scenario in which supporters greet Wayne Rooney during the warm-up with a deeply approving chorus of 'Rooooney, Rooooney', only for him to play like a complete lump with a cheap firework sticking out of it for the ensuing sixty minutes or so, until he has to be rescued from himself by substitution?

All in all, then, it would clearly be best if fans remained silent throughout games, reserving their judgement until later, when all the relevant facts are to hand. Supporters could then gather after the final whistle and, having duly reflected on what they had just seen, record a series of appropriate noises for players to download and listen to later, on the bus or at home, at a moment that suits them. (I'm sure the FA's website people would be able to help out with the practicalities here.)

By this simple means, we can spare the players the gross inconvenience of spontaneous reactions from the paying customer and promote the culture of reasoned, constructive and timely critical response that not just the England captain but everyone connected with football wants to see.

The Referee's a Conduit

Graham Poll's alleged 'arrangement' with Alan Pardew, the manager of Charlton Athletic, saw him heavily panned this week in many media outlets. (Pardew says the referee agreed to signal to him when Charlton's Alex Song was closing in on a second yellow card, enabling the manager to pull his player out of danger by substituting him. Charlton went on to draw 0–0.) But for those of us with a keen interest in information flow and its impact on performance enablement within the workplace environment, it was another chance to learn key lessons from a man who has long since attained the status of guru within the realm of people-management.

The mistake, of course, is to see the referee as a mere official, or passive arbitrator, rather than as a creative facilitator or, if you will, conduit. Poll has done more than any practitioner in this area to break down traditional, reductive notions of the referee as 'the man in the middle', encouraging, by his own work in the field, a more flexible mindset which enables us to think of the ref also as 'the man at the front', 'the man down the sides', and above all 'the man at the centre'. Not for nothing is the elite list official from Tring regarded within the game as a complete conduit.

We've come a long way from the days when referees were faceless administrators called things like Keith Burge of Tony-pandy, who blew the whistle when necessary and occasionally ticked players off for elbowing each other. In 2007, refereeing is re-strategizing to face its challenges going forwards. And chief among those challenges is keeping players and coaching staff on-task while providing a resource-based framework in which they can maximize their potential.

The three essentials of effective game-management? Communication, communication, communication. Watch Graham: plenty of eye contact, lots of encouraging smiles. An example to all people-managers, he's not afraid to be hands-on – a touch on the arm, even a gentle and consoling pat on the buttocks (single-sex workplaces only).

And now, apparently, he also specializes in sitting across emerging situations on a bud-nipping basis. In this light, the supposedly controversial business with Pardew really only falls under the category of intervening early to have a word with a supervisor about a troubled workforce member. Those who criticize Poll for micro-managing to this degree need to reflect on the potential consequences of doing nothing in such a situation.

This is probably best expressed as a flow diagram, but let me, for convenience sake, do it in words. Let's first consider the passive course of action. We'll call it Action Plan A. Under the terms of Action Plan A, the referee (we'll call him Poll) fails to devise an inter-personal strategy involving the manager of one of the competing teams (we'll call him Pardew). Accordingly, with no warning system in place, a key player (we'll call him Song) gets the red card that was coming to him, followed by a suspension, thus weakening a team (we'll call them Charlton) during the run-in to the end of the season, with the result that Team X (we'll call them Sheffield United) stay up.

Now let's look at Action Plan B – the proactive course. In this case, Poll does take the trouble to bring on-stream an applicable communication mechanism. Pardew is, accordingly, in a position to withdraw Song. Charlton are thus unweakened by suspension for the season's vital phase and Sheffield United go down.

Now, you will note that the eventual outcomes of Action Plan A and Action Plan B are not wildly dissimilar. Both lead to a club getting relegated at the end of the season, which was going to happen anyway. The critical distinction is that it's a different club – Charlton in the case of Action Plan A, and Sheffield United in the case of Action Plan B. 'So what?' you might well ask. But effective workplace-management isn't always about making a difference to the big things; it's about making a difference in little ways, too.

Poll teaches us that, in the future, the best game-managers will thrive by facilitating the flow of information. This facilitation could take many forms – be it the shouted warning to a player about to stray into an offside position or the nod that informs a goalkeeper that his opponents might be planning a quick free kick – but it must inevitably extend to the sidelines, too.

In this area, would it really be so difficult for referees and managers to communicate with each other via Blackberry or hands-free mobile during the match? We see too many managers with their blood up, rushing into the technical area in a flurry of loose Lucozade bottles, when a quick e-mail or text message from the referee – even a fax, if we're talking about a match in the lower divisions – could have cut straight to the heart of the problem and removed the need for unnecessary and counterproductive confrontation. The technology is there. It seems perverse not to use it.

Over to you for a Powerpoint presentation on this one, Graham.

Of a Fire on the Moon – or, at Any Rate, at Villa Park

Aidy Boothroyd, the erudite manager of Watford, seemed to be vigorously playing down his team's chances of turning over Manchester United in their FA Cup semi-final. You could even say he sounded defeated already. 'It would be a major shock,' he said, 'up there with man landing on the moon.'

It's a striking analogy, in the context of a meeting between the Premiership's top and bottom clubs, although, on reflection, perhaps not the perfect one. At any rate, it may not be entirely accurate to suggest that, in the immediate aftermath of the Apollo 11 landing in 1969, the presiding emotion was shock. Elation, perhaps, coupled with wonderment. And relief, definitely. But few genuinely regarded America as the minnow in that particular encounter and, having been years in the planning, the moon landing necessarily lacked the surprise element that would have lent it the shape of a classic, fully fledged cup upset.

Drawn to face a daunting away trip to the lunar surface, the NASA crew did what one was hoping Watford would do: prepared and trained fastidiously, established beyond doubt what was physically possible and steadied itself to perform accordingly. When the rocket bearing Apollo 11 to the moon ignited on the launchpad, monitors measuring the vital signs of Buzz Aldrin revealed that, far from being all a-jitter, his pulse was sitting just below its normal rate. That's the kind of calm under pressure Boothroyd ought to have spent the week encouraging in the likes of Gavin Mahon and Hameur Bouazza. Better that, certainly, than feebly and discouragingly talking up the ominous scale of the mission.

It sounds like Boothroyd could do with some of the determination and self-belief of Gene Kranz, the Mission Control flight director, who famously announced to his staff, 'Failure is not an option.' So, come on, Boothroyd. Get a grip. Dare to dream. History amply demonstrates that far more remarkable things have happened. As NASA used to say: 'For all mankind.' Or the big bit of it that doesn't support United, anyway.*

Football: Still Value for Money

'Tickets for the West End are nothing like the prices for football matches,' said Andrew Lloyd-Webber, the lord of musical theatre, this week.

Indeed they are not. Total cost of tickets for two adults and two children to see the FA Cup semi-final between Blackburn and Chelsea at Old Trafford (cheapest available seats): £75. Total cost of tickets for two adults and two children to see *The Sound of Music* at the London Palladium (cheapest available seats): a stonking £140.

Solve *that*, Maria. And that's before you factor in the wallet-stripping cost of an interval ice cream and a replica wimple. Also, more likely than not, you already know how *The Sound of Music* ends. So which is the bargain outing here?

Woman Commentates: Hell Grows Cold

Dave 'Harry' Bassett, the former Premiership football manager, may not have seen much meaningful frontline action lately but he remains one of the game's leading thinkers, and a first port

---

* United beat Watford. Defeatism, though undoubtedly bags of fun when you do it yourself, ultimately gets you nowhere.

of call on matters ethical and political affecting his sport. Hence
one's keenness to take a sounding from him on the topic of the
first woman commentator on *Match of the Day*. 'I am totally
against it, and everybody I know in football is totally against it,'
Bassett said. 'The problem is that everybody is too scared to
admit it.'

He must mean Lawrie Sanchez, the manager of Fulham, on
whose ground the BBC's Jacqui Oatley makes her television
debut this afternoon. Sanchez has described Oatley as 'a commentator of great quality whose knowledge of the game and its
personnel is every bit as good as anyone else I have heard'. But
presumably that's just because he's a scaredy-cat, running in fear
of the PC legions, like so many in today's game.

It takes a certain kind of man to stand up and speak for
football's silent and cowed majority, and, in the area of sexual
politics, Bassett is probably the first to do so since Joe Royle,
then the manager of Everton, expressed surprise that Eleanor
Oldroyd of Radio 5 Live wasn't at home cooking the tea. A
woman commentating on the football? They'll be letting them
drive cars next. And, before you know it, they'll have the vote,
and then where will football be?

Bassett, we should note directly, is not an unreasonable man:
he's not dismissing women altogether from football broadcasting. 'I'm completely relaxed about women presenting football
shows,' he said, generously. 'Women like Clare Tomlinson are
very good.' Tomlinson will be proud, we can be sure, to receive
the Bassett seal of approval – something to put on her CV.
'April 2007: highly recommended by Harry Bassett – as long as
I stay in my place.'

But, as Bassett emphatically points out, smiling nicely at the
start and end of the show and offering an informed and accurate
commentary on a match are tasks of a quite different calibre
requiring a totally different skill-set and, indeed, sex. If you're
going to commentate, Bassett notes, 'you must have an understanding of the game and the tactics', which, he suggests, means
men only.

Fair enough. Imagine that Fulham, at some point this afternoon, switch from 4—3—3 to 4—4—2. How is Oatley, as a woman,
not to be mentally overwhelmed by the sheer brain-confounding
complexity of this change and the NASA-standard science
behind it? Or say Blackburn, Fulham's opponents today, leading
1—0, suddenly, in the game's closing phases, take off a forward
and bring on a central defender. How is Oatley's by definition
female mind to cope with the dauntingly chess-like implications
of that shift in the game's tactical set-up? Indeed, will she even
see it? Or will she have popped out to re-do her make-up?

Not for nothing, then, does Bassett insist that, in order to
work as a commentator, 'you need to have played the game'.
Quite so. Which is why, when one thinks of the chief representatives of unquestionable authority in the commentary box, one
thinks first and foremost of John Motson's twenty-two goals in
forty-seven appearances for England, and of Guy Mowbray's
four championship medals and two FA Cup victories at Liverpool, not to mention Simon Brotherton's legendary role in the
great Brazil team of the 1970s. (Note to editing team: bit rushed
for time. Could you check these facts? Ta.)

Another disappointed football analyst raises a further germane
point when he accuses Oatley of sounding, at moments of excitement, 'like a fire siren'. You wouldn't get that kind of undignified
performance from, say, Alan Green, the analyst observes, and
quite rightly. As a man, Green is naturally in a position to
exercise a greater degree of control over his emotions, and
thereby ends up merely sounding like a car alarm or a cat under
the wheel of a slowly reversing lorry. And you wouldn't hear it
on the television from Jonathan Pearce, either, whose superior
male discipline under pressure ensures that he only ever comes
across like someone who has accidentally closed his cock in a
biscuit tin.

We can all agree, I think, that a football commentator is,
above all, someone who knows the value of the single, well-
chosen word. That's why the commentary box is properly the
realm of quiet, reserved, non-attention-seeking men like Clive

Tyldesley. You can't put someone in there who is just going to twitter on. People simply won't wear it.

And while we're on the subject of not wearing things, Black-burn have already sent Oatley a replica Rovers shirt, signed by the squad, as a token of their congratulations and support on this era-changing occasion. Furthermore, the club's marketing director has gone on record to welcome what he called, in a phrase that just possibly backfired on him slightly, 'a ladies' perspective'.

Again, though, you have to ask: a shirt? Couldn't they have got her something pretty? A signed box of chocolates, even. Or some signed flowers. It's political correctness gone mad. Harry Bassett will be shaking his baffled, grey head.

So, a woman commentated on *Match of the Day* and the world did not, after all, end in a cataclysm of thunder and boiling rain amid the bloodless laughter of hooded figures on horseback. People rose from their sofas afterwards, as usual, and, entirely unaffected by scarring or famine, proceeded to bed in still intact bedrooms – those who hadn't dozed off at some point during West Ham *v*. Everton, that is. But even they came round in the usual state of mild and slightly dribbly confusion, sometime after mid-night, part-way into the repeat of *Friday Night with Jonathan Ross*, and found their homes still standing and their families safe.

Given the build-up, it was easy to forget that the person driving a king-size battering ram into a heavily fortified bastion of maleness and writing her own chapter in the history of the sisterhood, was also merely doing the five-minute highlights slot for Fulham *v*. Blackburn. Rarely can so much have seemed to rest on someone's ability to call a 1–1 draw at Craven Cottage, and if the mountain of contentious pre-publicity had an unfair effect, it was in depriving Jacqui Oatley of the virtual anonymity that the show's regular pool of staff for this job – sundry Jona-thons and Simons, honeymooning from unglamorous shiftwork on Radio Fab FM – enjoys by right.

Clearly the coolest thing *Match of the Day* could have done in the circumstances was ignore the fuss entirely – just slide in and out of the Fulham segment without ceremony, exactly as if they had sent along a Jonathan or a Simon. 'Your commentator at Craven Cottage – Jacqui Oatley.' End of story.

But when was *Match of the Day* ever cool? OK, sometimes under Des Lynam. But not once since. And so we got a gigglesome build-up from Gary Lineker ('After all the publicity, a little moment of history . . . Lawrie Sanchez's first home game in charge of Fulham') and a wince-inducing coda to the effect that 'not even the presence of our female commentator' could inspire Fulham to a home victory – which merely left one wondering how often the appointment of, say, Simon Brotherton has been expected to produce vital points for a side sinking towards the relegation zone.

As if this didn't constitute a heaped serving of condescension, complete with cream and a cherry on the top, Oatley then knew the indignity of having her performance analysed by her own colleagues on her own show. 'She did well, didn't she?' said Lee Dixon, the former Arsenal full back.

Again, one felt that different standards were operating. At any rate, it was hard to think of Lee sucking on his pencil and saying, 'I think Jonathan/Simon did OK there,' or furrowing his brow to opine, 'Not bad, that, considering it was Simon/Jonathan.' Or even, 'One or two nerves showing from Jonathan/Simon, I thought, but don't forget that as recently as last week, he was lumped with the cross-country running on Medway SMOOTH.'

If we must pass judgement on Oatley, on the basis of such limited exposure, then surely all we can say, in fairness, is that she seems to speak perfectly fluent Commentary – that archaic branch of English spoken on the nation's gantries since time immemorial, and quite distinct in its rigid formality from the language spoken by people who aren't holding a wind-resistant microphone to their chins. Sample sentence: 'It's the Italian on loan from Roma who has sent Craven Cottage into raptures.' See also 'rocket of a shot . . . didn't deal with it initially . . . found himself in acres of space . . . rattled against the crossbar . . .' etc.

In other words, and despite the programme's own best efforts, the new woman blended in completely. In fact, in some ways, had the worst fears of the game's unreconstructed blowhards been even partly realized, and had Oatley revealed bafflement about the offside rule, or broken off in the middle of a threatening forward surge by Blackburn to rhapsodize on the cuteness of Benni McCarthy's thighs, at least it would have marked her out. But that would have been asking a lot, considering the pressures she was under – not least the pressure of time. And it's a job of work, after all. It just happens to be officially women's work now, as well as men's.

Oatley, we understand, will be back for more of the same next season, when presumably she will be allowed to get on with the job in conditions approaching peace, just like a Jonathon or a Simon. And good luck to her, in those less artificially heated conditions – though, personally, I hope the BBC suddenly decides to give her the FA Cup final. Nothing against John Motson. It's just that the following morning's *Daily Mail* would glow so hot with appalled shock that it would actually burn on the news stands, and who wouldn't want to see that?

The Yo-yo Analysed

Graham Taylor had some consoling words to say this week about the rise and fall of Watford, a club he used to manage, who were promoted to the Premiership last year, but have gone straight back down again. 'There is absolutely no disgrace in a club the size of Watford being a yo-yo club,' Taylor pointed out, 'providing eventually you go upwards.'

I imagine a lot of Watford supporters will take heart from that thought at this disappointing time for them. That said, what kind of yo-yo eventually goes upwards? Taylor may have played with one more recently than me – but isn't it a fundamental aspect of one's experience with a yo-yo that its ability to bounce back gradually weakens, that its rises gradually get shorter and shorter, until eventually it is left dangling as low as it can go?

I don't know. I never really got the hang of them, if I'm being honest. It's over to Taylor on this one. He seems to have a more confident grasp of the physics.

Portsmouth Fail to Push the Boat Out

The plans for a gleaming, bowl-shaped, 36,000 capacity, state-of-the art arena, poised on a thirteen-acre floating platform at the heart of historic Portsmouth harbour, disappointingly illustrate, once again, the general timidity and lack of imagination constraining football ground planning in this supposedly boom time for the game. By opting merely to spend £600 million constructing the world's first sea-borne Premiership venue, Portsmouth have missed a significant opportunity to signal their ambition and make a properly emphatic statement about themselves as a club prepared to think big.

Not that the proposal isn't entirely without its aspiring aspects. You don't call in Herzog & de Meuron, the designers of, among other things, the Tate Modern in London and Munich's extraordinary Allianz Arena, without expecting a bit of architectural bang for your buck. (Note to Harry Redknapp: Herzog & de Meuron are Swiss architects rather than potential short-term signings currently attracting interest at FC Schalke.) And, clearly, devising a stable water-bound podium that is sufficiently level for football, and that doesn't bob up and down every time the Fast Cat from Ryde comes in, must have provided a few afternoons at the drawing board for the boffins.

Also, you've got to hand it to everyone involved for having the nerve to sit squarely behind a project which, even if successful, offers a gift beyond the dreams of avarice to the nation's headline writers ('Man Overboard! Harry All At Sea As Portsmouth Get That Sinking Feeling', etc.).

Nevertheless, one can't ultimately quell the deflating feeling that, in thinking beyond their current corrugated home at Fratton Park, the club which is currently eighth in the Barclays Premiership have gone coyly for the safe option – almost as if anxious not to appear to be getting ahead of themselves.

We see such hesitation all too often at the moment. This, it is rapidly becoming clear, is the age of the modest, unassuming football stadium – one thinks of the new Wembley and Arsenal's Emirates Stadium, to name only those – with too few architects and planners rising to the challenge of creating non-hidebound, future-driven buildings which might properly reflect the game's advancing sense of its own importance and standing within the culture. With this surprising harbour development, involving 1,500 luxury waterside apartments, Portsmouth, too, seem dispiritingly content to follow the humble precedent set by, for example, the expansion of Old Trafford, and merely blend in as quietly as possible.

How differently one might be feeling about the south coast club if they were planning to approach the council in August with something a bit bolder. Given the problems already encountered and solved, at the blueprint stage, in founding a stadium on the seabed, would it really have been asking too much to go that little bit further and make the new ground fully ocean-going, thus honouring the mighty naval traditions of its host city?

The advantages accruing to Portsmouth from playing on board a sea-faring, engine-powered craft would be immeasurable. Quite apart from yielding a variety of unique corporate entertainment possibilities and a potentially stunning location for the Player of the Year dinner dance, it would enable the arena to double in the busy summer months as an overspill car-ferry service to the Isle of Wight.

Concerns have already been raised about parking around the new development, but these would have vanished at a stroke, under more far-seeing planning. Fans could have assembled at pick-up points along the shoreline and the stadium could have come round, shuttle-style, and collected them.

And imagine the scenes when Portsmouth eventually made it

into Europe. Amid copious bunting, and with a band playing on the quay, the club and its supporters would set sail for Spain, with teary family members waving passionately and a flotilla of small craft flanking them encouragingly on all sides, sending an old-fashioned but nevertheless highly resonant message about the dominance of English football in Europe.

It's called making a splash – literally. And that's not the limit of it. It could have been the first ground to admit fans on a women-and-children-first basis – and the first in which spectators needed to be advised over the PA before kick-off about the whereabouts of the muster stations. And if the wearing of lifejackets had been compulsory, they could at least have come in club colours.

How does a small club become a big club? Not just with investment, but by daring to dream. It's a chance gone begging.*

'Big Sam', Festival Man

A plausible theory is finally emerging to explain the abrupt exit of Sam Allardyce from Bolton Wanderers. Since the club announced its manager's departure a week ago, mystery has shrouded both the timing of the decision, when only a fortnight of the season remained, and the reasons underpinning it, given the relative strength of Bolton's position and the esteem in which Allardyce appeared to be held at the club.

Insiders now believe, however, that this surprise farewell is directly linked to a single financial transaction – namely Allardyce's purchase, on 20 March, at a charity auction, of two tickets for the 2007 Glastonbury Festival, which commences in Somerset on 22 June.†

---

* No sign, as yet, of this exciting new stadium in Portsmouth harbour. But stadium-building is very much a wait-and-see business. See also the new Wembley.

† This is all true, by the way. The bit about buying the Glastonbury tickets for £10,500 at a charity auction, I mean.

The outspoken and frequently controversy-embroiled boss secured the tickets at a special fundraiser for the Nordoff-Robbins music therapy charity, thus successfully avoiding the massively oversubscribed public ballot in April. His bid of £10,500 signalled in no uncertain terms the strength of his desire to join 150,000 other revellers watching the Arctic Monkeys and sitting around bonfires in a daze – a desire further underscored by an unconfirmed sighting of Allardyce on Monday this week in the Altrincham branch of Millets buying a sleeping bag.

In and of itself, a determination to camp out at Britain's leading counter-cultural performing arts festival would not automatically require a football manager to walk away from the club lying fifth in the Barclays Premiership – or anywhere else, for that matter. Alan Pardew is believed to have been a regular in the Field of Avalon down the years – indeed, the cry 'All back to Pards' tipi for tofu' is something of a festival staple – without ever needing to quit football in advance. Similarly, Neil Warnock almost routinely gets spotted trance-dancing in the Acoustic Tent, or just generally chilling with a vegetable samosa in the Green Field, but up to now has always managed to shower and report back in time for pre-season training afterwards.

However, as Phil Gartside, the chairman of Bolton, pointed out this week, Allardyce was never less than meticulous in his preparations, and it is clear that, by walking away after last week's match at Chelsea, he has put himself in a convenient position to attend the Puravida Bank Holiday Weekender, which starts today in Gillingham, Dorset, featuring DJ Marsh and Subgiant. Many believe this will be the first stop on a detailed schedule of preparatory festival-hopping which will take Allardyce, on 18 May, to the Evolution Music Festival in Gateshead, with Maximo Park and Groove Armada, before leading him to the Isle of Skye for Kasabian. After which it will be down to the Isle of Wight Festival at Newport, with the Rolling Stones, followed, one week later, by the O2 Wireless events in London and Leeds (Daft Punk, Kaiser Chiefs), before Allardyce finally arrives at Glastonbury for the showpiece occasion in what people are already calling 'Big Sam's summer of love'.

A close friend insisted, 'I don't think there's anything particularly new here for Sam. I just think he's looking to cut loose and explore the spiritual side of himself which has always been there and which was already beginning to come out when he signed Ivan Campo.'

And if it's a muddy Glastonbury this year?

'He's more than capable of coping with that,' the friend said.

Suspicions about Allardyce's future direction were fuelled as long ago as February, when he allegedly tried to bring in Pete Tong as an assistant fitness coach. Reports indicate that the manager was increasingly barefoot on official club occasions. In addition, there were rumours of a furious argument with Stelios Giannakopoulos over the question of whether lighting joss sticks on the team bus constituted smoking in a public space.

Anyone predicting an immediate return to football for Allardyce at Newcastle should note that the annual Cropredy folk festival, featuring Flapjack, the Parsonage Brothers and Farley's Rusk, takes place between 9 and 11 August, directly overlapping with the start of the 2007–08 season. That could well rule out, among others, Newcastle United, even leaving aside the question of whether Freddie Shepherd would be prepared to meet Allardyce's contractual demands for an on-site yurt. In any case, by then the former Bolton boss may well have renounced materialism altogether and be living under the name Oberoth on a hill in Wales.

Attention now shifts to the critical matter of who is in the frame for 'Big Sam's spare ticket. Chris Coleman is obviously well placed to consider any suggestion that comes in. Lawrie Sanchez, similarly, may well find himself free to listen to festival offers in a week or so. Mike Newell, formerly in charge at Luton Town, is always likely to be there or thereabouts. And it would take a bold person to dismiss out of hand the rumour that Stuart Pearce, no stranger to the outdoor festival scene, is ready to be

tempted away from Manchester City, if the timing is right and
the tent big enough.

Football and Art: the Age-old Discussion Revived

Jorge Valdano, the former Argentina international, ex-manager
of Real Madrid and widely acclaimed 'philosopher of football',
was witheringly critical this week of the acclaim heard at Anfield
for the work of Rafael Benitez and his team. 'Put a shit hanging
from a stick in the middle of this crazy, passionate stadium, and
people will tell you it's a work of art,' Valdano said. 'It is not:
it's a shit hanging from a stick.'

Is it, though? Alan Curbishley, the curator at West Ham, begs
to differ. 'Our decision about whether something does or does
not constitute a work of art comes down in the end to our
decision to regard it as such. Was this not the point the great
Marcel Duchamp was making in 1917, when he sought to
exhibit a urinal? Artistic value does not inhere in the object
itself, but in our perception of it and its context. A stick in the
middle of a football stadium becomes, by definition, a work of
art, if people perceive it to be one, no matter what is hanging
from that stick and no matter whether it's at Anfield or, as is
equally likely, St James's Park.'

However, Lawrie Sanchez, temporarily responsible for exhi-
bitions at Fulham, argues, 'Personally, I don't find the Duchamp
analogy to be helpful here. If you put a urinal in the middle of
a football stadium, people are going to queue for it. But that
doesn't make it a work of art, does it? That makes it a urinal. Or
possibly a health hazard, depending on the drainage situation.'

According to David Moyes at Everton, though, 'It's irrelevant
whether what's on the stick is nice or not. It is not the duty of
the artist to be merely pleasing to the senses. It is the duty of the
artist above all else to confront, to unsettle, to challenge the
complacency of his audience. If this involves doing unpleasant
things with sticks in stadiums, then so be it. For when an artist

ceases to unnerve, he ceases to be an artist. I have observed the work of Benitez at Liverpool. Let me tell you: this man is an artist.'

However, Mark Hughes at Blackburn said, 'Shit on a stick? A child could do that. I like art which actually looks like what it's meant to be: a bowl of fruit, a vase of flowers. There's skill in that. I certainly can't be doing with all these isms – situationism, contextualism. The game has gone ism mad. It's just mind games, as far as I'm concerned.'

So who is the Spanish artist at the centre of the great conceptual art debate that is currently splitting football down the middle? Born in 1960 in Madrid, 'Rafa' Benitez Maudes moved to England at the age of forty-four and first came to attention with a striking situationist piece, 'Crouch Up Front' (2005), also known as 'The Bride Descending a Staircase Backwards'. The art world was quick to hymn a groundbreaking talent, observing how 'Crouch Up Front' offered 'something different'. Subsequent notable works have included 'Bellamy Out Wide, with Pennant' (2006) and 'Trusting Gerrard to Get Us Out of Trouble with a Hopeful One from 45 Yards' (2004–7).

Benitez is most famous, however, for the large-scale series-in-progress which began with the piece commissioned to mark the Champions League final of 2005, titled 'Nicked It on Penalties II'. Regarded in some circles as Benitez's masterpiece, this was an open homage to an earlier piece by the French artist Gerard Houllier, dating from the time of the 2001 Worthington Cup final and entitled 'Nicked It on Penalties'. Benitez then returned to the same theme, producing, for the occasion of the 2006 FA Cup final, 'Nicked It on Penalties III'. That was followed as recently as the beginning of this month by a piece unveiled for the semi-finals of the 2007 Champions League called 'Nicked It on Penalties IV'.

Critics note that each of these works, when taken on its own, has at best superficial merit. However, when the series is considered as a whole, there emerges a work of mesmerizing scope and ambition, playing with nothing less than the concept of time itself, in which things appear to be moving on, while, in fact, nothing changes. The hypnotic effect of this piece explains why, even though he sells sluggishly on the domestic market, everything by Benitez has been snapped up eagerly by private American collectors.

Nevertheless, the theoretical arguments won't go away. Sam Allardyce, now linked with the major curatorial vacancy at Newcastle, says, 'I look at Benitez's stuff sometimes and I don't know what anything is. It seems a complete mess to me. Most of the time I don't even know which way up it's supposed to go. And I end up asking myself, "Is it art?" And I end up answering myself, "No."'

On the other hand, Alan Pardew, in charge of acquisitions at Charlton, appears to speak for the pro-Benitez side of the argument when he says, 'I don't have a problem with an artist working small, and using a very limited palette. I don't have a problem with an artist repeating the same theme, either. I liken it to George Stubbs and his paintings of horses. Always those bloody horses! But, you can't deny, he got good at it.'

So, Liverpool by Benitez: a work of immense power, profound meaning and expressive beauty from a man destined to be numbered among the leading artists of our time? Or dung on a pole? This one isn't going to die down.*

The Clap They so Richly Deserved

I bore witness this week to Chelsea's heavily trailed 'guard of honour' for Manchester United – a highly collectable piece of theatre in which Chelsea lined up to applaud the title-winners on to the Stamford Bridge pitch. And, like all acts of tenderness between rival football teams, its effect was fundamentally destabilizing. Gabriel Heinze, the United defender, looked slightly

---

* Later, England would acquire a bona fide, art-collecting manager who would be able to adjudicate on these slippery issues once and for all. See p. 369.

thrown by it – and he knew it was coming. It led one to consider, then, whether there might be an exploitable tactical use in the future for the surprise guard of honour at random moments of the season in order to spread confusion.

On any ordinary Saturday in October, for instance, Blackburn, say, would break out of the tunnel and form a line for Tottenham, for example, who wouldn't have a clue why they were being clapped on to the pitch and would be left wondering whether they had forgotten something and working out how they should react.

The overall effect could be radically enhanced by the unannounced presentation of confusingly substantial gifts – a pony, for example, or a grand piano. The state of disorientation and general distractedness thus procured would surely be good for at least twenty minutes of any ensuing match. And as the pundits are always telling us, the first twenty minutes are critical.

So Ironic

'It's so ironic that he's been the man that turned their season around,' Gary Lineker said, referring to Carlos Tevez's season-saving input at West Ham. The presenter was, we take it, using 'irony' in the football-related sense, to mean an entirely intended, wholly plausible and utterly twist-free outcome. We have to assume this, because Tevez's contribution to West Ham's safety would only be ironic, in the usual sense, had the club specifically appointed him to produce a sequence of bizarre on-pitch errors designed to lead them down into the Championship. Only in that circumstance would Tevez's provision of the goal that kept West Ham in the Premiership be ironic. Except in football, it seems, where 'irony' now officially describes the straightforward fulfilment of someone's carefully laid plans. Ironic.

Le Saux in Marathon Bounce-back

Quietly, stealthily, unannounced, with only a few million people tracking his progress, Graeme Le Saux has made his way to the semi-finals of *Vernon Kay's Gameshow Marathon* on ITV. Having sailed convincingly through *The Price Is Right*, the former Chelsea and England full back returned with his wife to see off full-strength opposition, including Ben Fogle and some bloke off a soap, in the 'Mr and Mrs' round.

Accordingly, Le Saux now stands on the edge of a major primetime television success that would have seemed unlikely as recently as last summer, when, on the eve of the World Cup, he walked out on the BBC's football coverage, alleging broken promises on the corporation's part regarding his role during the tournament.

At that point, the future looked bleak for the personable ex-international with the ready smile. Shortly before Christmas, though, as an advocate on *Extinct*, ITV's pro-celebrity conservation smackdown, Le Saux silenced the boo boys by hoisting the Rwandan mountain gorilla into a top-three finish – a spectacular outcome for an animal with such limited resources. (I'm talking about the gorilla, obviously.)

On that occasion, his quest ended in disappointment when he was beaten back by Pauline Collins and the Bengal tiger. But there was no ignominy in that and *Gameshow Marathon* found Le Saux in buoyant form, effortlessly emerging from the soundproof booth to concur with his wife that, if obliged to choose between wearing a German football shirt, a thong and a flowery swimming cap while on holiday, he would take the flowery swimming cap.

We are used to seeing ex-footballers forging media careers in punditry. What we are less used to thinking about is the kind of media careers ex-footballers might forge when they are ex-pundits. Le Saux is very much at the cutting edge in this respect, inspiringly putting himself on the line for more substantial challenges, and making Mark Lawrenson look very timid indeed.

Such are the rewards for daring to think big. Instead of inspecting replays of squandered shooting opportunities and saying 'he'll be disappointed with that', Le Saux has played his part in saving a gorilla and, now, at least two antiquated gameshow formats. Ironic, Gary Lineker would call it. And he'd be wrong.

First Thoughts on the First FA Cup Final at the New Wembley

First team to lift the FA Cup at the new Wembley? First goalscorer in an FA Cup final at the new Wembley? First players to be booked / substituted / sent-off in an FA Cup final at the new Wembley? We'll find out the answers to some, if not all, of these questions after the first teams to compete in an FA Cup final at the new Wembley have walked out together for the first time in an FA Cup final at the new Wembley.

But it's not only the elite stars who awake today in the hope of securing their place in the Wembley legend. The clean slate provided by the new stadium means that the history books are thrown wide open and records arc up for grabs in all categories.

First streaker during the first FA Cup final at the new Wembley
The opening of a new venue and the attendant media frenzy make the big occasion a 'must do' for freelance exhibitionists, many of whom will have been encouraged by a stadium design which has brought pitch and stands so much closer together and has entirely removed from the equation the potential discomfort of sand. Today's quick-change artists represent a tougher policing challenge than any the old Wembley faced, so expect stewards at the turnstiles to be frisking, not only for bottles and sharp objects, but also for Velcro fastenings.

First person to burst into tears during 'Abide With Me' before the first FA Cup final at the new Wembley
Fingers on the buzzers for this one, because you'll need to

be quick. The existing, old Wembley record for 'Abide With Me'-based lachrymosity is 0.047 seconds, held by Carl 'Poodle' Besterman of Kirkdale, who set it before the 1974 final between Liverpool and Newcastle United. It's a category in which Liverpool supporters have traditionally done well and, on that occasion, Besterman is reported, not only to have come off the blocks with startling pace, but also to have gone into a crying jag so intense that it only formally ended with a cup of tea at half-time. Today's competitors are going to have to go some to match the legendary Besterman, but a time within the 0.05–0.06 second bracket ought to be enough to secure a new era record.

First person to jump up and down in the background while a roving television reporter is trying to interview a celebrity fan ahead of the first FA Cup final at the new Wembley

The classic category for anyone seeking unauthorized television exposure while a minor British film actor, wearing a suspiciously new scarf, is explaining to the BBC's Hazel Irvine that they get to see their team 'whenever work commitments allow'. One notes how the event has grown more physical down the years. Originally passers-by were content to stand mutely to one side. This was followed by the great waving and gurning era of the 1980s and 90s (the so-called 'Hello, Mum' years), which has in turn given way to today's situation, in which brazen interruption, intrusive chanting and massed bouncing in such a manner as to jostle the celebrity are all deemed perfectly acceptable. Not for the faint hearted.

First person to complain in writing about the catering for the first FA Cup final at the new Wembley

Expect many to seek glory here. Becoming bitterly upset about the price and standard of food which one has no obligation to eat is a fundamental part of the Cup final experience. The earliest complaint on record dates back to 1907, when Arthur Pippin, of Stannington, wrote to Crystal Palace, then home of the final, as follows:

Sirs, it pains me to say so, but that tripe was absolute tripe. What is more, at tuppence ha'penny per paper bag-full, it was dismally overpriced and, which is worse, there wasn't enough of it.

In the modern era, records in this area tended to be held by David Mellor, the former Tory MP, whose position at the helm of the short-lived Football Task Force essentially made him a government-appointed burger supremo and a fierce advocate of the football supporter's inalienable right not to have to go more than two hours without a hot meal. As of today, though, the door is wide open again.

Actually, I quite fancy myself for this one.

Dear new Wembley,

Call that a slice of pizza? I didn't know which bit was the pizza and which bit was the box. And £15.99 for a hot dog? You're having a laugh.

There. Record claimed. And I haven't even arrived at the ground yet. Get in.

First person to miss a goal because they were in the lavatory during the first FA Cup final at the new Wembley

The original record holder in this area was Silas Staplemarsh, of Kidlington, who, during the 1874 FA Cup final at Kennington Oval, popped out to relieve himself exactly as Oxford University were mounting the attack which would lead to their second and decisive goal against Royal Engineers. Legend also reserves a special mention for William Formby of Thornton-Cleveleys whose poor bladder control led him to miss all seven goals in the fabled 'Stanley Matthews final' of 1953. Fifty-four years on, the fact that the new Wembley has, allegedly, more lavatories than any other public building in the world (2,618) makes this, as it were, a barn door target for the wannabe history maker.

First fan of the losing side to appear on the big screen weeping desolately into their scarf, only for the person in the next seat to nudge them, alerting them to their projected image and leading them to grin and wave ecstatically instead, at the first FA Cup final at the new Wembley
My tip for this afternoon (OK, more of a prayer, really, than a tip): it will be someone at the Manchester United end.*

You'll Win Nothing with Kids

On 29 April, Sam Allardyce left Bolton after eight years as manager. 'It became clear that he wanted some time with his family,' Phil Gartside, the Bolton chairman, explained.

Just sixteen days later, on 15 May, Allardyce became the manager of Newcastle United. It's a shocking turnaround which illustrates all too clearly the desperate toll that spending time with the family can exert upon a man in 2007. These days, the pressures of family life mount with worrying rapidity. The long hours, the ceaseless scrutiny, the constant decision-making, the perpetual judgement by results, not to mention the meals in Nando's – one sees how the stress of coping could quickly build to the point where it would ultimately force a man back into football management.

Sure enough, it took little more than a fortnight at home for 'Big Sam' to decide that enough was enough. It's a sorry tale, but a tale which is very much, one fears, of our time.

---

* Correct, narrowly – Didier Drogba's goal late in injury-time winning the Cup for Chelsea after what was widely agreed to have been the least entertaining FA Cup final of the televised era, and certainly the worst ever staged in the new Wembley at that point. Not that Chelsea fans particularly noticed.

A Farewell to Graham Poll

Come with me, if you will, on a journey of the imagination to a hotel room in Germany in the summer of 2006. It is the hotel room of Graham Poll, the football referee, and, as we slip undetected through the door and take up an invisible position beyond the standard lamp, the digital clock by the bed shows that it is merely hours since England's premier match official accidentally showed three yellow cards to the same player, thus critically undermining his authority, ending his World Cup and inadvertently scoring a forty-five-yard net-buster for comedy.

A television, perhaps, flickers silently from its cabinet. A Corby trouser press sits unused by the wall. And on the puckered bedspread, in the hour of his desolation, Poll is seeking manful solace in the arms of Carlos Simon, his FIFA-endorsed colleague from Brazil.

'Graham, you are a top guy,' Simon is saying. 'Football is shit . . . football is nothing . . . don't worry about it . . . your family is what matters and you are a really nice guy.'

We take these words from the account of Poll himself, who described this touching moment in an interview given to mark (and mark well) his retirement. 'He said that to me in my bedroom in front of Jose-Maria Garcia Aranda, FIFA head of refereeing,' Poll reported. 'A lot of tears were shed and it will always live with me.'

So, the referee does not walk alone, after all. Why, he only has to make one high-profile rick for his room to fill with Latin American FIFA representatives, crying and hugging. In the movie of Poll's life (don't rule it out), this surely will be the clinching scene, the tipping point that has our shoulders heaving, the salt tears plopping into our Revels. I see Antonio Banderas as Simon – maybe Joe Pesci as Aranda. And for Poll? Well, Poll himself, probably. I can't think of anyone else who plays Poll as well as Poll does.

That Crazy Hellzapoppin Burns Report in Full

It's the independently commissioned, soon to be implemented, far-reaching structural review that simply everyone is talking about – and when the shareholders of the Football Association voted overwhelmingly to accept its reforms it was 'one of the most important days in the FA's 144-year existence', according to Geoff Thompson, the FA chairman. So party like it's 2007 with our handy cut out 'n' keep guide to the FA before and after the Burns report.

Before: Geoff Thompson
After: someone who isn't Geoff Thompson

Before: internally monitored stationery cupboard
After: independently monitored stationery cupboard

Before: men in suits
After: men in relaxed-fit, free-breathing, easy-wash, nylon play-wear. Or maybe suits

Before: plates of slightly stale ginger nuts
After: plates of slightly stale but independently sourced ginger nuts

Before: out-of-control spending on vainglorious public building projects
After: no need. Wembley finished

Before: open season on attractive personal assistants
After: enhanced availability of mid-life crisis counselling

Before: Brian Barwick
After: Brian Barwick

Hatton's Low Blow

Sometimes sport lobs us a moral quandary so knotted that one hesitates even to catch it, let alone to begin to unpick it and attempt to arrive at an opinion about it. And so it is with the case of Ricky Hatton and his belt.

As a Manchester City fan, should Hatton have invited a Manchester United player (Wayne Rooney) to carry his belt into the ring before his light-welterweight fight against Jose Luis Castillo in Las Vegas? Does the friendship and affinity between two, young sporting icons transcend mere tribal divisions? And are City-supporting Hatton fans small-minded to threaten to boycott the fight unless the boxer rethinks his strategy?

And the answer, obviously, in the first place, is no. I mean, whose side are you *on*, Hatton?

Big Day for Blushing Steve McClaren

It's a huge weekend for Steve McClaren – you could even say, an enormous one, a period that may come to define the England manager and his era. It's the weekend of the weddings.

We assume, at any rate, that McClaren is one of a relatively small number of people in Britain who was sent invitations to all four of the week's nuptials featuring England footballers. We assume, moreover, that he is one of an even smaller number who will feel professionally obliged to turn up at all of them.

Priding himself on his man-management skills, and recognizing the importance of squad morale, McClaren will know only too well what kind of message it would send to Michael Carrick if the manager attended the nuptials of Steven Gerrard and Alex Curran at Cliveden House Hotel in Berkshire, and didn't bear witness to the betrothal of the Manchester United midfielder to Lisa Roughead at Stapleford Park in Leicestershire.

And he must know that Gary Neville would never forgive
him if he went to see John Terry and Toni Pool plight their troth
at Blenheim Palace in Oxfordshire, but neglected to witness the
splicing of the Manchester United full back and Emma Hadfield,
his childhood sweetheart, at Manchester cathedral, and after
awards back at their place.

McClaren will be grateful to Terry, at least, who had the
foresight to get in early and marry a day before the other three,
thereby beating the rush and having his pick of the flower
arrangers. Talk about tactically astute. But McClaren would
expect no less from the Chelsea centre back. It's why he made
him captain.

Even so, it's still a three-wedding assault course the manager
faces. In terms of the driving alone, that's a mighty prospect, as
McClaren heads south from Oxfordshire to Berkshire for the
Gerrard splicing, before turning north again to Leicestershire,
for the Carrick do, and then heading on to Cheshire and the
exotic home of the Nevilles.

Also, ask yourself, how much coronation chicken can one
man be expected to eat?

Yet this is a rare opportunity for the England boss. Thus far
in the role, McClaren knows, he has failed to impress. Even
now, after a victory in Estonia, the feeling persists that he is a
struggler, one of life's natural assistants, promoted beyond his
capacity to cope. Today, though, he gets the chance to prove
himself on his own terms. By tonight, if all goes well, McClaren
will have become the first England manager to have danced to
'The Birdie Song' in four different counties inside a twenty-
four-hour period. And if that doesn't finally silence the doubters,
then what will?

If you still question the scale of the challenge, consider the
outlay on presents. I don't know where Gerrard and Curran had
their wedding list, but I wouldn't be surprised to discover it was
at a Porsche garage somewhere. And if McClaren thinks he can
get away with buying a key fob, he's kidding himself. I don't
suppose Gary and Emma are the kind of people to settle for an

IKEA salad bowl, either. The combined effect of the weekend's multiple wedding coincidence could wipe out someone on a humble FA salary until Christmas at the earliest.

Then there's the question of what to wear. Ideally, McClaren will be after something that looks shop-fresh, but which won't crease up in the car between weddings. In many ways an England tracksuit would be perfect. It's not formal, it's true, and it would probably lead to him being asked to stay out of the photographs. But everyone would understand in the circumstances. And it would give the parents a greater chance of working out who he is and what he is doing there. Ditto the bouncers.

All in all, it will be well after midnight when McClaren nears home tonight. He will be exhausted and nearly broke. His ears will be ringing from four doses of the Blue Satin mobile disco, with DJ Mikey Mike (or similar). He will have heard, up to four times, a best man request a photo of the bride and groom, mounted if possible – just holding hands if not. He will be experiencing an uneasy, cramping sensation in his stomach that comes only from driving 360 miles and eating an inadvisable number of miniature smoked salmon roulades. He will never want to see a piece of fruitcake again. Nor anyone's granny. But he will have seen off the biggest challenge of his international career. He hopes. And if not – well, hey, that's why they call it the impossible job, Steve.

Just the forty-eight pages on John Terry's wedding in *OK!* magazine, then. Just sixty-one colour pictures of the Chelsea centre back and/or his wife on the most important day of their lives, only seven of Ashley and Cheryl Cole looking happy for them and a measly four of Lionel Richie providing the cabaret, making a little under a third of the issue in total. Fair enough, there's a full account of the telegrams sent by Prince William, Gordon Brown and the Beckhams. And a random quarter-page shot of a tower of cupcakes. But even so, it's a massive disappointment for those of us who had been hoping the magazine would really splash with the story – to the extent, in fact, that you wonder whether the commitment was really there, in the end, on *OK!*'s part. Show some respect. He's the England captain.

Fruit Selection with Jose Mourinho

'Young players are a bit like melons.' Who didn't emphatically agree with Jose Mourinho? 'Only when you open them up and taste the melon are you 100 per cent sure that the melon is good,' the never less than fascinating manager of Chelsea elaborated. 'Sometimes you have beautiful melons but they don't taste very good. Other melons are a bit ugly and when you open them the taste is fantastic.'

Absolutely. Been there, done that and chewed the cantaloupe.

But hang on, though. Does it have to be that complicated? Seeking practical enlightenment in this area, we did what we always do at times of food-related uncertainty – consult Delia Smith. And lo, on page 75 of *Delia Smith's Complete Cookery Course*, the queen of the fuss-free kitchen has this to say: 'To test melons for ripeness, press the opposite end of the fruit from the stalk with your thumb. If it gives a bit, then the fruit is ripe. A ripe melon should smell fragrant too.'

Simple as that, then. A little squeeze and a sniff, and bingo – that transfer fee or long-term developmental investment need not be in vain. Was Khalid Bhoularouz fragrant? Did he give a bit when pressed at the opposite end from his stalk? There's a fair amount of money and trouble that could have been saved, right there.

Other top tips in this area from Delia: 'Always store melons in sealed polythene bags [to prevent them absorbing refrigerator smells] and remember to bring them out of the fridge in time to reach room temperature.' Right again. Nothing more disappointing than an over-chilled melon. Ask Shaun Wright-Phillips.

Caning the Plastic

England's tricky Euro 2008 qualifier in Russia will almost certainly take place on a plastic pitch, it was announced – and, ah, how the mind reeled back to the golden, if short-lived, age of synthetic football. Loftus Road, isn't it? Kenilworth Road, too? Early 1980s? All-weather frolics? Hmm? Small shorts and nasty grazes? Polyester-mix jumpers for goalposts?

Was it not the great Bill Shankly who said, 'If God had meant football to be played on grass, He wouldn't have invented nylon-based polymers'?

Innocent times – before affordable undersoil heating and the introduction of global warming nipped the plastic pitch in its man-made bud. Remember how the fashion briefly raged hot enough to propel Subbuteo into producing a mock Astroturf surface, challenging the orthodoxy of the time-honoured cloth? It came in a giant cardboard tube and had a nap like an exhausted Brillo pad. The ball skittered and bobbled uncontrollably across the surface and left it altogether at the slightest encouragement. Brilliant. Just like the real thing.

Your artificial top is a totally different kind of surface – a proper, man's surface, you might say: stiffer, more abrasive, more conducive to the casual production of static electricity. Statistics suggest that, in a particularly physical encounter on an artificial pitch, the averagely involved defender can expect to suffer anything up to 82 per cent carpet burns and that box-to-box midfielders will generate, in their socks alone, enough electricity to heat a municipal swimming bath for up to a month.

Legends are rife within the game of the central defender who caught fire attempting a sliding tackle, not to mention the unfortunate right back who, having been given a torrid time for more than an hour by an overlapping wing-back, inadvertently touched an advertising hoarding and shorted the floodlights. It is often said of Gary Lineker that, following especially intense encounters on artificial surfaces during his time in Japan, it was sometimes more than two hours before his shorts finished discharging.

What a wake-up call lies ahead for today's salon-waxed stars. And what a challenge for Steve McClaren's as yet undemonstrated tactical nous. On unforgiving Russian plastic at sub-zero temperatures, a team is going to need all the protective leg hair it can muster. But who in the game has that kind of leg hair these days? It's why the England manager would be well advised to pick a team for this one with, first and foremost, hirsuteness in mind.

McClaren will already know who his hairiest players are. Wayne Rooney, Gary Neville – those names pretty much write themselves on to the team sheet for a match like this. But what about other key players – your Steven Gerrards, your Frank Lampards, definitely your David Beckhams – who may well have all but abandoned body hair as part of their high-maintenance male grooming routines?

At the very least, McClaren needs to issue a memo to all players in contention for a squad place, instructing them to swear off leg-waxing and emollient massage oils between now and October. A nightly, before-bed application of candle wax and refrigerated lamb fat, removed in the morning with a pan-scourer, should help both to encourage hair growth and to ensure leg flesh of a suitable robustness come the day.

Thickness of knee skin, after all, will be a huge factor in Russia – possibly the clincher. Accordingly, one can only lament the timing of Jamie Carragher's retirement from international football. The uncomplaining Liverpool lung-buster may be only fifth or sixth in the queue for a place in the centre of England's defence, but the thickness of his knee skin is pretty much unparalleled within the modern game. Probably only John Terry among today's Premiership big boys has thicker knee skin. Certainly there are major question marks over Rio Ferdinand in this area, while Ledley King's knee skin, however thick it might be, is relatively untested at international level. Carragher, one fears, has walked away from the international scene exactly at the moment the door was opening up for him and some diplomacy from McClaren may be in order.

Backroom staff are going to need a thorough briefing, too. It goes without saying that tossing an open Lucozade bottle to a player who is outputting 240 watts of direct current through the sleeves of his shirt is courting disaster of a very high order. McClaren can ill afford at this sensitive moment in his England career to reopen the tiresome club *v.* country debate by returning home with players who are, literally, frazzled from international duty.

Plenty for the beleaguered boss to think about, then, in the run-up to this critical and now additionally complicated game. But at least the rest of us can enjoy the reverie. Nasty bounce? Sore ankles? Goalies in track pants? Enduring image, hmm? Rubber granules? Isn't it?

So, how did you get on with the plastic pitch? Any niggles? Any problems changing direction at pace? I had a little panic about thirty-five minutes in when I turned quickly in my chair to pick up my mug and thought I felt something go in my knee. But it was nothing much and I was able to flex it off well before half-time. Apart from that, it was like watching football on any other pitch for me. It's hard to know what all the fuss was about.

Nevertheless, questions about the surface dominated the build-up, to the exclusion of pretty much everything else. It was matters like these, surely, for which high-definition television was invented. The unforgiving clarity of its gaze would have told us directly what kind of plastic we were dealing with in Moscow. Was it the soft, yielding material found on drinking straws or the vicious stuff used to bubble-wrap children's toys? Or was it simply a green tarpaulin, held in place at the edges by tent pegs?

Unfortunately, our Russian hosts weren't in a position to offer an HD feed, any more than they were in a position to offer a grass pitch. Sky were lucky, though: at least their commentary team found something to plug their microphones

into, unlike the Radio 5 Live team who, following an administrative slip-up, were reduced to commentating via their mobiles.
So small and tinny were the results that Alan Green sounded
like he was speaking from a position astride Sputnik. Now,
there's a thought.

Anyway, in the absence of detailed pictures of the plastic, we
were left to fall back on our worst fears. The terrifying prospect
had been raised of balls bouncing randomly and to a height of
anything up to 110 feet. We had come to be concerned that
under-prepared English knees would find the surface heavy
going and swell to the size of water melons within twenty
minutes of the match kicking off. We were worried that Paul
Robinson would become confused by a back pass and slice the
ball into his own net – though, of course, we worry about that
on any surface, in any country.

And so the worrying continued, right up to kick-off time,
courtesy of Sky's punditry panel, which was itself the rich mix
of natural and synthetic fibres which has been making people's
hair stand on end since time immemorial. 'I think it's an absolute
disgrace that we have to play on this pitch,' Jamie Redknapp
said. 'It's not a good surface – it's not grass.'

'It's not plastic,' Glenn Hoddle explained. 'It's a decent Astroturf, one of the best you can get. But it's not as true as grass.'
The former England manager also had plastic-related reservations about Joleon Lescott, the debutant left back. 'I had him
at Wolves. When we trained on the Astroturf in the winter, he
never wanted to train on it. Physically he didn't feel good
on it.'

Blimey. It was becoming almost impossible to cling to the
solitary optimistic outlook on this situation that one had managed to come up with – namely, the more something resembled
a credit card, then surely the better the present generation of
England internationals would be likely to understand it and feel
at home using it.

Anyway, a fat lot the pitch had to do with anything, in the
end. Before long, England were in control, Wayne Rooney was

lashing the ball in and David Platt, the co-commentator, was demonstrating that, when using the expression 'the full volley', it is perfectly acceptable for the word 'volley' to be silent, hence: 'He's just caught that so sweet on the full.'

It was the perfect complement to the broadcast's unashamedly grand and portentous opening wherein, after some stirring preliminary images of Moscow (black and white, naturally), Richard Keys announced, 'Russia is reborn. There's a new confidence about the biggest country in the world.'

Wouldn't you have loved to have heard Sky Sports' number one football presenter talk some more about post-communist optimism in the former USSR? And with Michael Palin talking about retirement, a space might be opening up for a thoughtful travel writer with an engaging on-screen personality. But unfortunately Keys had to move on to the football so there just wasn't time.

Of course, everything changed with the entry of Roman Pavlyuchenko, – or as Platt, risking nothing, tended to call him, 'this guy'. This guy scored twice to give Russia a 2–1 victory. 'I don't think the pitch was a factor,' said Hoddle. 'The pitch was OK.' Now you tell us. By then we had seen shots of defeated England players lying ruefully on the surface. One genuinely nasty thing about Astroturf: no matter how badly you want it to, it very rarely opens up and swallows you. Not the good quality stuff, anyway.

Spin it Like Beckham

You'll have been wondering, I don't doubt, in your quieter moments, about David Beckham. What's he up to these days? How is that wife of his? And the kids. They must be growing up. What are they all doing, do you suppose? We hear so little about them.

A big shout-out to ITV, then, for screening *David Beckham: New Beginnings* and bringing us up to speed with the family and their news. Obviously we won't have all the details until we get the round robin with the Christmas card. But in the meantime, it was something.

And what a lot there was to catch up with. David and Victoria have, it transpires, left Spain and moved to America. Very happy, thank you. Beautiful home in the hills, nice school for the kids, who are doing well. And David's got a new job with LA Galaxy earning approximately $80 bazillion an hour, so he's not doing too badly, either. 'I believe in this move,' said Beckham during the show. And, as the sun glinted off the swimming pool and the distant towers of downtown LA shimmered beyond his T-shirted shoulders in the brilliant Californian light, it was hard not to believe in it with him.

Other bullet points: David was gutted to get the call from Steve McClaren dropping him from the England squad, and would have burst into tears there and then if he hadn't been sitting next to Jonathan Woodgate, who would have 'had something to say about it'. In Woodgate's absence, though, Beckham cried all the way to the press conference at which he announced his retirement as England captain, and all the way home afterwards, whereupon he threw up. 'I'm one of the most emotional people you'll meet,' he explained.

These travails apart, it seems to have been business as usual *chez* Beckham. ITV's continuity announcer had warned us to expect 'scenes of flash photography from the outset'. Well, obviously. What are the Beckhams about if not the crackle of flashbulbs? This programme called David 'the most recognizable sports star Britain has ever produced' – 'recognizable' being, in our time, the optimum accolade. To hear him marvel at his own reception at Los Angeles airport ('Just to walk through and see the amount of coverage that we got . . .') was to be in the presence of a man who has measured his life in paparazzi ambushes.

The degree to which he has courted and resisted the attention must, alas, be a question for another day. Let us simply remember the ancient philosophical conundrum: if a celebrity falls over in a forest and no one photographs it, did it happen? Outside Beckingham Palace in Hertfordshire, the cameras briefly alighted on a sign saying: 'No Photographic Equipment Allowed On These Premises'. Is that why they moved?

Meanwhile, here's Alexi Lalas, general manager of the Galaxy, on the value of 'recognizable': 'That's a wonderful thing for any product, to use that as a platform to brand yourself all over the world.' Product? Platform? Brand? Wo! These are tough words to swallow for those of us with a copy of *Woodland*, Alexi's 1994 rock CD, recorded back when he hadn't cut his hair and sold out completely to the Man. Dude, what happened?

Few regrets for Becks, of course, although he's going to miss 'English pubs', he says. Who knew? Becks is a sucker for a lager top, a pickled egg and a game of dominoes. Expect scenes of flash photography in the Dog and Duck from the outset. And he'll miss the England branch of the David Beckham Soccer Academy, though, as he reasoned, 'I might be over in Los Angeles, but I'm never far away.' No kidding.

The last word belongs to Becks: 'Sometimes you have to look at the big picture.' Also the small print. This hour of television was brought to us by 19, the Beckhams' management company, and was 'copyright Brand Beckham Limited, 2007'. Enjoy the show? Good. You have just been branded by the Beckhams. People talk about the media being out of control, but clearly not all aspects of it are.

Top-drawer Draw

Two Champions League third-round qualifying ties that we're really looking forward to: FH Hafnarfjordur or BATE Borisov *v*. Zaglebie Lubin, and FK Ventspils *v*. Pyunik. When astonishing match-ups of the quality of those two are produced, UEFA must wonder why they go to all the trouble of organizing a proper draw, when they could equally well get someone to sit on a keyboard and see what comes up.

Exposed: the Sordid Secret Life of the Referee

Slowly, the lid begins to lift on the football referees' official fortnightly get-togethers at Staverton Park. 'We used to do Arthur Askey impressions,' Graham Poll confesses in *Seeing Red*, his gripping new book. 'Nobody missed the Thursday night quiz, either – or the bingo nights that were funny and rude.'

These regular, three-day gatherings for the elite list officials were the brainchild of Philip Don, the FA's head of refereeing, back in 2001, at the dawn of the professional era. He had in mind fitness training and briefings on matters of law. He can hardly have known that he was laying the foundations for a hotbed of depravity, hitherto shrouded in secrecy, in which bingo and quizzes were allowed to flourish, and wherein graphic allusions to sadly missed stalwarts of the British entertainment scene were not only tolerated but encouraged.

Poll isn't the first retired official to break the code of *omertà* relating to Staverton. In his acclaimed memoir *Who's the B*****d in the Black? Confessions of a Premiership Referee* (Ebury Press, 2006, 312 pages, 30 colour plates), Jeff Winter fingers Peter Jones as the 'social secretary' behind 'a multitude of events that were a laugh a minute' at the get-togethers, including 'a game of Connect Four'. 'We also got involved in fund-raising events for local charities and sports clubs,' Winter writes.

Poll pleads for mitigating circumstances to be taken into consideration. 'We were fit, youngish and, for the first time in our lives, were being supplied with proper, co-ordinated kits,' he writes. Well, true: take a group of men in the first flush of youngishness and grant them complimentary access to name-brand sportswear, and there may be no limit to the devilment they will wreak. But just because the outcome was predictable, it doesn't make it any less shocking.

Our own investigations into goings-on at this purpose-built hotel and conference facility near Daventry, Northamptonshire, offering twenty-two meeting rooms and convenient access to the M1, and accepting all major credit cards, make disquieting reading. They confirm the worst fears of a deep-set and possibly permanent culture of draughts at the heart of top-flight ref-ereeing. They paint a picture of a world in which people think nothing of playing Beggar My Neighbour on their evenings off, and where Uno is rife. They reveal a group of men away from home and out of control, no longer recognizing any normal boundaries of behaviour and in frenzied search of dominoes.

One insider told us, 'It all went along perfectly nicely for a while. In the day we trained hard and had meetings about the offside rule. But then there were the evenings to cope with. I suppose it changed the day that Steve Dunn brought along Pictionary. Some of us were worried about it. You know how these things go. It starts out harmlessly enough, with Boggle. But then it moves on to things like Mousetrap and Kerplunk and, before you know it, someone is suggesting Twister. It never did get as bad as Twister, by the way. But you know what I mean.'

Our source remembers looking on in horror one night as Graham Barber initiated a paper/scissors/rock championship. 'I don't mind admitting that I was a bit frightened. I went round the room, saying to people, "Don't you think we ought to be in bed?" But it went on until gone 9.00, when finally Uriah Rennie went scissors to Howard Webb's paper and the evening broke up. Imagine if word had leaked out that this is what we were getting up to behind closed doors. We were supposed to be professionals.'

Things rapidly worsened. 'I can't be 100 per cent sure about this,' our insider says, 'but I think the person who introduced the monthly tombola was Alan Wiley. I went along with it. Which, I know, makes me sound weak. But a lot of us did, on account of peer pressure.

'It was a slippery slope, of course – but how slippery I didn't appreciate until Mike Dean beckoned me into his room one day with a furtive look, and closed the door. He threw his suitcase on the bed and opened it up, and there, wrapped in a towel, were all these jars. "Deano," I said. "What are you playing at?" He just grinned. "Home-made jam," he said. "For the tombola. Don't tell anyone, eh? It's our little secret."

'I was worried. I was thinking, "This is going to get badly out of hand." But what could you do? I seriously contemplated having a word with Philip Don about it and I mentioned as much to Dermot Gallagher one night, when the day-room was empty. "You can't do that," Dermot said. And then he lowered his voice to a whisper. "Don't you realize? Oh, you poor innocent fool, where have you been? Don is in on the tombola thing. It was him who donated the tin of cling peaches."

'I was devastated. If I hadn't been in with a chance of ref-ereeing the FA Vase final that season, I would have packed my bags and walked right then. But I stayed. And, as it happened, later that night I won the cling peaches. Result.'

On the eve of a new season, Neale Barry, the FA's head of senior refereeing development, has already declared his hope that referees will not be regarded as 'celebrities'. This latest evidence that the men in the middle are, in fact, crazy, fast-living renegades could not have come at a worse time.

Incidentally, how *do* you do an Arthur Askey impression? Is it just a matter of shouting 'Ay Thang Yew' and 'Hello, play-mates' at random moments? Or is there more to it?

There is so much to enjoy in *Seeing Red*, Graham Poll's luminous autobiography, that one is reluctant to pick out favourite moments for fear of not being able to stop and simply reproduc-ing the entire text. Nevertheless, I must mention how I keep going back with especially renewed amazement to the appen-dices, which offer a full statistical breakdown of the much-missed referee's career (results, attendances, cards given, etc.), and include a table showing how the Premiership would have looked if only games refereed by Poll had counted – an illusion lavishly entertained, you would have to say, in the preceding 351 pages.

For me, those tables almost, but not quite, eclipse for majesty the moment in the acknowledgements where Poll writes, 'I

would like to thank the people of Tring for their quiet solidarity.'
So many questions here – such as, how quiet, exactly, was that
solidarity? And how quiet does solidarity have to get before it
stops being solidarity and starts being ignoring someone? Truly,
this is a magnificent volume.

Thinking of England

(A rare clash of international fixtures caused a rare moral quandary.)

The football or the rugby? England's Euro 2008 qualifier against
Israel at Wembley, or England's opening World Cup tie against
the USA at Stade Felix Bollaert? It's a no-brainer for Alex
Curran. As large parts of the country prepare to reach a decision
over the choice of viewing presented by this evening's clash of
internationals, Steven Gerrard's partner knows exactly where
her attention will be directed.

'Steven is away with England,' the distinguished wag wrote
this week in her newspaper shopping column, 'so on Saturday I'm
having a few of the girls round for an Ann Summers party. We'll
have a few drinks and some food, and a good laugh, I'm sure.'

Well, I suppose lying back and thinking of England takes
many guises. But surely this is no time to be perusing novelty
bedroom apparel in a relaxed home setting. For heaven's sake,
there's a war on – or, at any rate, a World Cup, clashing inconveniently with the qualifying stages of a European Championship.

England is calling. Twice. And at the same time. Put down
that see-through camisole and heed the cry. But which cry? It's
a huge decision, however you look at it. On the one hand, a
patched-together team scrabbling wildly to keep its chin above
water after a dire period of unfathomable underachievement.
On the other hand, a patched-together team scrabbling wildly
to keep its chin above water after a dire period of unfathomable
underachievement.

Let's not pretend, of course, that we don't know how the majority of the country will vote. For most of the nation, the idea of watching rugby when there is football on seems about as alien as the alien in *Alien*. You could even say it seemed Welsh. At the very least, it might be the kind of thing someone would do in Gloucestershire, but almost nowhere else.

But that's not to say there aren't sports fans everywhere – moderate, thoughtful sports fans, with their country's best interests ever at heart – for whom this rare and unfortunate piece of fixture congestion forms a proper dilemma. And maybe a few more of us – those of us apt to press the football button right away in these circumstances – need to consult our consciences in this area.

Yes, it may 'only' be England *v*. USA – and who knew that the United States even played rugby? (In terms of pure anthropology, World Cups can be tremendously enlightening in this way. See also the presence of Ireland in this year's cricket World Cup.) But are our memories really so short? This is the rugby World Cup we're talking about. The last time English players competed in one of those, in Australia in 2003, they won it and the nation melted all over them in helpless adoration.

Remember that? We went to Heathrow Arrivals when they flew home, stood cheering on the tables of Costa Coffee and waved at them, teary-eyed, from the roof of Tie Rack. We put them on an open-top bus in the centre of London and forgave them for being drunk and looking pretty silly in ties. We helped ourselves to 'the feelgood factor' as though it were the all-you-can-eat salad bar in Pizzaland. Can we really just turn our backs as our brave boys set out to defend the title we once gurgled over, abandoning them now like so many unwanted puppies in a bin liner, simply because they've become a bit rubbish since then?

At the same time, this could hardly be deemed a sensitive moment not to be tending unconditionally to Steve McClaren and his national football project – not when qualification for Euro 2008 is looking so iffy, when the manager's job is teetering on the line and when half his squad is either injured or pretending to be. The responsible nationalist may be tempted to ask, 'Who needs my support more?' Well, good luck with that. It's one ambulance, two crash scenes, patently.

Practically speaking, then, what are the options? Well, there's . . .

Watching the rugby and recording the football

Principal advantage: seen after the event in fast forward, the strike partnership of Emile Heskcy and Michael Owen may attain pace and a convincingly threatening aura. Other key advantage: a major saving on miserable counterpoints from Mark Lawrenson. Disadvantage: noise from the neighbourhood may disclose outcome of football match, spoiling it for later. Neighbourhood noise is rarely generated by televised rugby matches, apart from in Gloucestershire. Which is why it might be better to go with plan two . . .

Watching the football and recording the rugby

John Motson's increasingly unhinged perorations could handily serve as distraction during large periods of play in the rugby when the ball is entirely invisible under a pile of large, American bodies. Also, seen later in fast forward, Lawrence Dallaglio may still look like he has it. Lots to recommend this approach then . . . except that doesn't it still amount, in the end, to a feeble capitulation to the behemoth football, of the kind we were trying to avoid? So, how about . . .

Television tuned to the football, radio commentary from the rugby

The magnificent roar of Radio 5 Live's Ian Robertson could lend the dying agonies of the Steve McClaren era a whole, new, Wagnerian grandeur which Mark Lawrenson's moaning is unlikely to supply. Potentially confusing, though. Could try . . .

Television tuned to the rugby, radio commentary from the football

But no: equally confusing and, worse, would lead to unwanted exposure to Alan Green. Perhaps, then . . .

Flicking backwards and forwards

Technically perilous. Likely to be watching meaningless ruck in the rugby – or, for that matter, in the football – as key action happens on the other side. Worse still, likely, following un-planned fumble with remote control, to be watching mean-ingless ruck between Jack Lemmon and Walter Matthau in *Grumpier Old Men* on Five as key action happens in both rugby and football.

Actually, you know what? The whole thing is a minefield. Ann Summers party, anyone?

In the Interests of Competition

When people say the Barclays Premier League is 'wide open this year', they tend to mean, on closer examination, that Arsenal or Liverpool might win it, rather than Chelsea or Manchester United. Which makes it 'open', up to a point, but hardly 'wide open'.

So it was intriguing to hear from an Arsenal supporter this week about his team's match last Sunday with Portsmouth. Arsenal went down to ten men, following a sending-off, and apparently the game then became something like a proper con-test. Portsmouth ventured into Arsenal's half a couple of times, and there were some exchanges of open and plausibly competi-tive play, before Arsenal won 3–1.

The suggestion was that if the top four clubs were obliged to field diminished teams from the start (ten or nine men, say, against bottom-half clubs, and perhaps as few as seven against Derby), then fewer matches would be mere formalities and the league might genuinely move towards the wide openness that everyone seems to crave. It sounds a sensible and exciting notion to us, and we look forward to hearing back from the Premier League on this.*

---

* Complete silence from the authorities. But I guess they're busy.

Proper Representation

There was much cynical and tiresome sniggering from people who ought to be above that sort of thing after Jay Jay Okocha, the former Bolton Wanderers midfielder, revealed that he had been sent to his latest club by God.

'I always ask God if it is His will, and if so, let it be,' the Nigerian international explained. 'That's the message I got, and that's why I'm here at Hull City.'

Well, good for him, we say. Better to get God to do the negotiations, surely, than some unscrupulous agent.

The Crisis in Female Goalkeeping

The women's football World Cup is underway in China, and everyone is talking about it. Well, some of us are. The problem is that not everyone who is talking about it is doing so in an especially helpful way. On Radio 5 Live's '606' homepage yesterday morning (slogan: 'Comment, Debate, Create'), as England readied themselves for their critical group stage match against Germany, contributions relating to the topic were limited to one. It read, 'Are their [*sic*] any hot female footballers?'

Thanks for that, 'Torres Right Peg'. The name doesn't give a lot away but I've got a hunch that you might be a bloke. Am I right?

It's a shame because the football in China has frequently been as entertaining as the more frequently screened version of the game involving men. It's been fast and slick and watching Brazil has been just like . . . well, watching Brazil.

Until, at any rate, someone shoots from distance, high and on target. At which point, sadly, it all goes a bit wrong.

Too often do we see the looping, long-range effort drop behind the goalkeeper's head, spoiling the otherwise perfect veneer of professionalism and seriousness. In a related manner, corners and lofted free-kicks are apt to induce small flurries of flapping and scrambling, leading to easily satirized mayhem. You could say the same thing happens when Paul Robinson is in goal. As, indeed, it does. But not with anything like the same frequency.

The tournament's opening match has proved emblematic. It finished Germany 11 Argentina 0. Now there's a scoreline you don't often see. And reluctant though one is to single anyone out, much of the blame for the match's implausibility had to be laid at the door of Vanina Correa, the Argentina goalkeeper. She pushed a corner into her own net after eleven minutes, and opinions vary over how many of the subsequent ten goals she was implicated in: certainly the third, possibly the fifth and the seventh, maybe the ninth and tenth, and definitely the final, match-clinching eleventh, the one that finally put the game beyond Argentina's reach. Suffice it to say that so often has the phrase 'the hapless Correa' been used in reports from the tournament, that many are now convinced that 'the hapless' is her first name.

Yesterday, Correa was, understandably, rested for Argentina's second match, against Japan. Even then, Japan's late winner came from a fumble by her stand-in. Meanwhile, Ghana's match against Australia presented a rare opportunity to see a goalkeeper put the ball into her own net from four yards out, with the side of her foot. That was soon after the Korean and US goalkeepers had exchanged soap bars. And yesterday afternoon, Nadine Angerer, the veteran German goalkeeper, suffered the unusual indignity of seeing the ball bounce over her head as she stood just inside the eighteen-yard line. (It went out for a corner.)

So, how do we explain this running faultline? A global crisis in female goalkeeping? It seems unlikely. There is no crisis in any other area of the women's game – quite the opposite, in fact: every other aspect of the women's game appears to be booming. 'Ah,' you are going to say, 'but goalkeepers are different.' Well, yes, but there is no reason, surely, in 2007, why female goalkeepers should be regarded as any more or less different than male goalkeepers.

In the end, it must come down to height. It wasn't Correa's fault that the goal seemed to loom dauntingly high over her. And by no means is she alone in China in making the bar seem to have been set implausibly high. Brazil's 5–0 victory over New Zealand included a goal struck, high and with force, from several miles out by Daniela. 'You just don't save those,' Guy Mowbray, the BBC's commentator generously suggested. Actually, though, you do save them, sometimes, if you're taller than 5ft 7in.

So where are the tall women goalkeepers? After all, though not all women grow to be as long as Petr Cech, some women do. Maybe, in the playgrounds of the world, girls could be encouraged to start picking on the taller ones ('Oi – you're going in goal') rather than, as seems to be the case, picking exclusively on the smaller ones, easier though that is. Maybe then, in a new climate of positively discriminatory bullying, some lengthier goalkeepers would start coming through from grass roots.

There's a far simpler solution, though: smaller goals. Nothing radical: just a few inches off the height and width to bring the goal into proportion and give the average female custodian a shouting chance. One is aware that, historically, proposals to make things smaller in the women's game have been received poorly. Sepp Blatter, the president of FIFA, for example, a man who has spent so long thinking 'out of the box' that many now doubt whether he even knows where the box is any more, proposed in 2004 that women compete in smaller shorts, and, quite rightly, has never been allowed to forget it.

But we are not seeking, as Blatter apparently was, to narrow the gap between women's football and lap dancing. We are merely positing a minor adjustment of scale that would suddenly bring a sport, rapidly shaking off minority status, into serious contention for a major audience, to the point, even, where the currently distracted constituency represented by 'Torres Right Peg' would be convinced.

Interlude: Premier League All Stars

(Sky One's ground-breaking reality football format brought together ex-pros, celebrities and 'ordinary fans', some of whom were even less well known than the celebrities. And as if that wasn't enough, it also saw the return of not one but two disgraced pundits and featured an appearance from the prime minister's wife.)

Let me break this to you as gently as possible: there will be no series of *The Match* on Sky One this year. It's a sickening blow for fans of schedule-filling programming at the reality/football interface – and also for Graham Taylor, who will have no opportunity in 2007 to manage a team of celebrities against a side of portly ex-pros and end what now amounts to fully three years of hurt for followers of the celebrity game. (The ex-pros have always nicked it, usually with a solitary goal from a heavily breathing Ally McCoist, and always in front of an amazingly jam-packed St James's Park in Newcastle. But you know what they say: they love their football in that city.)

Don't despair, though. Warming up gingerly on the sidelines, and waiting to come on as a sub in the way that certain members of the cast of *Doctors*, or similar, so often did for Taylor's celebrities, though preferably with more impact, is *Premier League All Stars*.

The last time I looked, a Premier League All Star was a 2-in-tall, collectable plastic bust of a footballer, bearing only a passing resemblance to the footballer in question beyond the colour of its strip and, occasionally, on some of the more thought-through ones, the colour of its hair. Now, though, it's an all-new television format, promising to bring together legends, celebrities and total unknowns in an orgy of indoor football, played in replica strips to draw on our pre-existing sympathies.

Obviously, even before any other viewing challenges arise, the fundamental business of distinguishing between the celebrities and the total unknowns is going to keep us all on our toes. And let me say straight away, if you can separate *Casualty*'s Kip Gamblin from someone who has just walked in off the street on the off-chance of a televised kickabout, then you are already ahead of me.

But essentially the idea is that some football–mad stars of stage and screen, or thereabouts, will know the rare pleasure of turning out alongside some *bona fide*, if retired, club legends. Moreover, at the same time, a few hand-picked blokes with no record in either football or soap acting will know the even rarer pleasure of 'representing their club' alongside both the legends and the celebrities. We at home, meanwhile, will know the rarest pleasure of all, which arises from watching a programme that can flash up, without comment, a caption reading 'Gareth Gates, Aston Villa'. In your dreams, Villa fans. Or maybe not.

In the show's opening episode, the burden of picking the lucky unknowns from a crowd of eager triallists fell to Neil Warnock, fresh from piloting Sheffield United back into the Championship and ready, clearly, for new and exciting challenges. The tact and sensitivity for which he is renowned throughout the game were much in evidence, not least when he told the players trying out for Liverpool, 'To me, you all look like convicts.'

Moreover, Warnock still seemed to be nursing a few unhelpful grudges about his last season in the Premiership. Those Liverpool triallists were asked, 'Why didn't you play your full team at Fulham last year?' – a decision which none of them, in all honesty, could be said to have been in control of. Later, Warnock found himself muttering, still more trenchantly, 'West Ham – my favourite.'

Still, grievances aside, Warnock was pleased to discover that some of these people could really play. Better still, a handful of them could really play at the level that they boldly announced they could play at before the trials began. (In the flint-hearted manner made popular by *The X Factor*, contestants were allowed to build themselves high before betraying themselves in action, and the player who described himself in advance as 'one of the best unfounded talents in the world' spoke with greater wisdom than he knew.)

Those chosen to wear the shirt in the weeks to come gave shaky-voiced interviews in which the honour was rarely under-estimated. 'To be playing for Manchester United is something I thought I would never do,' said one. As for the Blackburn fan who declared, 'I try to base myself on the Robbie Savage work ethic' – well, let's just say he seemed to be choosing the long way to the nation's heart.

But who wouldn't be pleased to compete alongside the likes of Jamie Redknapp and Donny Tourette in a game devised by Craig Johnston, the former Liverpool player, described in the programme as 'a football visionary', mostly on account of the fact that he once designed a boot? Johnston's visions for *Premier League All Stars* amount, less than startlingly, to a drop-ball instead of a kick-off and the use of sin-bins for miscreants. But he hymned the selection policy. 'Legends/celebrities/fans is a priceless format,' Johnston enthused. We'll see. The un-knowns certainly look quite good. The celebrities are usually quite good. And the legends, formerly great, are now, with age, quite good. At the very least, it should be quite good.

Finally the waiting is over and the inaugural *Premier League All Stars* season is underway. Speaking to us amid no shortage of chrome from an open-plan punditry platform beside the indoor pitch at the David Beckham Football Academy (duly rechrist-ened the All Stars Arena for the occasion), Ian Wright explained, 'It's about pride, it's about passion, it's about dreams being realized.'

It's also about Angus Deayton robbing the ball from a stum-bling Matt Jensen in the centre circle and attempting to play in Detective Sergeant Dave Rimmer down the channel. And I know what you're assuming, but no: as much as the context would seem to insist that he was, Detective Sergeant Rimmer isn't a peripheral character from *Heartbeat* – he's an actual Detective Sergeant, the unique selling point of this week-long, nightly seven-a-side festival on Sky One being that it brings together not just legends and celebrities, in the time-worn manner, but also fans, to create what I suppose we need to describe as a 'pro-celebrity-am' format.

Note how the human interest is thus increased tenfold. All right, maybe only threefold. Some number of fold, anyway. The point is, as moving as it is to see Lee Latchford Evans from Steps given the chance to pull on an Everton shirt and do a job for the club he loves, it's even more moving to see the same opportunity handed to a window-fitter with no previous experience of live television at the reality/challenge interface. Especially when that Everton side includes the likes of Dave Watson, Adrian Heath and Neville Southall – figures who bulk large in the Merseyside club's storied history and, indeed, have never bulked larger.

And none more so than Southall, the legendary shot-stopper, who appears to be no easier to put the ball past these days, and is possibly even harder to beat. 'I've still got it,' Southall insisted, undeniably, before kick-off. Though he immediately admitted, 'I'm just not sure what it is.'

All in all, with a squad that included Donny Tourette, the punk-rock throwback, Everton were the kind of side one could have stood to have seen a lot of. A shame, then, that they had to go and get bundled out of the competition at the first time of asking by 'rogue trader' Nick Leeson and Rodney Marsh's Manchester City (final score, 3–0).

Yes, that's Rodney Marsh the ex-footballer, not Rodney Marsh the window-fitter, or Rodney Marsh the detective sergeant. It's been a while since the maverick former City striker cut a swathe across the screens of Sky – two years, in fact, since Marsh lost all his punditry work with the channel after attempting a slightly ambitious tsunami gag during a football phone-in. 'You're on Sky Sports?' Not any more you're not. The punishment seemed harsh – not to say self-sacrificial, when you consider that the phone-in in question is not famously spoiled for contributors prepared to risk a stab at humour, well advised or otherwise.

Still, it would appear that Marsh has done his time and that some kind of rehabilitation is underway, even to the point where the striker was trusted to share his thoughts with the nation, from a seat on Wright's chrome platform. It's a pleasure to report that Marsh acquitted himself happily enough without any reference to the tsunami or any other natural disaster greater than the show under appraisal.*

But Marsh is not the only disgraced football pundit who has come cap-in-hand to *Premier League All Stars*. The show also represents the formal return to the commentary box of Ron Atkinson, who was Big Ron until a live microphone picked up his lecture on Marcel Desailly's workrate, but who has been Diminished Ron ever since. The road back towards bigness for Diminished Ron has been long and tortuous. It has seen him attempt to underscore his cultural openness by learning a foreign language in *Pardon My French*. And it has seen him try to reclaim his authority by taking on the role of football troubleshooter in *Big Ron Manager* – albeit that any trouble shot by Diminished Ron during that series tended to come back to life in a much bigger and more terrifying form, as in some kind of horror movie.

Finally, though, Diminished Ron finds himself entrusted again with an open mic, and, as David Platt remarked, referring to Simon Garner of Blackburn's predatory instinct, 'You never lose it, do you?' So far we've heard Atkinson note that a team was 'a man light in the celebrity situation' and commend someone on 'a tidy lay-off', which is something Diminished Ron and Marsh alike would know all about.

Actually, you look around the All Stars Arena on match night and you see a surprising percentage of people who might be thought to have something to apologize for – be it Deayton,

* The comeback was officially underway, and, confirming as much, Marsh went on to appear in *I'm A Celebrity . . . Get Me Out Of Here!* soon afterwards. See p. 358.

who lost a job to tabloid infamy, be it the man who brought down Barings bank, or be it, on a very simple level, Neil Arthur of Blancmange, the 1980s synth band. So, yes, *Premier League All Stars* is about pride, passion and dreams. But it's also about forgiveness.

Crisis at Chelsea? Show me where. Playing with flair, coherence and a genuine sense of unified purpose, the side tucked five past Bolton Wanderers. And it could so easily have been seven – nine, in fact, if those two extra strikes had come during the Powerplay period, when goals count double. What's more, in stark contrast to last week's bare stands at Stamford Bridge for the Champions League match against Rosenborg, the fans turned out in numbers – a strong signal that the support is there when it matters, which is to say during the *Premier League All Stars* tournament on Sky One.

People deride the All Stars as a tin-pot trophy and an unwelcome burden on an already overloaded fixture schedule. With its innovative three-way blend of retired professionals, celebrity fans and fans who aren't celebrities, we prefer to regard it as 'the people's tournament'. If, as seems increasingly likely, this is the only silverware that Chelsea lift this season, I can't see how Roman Abramovich could possibly be disappointed.

Yes, it's only seven-a-side. And yes, there is no place in Europe on offer for winning it. Yet in a world of woe, the All Stars offers the troubled viewer a comforting parallel universe in which Ruud Gullit is still a silky presence in midfield, in which Kerry Dixon continues to rise imperiously in the box, and in which a recruitment consultant from Milton Keynes can clatter Liverpool's Jason McAteer from behind for the price of just sixty seconds in the sin-bin. What's not to like?

Not that McAteer enjoyed it very much. From that moment on, the former Republic of Ireland international found himself involved in a running battle with the said recruitment consultant, which included an off-the-ball incident from which McAteer's dignity did not emerge completely intact.

'McAteer reminds me of one those dogs that hasn't been walked and gets a bit aggressive,' Steve Claridge, valuably on duty in the commentary box, mused. But then I suspect that *Premier League All Stars* has a similar effect on all of us. It's two long hours spent indoors every night, and we could all use some fresh air and a tree afterwards, and possibly, not long after that, a basket.

Right now, though, looking away doesn't seem a sensible option. Not when Frank Worthington and Craig Johnston appear to be battling so compellingly for the Worst Hairstyle Overall award. (Johnston's grey pony-tail makes it look as though he is being followed closely at all times by a squirrel, but Worthington probably nudges ahead with his unique combination of abundant hair and completely absent hair, unmanageable and manageable together in the one ambitious styling.)

And how can anyone sensibly turn over when Euan Blair, the son of the former prime minister, is making his debut for Liverpool? 'People have been asking me, are you going to be playing on the left wing or the right wing?' Blair revealed. Ah, those old political gags. I bet he never tires of hearing them. And, of course, as it turned out, Blair landed up somewhere around the middle, neither significantly one thing, nor the other. (Boom, and again, boom.)

He looked promising enough in the dressing room beforehand, where he joined his team mates unselfconsciously in a rousing chorus of 'We all dream of a team of Phil Neals'. In truth, though, his opportunities to make a significant contribution where it mattered were hampered by the knee injury he was carrying, and also because, in all the excitement, his boot came off, not once, but twice. The close-up shot of Blair's unoccupied trainer, abandoned somewhere near the centre circle, was one of the more forlorn and unprepossessing television images we have seen in recent days, even though this is the party conference season.

'I think Cherie might have made more of an impression,' was Claridge's unforgiving summary. Euan's mum was, indeed, available for selection. At any rate, she was in the crowd – and roundly booed by it, too, though we should add, in fairness, that pretty much everyone involved in *Premier League All Stars* gets roundly booed. Round booing is simply part of the overall, panto-style package, along with flashing lights, pumping music and ear-splittingly loud hooters to signal full time. (My favourite moment of commentary so far came at the end of Manchester City *v*. Blackburn, when Andy Burton remarked, 'I don't think they've heard the klaxon.')

The other significant innovation here (one which the FA might consider having a look at) is the removal of the old-fashioned kick-off in favour of a ball-drop. At starts and restarts, the match ball is simply released from a metal tube, high above the centre circle, meaning it is possible for someone to get an elbow in the eye as early as the game's opening second – a huge entertainment bonus.

All this, and Chelsea win. Perhaps.*

A Qualified Success for 'Student' Grant

(*Nobody quite believed it when Chelsea replaced the hyper-glamorous Jose Mourinho with the almost completely unknown and technically unqualified friend of Roman Abramovich, Avram Grant.*)

Let's be clear from the start: this column unreservedly supports the concept of a statutory professional qualification for football managers. By extension, it completely understands why, whenever a club tries to install a manager who lacks that statutory qualification, representatives of the League Managers' Association start jumping up at the window and barking. After all, if

---

* No they don't. They go out in the quarter final to Sunderland. The winners of the series were Middlesbrough, for whom Alistair Griffin, from *Fame Academy*, netted a last-minute title-clincher. A glorious moment for the club and also, in a way, for *Fame Academy*, which hasn't seen a lot of success in recent years either.

the idea ever took hold that just any old pal of the chairman
could manage a professional football club, anarchy would surely
ensue. In this sense, the UEFA Pro Licence is the slip of paper
standing between all of us and chaos.

Also, consider what would happen to the public standing of
football management as a vocation, if you didn't need to pass an
exam to get through the door. The job would lose its claim to
be taken seriously as a formally regulated, thoroughly disciplined,
professional calling involving a lot of shouting and pointing and
a fair bit of work in the week with cones. In the absence of
UEFA Pro, people would be able to say any old nutter could
do it, and that wouldn't be fair.

Nevertheless, despite all this, we can't help feeling that a little
flexibility might be in order, at least on a case by case basis. After
ultimately futile, badge-related non-scandals involving Glenn
Roeder and Gareth Southgate, the latest manager to have his
fitness to govern called into question on a technicality is Avram
Grant, who (it may well have come to your attention already)
has replaced Jose Mourinho as the manager of Chelsea. Grant
has no UEFA Pro Licence – and, indeed, for all we know, may
until very recently have thought UEFA Pro was only available
on Xbox.

Now, there may well be significant reasons why Grant should
not have been handed the reins of a top Premier League club
with ambitions to dominate in Europe. Some of those reasons
may become painfully apparent in the forthcoming weeks.
Alternatively, they may not. But, as our researches over the last
few days unignorably reveal, a lack of relevant qualifications on
paper is not one of those reasons.

For instance, Grant is, we have come to understand, the
current holder of an internationally valid driving licence. Moreover, it is our belief that he passed the associated driving test first
time. Or, if not first time, second time. Early doors, anyway.
And people may carp and say it was easier in those days, without
the written exam aspect. But you still had to reverse around a
corner and not run anyone over, so credit where it's due.

Furthermore, in swimming, we believe Grant to be in possession of the following three certificates: Prelim 1, Prelim 2 and 200 metres freestyle. We also believe he is the holder of a Life Saving Skills badge, grade one, which is the one where you have to jump in wearing your pyjamas and then get out again without drowning. They don't just give those away with cereal, you know.

As a scout, meanwhile, Grant's credentials are not open to question. He has, we are led to believe, badges for knots, cookery, campfire safety and singing, and received a gold woggle for his efforts in bottle-top collection. We also understand that he was accepted as a member of the Tufty Club in 1961 and maintained that membership, unopposed, until 1964.

In addition to this, we are persuaded that, at an unspecified village dog show in 1989, Grant was the handler of a pale brown, soft-coated Wheaten Terrier which took the first place rosette in the Obedience (Sit, Stay and Recall) category. The dog was also placed second in Best Turned Out Dog and third in Dog Most Like Its Owner – a tidy afternoon's work by anybody's standards.

Plus, of course, Grant brings to the table sixteen years of club management in Israel (for which he acquired the relevant badges) and four years in international management. And let's not forget his year as technical director at Portsmouth, which must surely count for something, even if no one at the moment seems to be quite sure what.

All in all, then, if you're going to tell me that Grant isn't amply equipped to shout, point, use cones and take off Andriy Shevchenko after sixty minutes, I'm going to tell you that you're an unusually fussy person. In fact, with all due respect to the LMA, and looking at some of the people currently operating *with* UEFA Pro Licences, Chelsea's new boss may be significantly overqualified and to make him sit an exam that he doesn't strictly need, during a time when he must already be pretty busy, would be an insult to him and to the people who are placing their faith in him at this difficult time.

Arsenal Getting Better and Better

Those glowing Arsenal-related headlines continue to flow. Whether beating Newcastle with their third team, knocking back acquisitive Russian billionaires, declaring record-breaking profits and perpetual full houses, or simply mocking the humble business plans of other, less fortunate Premier League outfits, it's the north London club who currently lead the good news agenda. So get ahead of the game with our guide to next week's daily drip-feed of feelgood Arsenal stories before they appear.

Monday. Arsenal Unveil Plan to Expand Capacity of Emirates Stadium to 4 Million.

'The demand is clearly out there,' Peter Hill-Wood states. 'We are merely rising to meet it in our own, humble and entirely self-sufficient way.'

Tuesday. Gunners to Pay Off Season-Ticket Holders' Mortgages.

'It's just our way of saying thank you,' explains Hill-Wood.

Wednesday. Arsene Wenger Finds Five More Charismatic, International Standard, Attacking Midfield Players Sitting in a Bus Shelter in France.

The club announces that it will divert its transfer budget for 2008–09 into an ambitious 'laptop computer for every UK schoolchild' scheme. 'I feel we're only doing our duty as a football club,' Hill-Wood maintains.

Thursday. Nelson Mandela: 'I Was Always a Gooner'.

In an updated edition of *The Long Walk to Freedom*, the former president of South Africa reveals that, on that iconic, nation-healing day when he presented the 1995 rugby World Cup in a replica Springbok top, he was wearing his lucky Tony Adams shirt underneath. 'Obviously we're quietly flattered,' admits Hill-Wood. 'Though it stands to reason that someone who so passionately dedicated his life to human rights would support Arsenal.'

Friday. Football at Emirates Shown to Reduce Global CO_2 Burden.

A scientific study conclusively demonstrates that the playing style under Wenger is causing the polar ice caps to re-form while simultaneously increasing biodiversity by encouraging rare species to mate. 'This is a significant day for polar bears,' says Hill-Wood, 'and a significant day for the world.'

Razor Stays Sharp in Retirement

Slowly, steadily, and in a way that would have been impossible to foresee when he first pulled on a Millwall shirt, Neil 'Razor' Ruddock's portfolio of television appearances expands. Indeed, in this area he now stands alone among football's post-playing-career hard men.

We probably don't need to mention that Ruddock has long since ticked the box marked team captain on *A Question of Sport* – once the media pinnacle for retired sportspeople, but these days, for the ambitious ex-pro with the right agent, merely the springboard to higher things.

And so we saw the stubbly central defender go on from there to share a damp jungle clearing with Peter Andre and Mike Read in the third series of *I'm A Celebrity . . . Get Me Out Of Here!* And that in turn led to the gilded Saturday night in April 2006, when a bewigged Razor strode through the dry ice provided by *Celebrity Stars In Your Eyes* and gave us his Neil Diamond.

These exquisite efforts alone would have been enough to guarantee Razor a place in the ex-sportsman's broadcasting pantheon, even before the other night when he pushed back the boundaries yet again to take part in the first *Celebrity Wife Swap* involving a same-sex marriage.

Who among football's fabled enforcers can match that? Yes, Vinnie Jones did *Ready, Steady, Cook* and launched a career in both Hollywood and RAC advertisements. But did he ever share his home for five days with a male pop star, while his wife was off with the pop star's male partner? No, he did not.

The pop star in question was Pete Burns, who knew chart glory twenty-three years ago with Dead Or Alive, and has more recently been dwelling in the dim but strangely persistent afterglow that can ensue from an appearance on *Celebrity Big Brother*. The time-honoured *Wife Swap* format placed Michael Simpson, Burns's husband, with Leah Newman, Razor's wife, who used to have a regular column on page three of the *Sun* but has set modelling aside to raise Pebbles, the couple's six-month-old daughter. Ruddock, by process of elimination, drew Burns at home.

What Burns knew about football in general and Ruddock in particular could have been written on the back of one of the pop star's eyelashes, and he was sniffy about the location. 'Is he top of his league?' Burns asked. 'If he is, why is he living in Hastings?'

Harsher critics, including people from Hastings, would probably see such a statement as another example of the traditional imaginative failure, with regard to other people's lives, of someone based in Notting Hill. We prefer, more neutrally, to think that Burns had momentarily forgotten the place of this great East Sussex fishing port at the heart of British history. And if it was good enough for William the Conqueror, surely it's good enough for the singer of 'You Spin Me Round (Like A Record)'.

Still, you know what they say: marry in Hastings, repent at leisure. Despite Razor's initial enthusiasm ('Pete Burns! This is going to be brilliant'), the couple's compatibility was ever in question. Razor is possibly no longer at the level of fitness he attained as a professional athlete, and his hobbies now include going to the pub, coughing, not shaving and wearing hats while asleep on the sofa. Pete's interests include make-up (a ninety-minute application routine, every morning), clothes and wigs.

There's nothing anyone could tell Razor about putting himself between the attacker and the goal. But how would he cope when it came to putting himself between Pete Burns and his dressing-table mirror?

In fact, allowing for the fact that Pete thought Razor's life was 'a living hell', they rubbed along OK. Pete sweetly woke Razor in the morning with a mug of tea and a plate of chocolate-glazed doughnuts. Pete was then disappointed when Razor failed to pamper him on his birthday. But Razor argued that stopping on his way home from the pub to pick up a Thai takeaway was as good as it got, pamper-wise. And the following morning, remorsefully and in order to demonstrate that romance isn't entirely dead, Razor went out and bought Pete a novelty feather duster.

So it went on, and if even two minutes of the show had looked natural, rather than nudged into place for the cameras, we might have felt we were getting a genuine insight into how the other half lives – or how Razor Ruddock's other half lives, anyway.

As it was, in a suspiciously tidy finale, Pete told Razor, 'I think, underneath it, you're extremely sensitive.' And Razor explained to Leah that living with Pete had made him realize how much he wanted to spend the rest of his life with her. Now, if living with Pete Burns had made Razor realize how much he wanted to spend the rest of his life with Pete Burns, we'd really have a story to write about. But even now, we must regretfully conclude, there are boundaries beyond which football's hard men, however sensitive, cannot be seen to venture.

Barnes Goes Completely Ballroom

I was having a discussion with someone the other night about the new *Strictly Come Dancing* season (one of a million similar conversations taking place, I'm sure, in the nation's pubs and clubs and wherever people gather to talk about pro-celebrity ballroom dancing) and he said he couldn't see any further than John Barnes.

Interesting. Because I appreciated, obviously, that Barnes has put on a bit of timber since his playing days. But in terms of him actually being an obstruction when the competition gets underway on Saturday . . . well, it hadn't occurred to me.

We'll see, of course. We'll see so many things. (Assuming we can see round Barnes, this is.) We'll see whether Willie Thorne has it in him to sustain a dancefloor title challenge over twelve gruelling weeks and end the hurt inflicted on snooker by the under-performance of Dennis Taylor in series four.

We'll see whether Gabby Logan, the television presenter and *Times Sport* columnist, can deliver on the promise of semi-professional levels of athleticism hinted at in last weekend's preview show. (Stephanie Beacham, the legendary actress, was forced to arch an eyebrow and remark, 'That Gabby creature can put her foot over her head.' I hate to break this to you, Stephanie, but no one gets to work for *Times Sport* without being able to do that. It's the first question they ask.)

Above all, we'll see whether sport can again build on its massive *Strictly Come Dancing* legacy. Darren Gough, Mark Ramprakash, Matt Dawson, Colin Jackson, Denise Lewis, Roger Black – these are names synonymous in the public imagination with donning incautiously see-through clothing and delivering a primetime paso doble on the back of a week's sweaty training and, just occasionally, on the back of a bravely smiling professional.

Sport's record in this competition speaks for itself: two winners and three semi-finalists in four seasons. Only *EastEnders* (one winner, two semi-finalists) comes anywhere near sport as a breeding ground for top-quality waltzers. What would the show be without sportspeople? I'll tell you what it would be. It would be the sight of Quentin Wilson dancing stiffly towards Gloria Hunniford, for ever.

And sport couldn't be better poised to write another golden

chapter in the *Strictly Come Dancing* story. The selectors have assembled the biggest sporting field in the series' history – Barnes, Thorne, Logan, and also Kenny Logan, Gabby's husband, the former Scottish rugby international. The Logans are the first celebrity couple to compete on *Strictly Come Dancing*, and their professional partners are also a couple – which is all very neat and cosy, I suppose, although it would be a shame if it gave anyone the impression that this is some kind of novelty family show, rather than the most serious test of character that live television knows.

So who among them will shine? The Logans have, apparently, been looking good in training. And Barnes has already pointed out that he comes from the era of tight-fitting shorts, so at least the costumes should hold no fear.

As for Thorne, we hope he was being disingenuous when he described himself as 'the biggest layman you've ever had on this show'. His background in snooker will have prepared him mentally for the live televised experience, but don't under-estimate the physical side of his trade, too. Sometimes snooker players have to go as long as three minutes without a sit-down.

On the plus side for Thorne is the fact that his professional partner is Erin Boag, who accompanied Colin Jackson to within one dance of glory and also, with both Martin Offiah and Peter Schmeichel, amply demonstrated that she could coax refined performances out of unpromisingly large sportsmen. Techni-cally, Thorne couldn't be better placed to make a dark-horse run here.

At the same time, concerns remain about the dry-humoured snooker man's trademark moustache. There may well be aerody-namic consequences, and possibly even some health and safety implications. Mostly, though, one worries about the possibility of unwanted meshing between face-fuzz and nylon, and the thought of Thorne spoiling the landing of an ambitious lift by becoming Velcro'd to his partner's stomach doesn't bear thinking about.

As for the likely challengers to sport's supremacy – well, Kelly

Brook will want to give it a go. And, obviously, the form book tells you to look out for anyone with *EastEnders* on their CV, which, this time, means Letitia Dean and Matt Di Angelo. What is it about the training methods at Walford that sees the long-running soap produce serious ballroom contenders, again and again? I don't know, but if I did, I would bottle it and sell it to GMTV, whose runners tend to be gorgeous but hopeless.

Every competitor, though, sporting or otherwise, would do well to pause in their preparations and hear the nerve-settling words of Ramprakash, last year's runaway winner. 'You get used to the Cuban heels,' the Surrey batsman explained. 'You accept the make-up.' Three words, then. Bring. It. On.

So, farewell, then, Dominic Littlewood. We never did work out quite what it is that you do. Something in daytime television. But not, clearly, the paso doble.

And on you go, John Barnes, whose dreams of *Strictly Come Dancing* glory are still alive – but only, and for the second time in the series, after a scalding immersion in the white-hot cauldron of the Sunday night dance-off.

How long can the former Liverpool and England playmaker dance with disaster in this way? After last week's American Smooth, which was more like ten miles of hard road in a wheelbarrow, we needed the confidence boost of an assertive foxtrot to rekindle the belief that Barnes can go all the way here and clinch it for sport. Indeed, we needed Barnes to foxtrot like the hunting ban had never happened.

Instead, though, we got a performance which, as Arlene Phillips on the judging panel put it, was 'lots of fox but not quite enough trot'. Personally, I thought it was all trot and no fox – but, hey, she's the expert, and the point is, *something* was missing, meaning that viewer indifference again kicked in and Barnes was once more obliged to dance for his life when the phone votes were tallied.

Wrong dance, wrong time? Quite possibly. As Phillips pointed out, with no hyperbole, one felt, 'the foxtrot is one of the most difficult challenges known to man'. The Eiger? The Apollo moonshot? Just another day at the office by comparison with donning the penguin suit and leading a woman in nylons around a BBC-built dancefloor, with Bruce Forsyth looking on.

Yet Craig Revel-Horwood was in no mood to make allowances. 'Laboured, sloppy, you looked absolutely terrified,' the waspish judge told a bravely smiling Barnes. Only Len Goodman – who is, I would hazard, the sole genuine football fan on the panel – came to the player's defence. 'You've got a naturalness about you,' the head of the judges said.

But naturalness alone is not enough. It never has been, and it never will be – not in pro-celebrity ballroom – and if Barnes is ever going to silence the boo boys, he's going to have to get back in the rehearsal room and put in some very hard yards indeed.*

Dida Dropped in Glasgow

Is this the end for Dida? Some say the AC Milan goalkeeper will never again be taken seriously after his reaction to an extremely light-looking assault by a pitch-invading fan at Celtic's Parkhead. I'm not so sure. If you weigh up the contributing factors, you see how it may be too soon to write him off.

He goes to ground late – I don't think there's any question about that. This is the reason people are now asking themselves, did he fall or was he pushed a minute or so earlier? But think how much has to go through the Brazilian international's mind in those critical moments after the 27-year-old pitch invader comes on and flicks him.

First he has got to respond to his natural instinct to go after his attacker and flick him back. Then he's got to remember that this might not, in fact, be so smart, from an escalation point of

* Barnes, incredibly, clung on until week eight, outlasting Thorne, Beacham and, controversially, Gabby Logan. But in the end the former Liverpool man was powerless to put himself between Alesha Dixon and the title.

view. Then he's got to travel back through his memory, recall the time in 2005 when a flare thrown by an Inter fan struck him on the shoulder, and realize that, if he falls over convincingly enough, the match gets abandoned and the points get awarded to Milan, thus, on this occasion, snatching an unlikely victory from the jaws of defeat.

It's an awful lot for a goalkeeper to process in a split second, especially within the pressure cooker atmosphere of the live match situation and just after he has conceded a goal. And some will say that Dida should have dropped to his knees quicker. But I don't think there is a footballer in the world today who would have had the speed of mind and reflex required to hit the pitch faster in this particular context, with the possible exception of Cristiano Ronaldo and, maybe, Ruud van Nistelrooy, back when he was in his pomp.

Another thing: I don't think the fan has done Dida any favours by going in with his fingers. Bear in mind this was in Glasgow, at night. You would have expected him to lead with the head at the very least. In fact, the full extent of the fan's ambition seems to be to deliver Dida a pat on the cheek in mock consolation after shipping the goal.

I'm not saying that this diminished version of an assault might not have been infuriating in its own way, had the fan pulled it off properly. But it's not exactly the bunched fist, broken bar-stool or lit firework that Dida's thorough pre-match preparations and previous experiences might have led him to expect.

In any case, the camera angle from behind the goal suggests the fan's outstretched fingers missed the cheek and ended up patting Dida on the collarbone. Again, we don't criticize the fan for that. The 'running chuck' is one of the most difficult patroniz-ing gestures in the pitch-invaders' repertoire. Attempting to pull off a 'running chuck' while 'on a mazy' (the technical term for a meandering run with arms outstretched, aeroplane-style) is ambitious to the point of lunacy. Nevertheless, from Dida's point of view, the result is a blow which is no blow at all, and, in the end, you can only work with what you're given.

In this respect, credit to the Milan medical team. It's so easy to overlook the efforts of the backroom staff on occasions such as these, but this was a night when the anonymous servants publicly came good. It's not just about knowing which prop to choose (the exquisite ice pack, in this case), it's about knowing how to use that prop to maximize the dramatic potential, and the decision to apply the ice pack to the prone Dida's temple was little short of genius in this context, suggesting, as it did, not just immense physical trauma but also the onset of a possibly life-endangering fever.

Worst of all, though, where is the back four? Review the tape once more, and you will see how Dida is utterly and unforgivably exposed. Nobody picks up the invader and he drifts across the penalty area completely unmarked. It's a criminal lack of protection that Dida is getting from his defence here, especially at Champions League level, and if more bodies had been around to get involved, then who knows what might have been made to seem to go on.

I hope the Brazilian took his team mates to task for it afterwards. And I hope those team mates, in turn, gave Dida due plaudits for at least having the courage to make a stand on their behalf, albeit by lying down.

Protect Your Face with John Terry

Doubtless it's only a matter of time before a replica John Terry plastic face mask is available in all sizes from the Chelsea Megastore and other leading outlets. Can't wait until then to achieve that 'I've just had my face busted by an elbow at home to Fulham, but that's not going to stop me from playing in central defence in a critical Champions League group phase match four days later' look? Then do it yourself at home with our easy-to-make, JT-style cheek protector.

You will need: a roll of clear Sellotape, a pair of scissors and a steady hand. Take the end of the Sellotape and apply it to the centre of your forehead, pressing down firmly with your fingers or thumb. Continuing to hold the end in place, pass the Sellotape across your forehead to the top of your left ear. Make sure to keep the tape as tight as possible. Now bring the tape around the back of the ear and pass it across the cheek to the bridge of your nose, avoiding the nostrils. Carry on across the face and travel around the right ear from below before returning to the middle of the forehead. Detach the roll with the scissors and smooth down the loose end.

Hey presto – you're ready to delight your family and friends with your resemblance to England's never-say-die captain and also to something off *Dr Who*. Hours of fun. (Warning: not to be attempted by anyone under sixteen without adult supervision. Face mask is only a toy. Surgery could still be necessary. Putting your head in where it hurts in defensive situations may not be advisable.)

Next time: an utterly convincing Petr Cech protective helmet from an old Shreddies box and some sticky-back plastic.

Opera-going Southerners

In a new book, *Born Winner*, the much-missed coach and philosopher Jose Mourinho returns to a topic that frequently bothered him during his time at Chelsea – crowd noise, and its periodic failure to be generated at Stamford Bridge. Eschewing some of the popular theories (lunchtime kick-offs, success breeding complacency, conservative tactics), he interestingly summarizes the problem as follows: 'The Chelsea fans create a different atmosphere because a lot of them also go to the opera, the theatre and other types of shows that don't lend themselves to lots of shouting.'

Naturally one hesitates to pick an argument with Mourinho, whose understanding of the English game in all its aspects was so meticulous. But is it at all possible that the former manager may have slightly misread the demographic here? The fact is, if you look around you in the Shed End at Stamford Bridge, or take a sounding in the Matthew Harding Stand (positively a-buzz at half-time with chatter about the latest West End openings), you will doubtless find people who would be at the opera all the time if it wasn't so damned expensive.

Have you seen what it costs to go to the opera these days? It can be upwards of £75 a head, even for some of the smaller, category B operas. And that's before you factor in a programme, a scarf and a hot dog. All respect to Mourinho, but the average fan was priced out of the opera years ago.

By the way, who said you can't shout at the theatre?

Steve Bruce and the Chinese Vibes

Things That Football Managers Never Had to Say in the Old Days, No. 42. 'I found out off Mr Sullivan on Friday that the vibes coming back off the Chinese consortium were negative' (Steve Bruce, considering his future at Birmingham City under possible new ownership). When did Ron Saunders (Birmingham manager, 1982–86) ever have to interpret the positivity or otherwise of vibes emanating from a Chinese consortium? When did Bob Brocklebank (1949–54) or Arthur Turner, who took City to Wembley in 1956? Truly, managing Birmingham is a completely different game these days. Not that there's anything wrong with that.

Suite FA

Disappointing to hear John Toshack, the embattled manager of Wales, rail against the pampered lives of today's travelling international footballers.

This column has long held the opinion that the possibility of a complimentary towelling bathrobe and some prestige slippers in a top-whack hotel and spa compound represents a perfectly legitimate sporting incentive in an age when simply 'pulling on the shirt' doesn't quite do it for people any more. In the case of Wales, the chance of an Indian head massage and an individually wrapped fondant chocolate on the pillow might even provide a minor compensation for having to go abroad with Craig Bellamy. At any rate, imagine travelling with Bellamy and *not* having the comfort of a walk-in power shower and a nightly turn-down service. It's virtually unthinkable.

But Toshack, alas, has begun to view things differently. 'I don't like seeing some of the things I see,' he said, shortly before his team squeezed past humble San Marino, 2–1, in a Euro 2008 qualifier. 'Another five-star hotel . . . but if the waves are making too much noise, boys, we can move you to another room.'

We beg to differ. If there is any problem here, it is with the accommodation. A truly top-quality hotel, surely, would offer to do something about the waves.

Pep Talks We Wish We'd Given

Viktor Zubkov, the prime minister of Russia, issued the following call to arms shortly before his national side met England: 'They have eleven players and we have eleven players. They have two arms and two legs and one head each, and we have the same. But do you know what the most important thing is? We Russians won World War Two. And we were the first in space. Come on, Russia, come on, come on.'

Exquisite. Eleven of them, and eleven of us, plus Yuri Gagarin. The Russian space project and overcoming Joleon Lescott down the left – one mission. Stalingrad and closing down Gareth Barry – same difference. McClaren's side never stood a chance.

Football in the Age of Communication

Franz Beckenbauer must have loved Wimbledon in the Crazy Gang era. That would have been the Kaiser's kind of team. Shouting in the dressing room, shouting in the tunnel, shouting on the pitch – they never stopped shouting. Vinnie Jones, Lawrie Sanchez, John 'Fash the Bash' Fashanu – top-class shouters ran right through that side. 'Yidaho!' That was one of their shouts. They shouted themselves all the way to the FA Cup. See where shouting used to get you?

And that's England's problem, for Beckenbauer: no shouting. 'When I played against England in 1965 and in the World Cup of 1966,' he said, 'there was always a certain spirit. They were shouting and yelling.' Not these days. Now England are 'like a school team. They are not talking and not supporting. That was for me the biggest surprise. There is no life in this team.'

Withering thoughts – and yet they found some reluctant takers even among paid-up subscribers to England's cause. Graham Taylor, the former England manager, said, 'I understand where Beckenbauer is coming from' and spoke in favour of shouting and yelling. He mentioned his own use of players such as Paul Gascoigne and Tony Adams who 'didn't just play with their feet, they played with their mouths. That is one of the things the present England team are short of. I don't think they are loud enough.'

Well, I hate to break it to you, everybody, but the world has moved on, and football with it. Shouting has had it. It's all over. Shouting and yelling is *so* last century. Which is not to say that the contemporary England international doesn't communicate with his peers. On the contrary, he communicates more than any other generation before him. It's just that he does so in new and more efficient ways – ways that don't involve shouting.

By text message, for instance. Points that used to have to be made at the top of a player's voice, above cacophonous crowd noise, can now be made quickly and silently with the keypad.

'Mrk up, mrk up', for instance, or 'Sqr it, sqr it', or 'Ovr hr, sn, on me hd'.

Sometimes it can go a bit wrong of course – as in, 'Th no. 4's styd out wd fr th crnr, bt if I go acrss to hm I'm gng to lve th frnt pst opn, so . . . hng on, I'll cll you.'

But, in general, Bluetooth and WAP-enabled mobile phone technology and high-end personal organizers have revolutionized communication between players in ways never even dreamed of by Nobby Stiles. Thus Ashley Cole doesn't need to waste valuable energy shouting across to Rio Ferdinand that he's gone to sleep and lost his man again. He can alert him to this effect via MSN instant messaging and, at the same time, send him over the new Timbaland single in an attached MP3 file.

Meanwhile a whole new generation of computer-familiar professionals is using web-based networking sites to connect with one another in cyberspace. A quick glance at Peter Crouch's MySpace page reveals that he has four friends, which is far more than most people assume. It might not actually be his page, of course. That's one of the drawbacks about MySpace. But there's no denying that players are creating a genuine social presence for themselves on sites such as Bebo and Facebook. It is common knowledge that Gareth Barry spent most of the second half against Russia poking Joleon Lescott. And you're trying to say these players aren't connecting with one another, Franz? It doesn't add up.

Altogether, today's pros have little need for guttural vocalizing. They use subtler means – a wink, a nod, a picture message. They know that, in the multilingual club game, you can shout all you like, but very few people will understand you, so you might as well save your breath. Now, more than ever, a player soon learns to let his play do the talking and there's just no room any more for an Alan Ball figure, barging about the place with a rocket up his shorts, piping and whistling.

Do you suppose Arsene Wenger sits down with the Arsenal board over the summer and says, 'I'll tell you what we need at this club – a jaw-merchant. A rabbit man, preferably with big forearms. Someone who can give it some serious bunny out there in the middle'?

Of course he doesn't. He goes out and buys a painfully shy, wafer-thin French teenager, teaches him how to pass and run very fast, uses him to build a collection of major trophies and then, just as he is beginning to go off the boil, sells him abroad for £24 million. Shouting never comes into it.

The same goes for Sir Alex Ferguson at Manchester United. Look at his most recent signings: Nani, Anderson, Carlos Tevez. No big shouters there. Silent as the grave, most of them. But quite good at football. That's the new emphasis. With Roy Keane gone, Ferguson has realized that the major shouter is irrelevant to the modern game. In any case, shouting at people is *his* job.

The era of the big noise is well and truly over. When a hurt and outraged Dennis Wise can report a referee for swearing at him, thus setting a new standard for 'man bites dog' news stories, the demise of the gobby prankster as an influence on top-level football could not be more emphatically underlined.

Indeed, insert a phlegm-flecked clogger like Stuart Pearce into one of today's top-flight matches and he would look about as antiquated as a radiogram, and a touch less pacey. And yet important people around the international game continue to prize noisy passion above basic aptitude. Why? It's a big mistake, and it has already been a costly one. While other nations were developing their skills, the English were still talking about 'heart' and 'commitment' and working on their shouting. The strangely tenacious notion that everything would be all right as long as you had at least seven players who were ready to sing the national anthem loudly, bawl each other out and play on through a catastrophic and possibly self-inflicted head wound is single-handedly responsible for ushering English international football into the age of trophyless darkness from which it is still struggling to emerge.

And you know what? I think Beckenbauer knows that, really. Cunning old Kaiser, then, with his teasing about shouting and yelling. He's trying to turn the clock back on us. It's a trap. Don't fall into it.

Sand in Our Faces

No wallcharts. No sticker books. No flags flying from white vans belonging to plumbers. Why, you would hardly know the FIFA Beach Soccer World Cup was on at all if it wasn't for Eurosport, where, at a rate of up to four matches per day, this showpiece occasion on the calendar of sand-based international football gets something like the rapt attention it deserves.

Of course, local indifference to events unfolding on Copaca-bana beach could well be connected with the fact that none of the home nations is represented. It's ignominy, though, however you explain it. Did England not give the world this game? A colder, wetter version of it, at any rate, played in boots. Yet there is no place for England on beach football's biggest stage in 2007. You'll have your own diagnosis, I'm sure, but it seems the talent just isn't coming through at grass roots. Or rather, at whatever you call that geological stratum where the sand stops and the rock begins.

Anyway, it can't be denied – they do it differently in Rio. This is beach football, but not as we know it from our holidays. The goal posts are considerably more substantial than a cricket stump and a plastic windmill. The ball is far less likely to take a wicked deflection off a passing Yorkshire terrier. The family from the hut next door simply aren't welcome to join in when they fancy. They have to qualify, the same as everyone else. And so far not even one match has had to be belatedly abandoned thanks to an encroaching tide.

And what about that official tournament ball? Not even partly emblazoned with full-colour pictures of the Mighty Morphin Power Rangers and/or Princess Barbie, it seems to boast a physical property not widely connected with footballs in this area – namely, weight. Not as much weight as a regular football, maybe. But definitely some.

The consequences for the play that we are seeing are massive. The ball doesn't go 'poink' when the players kick it and swerve in a bizarre and unhelpful way. It goes 'thump' when they kick it and swerves in a bizarre and unhelpful way.

Form sides? That would be Brazil, obviously – unbeaten for fifty-five games. Portugal, also – the reigning European champions. Italy, too. Nobody locks up a beach quite like the Italians.

Nevertheless, referring to the competitiveness of so-called 'lesser' nations such as the United Arab Emirates (where, you would assume, they know pretty much all there is to know about sand), Wayne Boyce of Eurosport got it slightly wrong, one felt, when he said, 'It's a much more level playing field in beach soccer these days.' True, the pitch seems to have been carefully combed beforehand for stones, seaweed and stray parasols. But the lumps, the clumps, the thickness of the sand . . . if there is a less level playing field in sport right now, I should hate to see it.

And so one begged to differ again when Boyce chastised the USA for an error in front of goal in their match against Portugal. 'You cannot afford to give the ball away there and expect to get away with it,' Boyce said. On the contrary, the pitch is so unpredictable that you can give the ball away almost anywhere and expect to have a pretty cheerful, 50/50 chance of going unpunished.

I'm not saying the game is riddled with randomness to the point of absurdity, but in the group phase, now completed, Hamed Ghorbanpour, the Iran goalkeeper, scored three goals in three matches. That wouldn't happen on grass, would it?

At least England would have responded well to the weather in Rio this week. It's been grey and windy and the rain has been falling in droplets the size of dishwasher tablets. Still, this has meant that collectors of exotic television memorabilia have been able to enjoy the all-too-brief sightings of the mighty Eric Cantona, in a drenched tracksuit top, watching imperiously from the sidelines in his role as coach of the French team.

Few, I would hazard, would have predicted that the philo-sophical Manchester United legend would go into international management. And even fewer would have predicted that he would go into international management at the seaside. But there it is. It turns out that these days, when the seagull follows the trawler, he is merely looking for a decent kickabout on the shore.

Incidentally, on the topic of ornithology, Nigeria are known as 'the Beach Eagles'. I hate to quibble, but when did you last see an eagle on a beach? Unless it was on holiday, obviously. Anyway, Nigeria beat France on penalties, leaving Cantona looking even more existentially bleak than usual. Like the philosopher said (not Cantona, this time): life's a beach football match, and then you die.

Becks: He's Still Got It

Steve McClaren couldn't stick around in Los Angeles to watch David Beckham take part in last Sunday's big charity match at the Home Depot Center – ninety minutes of first-team football that could have provided some vital pointers, as the England manager was weighing up whether or not to restore the former captain to the international squad. That doesn't mean McClaren was under-informed, though, when he made his eventual decision to pick Beckham. Staff were on hand to prepare the manager a detailed scouting report.

Third minute
DB, looking lively early doors, collects ball just inside centre circle, looks up and picks out Viv Campbell of Def Leppard, surging out wide on left. Pass is overhit but the guitarist brings it down with his tongue before firing narrowly over. Nice move. Settles a few nerves.

Ninth minute
First big test for DB – a 50/50 challenge with Jennifer Aniston. If there's anything niggling in the back of his mind about the

ankle it doesn't show, as DB comes crunching in, full-blooded. So does Aniston, though, and the impact puts DB up in the air and over the touchline. Referee blows and cards Aniston, but it's a fussy one and the *Friends* star is right to complain that the ball was there to be won.

Eleventh minute
DB back up after treatment.

Thirteenth minute
DB very quiet.

Fifteenth minute
DB still very quiet. Trying to run off that Aniston challenge.

Seventeenth minute
Moving more freely now, DB wins corner and then pats Frank Leboeuf's shaved head. Good to see the old playfulness returning. Leboeuf goes down clutching his eyes, though, and DB is booked. Fingers crossed it can be overturned on appeal.

Twenty-fifth minute
DB needs to work much harder to shake off Tom Cruise. Wherever DB goes, Cruise shadows him. If DB pops up in the box, so does Cruise. If DB drops back into a holding role, Cruise does, too. It's a proper man-marking job. Kind of spooky, too, given that they're on the same side.

Thirty-second minute
DB beaten to a loose ball by Steven Tyler of Aerosmith who continues his run before shooting across the face of the goal when other options looked more promising. In particular, had Tyler cut the ball back to Macaulay Culkin, unmarked on the edge of the six-yard box, there was real danger. DB possibly lacking a yard of pace?

Forty-first minute
DB makes intelligent burst down left-hand channel, screaming
to be played in by Oprah Winfrey. Unfortunately, Winfrey
doesn't see him and instead squares to Pierce Brosnan, who
blasts wide. DB bawls out Winfrey. Then he bawls out Brosnan
for good measure. Great that the competitiveness is there, despite
the lack of match fitness.

Forty-eighth minute
Lovely marauding run through midfield by DB. Shrugs off Rod
Stewart just inside his own half and leaves Zak Starkey for dead
before being scythed down from behind on the edge of the
penalty area by Joan Rivers. DB takes the free-kick himself and
manages to get the ball up and down, but Gwen Stefani in goal
is equal to it.

Forty-ninth minute
Goal. Aniston from thirty-five yards, top corner. Nothing DB,
or anyone else, could do.

Fifty-fourth minute
DB growing increasingly frustrated with lack of service from
Ruud Gullit and Tom Hanks. Tension finally boils over with
Rivers (who's been giving DB all manner of lip, all night long)
after some jostling and shirt-pulling by the comedienne in the
box. But it's just handbags.

Fifty-ninth minute
DB gets on the end of a Sheryl Crow cross, but badly mistimes
his header which flies well over for a goal kick.

Sixty-first minute
Substitution: DB off, Henry Winkler on. DB looks furious and
goes straight down tunnel, refusing the proffered tracksuit top
and Donna Karan goodie bag. No harm in that, though. You'd
be more worried if a player *wanted* to come off.

Conclusions

Not sure about DB for Austria. Could be too early. Then again, it's only a friendly. And he's got to offer more than Gareth Barry, so why not?

Jennifer Aniston, though – she's definitely worth a look. Could come in and do a job, especially if we lose any more centre backs. Liked the Def Leppard guy, too. How many of the England squad could do that with their tongue?

Recommendations

Another LA fact-finding trip for SM and scouting staff as soon as possible. Perhaps stay a bit longer next time and make sure to do the Universal Studios tour. Huge value.

Pants-exposure: a Briefing for Refs

Quite the most beguiling and least predictable outcome of the Stephen Ireland shorts-drop goal celebration was hearing Gordon Taylor, the habitually buttoned-up chief executive of the Professional Footballers' Association, on a national radio phone-in the morning afterwards debating the critical distinction between pants and undershorts – not a discussion he necessarily imagined himself needing to get involved in when he ascended to the head of the players' union, but the game moves on so fast.

Obviously, though, if footballers are going to start exposing their underpants as an expression of the unfettered, manly joy that clearly arises from sticking one past Roy Keane's Sunderland during a televised Monday night game, legislation will need to be rapidly hammered out on what is and is not acceptable in this area. Our suggestion for a rough 'FA pants rubric' would be as follows.

• Plain, unfussy, M&S boxers: play on.

• Brightly coloured Y-fronts emblazoned with *Star Wars* characters or jokey slogans relating to their contents, and almost certainly secured in a three-pack from Tesco: word of warning
from the referee.

• Designer trunks as advertised by Freddie Ljungberg with boast-
ful elasticated waistband, costing roughly the same as shoes:
yellow card.

• Tasselled Peter Stringfellow-style thong-wear or Eastern European posing pouch in metallic silver or gold finish: straight red,
automatic nine-match suspension, £100,000 fine, suspended
prison sentence, four months community service.

Marsh in the Jungle

Mixed fortunes for Rodney Marsh in the opening exchanges of
I'm A Celebrity . . . Get Me Out Of Here! On the one hand, the
weather closed in and cancelled the football pundit's scheduled
1,000-ft bungee jump off the side of a helicopter. Marsh was
almost convincing when he described himself as 'disappointed'.

On the other hand, he lost the first public-appointed Bush
Tucker Trial of the 2007 series 9–8 to Janice Dickinson, and the
perceived indignity of being taken down by a surgically enhanced
former American supermodel seemed to hit the Manchester City
legend hard.

'I come from a mentality where second is not second,' Marsh,
in self-punishing mode, explained afterwards. 'It's the first loser.'

Stirring stuff, though, as Ant and Dec were quick to point
out, in this particular contest 'there were only two of them',
meaning that, technically speaking, Marsh wasn't 'the first loser'
but, more straightforwardly, 'the loser'.

Still, however you frame it, this was a defeat – one suffered
in a sinking Range Rover from which Marsh, armed only with
a pair of goggles, was obliged to retrieve plastic stars. Going for

his eighth, the maverick striker was underwater a worrying length of time before bursting out through the sunroof, but as Marsh said, 'If you've taken a penalty at Wembley in front of 100,000 people, why would you be afraid of getting drowned?'

Has Marsh taken a penalty at Wembley in front of 100,000 people? We can find no record of this moment. But we'll take his word for it, merely adding that he might also have mentioned *Gillette Soccer Saturday* at this point. When you've spent as many hours as Marsh has interrupting Jeff Stelling with news of a squandered chance for Southampton at St Mary's, there is nothing anyone can teach you about scrambling out of a floundering 4x4.

Those of us with much invested in a Marsh victory in Australia will note with concern that he is already suffering from the internal complications for which the world's most important in-the-raw celebrity challenge is famous. Or as Marsh put it, 'I haven't had an Eartha Kitt for seven days.' This announcement would have been alarming at any time, but was the more so for coming on just day three of Marsh's jungle existence. One hates to sound all parental about it, but why didn't he go before he came out?

Alternatively, could it be that the problem preceded his arrival in Australia? And should we attribute this inconvenient backing-up to nerves? Marsh conceded that he had been belatedly wondering whether following the likes of Tony Blackburn, Jordan and the bassist from Busted into the jungle was entirely 'a good idea'. He also reported how a disquieting dream had disturbed his sleep on the eve of the show – a nightmare in which he had bitten the head off a rat and spat it on the floor, only to realize that 'it was Glenn Hoddle'.

But we feel confident Marsh will settle. He can at least count himself lucky that he has been drawn to bed down amid relatively amicable co-contestants in Croc Creek rather than in Snake Rock, the opposing encampment, in which the professionally volatile Dickinson spends a lot of time threatening to stab people while they sleep and in which Lynne Franks periodically requires silence for her meditation routine.

Like so many of us, the award-winning publicist likes nothing
better of a morning than to kick-start her bio-rhythms by chanting a passage of ancient Sanskrit. It seems to work, too. 'I just
remembered who I was,' Franks reported.

It's encouraging to know that the problem of remembering
who people are afflicts those on the inside of the camp, as well
as those of us watching from the outside. It probably should be
added, in this context, that the names on the backs of the jackets
and undershirts aren't always a reliable help. 'Marc', anyone?
The chances are it will take more than one of Franks's mantras
before most of us remember who *he* is.*

But, of course, we're all still dizzy after Malcolm McClaren,
who used to manage the Sex Pistols, set a new world and
Commonwealth record for quitting the show, walking out
before it began. He then gave a press interview in which he
sensationally revealed that, far from being utterly wild, there
were cameramen all over that jungle clearing. 'The public is
being hoodwinked,' he declared.

Until then, I had no idea that cameras were involved at all in
the broadcasting of *I'm A Celebrity*, being firmly under the
impression that the action was provided in real time by a set
of tiny figures scurrying around inside my television set. Now
that I think about it, the advent of the flat-screen TV, with
its limited rear cabin space, should probably have aroused my
suspicions. But sometimes it takes the courage of a fearless
whistle-blower to raise consciousness in these mystifying areas
and advance us all to a state of enlightenment. Many thanks,
Malcolm.

News of England's dismal failure to qualify for Euro 2008 even
penetrated the jungle, where the isolated and starving contestants
on *I'm A Celebrity . . . Get Me Out Of Here!* were offered a

---

* Actually, the Marc in question (Bannerman, an actor) went on to achieve
lasting tabloid notoriety after an in-camp dalliance with singer Cerys Matthews
destabilized matters with his live-in girlfriend at home. I should have seen that
one coming, but didn't.

chocolate treat if they could correctly decide whether the final score had been 3–2 to Croatia or 3–2 to England.

Rodney Marsh, boldly carrying the candle for sport and disgraced football punditry in the present series, thought it was too tough to call, but the overwhelming opinion of the camp was that it was more likely that Croatia had won. Have England really become so predictable? Answers on the back of a witchetty grub.

Here, though, was an enclave in which the soggy closure of the McClaren era was an occasion for almost unalloyed joy and feasting – or, at any rate, snacking. As the truth and its consequences became apparent, Marsh alone turned unusually quiet, staring distantly into the smoke rising off the campfire and muttering, 'I can't believe it. They've not qualified.'

Later, in the intimacy of the Bush Telegraph, the Manchester City legend expressed his feeling that this had been a cruelly abrupt and painful way to learn the fate of his national side. Many England fans, though, would probably beg to differ, arguing that, in the pain and cruelty stakes, sleeping rough in a camera-infested clearing with Lynne Franks beat watching the game by a factor of about nineteen. At least Marsh got a free chocolate out of it. We should all be so lucky around England.

The blows just keep on coming for English football. No sooner had England been handed a return ticket to Croatia in the 2010 World Cup qualifying draw than the public phone vote ensured that it was the end of the jungle for Rodney Marsh on *I'm A Celebrity . . . Get Me Out Of Here!* No wonder people are already calling it 'Black Sunday'.

Marsh, clearly, was a victim of the nationwide public disenchantment which saw England players ritually booed during their club matches at the weekend – even the ones who, through injury or non-selection, didn't play in the side that lost to Croatia and went out of Euro 2008 before it had even started. The withdrawal of affection has been immediate and absolute, meaning that anyone connected even remotely with the Three

Lions cause is now discovering what it felt like to be Les Dennis, *circa* 2003. The national game will be a long time recovering from this.

Marsh, one has to say, had only himself to blame. He took a time-worn game plan into the jungle, only to find that the game has moved on. It's no longer enough, in 2007, to lie around on your camp bed being sarky and expect the votes to flow. These days, when Welsh former pop singers are openly falling in love with former *EastEnders* actors whose girlfriends are waiting for them at a nearby hotel, and when American supermodels are threatening to cut off other contestants' breasts while they sleep, there is only so far that a basic, lump-it-long, grumpy old man act is going to take you.

True, Marsh garnered some public approval by doing battle with the cosmically attuned and yet wildly aggressive Lynne Franks. But his failure to say goodbye to her on the grounds of 'sincerity' (so often the first recourse of the terminally rude) was a disastrous error of judgement which made him look small and scanted the basic sporting tradition of shaking hands at the whistle.

Marsh will doubtless blame the knee injury he picked up collecting firewood in the first week, which saw him removed overnight to a nearby medical facility. Incidentally, exactly how remote is this jungle clearing in which the contestants find themselves so mind-bogglingly marooned? The celebrities ritually arrive by helicopter, bungee cord and six-mile yomp. But Ant and Dec manage to commute in and out on a daily basis, and when a former Manchester City player needs an ambulance, one backs up almost to the nearest tree.

Anyway, the point is, beyond that midnight hospital dash, there was in the broader sense quite simply no journey for Marsh – and no openness to the possibility of a journey. 'I can honestly say,' Marsh announced one night in the Bush Telegraph, 'hand on heart, that I have learned nothing about Rodney Marsh that I didn't already know.' And there you had it – the complacency affecting English football in a nutshell.

It logically followed that we, too, learned nothing about Marsh that we didn't know in advance – leaving aside his fondness for goats, perhaps. Marsh's touchingly hands-on approach to 'Kylie', who visited the camp the other day, seemed to hint at a softer, more rural side to the maverick ex-striker than ever came across in conversations with Jeff Stelling on *Gillette Soccer Saturday*. 'It brightened the place up,' Marsh said later. 'Nice little goat.'

Moreover, one suspects that he will stand for a long time as the only ex-professional footballer to go on a reality television show and lament the lack of a book to read. Yet this was, overall, a dismally under-powered and backward-looking performance and one which practically screams out for a root and branch overhaul. And which footballer now, in the current hostile climate, would put themselves forward for public approval in a pro-celebrity ballroom contest or jungle-based, all-in insect-wrangling contest? Mark my words: it will be years before football comes back from this. Or at least until ITV recommissions *Celebrity Love Island*.*

Playing for England? What's the Motive?

Everyone agrees that the biggest problem is motivation. England players appear to have mislaid that vital drive to succeed. You can see it in the uneasy and fundamentally lacklustre nature of their performances in the workplace. Tasked with routine assignments, ostensibly well within their individual skill-sets, such as seeing off Macedonia or taking a point at home to Croatia, the will to excel deserts them and the players underperform. Naming no names, but especially Steven Gerrard.

So what's the solution? Replacing the manager? Got to be worth a go, but it's a short-term fix. What is required is a far-reaching reincentivization process, involving a company-wide

* A mid-table finish for Rod. Not bad. Christopher Biggins took the title.

motivation programme that addresses the full range of perform-
ance-based issues.

Honed over years of motivational speaking to industries up
and down the country, our seven-step strategy can, if rolled out
carefully, yield an experienced, driven and reliable workforce,
capable of the consistent delivery of desired performance goals.

Step 1: Reward your employees
Everyone is familiar with the truth that you can lead a horse to
water, but you can't make it drink. What you can do, however,
is *increase the horse's propensity to thirst*. Employees want to feel
appreciated and, at Wembley, it just isn't going to happen,
especially if you are Frank Lampard. Best, then, to set in place a
system of simple rewards for exemplary performance – a dinner
out, tickets to a show. That way lies a thirsty horse. And a happy,
motivated Frank Lampard.

Step 2: Empower people
Studies indicate that 39 per cent of the variability in workforce
performance is attributable to the personal satisfaction of the
staff. And *satisfaction arises directly from recognition*. Recognition is
a critical element in the management toolkit. You could say it
was the screwdriver. Or one of those wrench things that you
adjust. What are they called again? Never mind. The point
is, recognition needs stimulating, whether in the form of an
Employee of the Month plaque, or more straightforwardly, in
the form of a personal workplace greeting, such as, 'I recognize
you – you're Joleon Lescott, aren't you?' You'll be astonished at
the difference it can make.

Step 3: Minimize the we–they syndrome
In some of the best-functioning companies, employees rotate
jobs every Friday, encouraging an easy fluidity between staff and
management. Thereby, on the appointed day, Joe Cole would
become the kit man and the kit man would train in midfield.
And thereby Peter Crouch would become the team doctor and

the team doctor would do whatever it is that Crouch is meant to be doing.

Incidentally, Nike employees at Beaverton, Oregon, have 'Thrilling Thursdays', where work stops at 4.30 and 'after some beer and soda', workers at all levels 'kayak across a lake, race bikes and compete in a 600-yard run'. Obviously the 600-yard run would be a bit of a busman's holiday for England players. But the bikes and the kayaking sound good. So do the *beer and sodas*.

Step 4: Involve everyone
A company's most precious resource? Its staff, of course. Or, at any rate, its staff and the money it generates from television rights and top-line sponsorship tie-ins. But the extent to which staff feel involved has a major impact on *morale and motivation*. Branded uniforms are a start – but what about an employee photo wall, or a dedicated parking space for the team bus? It's all about making people feel they belong, including Keiron Dyer.

Step 5: Take time out
When was the last time an England manager in an international week said, 'OK, lads. Forget the upcoming friendly against Estonia. We're off to Alton Towers for the day.' Think how much team spirit and morale in general would be boosted by the opportunity to *come down a giant flume with Rio Ferdinand*.

Step 6: Offer Air Miles
It's worth a try, if none of the other stuff is working. Or money-off vouchers at Curry's. Or just *money*.

Step 7: Insist on summer vacations
What kind of company rewards exemplary employee performance with the prospect of more work? Specifically, what kind of company rewards its employees with the prospect of more work in their holidays? Not even McDonald's do that. Yet,

again and again, the prospect of having to go through it all over again, in their downtime, is the so-called carrot dangled before England teams. Thus, Gerrard and company went into Wednesday night's game knowing that victory would merely secure more of the same in Austria and Switzerland next June, when they could have been at the Forte Village in Sardinia with every other footballer.

Some basic restrategizing is needed in order to *reposition the incentive*, and we can do this by initiating a rule that says, if you are part of the qualifying team, you don't have to take part in the tournament. That's your reward for qualifying. Come the summer, you stay at home, packing for Sardinia, and the subs go. And they in turn can earn exemption from the next summer tournament by winning it. Hey presto: *a dedicated, high-achieving, motivated and on-task workforce* – and a properly rested one, too.

No Tragedy without a Feast

The FA's decision to convene a breakfast meeting and deal immediately, at the start of the working day, with the removal of Steve McClaren from his post as England manager was a piece of commendably swift planning. It enabled the organization to complete, without unnecessary and potentially painful prevarication, a solemn task for which the likes of FA dignitaries such as Brian Barwick and Geoff Thompson can have had little appetite.

That FA breakfast menu in full: flute of Bucks Fizz. All-day FA Sizzler – sausage, bacon, fried egg, kidneys, black pudding, hash browns, grilled tomatoes. Selection of toasts and carousel of locally sourced preserves. Choice of sugar-coated cereals from the buffet. Basket of assorted chocolate muffins and continental pastries. Tea or coffee or both at once. More Bucks Fizz. Another sausage.

Forgotten Heroes of '66 Get Their Due

Even now, after all this time, their names trip effortlessly off the tongue: Bonetti, Hunter, Armfield, Greaves, Callaghan, Eastham, er . . .

Hang on, I've got it written down here somewhere . . . Yep, here we go: Springett, Connolly, Paine, Flowers, Byrne.

These are the eleven men for ever more engraved on history's pages as the players who, on 30 July 1966, sat on the bench while eleven other players were winning the World Cup. And now, finally, following eager and important lobbying by Richard Caborn, the clearly phenomenally busy sports minister, the unused subs are set to get the winner's medal that was not offered to them on the day. Justice at last for 'the forgotten heroes of '66'.

Jimmy Armfield said, 'Wouldn't it be nice if all the players from 1966 who are still alive could get together for a proper presentation ceremony at Wembley?' Too modest by half. We're thinking more along the lines of an open-top bus tour and a commemorative stamp issue. English football needs a good news story right now, and eleven players who were just off to one side when the World Cup was being raised are clearly as good as it is going to get for a very long time.

In any case, their contribution has been shockingly overlooked for too long. Talk about strength in depth. When players of the calibre of a George Eastham or an Ian Callaghan sliced up the half-time oranges, make no mistake about it, they stayed sliced. Did anyone pour tea on the big occasion like Ron Flowers? I hardly think so. And when it came to folding up the tracksuit bottoms in a crowded dressing room, there was no one you would rather have seen standing at your shoulder than Norman Hunter of Leeds.

'This is something that I have always felt was not right,' Hunter said this week, of his long period in the winner's medal wilderness. 'And I have to admit that over the years it has rankled.'

Well, it would, though, wouldn't it? Just because it was your unfortunate destiny to play in the position occupied rather emphatically at international level by Bobby Moore, and just because, as a result, you never got the chance to get out on the pitch on the biggest day English football has known, it doesn't mean you should be subjected to forty-one years of under-appreciation for what you might have done had circumstances been different. No one should be expected to take that kind of neglect lying down.

At the same time, a lot of water has passed under the bridge since that magical, epoch-defining summer afternoon in the 1960s. And, more particularly, a lot of goals have passed under the body of Peter Bonetti – not least those three rather critical ones that England shipped against West Germany in the quarter-finals of the 1970 World Cup in Mexico. That was the spirit-sapping occasion in the Estadio Guanajuato in León, when Bonetti finally did get to fill in for a sick Gordon Banks and endured an experience which, thirty-seven years later, is still as good a definition as any of the term 'mare'.

So, inevitably, one can see the argument of those who are now saying that, having at last been handed his medal in acknowledgement of the part he played in the 1966 victory, Bonetti should then, in a separate ceremony, have it officially rescinded as due reparation for his contribution to that later disaster.

In the end, though, and whatever the appeal of the logic here, this is not a position that we feel able to support. Yes, 1970 was a dark moment and maybe there is still a way in which Bonetti needs to be made publicly accountable for it. At the same time, it surely wouldn't be appropriate to make him pay the price with his belatedly received World Cup winner's medal, because, in the end, nobody can ever take away from the man what he didn't do in 1966.

One thing is clear: the subs of '66 have missed out on more than four decades of lecture tours, cruise ship speeches, store-openings and television appearances. Let's hope they set about redressing the balance now. Who knows? It could even be that one of them has the definitive angle to offer on the still vexed issue of that second Geoff Hurst goal, the mystery of which has teased us so tantalizingly for forty-one years now. Did it cross the line, or did it not? How well placed, really, was that Russian linesman? We'd certainly be interested to hear their views.

Meanwhile, join us now, won't you, in a new campaign? Oscars for body doubles. When Tom Hanks won Best Actor in 1994 for *Forrest Gump*, that wasn't always his body we saw, was it? At any rate, someone will have been coming in to stand in place while they set up the lights and the cameras. Whoever that was, we haven't had the chance to say thanks. Let's get on and put it right.

Latest Hangings at the Football Association

(*As a replacement for Steve McClaren, the FA appointed the veteran Italian manager Fabio Capello, who, being both Italian and veteran, was agreed to be a man of great taste and distinction.*)

'Fabio Capello's art collection is thought to be one of the most impressive in northern Italy' (news report, *The Times*).

From Capello's diary

Tuesday
I am given a tour of the FA's premises at Soho Square. Quite good, if a little limited in terms of overall ceiling height. Plenty of natural light in the lobby, though, and some promising wall-space in that area, as well as in the stairwells.

What would become my own office is pretty much as the previous incumbent left it. Obviously the poster of the tennis girl with her bum out will have to go. The space would probably suit one of the Picassos. However, I might keep the 'Super Footie Wall-Planner' issued free with something called *The*

Match. It needs a frame, or some kind of surrounding device, but it's quite colourful and bold, in a proto-naïve kind of way.

Outside by the lift, I say to Brian Barwick, 'I can really see the big Kandinsky just here.'

He says, 'Listen, any assistants you bring in can have their own offices. There's room.'

Amusing man.

Wednesday

The overnight structural assessment I commissioned confirms that the floor-load capacity on the second level is insufficient for the Henry Moore. Happily though, with the removal of some internal walls, and the insertion of a cast-iron underpinning, it should be possible to accommodate the piece. However, Adrian Bevington, the director of communications, is complaining that, with the statue in its proposed position, he will have to climb through the hole in the woman's stomach to get into this office. My advice to Bevington is to stop moaning. Where I come from, people would kill to live and work among art of this quality.

In the afternoon, my tour of the building resumes. I express my opinion that the portrait of Geoff Thompson on the stairs isn't really doing anything for me and that the space would be more fruitfully occupied by one of my Chris Ofili pieces, using varnished elephant dung.

'It's a matter of opinion,' says Barwick.

'So much of what I see here is backward-looking,' I go on. 'These traditional, unreconstructed forms – photography, paint – have long been superseded. By far the most exciting work these days is going on in multimedia pieces and installations.'

'I suppose we have taken our eyes off the ball a bit,' Barwick agrees.

On the way up, I get into a conversation with Trevor Brooking.

'Are you familiar at all with Luigi Russolo?' I ask.

Brooking says, 'Was he at Milan?'

'Frequently,' I say. 'And also in Rome and Florence – he exhibited all over Italy. A wonderful worker with both paint and charcoal.'

'We're interested in any new methods you can offer,' says Brooking.

'And such a sure handler of the media,' I add.

'We certainly need one of those,' Brooking says.

I open a door on the third floor and discover a room that excites me profoundly. It's a perfect situationist piece – a disturbed bed, some dirty crockery, tangled clothes, the detritus of daily life laid punishingly and yet somehow sympathetically bare.

'A Tracey Emin,' I say to Brooking. 'Quite superb.'

'Actually,' Brooking says, 'that was Sven's old conference room.'

Thursday

Negotiations continue fairly smoothly, but we reach a small sticking point when I mention to Barwick my most recent acquisition – Mark Wallinger, the man in the bear suit who won the Turner Prize. The sense of alienation, the strange, overwhelming sorrow induced by this displaced, mute figure caught on film, apparently imprisoned at night within a locked environment – all of this moved me profoundly. I've done a deal with Wallinger whereby I get the use of him, in the bear suit, for a month next year, and Soho Square seems to me to be a perfect place to explore those themes again. I can already see the bear, staring mournfully through the front doors at night.

Barwick says we'll have to clear it with the overnight security guard behind the desk.

'Lose him,' I say.

'I think there might be insurance issues,' says Barwick, a little nervously.

I find myself shouting, 'You put another man in there, you lose the sense of alienation, which is the whole point of the piece.' I'm about to let rip even further, when suddenly I have one of those brilliant ideas which occasionally come to me. 'Would the security guard consider wearing the bear costume?' I ask.

Barwick promises to look into it.

Moving forwards gradually.

Friday

A good day, with many decisions taken and many arrangements finalized. The medium-sized Monet water lily replaces the portrait of Sir Bert Millichip. The bust of Sir Geoff Hurst goes, and in comes the cow's bladder suspended in formaldehyde. And Kenny Greenberg has been commissioned to reimagine Ted Croker in neon.

'Now,' I say, 'there's just the matter of my assistants.'

'Whatever they need,' Barwick says.

'They have their collections,' I say. 'Not as big as mine, obviously. But Italo Galbiati, my assistant, has gathered some exquisite animal sculptures over the years. And Massimo Neri, my fitness coach, has amassed a lovely selection of nineteenth-century seascapes. I was thinking of the top floor.'

Barwick suddenly looks very tired, but he manages a kind of smile. 'Right,' he says. 'Let's go back up, then.'

Excellent. It all begins to come together. Pretty soon I shall be able to turn my attention to Wembley. That statue at the front can go for starters.

Tonight We're Going to Party Like It's 1899

What were they thinking of? The Manchester United players' Christmas party was, reportedly, a 'fifteen-hour drinking marathon' culminating at the Great John Street Hotel in Manchester, where 'the atmosphere soured in the early hours on the heady mixture of testosterone, booze and Barry White'. It saddens one to see shame brought down in this way, by association, on the good name of Manchester United – almost as much as it saddens one to see shame brought down in this way on the good name of the late Barry White.

The full extent of Sir Alex Ferguson's uncomprehending fury at these dark goings on, we can only tremblingly imagine. It was, though, claimed this week that the United manager had moved immediately to ban Christmas parties for his players in the future. You can see why. His anger and disgust are shared, though, and all across the country, other clubs, mulling over these events, will be, if not actually cancelling their players' festive celebrations, then at least sensibly reining them in to avoid any further ugly headlines and to reassert a sense of proportion, more in keeping with the happy messages of the season. Here, then, replacing any previously published lists, is your revised guide to the football club Christmas parties for 2007, as we have them.

Manchester City

Original plan: Stretch limo cavalcade to the Dirtbox for cocktails and Christmas dinner, followed by an evening of mud-wrestling at Slagz before bringing the evening to a close with nightcaps and a game of forfeits in the Nicole Richie bar at the Thistle Garden Hotel.

Rearranged plan: Lunch in the training ground canteen with Santa hats.

Everton

Original plan: Fuzz nite with DJ Spanky at the Bangin' Otter, including public appearance by US hip-hop legend Mos Pist feat. Krispi ('Gun Me Down, Say That One Mo Time And I'll Pop Ya'). Followed by fire-walking in the car park, and then home in a specially laid-on fleet of bicycle rickshaws.

Rearranged plan: Sausage roll round at Lee Carsley's.

Blackburn

Original plan: *Star Wars*-themed fancy dress party in the Park Hall Country House Hotel near Accrington, with all-you-can-eat seasonal turkey buffet, followed by flaming sambucas and pole-dancing at the Leather Fist. Optional fight under town centre Christmas tree later for anyone still standing up and holding a light sabre.

Rearranged plan: Mince pies and carols around the piano with Morten Gamst Pedersen, plus a round of Pictionary.

Liverpool

Original plan: Japanese Slippers at Bar Climaxx in Albert Dock, going on to a special festive lingerie and shaving foam evening at Peppermint Hippo. Entry only £8 before 7.30 p.m. with this flyer.

Rearranged plan: 2.40 p.m. screening of *Mr Magorium's Magic Emporium* at Edge Lane Retail Park Cineworld, with tea in Pizza Hut afterwards. No fizzy drinks. (PS Any parents willing to help out on the day more than welcome!)

Aston Villa

Original plan: Five-course Christmas Feast with all the trimmings in the Biggins room at the Sparkhill Ramada, followed by karaoke at the Dizzy Pixie, leading on to a pre-booked, seven-hour table-dancing session at the Sugarlump Pumphouse. Dress: fire-proof.

Rearranged plan: Cup of tea and a slice of Yuletide-style chocolate log from Iceland at Gareth Barry's mum's house.

Fulham

Original plan: Afternoon of go-karting. Drinks and dinner in Su Pang's Taiwanese Restaurant and Comfort Spa, followed by dancing at Chittychittybangbang. Afterwards, a private meet'n'mingle event at Madame Frou-Frou's quality escort lounge in East Cheam. Minicabs at 5.00 a.m. (Special note: please ensure that your go-kart is not still with you at the end of the evening.)

Rearranged plan: 5km charity run. In Santa hats.

Portsmouth

Original plan: Paint-ball battle at the WarZone, followed by happy hour cocktails in the Slime Bar. On from there to dinner in the upstairs private room of the Gandhi's Revenge curry emporium, followed by all-in cage fighting at the Dog Hut and a big old Christmas wind-up involving a shaved coconut and the tyres from Sol Campbell's Lincoln Navigator.

Rearranged plan: Cancelled – though not because of the new sensitivities surrounding Christmas parties, but because of the new sensitivities surrounding Sol Campbell.* Do you realize what he goes through in the workplace, week after week? In any other walk of life the abuse this noble campaigner for club and country gets as a matter of routine would be unacceptable. True, in any other walk of life he wouldn't be getting £40– £50,000 per week. But what's that got to do with anything?

Newcastle United

Original plan: There was no original plan. Christmas was banned by Sam Allardyce a long time ago. He's not stupid. If your family included Alan Smith, Nicky Butt *and* Joey Barton, you would ban Christmas, too.

Shearer at the Crossroads

It's one of those big decisions that affect all of us at some point in our working lives. You're holding down a steady job as a pundit on *Match of the Day*. But then along comes the opportunity to manage Newcastle United. What should you do?

Tricky one. They don't, in the careers advice business, call

---

* The tender stopper spoke out against the abuse levelled at him, and other players, from the stands. Some credited him with a brave and timely piece of whistle-blowing. Others reckoned that if you move from Tottenham to Arsenal at a sensitive moment in your career, you probably ought to be resigned to what's coming.

this crossroads moment 'Shearer's Dilemma' for nothing. Both positions, obviously, have their attractions. On the one hand, there's the *Match of the Day* role, offering fulfilling work, handsome remuneration and a high public profile, with a decent incentives package and plenty of time off. And on the other hand, there's the Newcastle job.

How to decide, then? Obviously, in the end, it's a decision that no one can make for you. It's a decision you have to arrive at yourself. But by applying the right strategies, you can at least cut through the complexity and alleviate some of the burden of deciding.

So let's begin. What we're going to do is take a clean sheet of paper and draw a line down the centre. Then, on one side of the line, you're going to make a list of all the positive things about the *Match of the Day* job, and, on the other side of the line, you're going to list all the positive things about managing Newcastle. It sounds corny, I know. But trust me. It will help you to achieve clarity, which will make the decision process that much easier later.

First, let's think about all the things that make that *Match of the Day* punditry position attractive. Under this heading, you might want to note down items such as 'quality time with Lee Dixon', 'paid-for trips abroad for England games, with nice hotels' and 'I get to put on a red nose and corpse amusingly in a hilarious pre-promote for this year's Sport Relief campaign'.

Something else you might consider writing here: 'easy-peasy lemon-squeezy'.

Right. So that's the positives about the *Match of the Day* job dealt with. Now let's consider the pluses on the Newcastle side.

OK. Now that we've done that, let's turn the sheet of paper over, draw a line down the middle again, and this time we're going to make lists of the negative things in each case – the drawbacks.

In the *Match of the Day* column, for example, you'll probably want to say something about pressure. *Match of the Day* is watched by some of the most passionate viewers in the land. If anybody deserves success, it's the viewers of *Match of the Day*. And that means that, as a pundit, you carry the weight of their expectation. And they're not after just any old success. They want success delivered with style and flair and with, preferably, minimal input from Garth Crooks. It's your duty to bring them that. Are your shoulders broad enough?

Also, *Match of the Day* does involve quite a lot of weekend work. But so does the Newcastle job, of course – although you wouldn't have to be there much into the evening on a Saturday. You would, however, have to work in the week as well. Again, you will have to measure up the pros and cons for yourself.

Also, the *Match of the Day* job can, at some stage, get in the way of your golf. Not often, nor for very long, it's true. How do you think Alan Hansen has managed to keep his handicap down around the scratch mark all this time?

Of course, the line 'unfriendly to golf' would be even more true of the Newcastle job. Did Sam Allardyce in the closing stages of his tenure, and particularly in the rain at Stoke, look like a man who had been spending a lot of time working on his short game? No, he looked like a man who had been beaten up for fourteen hours with the bunker rake. The last Newcastle manager to try to combine the job with a proper number of hours on the fairway was Ruud Gullit, and look what happened to him.

Something else to think about: can you manage Newcastle while sitting with your legs wide apart? I mean *really* wide apart. That kind of thing takes a studio and a free-standing, steel-frame chair, by and large, and today's dugouts just aren't built for it. In any case, managing Newcastle will, like as not, involve standing in the technical area at least some of the time, looking agitated, while as many as 50,000 people shout, 'You don't know what you're doing.'

There's no easy solution. As I say, in the end only you can decide what's right for you. And take all the time you can, because you want to get it right. After all, the chance to manage Newcastle doesn't come up more than three or four times a year. I'm often asked, 'How will I ever know?' But I promise, there will come a point where one or the other will feel like the right thing to do. Then you'll know.

We Need to Talk About Kevin

(And then, finally, unthinkably, amazingly, at the beginning of 2008, Newcastle United announced the reappointment as manager of Kevin Keegan – the return of the one true redeemer, descending in a halo of light, the leader of the Geordie faithful, the Messiah, albeit a Messiah who confessed that he hadn't been to a football match since he walked away from Manchester City nearly three years previously . . .)

Been out of the game for a while? Haven't seen a match since March 2005? Been brought in to rescue Newcastle United? No worries. Fill in the gaps right here with our one-stop catch-up service. Hey presto! You're ready for a visit from Bolton Wanderers.*

The offside rule
The summer after you tuned out, FIFA introduced some fiddly nonsense about 'active' and 'passive', as well as the brain-confounding distinction between 'being offside' and 'commit-ting an offside offence'. It's all very confusing. But essentially these days, a player is offside if the referee's assistant says so. You'll get the hang of it. Basically, flag up – offside. Flag not up – play on!

Two-footed tackles
What was just a bit of a lark in 2005, and a sure-fire way to break the ice at local derbies, is now officially the devil's work and a canker that threatens to destroy the very heart of the game from within. A clampdown is underway and players who even

---

* The first game of the new Keegan era finished Newcastle 0–Bolton 0.

look at both their feet get carded at the moment. But, hey, what am I saying? This is Newcastle we're talking about. Newcastle don't do tackling, they only do attacking. It's someone else's problem.

Diving

Absolutely everyone was at it, back in 2005. But since then there has been a sea-change in people's attitudes, and now it's only really Cristiano Ronaldo. On the whole then, best not to encourage diving. Unless, of course, there is someone in your squad who is especially good at it. Ask around in the dressing room.

The ball

It is, literally, a whole new ball game since the last time you looked. Fully two generations of sphere-related technological advance have come and gone since your day, and the Premiership now officially favours the all-new Sensurround Opta-Burst, which is much lighter than the balls you are used to and, in fact, goes up in the air and loops the loop, no matter how you kick it. It's certainly a vote-winner with the fans, though it has spelt career catastrophe for Paul Robinson. Remember him? Don't worry. You probably don't need to.

Available players

Many of the players who might have been 'unsettled' in March 2005 may not be unsettled any more. Some other players who looked good back then have retired (Alan Shearer), dropped down a division (Teddy Sheringham) or moved to America (David Beckham), which is like retiring and dropping down a division all in one go. So take care when drawing up your transfer window wish-list. Ask Arthur Cox. He'll know what's what.

Graham Poll

Gone, quite gone. Retired early, when the pressure of being England's leading bloke with a whistle became too much to

bear. Wrote a 384-page autobiography. Have you got that?
You're welcome to mine. We all miss him like mad, though.
Nowadays we've only got Mark Clattenburgh. It's not the same.

Christmas parties

We don't talk about these any more.

Joey Barton

Not quite as available for selection as he was when you had him
at Manchester City. You'll find a copy of the full police record
in your drawer.

The 2006 World Cup

Italy won it. England didn't win it. They were worse than
useless, and this highly publicized pratfall, combined with (sorry
to break it to you) the failure of England to qualify for the
2008 European Championships, means that the stock of our
home-grown internationals has never been lower. Wherever
they go now, England players get booed. Does this seem wrong
to you? It probably is. But it's quite fun, though.

Wags

Last time you checked in, your wife was straightforwardly your
wife. Now, she's your wag. On matchdays, she'll be asked to
join 'the other wags'. It sounds derogatory and reductive and
almost rude. And it is, in a way. But don't worry about it.
Nobody else seems to, least of all the wags.

Tony Blair

It's not him any more, it's the other one.

Steve Brookstein

When you walked away, Steve was just three months into his
reign as the winner of *X-Factor*, but an awful lot of water has
passed under Simon Cowell since then, and you'll earn no
changing-room props by mentioning the London-born crooner

now. Speak instead of Leon Jackson and – even more loudly – of Leona Lewis. Or better still, Mos Def, Kanye West and Basshunter. (Again, ask Arthur Cox.)

The bubble perm
Still no sign of a comeback for this one, I'm afraid. But give it time. After all, they said we'd never see flares again.

Appendix A
Where Are They Now?

Your handy catch-up guide to some of the figures featured prominently in the preceding pages.

DAVID BECKHAM

Following a frustrating first few months in America, marred by injury, the former Real Madrid star finally made his Major League Soccer debut as a wide receiver against the Cincinnati Moosejaws, when he was named Most Valuable Player after rushing a total of 224 yards in the third trimester. Nevertheless a recall to the England squad, under Fabio Capello eluded him until later.

JOSE MOURINHO

Fired as the manager of Chelsea for the crime of drawing 0–0 with FC Rosenborg of Norway in a Champions League group match, Jose Mourinho returned to Portugal where he now makes lobster pots in the quiet fishing village of Salema.

LEE SHARPE

The former Manchester United and Leeds star is still looking for love, but not live on the television which, some love experts believe, may improve his chances by a factor of anything up to 5,000.

VINNIE JONES

Tired of the soullessness of Hollywood life and the unvarying nature of the Californian weather, Jones returned to England to establish a chain of management consultancy offices in the east Midlands.

KITKAT KUBES

Still somehow gamely clinging on to a space in the nation's confectionery shelves, but when do you ever see anyone eating them? Certainly not at a football match. Still a better snack-choice, though, I would hazard, than a KitKat Peanut Butter. They're just weird.

SAM ALLARDYCE
Removed from his post as manager of Newcastle United amid the usual nonsense about 'failing to understand the unique nature of this great Geordie club', Allardyce sequestered himself in a recording studio near Liphook and began work on an as yet uncompleted debut album which, those who have heard some of it maintain, bears favourable comparison to mid-to-late period Supertramp.

WINSTON BOGARDE
The Chelsea wage-bill legend spent a year travelling by InterRail and then returned to his native Holland where he now specializes in glass-blowing and presents the late-night current affairs programme 'Hup the News!'

GRAHAM POLL
Following the success of his autobiography, *Seeing Red*, the retired referee went on to write the Tony Award-winning Broadway musical 'There Goes My Whistle!' as well as two novels, a collection of blank verse and a Pulitzer-nominated non-fiction work about the rise of Al Qaeda.

SEPP BLATTER
A long, unbeaten run of really dumb ideas – doing away with the penalty shoot-out, reducing the size of the shorts in the women's game – finally came to an end in 2008 when the President of FIFA stood up and made loud derogatory noises about the Premier League's idea to stage a round of fixtures abroad. Overnight, public perceptions of Blatter abruptly switched drastically and he went from being a man incapable of getting anything right to a man capable of getting one thing right.

RODNEY MARSH
Following a massive departmental shake-up in the spring of 2008, Marsh is now Parliamentary Secretary of State for Schools and Learners.

THE OFFICIAL BALL OF THE 2006 WORLD CUP (REPLICA)
Scuffed, deflated, slightly mouldy and under a bush in the author's garden.

WEMBLEY STADIUM
Still standing at the time of writing. 'So it should be,' you're probably thinking. But in February 2008, after a rugby international between France and England, the people responsible for the Stade de France lit off a massive firework display to celebrate the fact that the building was still in one piece after ten years, so obviously the expectations for longevity in this area have come right down.

STEVE McCLAREN'S UMBRELLA
Having written a memoir and toured the talk shows, the fabled 'wally's brolly' was last seen providing shade for Fernando Alonso on the grid at the Canadian Grand Prix.

Appendix B
The Soul of Chelsea in 50 Moments*

50   The goal that never was

Classic low strike from the furiously talented Alan Hudson, at home to Ipswich in September 1970, with the ball narrowly flying past the post, hitting the stanchion and rebounding on to the pitch. The ref, assuming the ball has struck the stanchion inside the goal, whistles and heads back upfield. Ipswich players protest, Hudson and others try to celebrate convincingly, goal stands. Cue cries for goal-line technology, referees with eyes, etc.

49   Culture Club attack the Shed End

1984, a home league game against Watford, and Boy George's chart-topping pop combo attempt to shoot a scene for the video accompanying their single 'The Medal Song' on the pitch at Stamford Bridge. The storyboard indicates that Mikey, the alluringly coiffed Culture Club bass player, in full Chelsea strip, must bear down on the Shed End goal and shoot past a compliant youth team goalkeeper. Alas, in a terrible and eerie pre-figuring of Diana Ross's penalty-taking problem at the 1994 World Cup opening ceremony in the US, Mikey misses. And continues to miss through many subsequent retakes. The Shed hails his efforts with a vigorous show of hand signals. Check the video on YouTube: the ball never hits the back of the net and the crowd are barely in shot for a split second. 'The Medal Song' was the first Culture Club single not to be a hit. Chelsea lost to Watford.

48   Celebrity fans

Ours tend to be genuine and stick around. OK, Raquel Welch only came once. But Lance Percival, Rodney Bewes, Michael Crawford – these people were always there, work permitting. Same goes for the

---

* First published by Times Online, as part of a series.

later generations. Damon Albarn? Bleeds Chelsea. They once shot an episode of *Minder* in the Shed, you know. Well, not the whole episode, obviously. But parts of it.

47 Willie 'Fatty' Foulke

An extra large goalkeeper and captain of the inaugural Chelsea side of 1905, Fatty Foulke checked in at 22 stone and 6 ft 3 in and minded the net by the highly efficient means of virtually filling it – a smart idea, rarely copied in later years, except, obviously, in the case of Neville Southall. On an away trip to Burton, Fatty is alleged to have consumed the entire team's breakfast before anyone else arrived. These days, when people set greater store by politeness, he would probably have to be known as Willie 'Morbidly Obese' Foulke. People in recent years have accused Chelsea of being over-reliant on imported players. They forget (or perhaps never knew) that almost the first thing the club did upon its foundation, to convince the Football League that their application was serious, was to sign Foulke from Sheffield United, as well as Bob McRoberts, a Scottish centre forward, from Small Heath. Bringing in foreigners is a long-standing Chelsea tradition, and we're rightly proud of it.

46 Chelsea Village

What if a football ground wasn't just a football ground? What if it was a purpose-built, 24/7, lifestyle campus, with ritzy apartments, four-star hotel facilities, buzzing restaurants and fizzy nightspots? What if it was Chelsea Village? Well, that was Ken Bates's plan, anyway – the conversion of Stamford Bridge into a cosmopolitan, all-hours entertainment centre. Unfortunately London already had one of these. It was called 'London'. Hence the sight of tumble-weed blowing through empty consumer facilities as the club expensively discovered that people had a limited enthusiasm for travelling to a football ground to eat fish and chips if they couldn't watch a football match afterwards. In any case – 'village'? Where was the green, the pub, the old well, the war memorial, the taste of warm beer, the distant clop of leather on willow . . .

45   Cars behind the goal

So vast was the gap between the Shed End at Stamford Bridge and the pitch that it allowed room for the cars of disabled or otherwise prioritized supporters to drive in and line up behind the goal-line. Therefore matches would routinely see a small forecourt-style display of motors and the ground would periodically ring to the evocative 'doink' of ball on near-side front-end car panel. Irregular, perhaps, but, at a time when the United States seemed much more remote than it does now, it loaned the Bridge some of the glamour of an American drive-in movie theatre.

44   Buying Winston Bogarde

The downside of the turn-of-the-century 'see 'em, sign 'em' frenzy. Bogarde was the surly Dutch stopper identified by Chelsea as the weak link in a storming Champions League home victory over Barcelona in April 2000 and then mysteriously signed by us the summer afterwards. People say Bogarde brought little to the table, but he was a tireless presence on the club's wage bill for four seasons, earning a rumoured £40,000 per week but making just four first team starts and eight further appearances as a substitute. All of which, incidentally, came in his first year. So, for three seasons, he did absolutely sweet Football Association. Apart from train, obviously, and go to the bank.

43   A brave new ground

Looking back, the middle of the worst recession since the Second World War wasn't perhaps the ideal time, economically speaking, for the Mears family to attempt a radical rebuilding programme which would see Stamford Bridge reformed as a glorious, leading-edge 60,000-capacity temple of football. Sure enough, only the East Stand got built – one brick at a time, between power cuts – the club almost died of poverty in the process and the long and bitter 'battle for the Bridge' was commenced. Tricky stuff, economics.

42   Beating Tottenham

Chelsea's unbeaten league run against Tottenham didn't really last for ever. It only seemed as though it did. In fact it went on for sixteen years – twenty, if you only count the games played at White Hart Lane, where, in November 2006, Graham Poll finally brought the streak to an end in the way that only he knew how – by sending off someone who didn't deserve to go (John Terry) and by disallowing a perfectly good goal (Didier Drogba). Highlights of the run? Well, the 1–6 pasting at Tottenham in 1997 had a certain poetry about it. But so, in its own quite different way, did the wintry night at Stamford Bridge in 2000 when George Weah, who had arrived on an aeroplane that afternoon, came off the bench and rose to a height of approximately fourteen feet in the Tottenham penalty area to head in an extremely late winner. We liked to imagine that, as he left the pitch that night, the former World Footballer of the Year put his arm around Jody Morris and said, 'That's the ten-year record safe, Jody.' He probably didn't, though.

41 *Disliking Liverpool*
Leeds will always be there or thereabouts. Spurs, too. And Manchester United, naturally. But recent seasons have seen Liverpool pull out of the pack and top the pile as the club we really don't like. Liverpool fans' incorrigible tendency to sentimentalize themselves in completely fantastical ways has, of course, always grated, but recently the irritation which comes by default with teams from Anfield has intensified. Reasons? Well, clearly the indignity of losing by a non-goal to the worst side ever to win the Champions League left a wound which going out of the same competition on penalties to them two years later didn't exactly heal. Another reason: Rafa Benitez. I mean, what a *plonker*.

40 *'Ten Men Went To Mow'*
And his dog, Spot, of course. Just one of those songs that Chelsea fans sing without really knowing why. See also the frankly pornographic number regarding celery, accompanied, in days gone by, by much hurling aloft of said underrated salad ingredient, although recently the authorities have effected a celery clampdown, banning the substance from inside the ground. (Those little sticks can sting, you know. Ask Cesc Fabregas.) 'Ten Men Went To Mow' involves a mass stand-up on ten, and is therefore one of only two examples of a chant specifically

adapted to the all-seater stadium era – 'Stand up if you hate Man U', being the other. Little known fact: Bryan Adams, the gravel-voiced Canadian rock star, likes to attend matches at Stamford Bridge when he can, and, walking up the Fulham Road on the way to the ground, has been known to ask, with considerable relish, 'Do you think there'll be some great mowing today?' There invariably is.

39   The White Feather Six

In October 2001, half a dozen Chelsea players, including Emmanuel Petit and Eidur Gudjohnsen, elected not to travel to Israel for a UEFA Cup game on the grounds that a bomb had recently gone off in an adjacent country. They were ritually denounced as 'weedy', among other things, but some of us prefer to dwell on how typically enlight-ened it was of Chelsea to let them make their own minds up. Sir Alex Ferguson, one feels sure, would have frog-marched all dissenters, shivering, on to the plane and made them have a cold shower when they got there. But at Chelsea it's all about respecting the individual, his feelings and his rights. Gudjohnsen, incidentally, holds the distinc-tion of being both a member of the White Feather Six *and* one of the Heathrow Four, who unwisely chose the aftermath of 9/11 for an airport-based public bender. Footballers, eh? You can never predict which way they're going to go.

38   Damon Hill burns rubber

At some point before he became a Grand Prix legend, Damon Hill was invited to drive a racing car up and down the gravel track in front of the old West Stand, by way of some slightly superior, cross-promotional half-time entertainment – superior to a cup of Bovril and a Wagon Wheel from the tea bar, anyway. West Stand mission completed, Hill then motored down to the Shed End and pulled out a demonstration of the legendary spin-trick known as 'doughnutting'. As a result, several hundred Chelsea fans found themselves pebble-dashed where they stood. There followed a show of hand-signals very similar to the one seen when Culture Club were our half-time guests. Hill never drove for Chelsea again.

37 Shocking away strips

You think the 2007–08 season's bright yellow, cycling proficiency outfits are the worst you have seen? You're forgetting the 'tangerine and graphite' assembly in which otherwise ostensibly serious Chelsea sides were obliged to see out the close of the last century. And as John Motson once found himself definitively obliged to announce, back in the 1980s, 'Chelsea in their slightly unusual away colours – jade.'

36 The away end

Brutally minimalist and entirely unsheltered concrete steppe which, for most of the 1960s, 70s and 80s, was the full extent of the hospitality extended to our visiting friends. It wasn't all hardship, though, for the people who might already have endured a six- or seven-hour coach journey – occasionally a disenchanted teenager with a tray would walk round on the dog track and push expensive snacks through the fence at them. Wolves fans once built a bonfire on the terracing to keep warm and the police, who also wanted to keep warm, turned a blind eye – or rather, a cold backside. Of course, health and safety regulations were less stringent in those days, and bonfires, like smoking, are now banned throughout the stadium.

35 Tromso in the snow

23 October 1997 and Chelsea head off up to the Arctic circle for the most bizarre game of football ever to be screened live on national television, played on a carpet of snow in a blizzard. The rules state that if the referee can't see both his assistants, the game must be called off. There is a very strong case that, at the height of the blizzarding here, the referee could barely see both his own shoulders. Even now the suspicion lingers that the match would have been postponed if the official party from UEFA hadn't decided that they couldn't face trudging back out to Norway at a later date and trying again. Dennis Wise, of course, wore a short-sleeved shirt, but the next time someone runs the hoary old argument about foreign players not fancying it on a cold night up at Ewood Park, set them down in front of a video of Gianluca Vialli, barrelling through a six-foot snowdrift late in this match and somehow managing to slap-shot the snow-encrusted ball,

ice hockey-style, into the icicle-decked net, thus securing the relief of an away goal, when Chelsea had fallen two goals behind in the confusion. In the event, we clobbered Tromso 6–1 on grass in the home leg, to cries of 'You only sing when it's snowing.' But it's the first leg we remember.

34   The Shed
The legendary, partly sheltered bank of terracing at the south end of Stamford Bridge, liable to provoke awe, wonderment and terror in equal measures and all at the same time. Undeniably, for a period in its history, the Shed was a fertile BNP and Combat 18 recruitment ground and a limited-hours drop-in centre for some of south-west London's most regrettable boneheads, but let's not say that was all it was. It housed (and continues to house) some of the firmest and funniest and friendliest and most patient supporters in football. Let's not forget, either, that even the people in the posh seats knew that a sizeable part of the attraction of going to Stamford Bridge was watching, and hearing, the Shed. In fact, for large periods of the 1970s and 80s, the Shed was the only thing going on that resembled entertainment.

33   The benches
The household fame of the Shed End should never be allowed to eclipse the part in the Chelsea story of the benches, a raw seating area at the foot of the old West Stand, available as an upgrade to standard ticket holders for a small supplementary fee. These days, Virgin Atlantic would call it Premium Economy. Those days, it brought you closer to the pitch and, more importantly, closer to the away fans. Hence the chant from the inconveniently distant Shed End of 'Benches, benches, do your job.'

32   *When Wise went up to lift the FA Cup – with his kid*
Ah! Little face! And the baby is cute, too. People think Wise was a gobby troublemaker and all-purpose one-man fire-starter. They are right. But he was also the midfield linchpin and captain of arguably the most technically sophisticated side that Chelsea ever produced, and a warm, cuddly family man to boot. Actually, 'to boot' is the wrong

expression, but you know what I mean. Carried up the Wembley steps by his father, Henry Wise became the youngest person ever to lift major silverware in the televised era and sparked a small vogue for sharing such moments with the fruit of your loins. The father and son duo returned to mark the opening of the new Wembley at the FA Cup final of 2007, which Chelsea also won, and where it was immediately apparent that Wisey's son is now nearly as tall as Wisey. Then again, he was in 1997, too. From *Dennis Wise – The Autobiography*. 'When Ken Bates took over in 1982 the club was going nowhere and had debts of £1 million. That was a lot of money then.' Only a footballer, of course, would think that £1 million wasn't a lot of money now.

31   Ken Bates's beard

The resemblance of Chelsea's argumentative former chairman to Father Christmas was, we must all agree, one of nature's better jokes. Bates rarely liked to be seen to be giving anything away that he could sell, and particularly not tickets. Allegedly Phil Collins once phoned up for some seats and was told to stuff off and buy his own. But doesn't that tale, however apocryphal, make you kind of love Bates, deep down? Chelsea fans have other reasons to hold this blunt, controversy magnet in high regard. He bought and saved the club. He brilliantly outman-oeuvred a business plan that would have seen the ground concreted over and Chelsea homeless. He turned a rubbish stadium into a spark-ling enormodome. He then saved the club a second time by selling it to a Russian football fan with bottomless pockets. Nice work. Note, too, that by selling his farmhouse in the country and taking a penthouse apartment in Chelsea Village, Bates became the only football chairman ever to live above the shop. This meant that he couldn't go in and out of his house without bumping into fans who, being fans, would want to ask him about season ticket prices and question the standard of the confec-tionery in the tea bars. You would have to love the place and everything it stood for to expose yourself willingly to that on a daily basis.

30   Vinnie Jones after three seconds

15 February 1992: whistle goes, ball narrowly departs the centre circle and the heart and soul of Wales goes in two-footed on Dane

Whitehouse of Sheffield United to earn the quickest booking ever seen at Stamford Bridge. Three seconds – staggering. And, what's more, it broke by a full two seconds Jones's previous early booking record, earned (unsentimentally enough) as a Sheffield United player, by ploughing into someone from Manchester City in January 1991. It's called 'letting them know you're there'. Many supporters were appalled when Chelsea signed Jones, and for perfectly decent moral reasons. But within ten minutes of his debut for the club, most of those same people were on their feet shouting, 'Vinnie! Vinnie!' Nothing about him had changed, of course. It's just different when they're family.

29   European Cup? No thanks

After Chelsea won the league title in 1955, the FA were asked if they would like to enter them in a new knock-out tournament that was being devised, featuring the champions of various European nations – working title, 'the European Cup'. But the FA said, 'Nah. What's the point? There's no future in it.' So we didn't go. Far-sighted, the FA, even then.

28   Players who live near the ground

Peter Osgood liked the district of Chelsea so much that he moved back to Windsor as soon as he could afford to. It was standard practice among the players of the 1970s and 80s to live somewhere leafy with a golf course. The signings of the 1990s changed all that. Albert Ferrer and Dan Petrescu used to walk over to the ground from Chelsea Harbour, five minutes away. Roberto Di Matteo took a flat near the Albert Hall and bought a restaurant near the Chelsea and Westminster Hospital. Ruud Gullit lived off the King's Road. Their English peers began to follow suit. Dennis Wise bought a mews house off the King's Road. So did Graeme Le Saux. Even now, when the new training ground at Cobham makes comfy Surrey a pragmatic option for many, Frank Lampard prefers to live within a thirty-yard volley of the Fulham Road. The sense of a team rooted in its local community was said to have gone out of the game with Brylcreem and the laced-up ball. It took an influx of foreign players to bring it back. But not just any foreign players – special ones who were interested in understanding the club and its culture. How many Liverpool players live within five minutes of Anfield by foot? How many live within forty-five minutes by reinforced SUV with tinted windows?

27 Official Peter Bonetti goalkeeping gloves
Thin, tight-fitting and indisputably green finger-protectors, as used in combat by 'the Cat'. About as far removed from today's padded Mickey Mouse mitts as it is possible for a pair of gloves to be, and offering minimal protection against the sting of either the ball or the weather, but a must-have accessory for the 1970s schoolboy.

26 Buying duff strikers
Are you a record-breaking Chelsea signing? Do you play up front? Uh-oh. There was Robert Fleck – big news in 1992 when signed from Norwich for £2.1 million, back when (as Dennis Wise would say) that was a lot of money. He appeared forty times and managed three goals. Cost per goal: £700,000. Then there was Chris Sutton – record signing in 1999 at £10 million. Made twenty-eight appearances, scored one league goal. Cost per league goal: you do the maths. And then, at £30.8 million, Andriy Shevchenko . . . but no. We love Sheva. He just needs time to settle. Believe it.

25 Rained on by Manchester United
1994: our first Wembley final in a quarter of a century unless you count the Zenith Data Systems which, thinking about it, for a long period we did. Oh, the hope and the painted faces on this dismal day in May. And oh, the 0–4 scoreline. *Are You Watching, Liverpool?*, Jim White's book-form account of that season from a United fan's perspective, has it that Chelsea were 'crushed like a pigeon beneath the wheels of a juggernaut'. Properly dispassionate historians, however, recall how the pigeon dumped on the juggernaut's crossbar at 0–0 in the first half, only to be cruelly poisoned by some marginal refereeing calls leading to two penalties after the interval. David Elleray was never warmly welcomed to Stamford Bridge again. The rain fell into my polystyrene cup of tea all the way to Wembley Central – the longest walk of all, in so many senses.

24   Chelsea Pensioners in the stands

Esteemed war veterans in bright red coats never miss a home game at the Bridge. 'But do they jump up when we score?' some of us are given to wonder. Unfortunately we've always been too preoccupied at the time to watch them and find out.

23   Ian Hutchinson's throw-ins

Following a quick polish on the insides of his sleeves, Hutchinson could sling the ball 112 feet into the opposition penalty area – which would have been impressive enough even without the physical quirk by which his arms would continue to rotate a couple of times after the ball had left his hands. Often imitated in the playground, this was football's equivalent of the Pete Townshend windmill, although when did the Who man's guitar antics ever mean that a throw-in was effectively 'as good as a corner'?

22   Roman Abramovich's yacht

. . . is bigger than Craven Cottage. Fact! Possibly. And it's got a sub-marine. Has Craven Cottage got a submarine? Not the last time I looked. Scene of several key business meetings in the Russian era, including the wooing of Jose Mourinho. Beats a conference room, a flask of Kenco and a plate of Bourbon biscuits in the St Alban's Ramada Inn any day. Also occasionally available to honeymooning players, some of whom will have to work weeks before they can afford luxury like this.

21   Electric fencing

Controversially agricultural approach to fan management proposed by Ken Bates in an era when Chelsea fans spent at least as much time on the pitch of a Saturday afternoon as the players did. The chairman talked a good game, electrocution-wise, but, revealing his not-frequently-enough commented on softer side, Bates never switched the fence on, meaning that its chief function was as a magnet for publicity rather than as a frazzling device for scrap-ready Sheddites and freelance exhibitionists.

20 Ruud Gullit dreadlock wigs

A BNP recruiting ground? Undeniably, it went on. But also let's not forget that Chelsea was the home of the first black manager in Premier League history. What's more, the first manager of any skin colour to be elected by public vote. At the end of the 1995–96 season, with Glenn Hoddle heading off to manage England, a rumour took hold that the board was about to appoint George Graham. During the season's final home game, repeated and ground-wide singing insisted, 'You can stick George Graham up your arse' – a suggestion emphatically followed up by cries of 'Ruudy, Ruudy'. The people had spoken, and that evening the job was Gullit's. Cue two happy, sun-dappled seasons of 'shekshy football' and widespread imitative wig-wearing. Emblematic moment of the Gullit era? Possibly the way he looked, suited and booted, leading out Chelsea at Wembley for the 1997 FA Cup final. Alternatively, consider the point where Chelsea take a 4–2 lead over Liverpool in that famous Sunday afternoon Cup tie, having trailed 0–2 at half-time. The television cameras cut to Gullit on the bench. Leaping up? Fisting the air? No. Bending down to tie his shoe lace. Eventually the Dutch legend's interest collapsed properly, to the point where he seemed to be managing by text message. But it was fun while it lasted. Shekshy, even.

19 Buying our way out of trouble

In 1910, only five years after foundation, Chelsea found themselves plunging towards relegation. Accordingly, they went out and signed five players at a cost of £3,575. Which, as Dennis Wise will tell you, was a lot of money then. As a direct result of this panic-buying, the FA introduced the March transfer deadline, forerunner of the transfer window. Unfortunately, at least three of those five players Chelsea bought turned out to be injured, so the cunning plan backfired and Chelsea went down. You see? You can't buy success, no matter what anybody tells you. Especially if you buy injured players. And Liverpool fans say Chelsea have no history.

18   The first all-foreign XI

Boxing Day, 1999. Team to face Southampton, away: De Goey, Ferrer, Thome, Leboeuf, Babayaro, Petrescu, Deschamps, Poyet, Di Matteo, Ambrosetti, Flo. Can you spot who's missing? That's right – England.

17   John Terry sees the light

You're saying the fielding of the first all-foreign XI was a bad moment for English football? We're saying it was a wake-up call. English players at Chelsea abruptly realized that the bar had just risen by about twenty-seven feet and that they would be obliged to go to Leeds United with Michael Duberry if they couldn't cut it. 'If I want to play for this club,' young English players were suddenly saying to themselves, 'I'd better be good.' John Terry, in particular, stood at a crossroads. He could either choose to concentrate and work hard with Frank Leboeuf and Marcel Desailly as his mentors, and with Claudio Ranieri (also not English) looking on protectively. Or he could continue the way he was going and end up in court again with Jody Morris. Hallelujah, he took the right path, and Chelsea now routinely supply the English national side with half its first-team personnel, more than at any other time in our history, and including its captain. Terry, Frank Lampard, Ashley Cole, Shaun Wright-Phillips, Joe Cole, Wayne Bridge . . . What riches. If only England had had a manager who had had the first clue what to do with them.

16   The Wizard of the Dribble

Also known as Charlie Cooke. Dazzling. Like Arjen Robben, only without the incessant diving, the crises of confidence and the perpetual injuries. And with an at times quite extraordinary moustache.

15   Giant-killed, again and again

How does this work? In the fairy tales, the giant gets killed once and that's it. In football, the giant gets painfully killed, but then gets up and is ready to be killed again, in almost identical circumstances, a year later, or even less. In the last quarter of the twentieth century, Chelsea made something of a habit of embarrassing themselves to sides of the quality of Scunthorpe and Walsall. It happened thirteen times in the

1980s and early 1990s. At some point in the middle of this dire era, Gareth Hall, a stocky right back, was asked by the club's magazine to nominate a song for the team to run out to. He suggested Talking Heads' 'Road to Nowhere'.

14 *'Always look on the bright side of life'*
Chelsea fans sang it first, while going down 7–0 at Nottingham Forest.

13 *Kerry Dixon and David Speedie*
Now, that was what you call a strike partnership.

12 *Jimmy Floyd-Hasselbaink and Eidur Gudjohnsen*
And so was that.

11 *Claudio Ranieri breaks the bank in Monte Carlo*
The semi-finals of the Champions League against Monaco and a series of inexplicable and ultimately catastrophic substitutions reveal why someone who is clearly the nicest man ever to manage a football team nevertheless had to be replaced. We hated to lose him. But he did have to go.

10 *Matthew Harding day*
Flowers and shirts at the gates, and a floral tribute on the pitch along with a fathom-deep silence in honour of the popular director who funded the North Stand and died in a helicopter crash returning from a night game at Bolton Wanderers. Somehow, in the wake of the solemnity, a game took place and ended in another victory over Tottenham. Form dictates that I now write 'Harding would have enjoyed that.' Of course, the truth is, he would have found it utterly predictable.

9 *John Neal's blue and white army*
The slick, quick-witted, easy-on-the-eye side (Nevin, Spackman, Dixon, Speedie) with which John Neal brought Chelsea out of the Second Division in 1984 went on to finish sixth for two consecutive years in the top division – dizzying heights by the standards of what

had gone before. It was all too brief. Neal succumbed to ill health. John Hollins took over and it all went pear-shaped.

8   *Jimmy Greaves leaves*

The best centre forward Chelsea ever knew left the club in high style, scoring all four goals in a 4–3 win over Nottingham Forest and getting chaired off the pitch before flying away to join Milan and make some money. Those four goals brought his total for the 1960–61 season to forty-one. He scored 114 goals for the youth team and thirty-two goals in his first senior year and managed a total of thirteen hat-tricks in four seasons. And to think that people now speak longingly of finding 'a decent, twenty-goals-a-season man'. That he would eventually be part of the Tottenham side that beat Chelsea in the 1967 FA Cup final was, of course, especially unpalatable. We think of him as pure Chelsea.

7   *4–2–4 versus Real Madrid*

4–3–3 hadn't worked. We drew with them in the first staging of the 1971 Cup Winners' Cup final in Athens. So Dave Sexton switched to 4–2–4 for the replay. Result! Chelsea's first European trophy.

6   *Roberto Di Matteo after forty-two seconds*

Typical. You wait three years for an FA Cup final to come around. Then Roberto Di Matteo runs through a nervous Middlesbrough midfield and cracks it over the goalkeeper's head and you spend eighty-nine minutes praying for the match to end. Eddie Newton made it 2–0 much later and, according to official time-keeping records, the celebrations on the pitch afterwards went on for longer than at any other FA Cup final in the history of the tournament. All together now, line up, hold hands, run and . . . *dive!* Excellent. Now, let's do it again. Only *across* the pitch this time. (Repeat for thirty-five minutes.)

5   *David Webb rising in the mud*

And putting away the winner in the 1970 FA Cup final with his cheek. And then running back up the knackered Old Trafford pitch and doing a lopsided jump in celebration. And no wonder. This was not just the victory of Chelsea over Leeds – this was also the victory of flair over cynicism, of artistry over violence, of good over evil. Ask Ron 'Chopper' Harris – he'll tell you the same. Chopper, incidentally, bought and sold a couple of golf courses after he retired from the game, and became a millionaire. Which was a lot of money, back then.

4 Jose Mourinho

His instructions were to improve a club that had just finished second. The next season it finished first. Few of us expect our team to have a manager as charismatic, clever, outrageous, well dressed and sometimes just plain funny, again. A vigorous celebrant of important goals, it was noticeable in general that he narrowed the traditional gap between players and coaching staff to an unprecedented degree. After a Champions League match at Valencia, Michael Essien stood in front of the usual logo'd board, giving a post-match television interview. Suddenly a figure jumped on him from behind, whooping loudly, and then ran off laughing. A typical players' prank, you were thinking, when the camera flashed up the corridor to reveal that it was Mourinho. It was always going to end in tears and a bust-up with the owner, of course – and lo and behold, it did, on, of all things, the night that Chelsea premiered a full-length feature film celebrating three glorious years under Mourinho. Inevitably there followed public displays of shock and mourning unlike any seen since the death of Princess Diana. Others say: cautious, attritional football, based on solid defending and lacking flair. We say: two Championships, two League Cups, one FA Cup and a whole barrel of laughs. Oh, and a Charity Shield. Jose never left out the Shield when making public declarations about his trophy tally, and neither should we.

3 Roy Bentley's lungs

Legend has it that Roy Bentley joined Chelsea from Newcastle because doctors advised him to head somewhere warmer for the sake of his lungs. Good idea. Seven years later, in 1955, he was the centre forward, captain and catalyst-in-chief of the first Chelsea side to win the League Championship and people have been coming to Chelsea for their health ever since.

2   *Peter Osgood's sideburns*

The King of Stamford Bridge, schooled in what is required of a monarch at this level by Tommy Docherty. Goals, more 1970s glamour than you could shake a stick at and, in his pomp, a pair of sideburns the size of adult weasels, but for many of us Ossie is perpetually frozen in midair, dive-heading the first Chelsea goal in the FA Cup final replay of 1970. Never to be forgotten.

1   *Gianfranco Zola's everything*

In particular there was the gasp-inducing moment against Norwich in which the original 'man with happy feet' and the best player ever to wear a Chelsea shirt (possibly, also, the nicest man ever to do so) runs on to a corner to the front post and scores with a flicked volley off the inside of his right heel. Brilliant in the same way that the moment he gave Julian Dicks of West Ham 'twisty blood' was brilliant, or in the way that he walked through the Manchester United defence one cold winter's afternoon at the Bridge was brilliant or in the way that he came on in Stockholm and won the European Cup Winners' Cup was brilliant, or in the way that . . . Actually, you could compile one of these 'Soul in 50 Moments' lists using Zola-related incidents alone, which explains why his is still among the first names to be sung when things are going well – as they so often seem to be these days.

Appendix C
Football Phone-ins of the Future*

HOST: Let's hear from Mick on the B 417 near Guangdong. Is that right, Mick?

MICK: Yeah, that's right, Alan. Just heading up into Hunan province, on our way across China.

HOST: Good game today?

MICK: Not bad, mate. We were a bit lacklustre in the first half, but we picked up after the interval and in the end I think we just about deserved the point.

HOST: You know, it's still pretty tight down there. Any danger of Birmingham getting sucked in?

MICK: I'd like to think, with this squad now, we're too good to go down. But, as you know, anything can happen. Let's wait and see how Sunderland get on in Riyadh . . .

HOST: Steve, you're breaking up a bit. Where are you calling from?

STEVE: We're just heading back from the Jakarta game in a rickshaw.

HOST: Do me a favour, would you, and ask the driver to turn the radio down?

STEVE: Hang on a minute . . . Better?

HOST: Much better. What is it you want to say?

STEVE: Well, I just want to say I thought Middlesbrough were brilliant today. Absolutely brilliant. We got players forward, we attacked well, we defended well when we had to. Every time Blackburn got the ball, we closed them down. The players showed a lot of

* Early in 2008, Richard Scudamore, the chief executive of the Premier League, announced a plan to extend the league season by one round ('the thirty-ninth match') and stage these extra games in various cities around the world, where people were, apparently, just gagging to bid big bucks for an in-the-flesh sighting of Fulham's Jimmy Bullard. How we laughed – until we realized Scudamore was quite serious.

commitment, especially when you consider how hot it was and the injections they all had to have . . .

HOST: Deggsy in Kampala – you're on.

DEGGSY: I'm absolutely spitting with fury at the moment, Spoony. I can't believe what I'm seeing, week after week. That's two more points we've dropped here today and, no disrespect, but we ought to be beating teams like Fulham.

HOST: Is that gunfire?

DEGGSY: Well, I don't blame them. People are fed up with it, Spoony. When you look at the money he's had to spend and we're still not competing for titles. Seventh place just isn't good enough for Liverpool Football Club and the sooner Benitez goes, I'm telling you . . .

HOST: Mark, what *is* it about Reading and Nairobi? You just can't get a result there.

MARK: I know, mate. It's incredible. What is that now? Four times? And there's always something – a penalty, a last-minute goal, a handball, or the ref has a shocker. But what can you do? I'm not saying the heat was a factor, because it's the same for everyone. Well, it's the same for the four teams who got sent to Nairobi, rather than the ones who got sent to Malmo. But you know what I mean . . .

HOST: Let's hear from a Newcastle fan. Rob.

ROB: I tell you, Alan – I'm made up tonight. There aren't many sides who are going to come to Volgograd this season and come away with three points.

HOST: Stand-out players?

ROB: Well, Joey Barton was on fire. James Milner had a good game, too. And Michael Owen looked back to his best. All of them, actually. I really think this could be a turning point.

HOST: It's great for the fans.

ROB: Absolutely. There's no supporters anywhere in the world that deserve success as much as these.

HOST: How did Derby look?

ROB: Shocking, to be honest. But you can only play what's put in front of you . . .

COCKNEY JIM: What I want to know, right, is why isn't London bidding to stage one of these big Premiership games? You've got all these other cities – your Sydneys, your Mumbais, your Pyongyangs – all jumping up and down and going 'I'll have some of that.' And yet London – nothing.

HOST: It's money, probably.

COCKNEY JIM: Yeah, but, Alan – we've already got the facilities. Look at the Emirates. World-class stadium, that is. Why not get a game on there? And it wouldn't just be for London. I think you'd see a feelgood factor that spread right the way across the country. We gave the world football, you know, and now we're getting left behind . . .

Acknowledgements

I would like to thank Ben Cairns, Dermot Clinch, Diana Eden, Nick Hornby, Anthony Lane, Paddy McAloon (who gave me the title, again), Ian Parker, Martin Smith (no relation), Jeremy Smith (relation) and Andrew Watson for their input and friendship.

It goes without saying, of course, that any errors of fact, taste or judgement enshrined in this volume are entirely attributable to these people, too.

All of the preceding articles originally appeared, in variously different forms, in the sports pages of *The Times*. I owe a lasting debt of gratitude and kinship to Keith Blackmore for taking me to the paper in the first place, and to Tim Hallissey, Jeremy Griffin, Craig Tregurtha, Tim Rice, Clive Petty, Adrian Drummond, Catherine Riley, Daniel Finkelstein, Tony Evans, David Chappell and the exceptional sub-editing team on the sports desk, for keeping me there. I would also like to thank the former editor of *The Times*, Robert Thomson, and his successor, James Harding.

I am hugely grateful to Tony Lacey, Jon Elek and Joanna Prior at Penguin and, as ever, to Georgia Garrett, my patient agent, at AP Watt.

With thanks, too, to Cas Knight and Paul Mason at Chelsea Media.

He just wanted a decent book to read ...

Not too much to ask, is it? It was in 1935 when Allen Lane, Managing Director of Bodley Head Publishers, stood on a platform at Exeter railway station looking for something good to read on his journey back to London. His choice was limited to popular magazines and poor-quality paperbacks – the same choice faced every day by the vast majority of readers, few of whom could afford hardbacks. Lane's disappointment and subsequent anger at the range of books generally available led him to found a company – and change the world.

'We believed in the existence in this country of a vast reading public for intelligent books at a low price, and staked everything on it'
Sir Allen Lane, 1902–1970, founder of Penguin Books

The quality paperback had arrived – and not just in bookshops. Lane was adamant that his Penguins should appear in chain stores and tobacconists, and should cost no more than a packet of cigarettes.

Reading habits (and cigarette prices) have changed since 1935, but Penguin still believes in publishing the best books for everybody to enjoy. We still believe that good design costs no more than bad design, and we still believe that quality books published passionately and responsibly make the world a better place.

So wherever you see the little bird – whether it's on a piece of prize-winning literary fiction or a celebrity autobiography, political tour de force or historical masterpiece, a serial-killer thriller, reference book, world classic or a piece of pure escapism – you can bet that it represents the very best that the genre has to offer.

Whatever you like to read – trust Penguin.